REMAINS

𝔥𝔦𝔰𝔱𝔬𝔯𝔦𝔠𝔞𝔩 𝔞𝔫𝔡 𝔏𝔦𝔱𝔢𝔯𝔞𝔯𝔶

CONNECTED WITH
THE PALATINE COUNTIES OF

𝔏𝔞𝔫𝔠𝔞𝔰𝔱𝔢𝔯 𝔞𝔫𝔡 𝔠𝔥𝔢𝔰𝔱𝔢𝔯

Volume XLII – Third Series

MANCHESTER
𝔓𝔯𝔦𝔫𝔱𝔢𝔡 𝔣𝔬𝔯 𝔱𝔥𝔢 𝔠𝔥𝔢𝔱𝔥𝔞𝔪 𝔖𝔬𝔠𝔦𝔢𝔱𝔶
1999

Macclesfield in the Later Fourteenth Century

Communities of Town and Forest

A. M. Tonkinson, M.A., Ph.D.

General Editor: P. H. W. Booth

MANCHESTER

1999

Macclesfield in the Later Fourteenth Century:
Communities of Town and Forest
by A. M. Tonkinson

Copyright © The Chetham Society, 1999
Text copyright © A. M. Tonkinson, 1999

ISSN 0080–0880

Published for the Society by Carnegie Publishing Ltd,
Chatsworth Road, Lancaster
Typeset in Linotype Stempel Garamond by Carnegie Publishing
Printed and bound in the UK by Cambridge University Press

British Library Cataloguing-in-Publication Data
A catalogue record for this book is available from the British Library

ISBN 1-85936-066-1

Contents

Acknowledgements

I am particularly indebted to Paul Booth for his advice and for allowing me access to his unpublished sources. I would also like to thank Phyllis M. Hill for her assistance when referring to her unpublished work on the Chester county court rolls. Finally I should like to record my thanks to the late Brian Harris for his help at the beginning of my research.

List of Tables and Diagrams

Abbreviations

SC 2	Public Record Office, Special Collections, Court Rolls.
Ch.Acc. (1)	*Accounts of the Chamberlains and other Officers of the County of Chester, 1301–60* (ed.) R. Stewart Brown, Record Society of Lancashire and Cheshire, 59 (1910).
Ch.Acc. (2)	*Account of Master John de Burnham the Younger, Chamberlain of Chester, of the Revenues of the Counties of Chester and Flint, Michaelmas 1361 to Michaelmas 1362*, Record Society of Lancashire and Cheshire, 115 (1991), (ed.) P. H. W. Booth and A. D. Carr.
C.C.R.	*Calendar of the County Court, City Court, and Eyre Rolls of Chester, 1259–97*, (ed.) R. Stewart Brown, Chetham Society, new series, 84 (1925).
C.P.R.	*Calendar of Patent Rolls.*
B.P.R.	*Register of Edward the Black Prince (1930–3).*
V.C.H.	*Victoria County History.*

TABLES

br.	brother of.	serv.	servant of.
d.	daughter of.	sis.	sister of.
h.	heir of.	o.	of a place.
jun.	junior.	w.	wife of.
s.	son of.	wdw.	widow.
sen.	senior.		

For a full list of the abbreviation of names see the introduction to Appendix Two, pp. 235–40.
Surnames have been standardised and kept as closely as possible to their original form.

Map One: Macclesfield Hundred

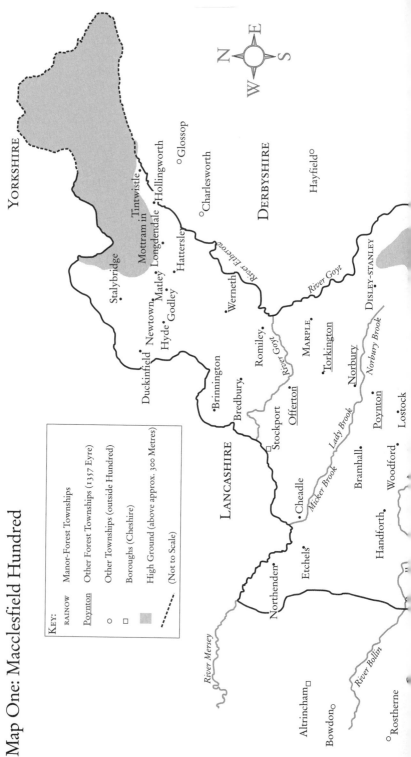

KEY:

RAINOW   Manor-Forest Townships

Poynton   Other Forest Townships (1357 Eyre)

○   Other Townships (outside Hundred)

□   Boroughs (Cheshire)

░   High Ground (above approx. 300 Metres)

- - -   (Not to Scale)

YORKSHIRE

DERBYSHIRE

LANCASHIRE

Glossop○

Hayfield○

Charlesworth○

Tintwistle

Mottram in Longdendale

Hollingworth

Hattersley

Stalybridge

Matley

Godley

Newtown

Hyde

Duckinfield

Werneth

River Etherow

River Goyt

DISLEY-STANLEY

Norbury Brook

Romiley

MARPLE

Torkington

Norbury

Brinnington

Bredbury

River Goyt

Offerton

Stockport

Lady Brook

Poynton

Lostock

Cheadle

Micker Brook

Bramhall

Woodford

Handforth

Etchels

Northenden

River Mersey

Altrincham□

Bowdon○

River Bollin

Rostherne○

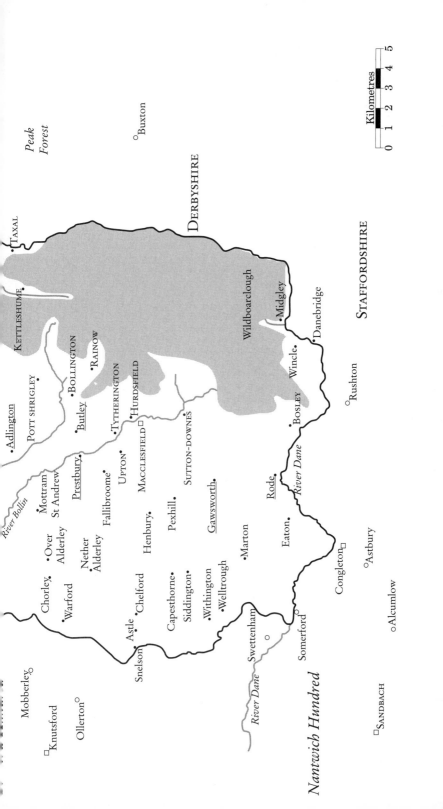

Peak
Forest

DERBYSHIRE

STAFFORDSHIRE

○ Buxton

• TAXAL

KETTLESHUME

Wildboarclough

• Midgley

• Danebridge

BOLLINGTON
• RAINOW
Butley •
TYTHERINGTON
HURDSFIELD

Adlington
POTT SHRIGLEY •

Mottram
St Andrew
Prestbury •
Fallibroome •
UPTON •
MACCLESFIELD □
SUTTON-DOWNES •

Over
Alderley •
Nether
Alderley •
Henbury •
Pexhill •
Gawsworth

River Bollin

Chorley •
Warford •
Astle •
Chelford •
Capesthorne •
Siddington •
Withington •
Welltrough •
Marton •
Eaton •

Snelsom •

Mobberley ○

□ Knutsford

Ollerton ○

Swettenham

Somerford ○

River Dane

Rode

River Dane

Wincle •
• BOSLEY

○ Rushton

Congleton □

○ Astbury

○ Alcumlow

□ SANDBACH

Nantwich Hundred

Kilometres

0 1 2 3 4 5

Map Two: The Topography of Macclesfield Forest

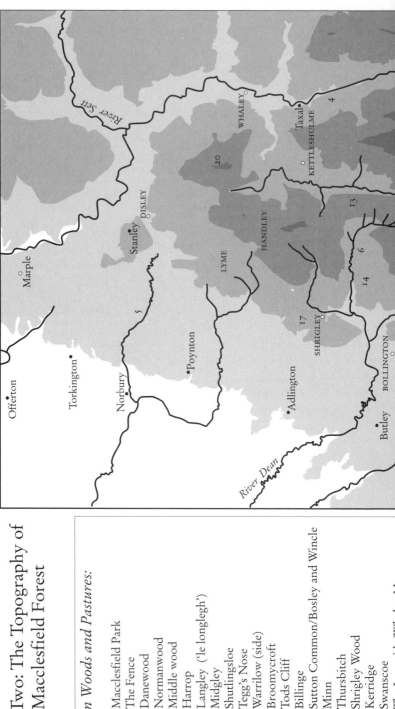

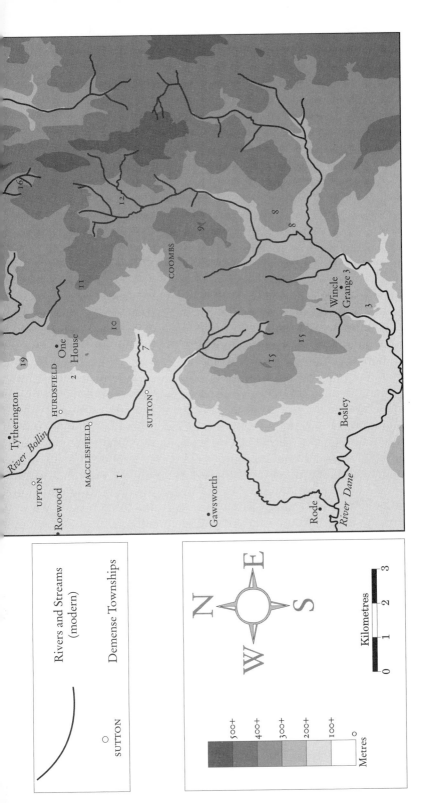

Rivers and Streams (modern)

SUTTON   Demense Townships

N W E S

Metres

500+
400+
300+
200+
100+
0

Kilometres
0   1   2   3

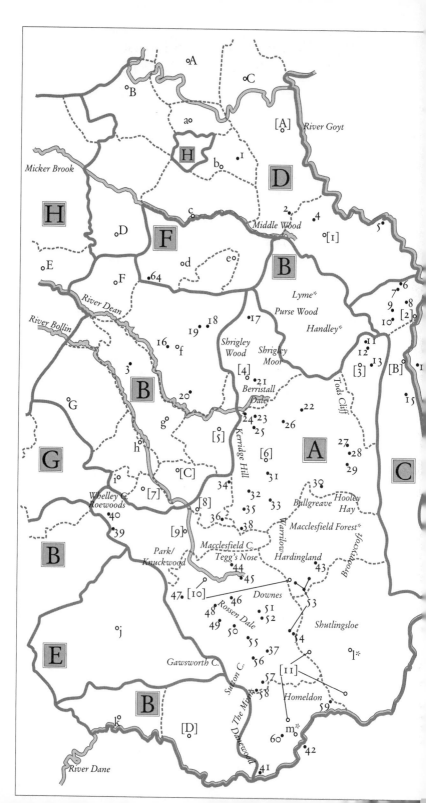

Map Three: Macclesfield Forest in the Later Fourteenth Century

ey and Guide:

wnship Boundaries: ....

vers (modern): ▬▬▬▬▬▬

rish/Chapelry: ▬▬▬▬▬▬

Kilometres

0   1   2   3

N
W ✦ E
S

rish/Chapelries:

A Macclesfield Chapelry (of Prestbury)

B Prestbury (part)

C Taxal (chapelry of Prestbury until 1377)

D Stockport

E Gawsworth (chapelry of Prestbury until 1382)

F Poynton Chapelry (of Prestbury)

G Alderley (Chapelry of Prestbury until 1328)

H Cheadle

emesne Townships:

] Disley
] Whaley
] Kettleshulme
] Shrigley
] Bollington
] Rainow
] Upton
] Hurdsfield
] Macclesfield
] Sutton
] Sutton

b-infeudated Township holly/partly in forest):

Marple
Taxal
Tytherington
Bosley

Township/Area that lay wholly or partly within the forest:

a Offerton
b Torkington
c Norbury
d Poynton
e Worth
f Adlington
g Butley
h Prestbury
i Fallibroome
j Gawsworth
k North Rode
l Wildboarclough*
m Wincle*

(* Indicates a Post-Medieval [14th C.] Township)

Township that lay outside of the forest:

A Bredbury
B Stockport
C Romiley
D Bramhall
E Handforth
F Woodford
G Mottram St Andrew

Other Later 14th C. Forest Settlements:

1   'le Graverslond'
2   Wybersley
3   Foxtwist (?)
4   Stanley
5   Warkmoor
6   Yeardsley
7   Ringstone
8   Hockerley
9   Stones
10 Hawkhurst
11 Coalhurst

12 Broadcarr
13 Walker
14 Shallcross (outside of forest)
15 Overton
16 Hollingsworth
17 Redacre
18 Pedley
19 Booth Green
20 Whiteley
21 Pott
22 Harrop
23 Oakenbank
24 Sowcar
25 Ingersley
26 Billinge
27 Jenkin's Cross
28 Saltersford
29 Redmoor
30 Lamaload
31 Thornset
32 Calroford
33 Hordern
34 Swanscoe
35 One House
36 The Fence
37 High Lee
38 Eddisbury
39 Gorseyknoll
40 New Field
41 Barleighford
42 Danebridge
43 Chamber
44 Pyegreave
45 Langley
46 Ridge
47 Shadeyard
48 Symondley
49 Knowles
50 Foghlegh (?)
51 Oldfield
52 Fernlee
53 Coombs
54 Oakenclough
55 Kinderfields
56 Hollinset
57 Cleulow
58 Butterlands
59 Midgley
60 Wincle Grange

1 *The Early History and Landscape of Macclesfield*

Macclesfield was a manor long associated with the earls of Mercia and then of Chester.[1] The name appears to mean 'Macca's open land' which is an early indication of its relationship to the clearance of woodlands and wastes.[2] By the eleventh century, when it had passed to the earls of Chester, it was the centre of a Hundred with an extensive area of arable, a hall and a mill.[3] The Domesday Survey gives the impression that it was situated in a 'ravaged and depopulated countryside' which, no doubt, related to its geographical setting.[4] Macclesfield sits in a border land where the productive soils of the Cheshire plain, of thick glacial till overlying sandstone, meet the south-eastern edge of the Pennines. Here the millstone grit crossed into neighbouring Derbyshire and Staffordshire and led, to the north-east, into Lancashire. Even when cleared of its original woodland cover, much of the uplands to the east of Macclesfield would have had only limited use for arable cultivation.[5]

The main area of settlement was centred on the River Bollin in low-lying land around Sutton and Macclesfield. To the south and east the land rises and this formed an extensive region of waste, pasture and common land that stretched from Sutton and Bosley Minns to Wincle and the River Dane, which marked the hundred and county boundary; at its highest point this reaches 506 metres

[1] *C.C.R.*, p. 218; *B.P.R.* iii, pp. 199, 259, 336; CHES 33/6 m. 36.
[2] J. M. Dodgson, *The Place-Names of Cheshire, Part One*, English Place-Name Society, 44 (Cambridge, 1970), pp. 113–14.
[3] *V.C.H. Chester*, I, p. 247.
[4] D. Sylvester, 'Cheshire in the Dark Ages: A Map Study of Celtic and Anglian Settlement', *Trans. Hist. Soc. of Lancs. and Cheshire*, 114 (1962), p. 4; J. P. Dodd 'Domesday Cheshire', *Cheshire History* (1986), pp. 10–20.
[5] D. Sylvester, 'Rural Settlement in Cheshire: Some Problems of Origin and Classification', *Trans. Hist. Soc. of Lancs. and Cheshire*, 101 (1949), pp. 1–37.

at Shutlingsloe hill. To the north-east of Macclesfield a collection of scattered hamlets were situated on gently rising land, and the later commons of Rainow, Kettleshulme and Whaley embraced the moorland ridges that extended to Peak forest and towards Buxton. The township of Yeardsley-Whaley, now part of modern Derbyshire, formed a more populous village on the River Goyt.

The geographical situation was thus ideally suited to the area's exploitation as a forest. Macclesfield Hundred contained one of the largest areas of woodland in England at the time of the Domesday Survey.[6] By the fourteenth century this survived as three separate woods: Lyme (Handley) to the north, the Coombs of the Forest, and Dane Wood, to the south. Other smaller areas of woodland or wood pasture, kept separate from the common waste and the arable demesne, are indicative of woodland management.

It is more difficult to establish the precise boundaries of the medieval forest of Macclesfield. It is first referred to in the later twelfth century when the tenement of 'One House' in Rainow was granted to Richard Davenport with the office of master-forester.[7] At this time the bounds of the forest extended to include Leek in Staffordshire but this area was later granted to Dieulacres Abbey. By the later thirteenth century there were eight or nine subordinate and hereditary foresters-in-fee who held their land by the service of grand serjeanty. These were based at Sutton (Sutton); Shrigley and the 'Ratonfield' (Downes of Shrigley); Disley-Stanley (Dycon); Disley (Sherd); High Lee (Foxwist followed by Cresswall); Downes and Taxal (Downes); Worth (Worth and later Downes); Marple and Wybersley (Vernon); and Gawsworth (Fitton).[8]

The borough of Macclesfield was already in existence at the start of the thirteenth century, and by its close there were at least 120

---

[6] For its situation within the wider district of 'Lyme', see *V.C.H. Chester*, II, p. 179; O. Rackham, *Ancient Woodland its history, vegetation and uses in England* (1980), pp. 112–18.

[7] G. Barraclough (ed.), *The Charters of the Anglo-Norman Earls of Chester, c. 1071–1237*, Record Society of Lancashire and Cheshire, 126 (1988), pp. 180–1.

[8] The land held by the foresters, therefore, extended beyond the manor townships. The holding of the Fittons at Gawsworth may have included part of Sutton. CHES 33/6 m. 36; *V.C.H.* II, 178; F. Renaud, *History of the Ancient Parish of Prestbury*, Chetham Society, Old Series, 97 (1876), p. 191.

burgages.[9] It was situated at the core of the manor of Macclesfield and close to the Domesday settlement. By the fourteenth century the manor had grown to encompass a number of townships which appear to have been formed either as a result of new assarting in the later thirteenth century or from the substantial clearances that were already present. These settlements were located close to the higher ground which was situated to the north and east of the town.

The manor thus consisted of the demesne townships of Sutton Downes, Bollington, Hurdsfield, Upton, Pott Shrigley, Rainow, Kettleshulme, Disley Stanley, Yeardsley and Whaley, whose occupants owed suit to the manor court. Under the control of powerful local tenants some of these townships effectively became 'manors' in their own right; Downes for instance, held by the family bearing its name, was already referred to as a manor by the mid-fourteenth century. In addition another four townships – Bosley, Tytherington, Taxal and Marple – owed suit to the Macclesfield manor court (the halmote) but were held by local lords as tenants of the earl of Chester.[10]

The forest boundary extended beyond the manor of Macclesfield and into the Hundred. Of 61 townships in the Hundred of Macclesfield a third came within forest jurisdiction as defined by the mid-fourteenth century forest eyre.[11] For some of these townships, most notably Adlington, comparable or even greater areas of woodland than that found in the manor were recorded by the Domesday Survey.[12] All these townships owed suit to the separate Hundred

[9] *Cheshire in the Pipe Rolls, 1158–1301*, Record Society of Lancashire and Cheshire, 92 (1938), pp. 35–6; Barraclough (ed.), *Charters*, p. 342; P.R.O., E 372/146 rot. 33 m. 1.

[10] Bosley by Montagu, the earl of Salisbury and later by John Macclesfield senior, clerk; Tytherington by the Worths; Taxal by a branch of the Downes family; and Marple by the Vernons.

[11] Bollington, Sutton Downes, Hurdsfield, Tytherington, Bosley, Rainow, Pott Shrigley, Disley, Yeardsley and Whaley, Kettleshulme, Taxal, Marple, Upton, Rode, Adlington, Poynton, Prestbury, Butley, Norbury, Offerton, Torkington, Gawsworth; CHES 33/6 m. 36.

[12] Eleven by two leagues in Adlington compared with six by four in Macclesfield, while significant amounts of woodland were also contained within the townships of Gawsworth, Bosley, Norbury and Butley, *V.C.H.*, I, p. 247. See also n. 65 below

court. In practice, however, the forest increasingly overlapped with the manor administration.[13]

The two centuries that followed Domesday witnessed a transformation in Macclesfield manor's fortunes.[14] In the 60 years between 1183 and 1247/8 its financial yield increased markedly, and by the end of this period the manor and mills were worth more than £50 a year.[15] Three factors can be linked to this development. The first relates to land use. The growing exploitation of the forest pastures led to the repair and restocking of the manor; by the twelfth century there were four vaccaries worth annually around £6 a year, and the pannage yielded between £2 and £11. Secondly, the founding of the borough by Earl Ranulf III of Chester acted as an economic and social catalyst: the fairs came to be worth as much as £10 a year and the common oven a further £2.

Thirdly, the burgeoning population led to an increasing pressure on the arable resources. The combined profits of the manor and borough courts, which, at £30 in 1237/8 were more than double the average for the second half of the fourteenth century, is evidence in itself of a thriving population; in the same year feudal aids (*de auxilio*) of £10 and £4 were raised from the tenants of the manor and borough. The bringing of new land into cultivation from the late twelfth century may correspond with the formation of new townships within the manor – none of which were mentioned in Domesday Book.[16] Indeed, such a process was taking place in some more northerly Pennine regions at this time.[17]

The evidence for settlement formation in Macclesfield mainly relates to townships on the periphery of the forest. Bosley, for instance, was largely the product of assarting by successive generations of the Montalt family between 1199 and 1319: 60 acres during the reign of King John; woodland of 87½ of acres, c. 1216–1272, and 60 acres, c. 1272–86, during the reign of Henry III; and a further

[13] See for example, the Cheshire Mize Book of 1405, John Rylands University Library of Manchester, Tatton MS, 345.

[14] From the later thirteenth century, and for more than a century, the lordship was granted to successive royal ladies, *V.C.H. Chester*, I, p. 181.

[15] *Ch.Pipe Rolls*, pp. 9, 12, 35–39, 44–47, 51–3, 56, 65–6 75, 87 and 92.

[16] The manor townships all first appear in thirteenth century records, Dodgson, *Place-Names of Cheshire*, pp. 106–287.

[17] For example, D. Postles, 'The Rural Economy on the Grits and Sandstones of the South Yorkshire Pennines, 1086–1348', *Agricultural History Review*, 15 (1979), p. 7.

122 (including ten houses) acres in 1319. Once permission for the assarting had been secured the freehold remained with the Montalts, and the tenants were charged in the forest eyre for their work.[18]

Any large scale assarting of land was a costly procedure and the presence of wealthy local tenants was an important determining factor. In addition to Bosley there is other evidence for the establishment of planned settlements and manors on the edge of the forest. The Vernons, for instance, brought a substantial area of land and wood into cultivation in Torkington, next to Marple, in 1290 along with a further 100 acres of wood and underwood in Marple in the 1330s. In 1344 John Legh built 'le Gravereslond' in Torkington which consisted of a manor-house with a hall, two chambers and a kitchen – all surrounded by a deep moat – and a large barn, a stable, an ox-shed and a kennel.[19]

These planned settlements were all associated with the clearance of woodland by important local families. This produced a landscape of hamlets, dispersed farms and numerous fields. In Adlington, held by the Leghs and already mentioned for its large amount of wood in Domesday Book, enclosures of sixteen, ten (twice), seven, four and one acres were created in the years leading up to the Black Death. The fields were named after individuals and all land was cultivated on a three-course rotation system, while in some townships marl-pits were dug to improve soil condition.[20]

The evidence for the demesne townships of the manor is less abundant. The earliest references in the Pipe Rolls, for instance, do not indicate any sizeable land clearance. In 1238/9, for example, one new assart worth 2s. 0d. and a licence of 20s. 0d. to cultivate six acres were recorded and in the two years following the land brought into cultivation amounted to two assarts worth 1s. 0d. and 2s. 0d.[21] A more detailed and reliable source of information is the forest pleas in the county court of the later thirteenth century. In Macclesfield Hundred just over a third of the 142 acres of assarts recorded between 1285 and 1290 were made within the manor itself. These were approved by seven men and were largely in the form of small intakes or enclosures: for example 3½ acres of alder and scrub by four men in Hurdsfield, and 20 by four men in Disley,

---

[18] *C.C.R.*, pp. 222, 233; CHES 33/6 m. 40d.
[19] *C.C.R.*, pp. 233, 245–6; CHES 33/5.
[20] CHES 33/6 mm. 40–41.
[21] *Ch.Pipe Rolls*, pp. 44–7.

including a one acre enclosure with a house.[22] This contrasts with Wirral, in the far west of Cheshire, where around 350 acres were asserted between 1258 and 1286, whereas in Peak forest an average of eight houses were built each year during the first 35 years of Henry III's reign.[23]

The forest eyres of the mid-fourteenth century detail the improving of land from around the beginning of the century.[24] Out of nearly 1,300 acres asserted throughout the forest between c. 1299 and 1349 all but 100 were approved within the townships around the perimeter of the forest.[25] Of the 70 or more acres within the manor townships a total of 61, along with two unspecified enclosures, were brought into cultivation between 1335 and 1349. The majority of these improvements, around 55 acres, were in the township of Shrigley where woodland was being enclosed under the influence of William Dounes (24 acres and a grange at the Redcar) and Jordan Macclesfield (10 acres). This is the only township that can be identified with very late clearance with between one third and half the land being approved from the mid-thirteenth to the end of the fourteenth centuries. The assarting in the remaining townships was small-scale and all under five acres.

It is not possible, therefore, to precisely date the formation of the manor townships although the increase in revenues indicates a substantial development from the late twelfth to later thirteenth centuries.[26] In the absence of wealthy local families most of the

[22] C.C.R., pp. 224–5.

[23] J. P. Dodd, 'The Clearance of the Medieval Waste, 1250–1350', *Cheshire History*, (1978), pp. 24–5; this assarting had almost ceased by the mid-fourteenth century, W. Fergusson Irvine, 'Trespasses in the Forest of Wirral in 1351', *Trans. Hist. Soc. of Lancs. and Cheshire*, 101 (1949), pp. 42–5; *V.C.H. Derby*, I, p. 403.

[24] The regards held in 1347–8, CHES 33/5, and 1353, CHES 33/6 mm. 40–1, the latter of which was dealt with at the full forest eyre for Macclesfield in 1357. The relationship between the recorded assarts and the development of the forest landscape, are discussed in *Ch.Acc.* (2), pp. xlii–xlvii.

[25] The approximate figures for assarting in the early fourteenth century are: around 400 acres in Adlington, 178 in Gawsworth, 177 (or possibly 297) in Poynton, 128 in North Rode, 100 in Marple, at least 71 in Torkington (excluding that approved by Marple above) and 69 in Norbury.

[26] See P. H. W. Booth, *The Financial Administration of the Lordship and County of Chester*, Chetham Society 3rd ser., 28 (1981), pp. 155–6. It has been suggested that part of the common fine of £87 paid by Macclesfield forest in the 1357 forest eyre, and not detailed in the regard, relates to

land appears to have been asserted on a piecemeal basis which, although largely complete by the end of the thirteenth century, continued right up until the Black Death.[27]

The fourteenth-century land holdings in the manor townships were mostly held by customary tenure.[28] These were rented at 8*d*. an acre, which was the standard figure for Macclesfield forest assarts. The tenants had full right to alienate their holdings in the manor court on payment of a relief or entry-fine of two years' rent. In addition some manor tenants owed a customary heriot while some landholdings were charged with the service of providing doomsmen, or judgers, in the manor court.

The customary acre of Cheshire was more than double the size of the statute measure.[29] The majority of tenants of the manor held between three and 21 Cheshire acres, with more than half holding under nine acres and only one in eight holding 22 or more. As these acreages are broadly compatible with holdings in other parts of the country, local tenants clearly had more sizeable holdings.[30] It is necessary, however, to take into account the subletting of tenancies before gaining an accurate view of actual landholding, particularly in the case of the large number of tenants in possession of fewer than three acres (see below).

However not all manor-forest land was rented at the usual 8*d*. for forest assarts, and this may be land which was occupied by tenants from an early revision. In the eleventh century there were four *servi* on the Domesday demesne, and by the thirteenth century four customary tenants (*custumarii*) were referred to in the Pipe Rolls.[31] In the mid-fourteenth century some customary holdings,

---

assarting by the demesne townships during the earlier fourteenth century, *Ch.Accs. (2)*, p. 23 n. 22.

[27] The one exception was Langley which was only referred to as a demesne pasture ('le Longlegh') during the later fourteenth century: nearby undated ridge and furrow may indicate later medieval cultivation.

[28] All were copyholders in the southern uplands of neighbouring Derbyshire by the earlier middle ages, L. Wharfe, 'Rural Settlement in Upland Derbyshire' unpubl. thesis (Manchester 1955), p. 50.

[29] 10,240 square yards, D. Sylvester, 'The Open Fields of Cheshire', *Trans. Hist. Soc. of Lancs. and Cheshire*, 108 (1956), pp. 27–8.

[30] M. J. Bennett, *Community, Class and Careerism. Cheshire and Lancashire in the age of Sir Gawain and the Green Knight* (Camb. 1983), pp. 101–104; M. M. Postan, *The Medieval Economy and Society* (1972), pp. 142–7.

[31] *Ch.Pipe Rolls*, for example, pp. 35, 40.

measured in bovates, were situated next to Macclesfield mill near the River Bollin; at least five were in Sutton and one in Hurdsfield. This land was also described as *terra nativa* and some of those holding it as villeins. By this time, however, the holdings had become sub-divided and most were held by free or copyholders (see below). The services to which they were liable related to the maintenance of Macclesfield mill, hunting, and toll collection at the fairs.[32]

It is likely that these customary holdings had formed the core of the manor recorded in Domesday Book.[33] Some of this land later became incorporated into the borough.[34] However, this might still not account for the 800 or more acres for Macclesfield manor mentioned in the survey, and it is likely that some further land had already been cleared for arable use.[35] One candidate for early clearance is the carucate of land that lay in Eddisbury (*Esebury*) within the township of Rainow; this was near to Onehouse, the tenement granted in the twelfth century along with the office of master-forester. In the later fourteenth century half an acre of land lying between them was rented at 4*d.*, while Eddisbury itself was later entered at a reduced sum after spending many years in decay after the Black Death.[36]

Another messuage and carucate in Whaley was held by forester John son of Richard Sutton in the later fourteenth century at a rent of only 15*s.* 0*d.*[37] There are very few references to land assarted in this township and by the mid-fourteenth century it was the second

---

[32] The services are set out in the 1383/4 rental, SC 11/898 m. 2: The mill and its pond were maintained (around fifteen feet each of the mill-pond and the cleaning of ten feet of the water channel beneath the mill beginning at the lower mill gate each year); the replacement and carriage (or payment of a moiety of the carriage) of the mill-stone when necessary; the carriage of the lord's game by the tenants' oxen and horses when he hunted in the forest; the making of a stall for the collection of toll at All Saints' Fair at Macclesfield; the cost of a gate for the lord's fold at Macclesfield; and the payment of a merchet at the manor court. See also, for example, SC 2/253/2 m. 2d.

[33] An inquisition into the holding of forester Richard Sutton in 1287 stated that he had held two bovates which formerly belonged to the demesne of Macclesfield manor, *C.C.R.*, p. 233.

[34] That described as 'terra antiqua' in the mid-fourteenth century rental, SC 11/899 m. 1d.; C. Stella Davies, *A History of Macclesfield* (Manchester 1961), p. 2.

[35] Ten ploughs or around 40 carucates, *V.C.H. Chester*, I, p. 181.

[36] See below p. 77 n. 144.

[37] SC 11/899 m. 4.

most populous demesne township after Sutton, with a number of other holdings rented at 4*d.* an acre.[38]

Apart from the bovates held on the demesne around Macclesfield mill there is no evidence of servility in the remaining manor townships. Services were, however, owed elsewhere. Those relating to stabling and the building of two deer hays in the forest were provided by the lords and tenants of the townships of the Hundred around its border: Adlington, Chelford, Butley, Bollin, Cheadle, Etchels, Bramhall, Mottram St. Andrew and Woodford.[39] Some tenants in the nearby townships of Bosley and Bollington also owed carting services. In Bosley there was only one holding held in villeinage at the end of the fourteenth century, but by the early fifteenth century it was no longer of this status and was rented at the customary 1*s.* 0*d.* an acre, or double its former rent.[40]

The eleventh-century manor of Macclesfield, therefore, was centred around the River Bollin and its mill and the townships of Sutton and Downes. By the start of our period, the mid-fourteenth century, the mill came within the bounds of a well established borough while the nearby customary land had mostly been divided and sublet. Although there is some evidence for earlier clearance, such as of land near Rainow and at Whaley, the demesne townships were predominately or even wholly made up of assarted land – the most likely date for which was from the late twelfth to later thirteenth centuries. This bringing of new land into cultivation was achieved largely as the result of piecemeal enclosure which continued, at a greatly reduced rate, until the eve of the Black Death. The resultant pattern of settlement was thus one of dispersed hamlets, farms and enclosures.[41]

---

[38] One further carucate in the manor was later granted by a Robert Pultrel to the monks of St. Werburgh's abbey, Barraclough, (ed.) *Charters of the Anglo-Norman Earls of Chester*, pp. 2–11, 38–47.

[39] SC 11/898 m. 1.

[40] 'An Edition of the John de Macclesfield Cartulary', J. L. C. Bruel, unpubl. thesis (London 1969), fo. 7, 202–3.

[41] For recent discussions on dispersed settlements see A. E. Brown and C. C. Taylor, 'The Origins of Dispersed Settlements, some Results from Fieldwork in Bedfordshire', *Landscape History*, 2 (1989), pp. 61–81. C. C. Taylor *Medieval Rural Settlement: Changing Perceptions, Landscape History*, pp. 5–17; C. Dyer, 'Dispersed Settlements in Medieval England: A Case Study of Pendock, Worcestershire', *Medieval Archaeology*, 34 (1990), pp. 97–121.

The earliest charter for the borough of Macclesfield dates from 1261. This established 120 burgages at a rent of 12*d.* each and allowed for a merchant guild and freedom from tolls throughout Cheshire.[42] In addition the burgesses had the right to housebote and haybote and free pasture within the manor-forest.[43] The arable lands of the borough may originally have been in the form of one (or possibly two) townfields situated in a broad area adjacent to the park and mill and to the west of the town. In Frodsham, in the west of the county, the borough land was separate from that of the manor and was either contained in thirteen fields divided into furlongs or in two open fields.[44] The Boothfield of Macclesfield was held by the principal tenant of the borough, for no money rent, and in the mid-fourteenth century this was Master Jordan Macclesfield who owed four barbed arrows a year.[45] Some burgage holdings had strips of land here, measured in fractions of an acre, and by this time organisation into furlongs had taken place: these included, for example, 'le Paghemarl' and 'le Naghtemare' furlongs, and 'le Blacacre'. The word for field as applied to this area was always in the plural (*campis*).[46]

At the beginning of the fourteenth century, 1305–6, the borough's territories were extended when an area of forest 'waste', in this context probably woodland, was purchased for the sum of £90 18s. 2d. in 1305–6.[47] This was situated near to the park and to the west of the town and came to be called the Roewood or Roughwood (*le Rowode*). At least one part became known as 'le Newefeld', and another part called the 'Smethelenemore', of which 29 acres were assarted in *c.*1313 and further 23 acres between *c.*1337 and 1349.[48] Some of this assarted land, whether held jointly or by

---

[42] A facsimile and translation is included in Stella Davies, *History of Macclesfield*, pp. 8–9.

[43] Unlike the tenants of the manor townships, they were allowed to fell oaks in the demesne woods in the later thirteenth century, *C.C.R.*, p. 213.

[44] P. H. W. Booth and J. P. Dodd, 'The Manor and Fields of Frodsham 1315–74', *Trans. Hist. Soc. of Lancs. and Cheshire*, 128 (1979), p. 37.

[45] SC 11/899 m. 1.

[46] For an example of a burgess holding an acre in the fields of Macclesfield, see SC 2/253/5 m. 3.

[47] *Ch.Acc.* (1), p. 77. As this was 'assarted forest land', tenants were later said to be liable to the same entry fines paid by manorial tenants, *B.P.R*, iii, p. 275.

[48] CHES 33/6 m. 40.

individuals, was in strips and measured in selions and all was sown on a three-course rotation system. The borough's 'Terra antiqua' or ancient lands in the 1352 rental, rented at 8*d.* an acre, totalled only around 43½ acres. Of these fewer than five acres had been assarted during the first half of the fourteenth century. They included land held as separate enclosures, such as the Millfield consisting of only 1½ acres, and a small close, held jointly and probably sublet by three men, which was sown with oats. Borough holdings also included pasture, and one grange with a yard contained both arable and marshland. The common fold for the burgesses' livestock, which were classed as escapes within the forest, was administered by the foresters and their officials.[49]

In the mid-fourteenth century the urban area of Macclesfield primarily consisted of the three main streets of Jordangate, Chestergate and Wallgate. The burgage-plots were separated by hedgerows, often of ash, which were sometimes broken and used for fuel by the town's poor.[50] There were several orchards in the town and many gardens and some of these also had apple trees. Even close to the town centre there must have been a rural atmosphere as Jordangate contained a grange with a garden and Wallgate a barn with a fold.[51] The town chapel, dedicated to All Saints, was a dependency of the parish of Prestbury, and there was a chantry dedicated to the Blessed Mary which had three reeves or churchwardens in 1364. From at least the thirteenth century the town also had a small leper hospital.[52]

Although the forest landscape was originally intended for the preservation of game there had been conflict from an early date

[49] The breaking of the fold was presented to the portmote, SC 2/255/2 m. 5. It appears to have been in the forest, and not in the town itself. For land held close to it, see 'John de Macclesfield Cartulary', fo. 82–3.

[50] One grant included the provision for a stone wall and gutter to be built to separate two plots, along a line measuring 44 feet in length and two feet in width, as well as a French louver over the nearby kitchen; for this and other descriptions, see 'John de Macclesfield Cartulary', fo. 52, 111–12, 126–7, and the rentals of 1414/5, fo. 196–201.

[51] T. Mclean, *Medieval English Gardens* (1981), p. 86 and C. Dyer, 'Gardens and Orchards in Medieval England' in *Everyday Life in Medieval England* (1994), pp. 113–32.

[52] SC 2/252/15 m. 5; *Notitia Cestriensis* I, Chetham Society, OS 8, (1845), pp. 289–91; G. Ormerod, *History of the County Palatine and City of Chester: The Hundred of Macclesfield*, 2nd edition, (Manchester, 1980), p. 751. For a further altar or chantry see p. 113 n. 95 below.

with its use as grazing for domestic livestock. Domesday Book recorded that Macclesfield contained one of the largest areas of woodland in England and we should view this landscape as one of enclosed clearings and pastures: of the 21 hays or enclosures recorded by the survey only seven were included within the manor of Macclesfield. In the later thirteenth century there were still wolves in Peak forest, and at the start of the fourteenth a trap was constructed at Macclesfield to prevent their entry into the park after deer had been killed on many occasions.[53] The presence of both red deer (*cervus, cerva* and *bissa*) and fallow deer (*damus* and *dama*) was recorded in the courts.[54] Fallow deer were primarily associated with the area around the park itself and the enclosure called 'the Fence' near Hurdsfield.[55] The red deer were more numerous in the upland areas and valleys to the east, particularly in the Pennines where Macclesfield and Peak forests adjoined, from Danebridge to the River Goyt. One indictment in the eyre of 1381 refers to eight men from Derbyshire who killed two red deer and drove 40 harts and hinds across the border.[56]

Domesday also records an ox meadow in the manor and from the thirteenth and fourteenth centuries the forest was increasingly exploited for its pasture.[57] Four vaccaries, worth more than £6, were situated at Midgley, between 1237 and 1241, and most likely at Swineshurst, Handley, and Tods Cliff. The pipe rolls record the sale of 79 cattle for £20 6s. 1d. in 1240.[58] The Chester county court attempted to restrict enclosures that interfered with the free passage of the deer. In 1286, for example, a hedge enclosing an area of thirteen acres in Disley was thrown down, while many buildings in the forest were ordered to be pulled down in the earlier fourteenth century.[59]

[53] J. C. Cox, *The Royal Forests of England* (1905), p. 33; *Ch.Acc.* (1), p. 25.
[54] Fallow deer were the most common in England, A. Grant, 'Animal Resources' in Astill and Grant (ed.), *The Countryside of Medieval England* (Oxford 1988), p. 165; only red were present in neighbouring Peak Forest, Cox, *Royal Forests*, 26–7; roe deer from Macclesfield forest were sometimes granted by the Black Prince, *B.P.R.*, *iii*, 112, 461.
[55] At least 40 were taken prior to the Black Death during the time of Queen Isabella (1331–47), CHES 17/13 m. 39.
[56] SC 2/254/3 m. 6d.
[57] *V.C.H. Chester*, I, p. 347.
[58] *Ch.Pipe Rolls*, p. 56.
[59] *C.C.R.*, pp. 224–5; CHES 33/6 m. 41d.

In 1291 the chambers at the Coombs were constructed for preserving the deer. At this time the queen's bailiffs were accustomed to mowing the forest pastures each year to feed her cattle and there were accusations of the overstocking of the pastures at Midgley; the foresters denied that they had 'greatly diminished' the hunting grounds by allowing their animals to graze there.[60] In 1326 a commission found that the forest was 'much destroyed' after complaints of the bailiffs' mismanagement and the tenants' usurpation of the common pasture.[61] In 1335 forest residents petitioned the Black Prince regarding the taking of large quantities of venison and timber by the queen's bailiff, who was refusing to let anyone be summoned to the eyre for forest offences.[62]

During the fourteenth century the culmination of its changing role from a game preserve to livestock pasture took place. These changes resulted in the felling of a significant part of the forest's timber and in the neglect, grazing and enclosure of the underwood.[63] At the beginning of the century a stallion was purchased, at £5 6s. 8d., for the stud and three haystacks were made in the park for this and for the deer. A further £1 3s. 0½d. was spent on stabling and hay in the two years following. At the same time oxen were purchased from Macclesfield fair for the prince's larder. In the first decade of the century the Coombs, Macclesfield park and the manor buildings and walls were extensively repaired using local supplies of timber. The enclosures consisted of an oak palisade (*Jarella ex planceis de quercu*), and other repairs used alder from the park; 5,000 were said to have been taken during the time of Queen Isabella and a further 800 in the early 1330s when the manor and the fencing of the park were again repaired extensively.[64]

In 1345 the tenants of the Hundred townships had their hedging service for Coombs commuted to a money rent on account of their complaint that the wood was 'so destroyed that scarcely any for

---

[60] *Ch.Acc.* (1), p. 9; *C.C.R.*, p. 225.

[61] *C.P.R.*, 1323–7, p. 293; *Cal. Chancery Warrants* I, 1244–1326, p. 581.

[62] During the time of Queen Isabella, *Rotuli Parliamentorum* II, p. 94.

[63] See, for example, J. McDonnell, 'Pressures on Yorkshire Woodland in the Later Middle Ages', *Northern History*, 28 (1992), pp. 110–125.

[64] *Ch.Acc.* (1), pp. 6–7, 9, 11, 25–6, 44; CHES 17/13 m. 39; *Cal. Close Rolls 1330–3*, pp. 233, 447; H. J. Hewitt, *Cheshire Under the Three Edwards* (Chester 1967), pp. 31–2.

such repair is found within three miles'.[65] In the 1357 eyre the felling and sale of 1,267 oaks was recorded from the beginning of Edward III's reign: most of these were charged at 2s. 0d. each and were taken by local inhabitants a third or more of whom were burgesses.[66] A few large oaks went outside the area, such as the four taken by the canon of Rochester at 3s. 4d. each, and the six by the earl of Huntingdon at 10s. 0d. from Hawksyard in Dane Wood. Outside the woodland enclosures timber oak trees, such as fifteen in Shrigley in 1332/3 and nine in Taxal, were cut down by tenants in the commons and wastes (see Tables 2 and 3).

After acquiring the manor in 1347 Edward the Black Prince was determined to raise revenues, and this was achieved by the introduction of an unprecedented forest eyre and the reorganisation and further exploitation of the demesne.[67] His improvements included the enclosure of the manor with an earthen wall and the Coombs, Lyme, the meadow and orchard with wooden fences. The lodge at Coombs, the great stable at the manor and the mill were all repaired, and a new fulling-mill and a lodge for the park-keeper were built using timber from Lyme. This timber was also used in 1359/60 when the valley of Harrop was enclosed as a pasture for the first time. The mill-pond was also enclosed and the manor waters were stocked with fish from Peckforton.[68]

The prince's administration also sought to exploit the demesne pastures by introducing a large number of cattle and purchasing horses for the stud. In 1353/4 three mares and foals were purchased for over £5 and there were around 20 horses until 1358 when the stud was transferred to Denbigh. In 1356–57 there were over 460 cattle, mainly consisting of oxen, cows and calves, and in 1362 125 animals were brought from Ashford in Derbyshire to be included in the Macclesfield herd. The stock account for this year shows an income of £70 2s. 9d. from stock sales (of which £30 came from this Ashford stock). The prince was using the palatinate to fatten

---

[65] C.P.R., 1343–5, p. 355; the nearest woodland was probably Dane Wood. In 1383/4 nine (Hundred) townships were listed as owing this service in the rental, SC 11/898 m.1. In 1388 Hamon Bollin was said to be responsible for making 72½ roods of the Coombs enclosure and for finding 33 men for making the stable, Deputy Keeper's Report 36 (1875), p. 180.

[66] CHES 33/6 m. 37d, m. 38.

[67] For the exchange of lands in Wiltshire, B.P.R., i, p. 147.

[68] Ch.Acc. (1), pp. 126, 167, 230, 254, 271; Ch.Acc. (2), p. 90; B.P.R. i, p. 158, v, p. 420.

large numbers of cattle for sale, and the 100 animals that were sent to London from Cheshire in 1352 and 1357 and 300 in 1361 had to be bought in. This use of the demesne pastures, however, declined and the peak of around 700 animals in the decade 1354–63 had halved by 1376.[69]

The demesne pastures were a combination of enclosed wood pastures (as at Coombs), upland hillsides and plateaux with enclosed crofts or folds (like Warrilowside, Broomycroft, Tods Cliff, Shutlingsloe, Midgley and Handley), and enclosed pasture in valleys (Langley, and Harrop which included some underwood on the hillsides, and at adjacent Billinge). These must have provided both summer and winter grazing. In 1347 the prince ordered that all beasts trespassing in the forest were to be impounded and then forfeited on their third offence.[70] The day to day supervision and presentment was carried out by the foresters and their servants.[71] Any animals belonging to tenants entering these areas were termed 'escapes' and a fine was levied. In most years during the later fourteenth century between 100 and 200 people can be found in the lists of escapes which appear alongside the records of the yearly eyres. These lists usually refer to the origin of the person, using the prefixes 'f' for forest, 'b' for borough (specifically burgesses), and 'h' for hundred, and state whether the escape occurred during the summer herbage or winter foggage. The overwhelming majority of those responsible were manorial tenants and in one year, out of a total of £7 5s. 0d., only 8s. 0d. was paid by burgesses and under 5s. 0d. by Hundred inhabitants. The annual fines levied at this time were between £6 and £9 compared to below £5 in the later thirteenth century, implying a significant increase in the numbers of animals. As many individuals repeatedly payed similar amounts and as the fines were not progressive some form of *de facto* licensing system was probably operated.

The impounding of escapes was recorded on separate rolls.[72] Some of these refer to the presentment of animals at folds within the

[69] SC6/802/13m.4d; for a full discussion of the revenues at this time see 'Profit and Loss: The Lordship of Macclesfield' in Booth, *Financial Administration*, pp. 86–115 and pp. 93–7 in particular. The increasing revenues within the lordship were primarily related to increased fines relating to justice rather than an exploitation of resources.

[70] *B.P.R.*, iii, p. 158.

[71] CHES 25/20 m. 26; SC 2/253/7 m. 1d.

[72] For example, SC 2/253/10 m. 7, SC 2/253/12 mm. 8–10.

demesne pastures and deal with large numbers of livestock which often belonged to the same individual; 70 and 68 sheep in Warrilow-side on one day, for instance, and 40 sheep of the rector of Taxal in the newly-enclosed Harrop. This is further indication that some form of licensing was in operation for the grazing of animals on the demesne pastures. In addition a few rolls, again filed alongside the yearly Hundred eyres, record the droving of animals within these areas (*Delib(er)atio p(er) viam*). Although this was supervised by the foresters a *custos falde* appears in one list of escapes and it was customary for one herdsman from each township to be allowed to enter the covert.[73]

The fine paid for escapes was dependant upon the time of year, and higher sums were charged for the summer herbage. The usual costs per animal were: oxen and other draught-beasts between 1*d.* and 2*d.* in winter, and 4*d.* in summer; working horses, between 1*d.* and 3*d.* in winter, and 3*d.* and 6*d.* in summer; and sheep, ¼*d.*, ½*d.* or 1*d.* throughout the year. An inquiry in 1373 referred to the pasture rights of under-forester Roger Oldhed who held part of the former vaccary at Midgley. It included a house at Over Midgley and a meadow rented at 12*d.* a year along with the pasture of many animals, at 2*d.* in both summer and winter and twelve cows twice yearly, within the bounds described. He was frequently mentioned in relation to the fold and the delivery of cattle and his office, as under-forester, may have been attached to this land; later he enclosed a further three acres of the *seperali*.[74]

As the century progressed, and following the decline in demesne stock keeping, the pastures were increasingly leased out. The most valuable were Handley at £10 yearly and the park which was leased for a similar sum, while Midgley had been leased in 1355 to parker Alexander Attecrosse for four marks. The escapes were of far less value and John Cresswall took a lease of those of Midgley and Dane Wood for 5*s.* 0*d.* in 1381–2, those of Warrilow for 10*s.* 0*d.* in 1387–8 and those of the Coombs, jointly with Nicholas Gardener, for the same sum in the following year. By the mid-fifteenth century all the pastures were leased at £16 in total, and their escapes at

[73] SC 2/254/4 m. 14–16, SC 2/254/5 m. 5. Robert Legh, the younger, received a payment in 1372–3 for the number of escapes received, Booth, *Financial Administration*, p. 100.

[74] SC 2/253/7 m. 10. For a full description, see his biography in Appendix One.

£5 yearly: these were Harrop, Tods Cliff, Midgley, Shutlingsloe, Saltersford (the high ground between Rainow and Kettleshulme) and Wildboarclough (adjacent to Shutlingsloe).[75] By the seventeenth century they were described as commons belonging to one or more of the manor townships.[76]

The exploitation of the Coombs (and possibly some other areas) as wood pasture, in which trees were pollarded to provide a regular crop, is indicated by the periodic sale of wood.[77] However, apart from a small number of free-standing trees it is unlikely that much timber remained on the higher ground of the forest by the mid-fourteenth century. The remaining woodland, or underwood, was contained within separate low-lying or valley enclosures that were managed as coppice to provide fuel and fodder. The most important resources of wood or timber were the Coombs (the *haie del Coumbes*) and Lyme Handley (*le defensum domini*, near Disley). The latter was divided into Lyme, which was used solely for wood and pannage, and the pasture of Handley. By the early seventeenth century Lyme contained eighteen different commons as well as a park, a mill and manor-house.[78]

The demesne underwood was situated at *le Fence* in Hurdsfield, Macclesfield park, Dane Wood, the severalty (*seperali*) that included timber in the Hawksyard, and the wood at Shrigley. Areas of underwood may additionally have belonged to each township and wood from the commons was sometimes taken. The main species of tree referred to were oak, hazel (*corulus*), alder (*alnus*), hawthorn, holly, birch and, to a lesser extent, ash. Smaller timber trees, probably birch, were described as *lentiscus*, while an elm was referred to on one occasion. The trees had three main uses. The leaves were used as a fodder; the crop and lop of branches were used for fuel as well as carpentry and crafts; and the timber was used for building.

The cutting, pruning and felling of wood was the responsibility

---

[75] Booth, *Financial Administration*, p. 96; *B.P.R.*, iii, p. 188, *passim*; *Deputy Keeper's Report* 37 (1876), p. 486.

[76] See Renaud, *History of Prestbury*, pp. 223–8.

[77] O. Rackham, *Ancient Woodland* and *Trees and Woodlands in the British Landscape* (1990); P. A. Stamper, 'Woods and parks' in Astill and Grant (ed.), *Countryside of Medieval England*, pp. 128–48.

[78] Restrictions on those holding lands and woods within the defence of Lyme were removed in the mid-thirteenth century, *V.C.H. Chester*, II, pp. 178–9.

of the rider of Macclesfield forest, the foresters, verderer and their officials. The right of the burgesses to housebote and haybote without view was confined to the woods of Shrigley, Sutton, Kerridge and 'Swanshagh' (later Swanscoe which was adjacent or contiguous with 'the Fence'). The tenants of the Hundred townships were also allowed to take timber from the demesne woods although, as already noted, this was a right the manor tenants did not possess. The foresters themselves had the right to take housebote and haybote, reasonable estovers for their soc throughout the forest, except within the severalty (*seperali*) and the *defens*, together with holly for their animals when it was sold. In 1347 the Black Prince disallowed their claim to windfalls and restricted their right to take wood to a fortnight after Whitsunday, and permitted other estovers to be taken only 'by view' (that is, under the supervision, officially at least, of the justiciar and chamberlain of Chester).[79]

In the second half of the fourteenth century the revenue from lop and crop (usually termed *stipit(is)* and *croppe*) was fairly small (see Table 4). In the 1380s three successive years of sales yielded a total of only £5 9s. 0d. Those purchasing wood were predominantly manor tenants. They also included foresters, burgesses, tenants from the Hundred who were responsible for more than a third of purchases in one year, and Robert Legh the younger. A more regular, if minor, income resulted from fines for *vert* offences in the manor courts and Hundred eyres which came to around £1 a year. As the fines levied against individuals were very small, and were invariably linked to the value of the wood taken, it is again appropriate to see these penalties as closer to a form of licensing.[80] Tenant John Brocwalhurst, for instance, made at least eight payments for legitimate wood sales, which totalled more than 12s. 0d., and paid a further 7s. 0d. in manor-court fines for carrying off old and dead wood from Handley. In this he was sometimes accompanied by a party of four or eight others.[81]

In the three year period 1382–5 Roger Oldhed's payments for wood totalled 8s. 8d. These included: 6d.-worth of loppings and one trunk worth 3s. 4d. in the Oakenbank; one lopping worth 1s. 8d. and one tree worth 3s. 0d. in the Echencliff; and two birches in Hordern worth 2d. In the cases of both John Brocwalhurst and

[79] *C.C.R.*, p. 213; *B.P.R.*, i, pp. 156–7.
[80] For example, SC 2/254/4 m. 5d., SC 2/254/5 m. 8d, SC 2/254/6 m. 8.
[81] SC 2/252/10 m. 5 – SC 2/253/4 m. 1d. He was also indicted, CHES 25/19 m. 5. For his biography, see Appendix One.

Roger Oldhed, both of whom were involved in the keeping of livestock, this wood was probably destined for fodder.[82] Holly was another important cattle feed that was regularly cut, usually from the commons.[83] In some areas, like West Derby, it was a customary payment and tenants gave 2s. 0d. for the right to cut it each year.[84]

The use of woodland was not unlike that found in other forests where the courts recorded the regular sale of loppings.[85] In the larger forests, like Dean, they rarely exceeded 2s. 0d. while in Needwood they were 'largely pro rata'.[86] In Hatfield forest the courts were 'almost always concerned with raising revenues from fines, rather than deterring people from doing things'.[87] In Macclesfield the enforcement of the law to preserve the vert was primarily intended to ensure that wood was taken only by view of the foresters; in one case, for example, a person was presented after a forester found him in the act of *capientem et abducentem vetus lign' quercum*.[88] The more serious offences, which involved an indictment in eyre, again largely ended in fines related to the value of the wood, and should be regarded as licensing in disguise. In 1381/2, for example, John Shydyort of Wincle paid 3s. 4d. damages for cutting down 40 oaks and small trees in Midgley ('Myggelesall') in the autumn of the previous year.[89]

The right of burgesses to take wood from the enclosures, such

---

[82] SC 2/254/4 m. 5d., SC 2/254/5 m. 8d., SC 2/254/6 m. 8.

[83] Those indicted include John Shotelsworth in 1378, for cutting 18d. worth from Disley common on many occasions, and Edmund Ashton for cutting it in Sutton common to feed 20 draught-beasts in winter 1368. SC 2/253/12 m. 10, CHES 25/20 m. 36; SC 2/252/13 m. 3, SC 2/254/3 m. 6.

[84] M. Spray, 'Holly as a Fodder in England', *Agricultural History Review*, 29 (1981), pp. 97–110; R. Cunliffe Shaw, *The Royal Forest of Lancaster* (Preston 1956), p. 66.

[85] For example, W. Linnard, *Welsh Woods and Forests, History and Utilization* (Cardiff 1982), pp. 33–8; A. J. L. Winchester, *Landscape and Society in Medieval Cumbria* (Edinburgh 1987), p. 103.

[86] C. E. Hart, *Royal Forest: A History of Dean's Wood as Producers of Timber* (Oxford 1965), pp. 42–3; J. Birrell, 'Common Rights in the Medieval Forest: Disputes and Conflicts in the Thirteenth Century', *Past and Present*, 117 (1986), pp. 33–4.

[87] O. Rackham, *The Last Forest: The Story of Hatfield Forest* (1989), p. 90.

[88] At 'Callerrake' bank in Disley, SC 2/254/15 m. 4d.

[89] SC 2/254/3 m. 6.

as Lyme, was monitored in the halmote court while the portmote also helped regulate their rights. Richard Neuton, for example, had to pay for the holly he cut for his servants, while non-burgesses, such as the poor, and especially women, were regularly amerced small sums of between 1*d.* and 4*d.* for collecting wood, mostly from the nearby park.[90] The licence to prune or fell underwood was sometimes given and in one year the profit from hazel (*hassellyn Warres*), by means of one axe, was granted as a fee to an outsider for 13*s.* 4*d.*[91] The Black Prince also made a small number of gifts of oaks in the forest.[92] The forest eyres of the mid-fourteenth century – sitting in 1347 and 1357 – introduced substantial fines for a large number of forest offences although the financial origin of these courts should not be underestimated.[93]

A further potential for exploitation of the forest woodland arose out of the foraging or pannaging of pigs. Pigs were common, if not universal, amongst medieval households and some forests, like Delamere in Cheshire, supported large numbers.[94] In Macclesfield forest they were the least numerous of the domestic animals although they appear to have been kept almost universally in small numbers. In the second half of the fourteenth century the pannage of six or more by an individual was rare and probably reflects the absence of any large tract of available woodland. The right to forage pigs was charged at a standard rate of 1*d.* a head, and of the 100 or more people charged each year for this the vast majority paid only 1*d.* or 2*d.*[95] Although the woodland was not usually referred to, Lyme was specifically mentioned and in one year the profits from acorns (*glandes in bosco de Lyme*) were sold there.[96]

[90] SC 2/252/15 m. 5, SC 2/253/9 m. 5d.

[91] SC 2/252/10 m. 5d.

[92] For example, *B.P.R.* iii, pp. 406, 460, 480 and 484.

[93] CHES 33/5, CHES 33/6. Forest men were fined £87, the burgesses £40 and Robert Legh, the elder, over £88 in the 1357 forest eyre, *Ch.Acc.* (1), pp. 248–9 and 262–3; Booth, *Financial Administration*, pp. 122–3.

[94] B. M. C. Hussain, 'Delamere Forest in Later Medieval Times', *Trans. Hist. Soc. of Lancs. and Cheshire*, 107 (1949), p. 38.

[95] This was the usual sum elsewhere, Birrell, 'Common Rights', pp. 37–40.

[96] For example, SC 2/253/7 m. 1, SC 2/253/9 mm. 11–12, SC 2/254/5 m. 7. The foresters' rights to pannage are summarised in *V.C.H. Chester*, II, p. 181: they were quit of both their own and their men's pigs, they were entitled to the lord's best pig, and 1*d.* each every day during the time of pannage; the foresters were, however, included in the lists of payments at 1*d.* per animal.

A number of other forest revenues were exploited in the later fourteenth-century either through sale or leasing in the manor court. The waifs and abstracts were purchased or leased annually for the sum of one mark. From 1362–3 to 1365–6 they were held by stock-keeper John Alcok and Henry Prestbury and from the later 1370s by forester John Cresswall and at least one other lessee, for terms of between one and three years.[97] In addition, coal was either sold or the right to mine was leased (*minera carbon(is) maritt(ime)*), for 6s. 8d. in 1354–5 and during the 1380s to forester John Sherd for 8s. 0d.[98] The profit from bees (*apes*), in terms of their honey, hives and nests (*mel* and *alviare*) was either sold or, during the 1350s and 1360s, leased to riding-forester Robert Legh.[99] Fines were imposed when they were taken without licence, as two men found to their cost in 1384. A fee, called *Ruddyngfee*, for the finding of three horses (*caballis*) as waif at Tods Cliff was granted to an outsider at 1s. 2d. per horse. In one instance woollen thread (*fil(etum) lane*) found within the forest was purchased for 4d.[100]

A further large-scale woodland enterprise were the iron forges operated, largely by successive bailiffs, during the first half of the fourteenth-century. These were usually charged at the customary sum of 18d. a week and the majority appear to have been short-lived. One which began in the 1330s was said to have consumed one thousand green oaks and underwood to the value of 100 marks over a period of ten years. At least three were located in both Midgley and Dane Wood and it is clear that they were operating under official sanction using wood from within the enclosures: one used two acres of underwood at Rogersbottom, while one at the Echencliff was known as 'le Quenesford'. In 1349 two forges worth

[97] SC 2/252/11 m. 5 – SC 2/253/3 m. 10d.; SC 2/253/6 m. 3 – SC 2/254/4 m. 5d.

[98] SC 2/252/6 m. 3d., SC 2/254/4 m. 5d., SC 2/254/9 m. 5d., SC 2/254/10 m. 6 and SC 2/254/11 m. 4. No precise location for the coal-mines can be given although at the start of the seventeenth century there were three at Disley, Rainow and Pott Shrigley, J. Laughton, *Seventeenth Century Rainow, The story of a Cheshire hill village* (1990), p. 27; later place-name evidence also relates to Lyme.

[99] For example, SC 2/253/5 m. 10 and SC 2/254/12 m. 7d. The term *vespetum*, usually referring to a wasp nest, was also used, SC 2/254/5 m. 8d. In 1447 'les bikes et les hiettes' were taken into the King's hands, *Deputy Keeper's Report* (1876), p. 485.

[100] SC 2/254/5 m. 8; SC 2/252/14 m. 4.

over £17 a year were in the lord's hands because of the Black Death.[101] After the pestilence their numbers and impact upon the woodland management rapidly decreased, and a decline in the demand for iron may well have been a factor here. In 1352 John son of Roger Sutton, the grandson of the person who had operated one of the largest forges, paid a fine of 10s. 0d. for erecting a forge using the wood growing in his own land. In 1359–60 forester Thomas Worth paid £3 for licence to erect a forge for eighteen weeks at the substantial sum of 3s. 4d. a week; he died, however, two years later. The one area where small-scale forges continued to work was in the borough where at least six were in operation in the 1380s.[102]

The medieval countryside supported a significant number of skilled carpenters while medieval peasants, especially those dwelling in forests, would have supplemented their income by making tools and furniture.[103] There are several examples from Macclesfield of individuals taking wood for these purposes. For example: Richard Broke of Adlington took one large birch (*grossum lentiscum*), worth 2d., to make cart-wheels at the Longside in 1391; William Whitehull from Whaley paid 20s. 6d. for various trees, cuttings and loppings including some curved pieces of wood or 'cubles'; and Richard Alcok, a carpenter who rented a cottage for 2d. in Bollington, made a 6d. fine in 1371 for carrying off curved pieces of wood.[104] Carpenter and wheelwright William Hayfeld held a burgage in Jordangate and, for a short period at least, fourteen acres of land, meadow, and wood in Hurdsfield. His court appearances reveal that he paid for loppings of trees, and cut small amounts of holly in Rainow common for his animals.[105]

The utilisation of fish and other animal resources was regulated in the manor court where the fines and amercements again more closely resembled a licensing system. There were many examples

[101] Booth, *Financial Administration*, p. 97; CHES 33/6 m. 40.

[102] SC 2/252/4 m. 4d.; SC 2/252/11 m. 6d., SC 2/252/13 m. 3; SC 11/898 m. 1.

[103] C. Dyer, 'English Peasant Buildings in the Later Middle Ages', *Medieval Archaeology*, 30 (1986), pp. 18–45; J. Birrell, 'Peasant Craftsmen in the Medieval Forest', *Agricultural History Review*, 17 (1969), pp. 91–107.

[104] SC 2/254/13 m. 4; SC 2/253/2 m. 3d. – SC 2/254/5 m. 8d.; SC 2/253/6 m. 3.

[105] SC 2/253/2 m. 3, SC 2/253/7 m. 3d., SC 2/254/4 m. 5d., SC 2/254/7 m. 2, SC 2/254/13 m. 6d.

of fishing and those presented were generally either outsiders or local smallholders. In 1371 five men were amerced 6*d*. each and in 1375 two men from Eaton near Congleton were similarly accused of fishing in the River Dane. The fines levied were in most cases very small: in 1384 one man paid only 2*d*., and in 1375 Ranulf Rathebon was amerced 8*d*. for fishing and hunting hares over a period of ten years. The taking of birds would have brought added nutrition to the diet of local peasants and in one instance outsider William Underclyf took game birds over a period of three years (*gallos silvestres*).[106] The foresters' rights included the taking of hares, foxes, squirrels, badgers, fish, otters, cats, male sparrowhawks and eagles within their own land.[107] The woodland names of Hawkhurst, Hawksyard and Hawksclough along with the tenement Sparhauke-sert suggest the presence of birds of prey, and in 1366 Henry Pot, a smallholder of Rainow, took a sparrowhawk (*espervarium*) from the woods in Echencliff – presumably for falconry. The eyre of 1357 also refers, more surprisingly, to a badger (*tessonem*) being taken at Rainow.[108] In 1371 Adam Shore, described as a common fowler (*ankepator*) was found guilty of fishing in the lord's waters and of cutting down an oak worth 6*d*.[109]

In addition to the separate demesne woodlands and pastures the manor townships contained extensive commons and wastes. These exploited the higher ground and were primarily a pasture resource reserved for tenants. Other forest dwellers, though, may have had some rights there and two outside men were fined 6*d*. each for trespassing in Sutton common – *sine libertate foreste*.[110] The ridges of the Minns were used by tenants of Sutton and Bosley, and Kerridge by those of Pott Shrigley, Rainow and Bollington. Some of these were situated away from the townships centres, such as Thursbitch, an area of upland close to the Derbyshire border, which belonged to Rainow. Although the manor tenants had the right to use all the commons, there could be disputes with neighbouring townships. In 1351, for instance, the lord of Bosley complained that Macclesfield men were daily pasturing their animals on the township's common

---

[106] SC 2/253/6 m. 3, SC 2/253/9 mm. 3–4, SC 2/254/5 m. 7.

[107] *V.C.H. Chester*, II, p. 181; CHES 33/6 mm. 42–3.

[108] The sparrowhawk, SC 2/253/2 m. 3, and the badger, CHES 33/6 m. 39. 'Badgers were probably the quarry of the peasantry', J. Cummins, *The Hound and Hawk: The Art of Medieval Hunting* (1988), pp. 151–52.

[109] SC 2/253/6 m. 3.

[110] SC 2/252/15 m. 3.

and that his tenants 'dared not … impound the beasts … because of threats'.[111] The borough charter allowed burgesses common rights throughout the manor and in spite of these complaints Bosley tenants were regularly presented for overburdening the common pasture of the adjacent township of Sutton (Table 5).

The rights to use the commons was presumably linked to landholding (in a similar way to Roger Oldhed's holding of Over Midgley) whereby individuals were allowed to graze a certain number of animals.[112] Excessive grazing was controlled by the manor court and in more serious instances by indictment in the Hundred eyre. The presentment of individuals for overburdening (*oneratio* and *superoneratio*) had a practical, as well as financial, role in maintaining the vegetation and thus the quality of the pasture. As with other forest resources the pattern of regular and repeated fines, assessed according to the damage, is suggestive of *de facto* licensing. When Rainow tenant William son of Roger Lowe was accused of overstocking the common with twelve draught-beasts, 30 sheep and three working horses in 1370, he incurred a fine of 2s. 0d.[113]

There were restrictions on the amount of wood that could be taken from the commons and fines were again levied in the local courts. At Kerridge, one of the woods where burgesses had common rights, a smallholder took a horse and cart-load of stakes and another man cut down 1,000 sticks of hazel and hawthorn eleven years later (to the damage of 2s. 0d.). At Whaley 1,000 holly cuttings were taken either from the common or from an attached woodland. It was not unusual for outsiders to pay to exploit these wood resources and a man from Derbyshire, for instance, cut down wood to the value of 3d. in Disley, whose common land contained both holly and hazel.[114]

Bollington wood had a woodward and contained hawthorn, holly, and hazel which was sometimes collected to make hafts. Elsewhere

---

[111] *B.P.R.* iii, p. 23. Although Bosley was part of the Montalt barony, its tenants were under the jurisdiction of the Macclesfield manor court.

[112] One cow and 20 sheep, for instance, were allowed on each acre of stubble in the neighbouring Derbyshire uplands, Wharfe, *Rural Settlement*, pp. 120–1; no such restrictions apparently existed on the seventeenth century commons, Laughton, *Rainow*, p. 8.

[113] SC 2/253/5 m. 10. He also cut down holly, SC 2/254/7 m. 2, SC 2/254/15 m. 3, and was indicted at least three times. See p. 116 n. 104 below.

[114] SC 2/254/15 m. 3, SC 2/254/3 m. 6; CHES 25/22 m. 15; SC 2/253/2 m. 3, SC 2/254/11 m. 4.

in Bollington common there were small amounts of birch and alder, such as that cut down and valued at 2*d*. Burgess John Boyle took four cart-loads of holly and hazel twigs valued at 16*d*. from the wood, while hazel was cut by two men from Alderley and Prestbury. On another occasion a probable outsider was indicted and fined 1*s*. 0*d*. for taking a cartload of raddling.[115] It is likely, therefore, that at least some of this land was enclosed and managed as coppice woodland. The other scrub vegetation (*browles*), consisting of the heather, gorse and bracken, was available once a year at the discretion of the foresters and under their supervision. A little over a century later there are references to ricks (*tasas*) being raised on the commons along with the encroachment of cottages.[116]

The records relating to both the demesne pastures and the commons help us to estimate the number of domestic livestock in the manor-forest. During the later fourteenth century more than 800 cattle or other young cattle, 300 to 400 working horses, fewer than 30 cows and nearly 1000 sheep were mentioned. Unfortunately as the rolls relating to escapes and folds exist for fewer than one in four years the figures should be treated with caution, and it is likely that far higher numbers were present.[117] In comparison the occasional sale of heriots in the manor court suggests that oxen, as in Lancashire, were the main draught animal.[118] The references to carts (*plaustra*) show that they were drawn by teams of either four or eight draught animals.

The ownership of a large number of working horses (*caballi*) was a consequence of both the landscape and settlement pattern, as these were better suited to small plots and could also serve as pack-animals.[119] The keeping of cows was not widespread among the

[115] SC 2/253/2 m. 3d., SC 2/253/9 m. 14, SC 2/254/1 m. 3d., SC 2/254/2 m. 9, SC 2/254/5 m. 10, SC 2/254/10 m. 6.

[116] *B.P.R.* iii, p. 15; CHES 33/9 m. 1.

[117] In 1399 it was claimed that 700 stock had been driven off by Staffordshire and Derbyshire men into these neighbouring counties, *C.P.R., 1399–1401*, p. 83.

[118] The word *averium*, meaning cattle in general, was distinct from that used for a working horse, *caballus*, in the lists of escapes. It was used in 70% of the heriots sold in the halmote, compared to 14% for cows and only 5% for working horses; for example, SC 2/252/4 m. 4d. Cunliffe Shaw, *Royal Forest of Lancaster*, p. 411.

[119] J. Langdon, *Horses, Oxen and Technological Innovation* (Cambridge, 1986), p. 295.

tenants and they tended to be concentrated in the hands of the more wealthy. The Calverhale family (of 'calves corner' or Calrofold), who were smallholders from Rainow, appear to be one peasant family involved dairying. As well as making payments for escapes their livestock in 1385 included three cows worth 5s. 0d., two bullocks worth 6s. 0d., and five yearling calves worth 1s. 4d.[120]

Flocks of between 40 and 60 sheep were grazed by a few well-established and wealthy peasant families, as well as by local clergy who would have placed theirs in the custody of shepherds. The grant of the grange at Wincle near Midgley to Combermere abbey had included, so the abbey claimed, the provision for a very large number of sheep.[121] These larger flocks, though, were rare and most of those grazed were in groups of under ten or 20, with even the poorest inhabitants keeping one or two. When wealthy peasant William Shoteswall of Whaley had his goods seized his livestock amounted to six sheep and two lambs, with wool to the value of 6d. Another wealthy peasant was John son of Adam Brocwalhurst of Kettleshulme, who has already been referred to in connection with wood sales for fodder. In addition to the more than 20 draught animals, including several working horses, and pigs that he owned in the later 1350s, he also grazed a flock of 100 sheep throughout the commons of the manor in the early 1360s – from Sutton and Macclesfield in the south to Whaley in the north.[122] The significant number of local tenants with sheep contrasts both with the rest of Cheshire and many other lowland forests.[123] The landscape may already have been contributing to the development of a woollen cloth industry.

Cheshire was outside the three-field system area and there was

[120] These were taken from their daughter Joan following her indictment for a felony, SC 2/254/5 m. 8. See the biography of Thomas Stanystrete in Appendix One.

[121] As well as sheep a smaller number of cattle and horses: however as the charter was a likely forgery these figures cannot be relied upon, *Charters of the Anglo-Norman Earls*, pp. 237–9.

[122] In 1385/6 Reginald Dounes (Parker in 1376, SC6/804/8 m. 4) was said to have cut holly in Lyme for four animals and 200 sheep, CHES 25/21 m. 25d. There were some large flocks of sheep by the end of the sixteenth Century in Rainow, Laughton *Rainow*, p. 20.

[123] M. M. Postan, 'Village Livestock in the Thirteenth Century', *Economic History Review*, 2nd ser., 15 (1962/3), pp. 219–49; C. Dyer, *Lords and Peasants in a Changing Society, The Estates of the Bishopric of Worcester 680–1540* (Cambridge, 1980), p. 329.

a tendency in the county for the common arable to be divided into either one or two townfields or multiple fields with divisions based on furlongs.[124] In forests and upland wastes the situation was more complex as assarts could be absorbed into open fields or formed into separate farmsteads or enclosures.[125] The landscape that developed within the manor of Macclesfield was a combination of open-field cultivation with strips, close to the township centres, together with enclosed crofts, fields or 'places', with or without dwellings, that extended a considerable distance into the outlying wastes and commons. The former included the land divided into bovates around the River Bollin in Sutton. The latter were, in effect, the forerunners of the later enclosed farms, and might include pasture, meadow and woodland in addition to arable.[126] The division of holdings into selions and furlongs, of below a quarter of a Cheshire acre or part of a rood, was common. The main crop in Cheshire and the north west was oats although a significant amount of wheat was grown in some areas.[127] In Macclesfield oats, rye and barley all occured in this period.

The bovates in Sutton well illustrate the complexities of landholding and service in the manor after the Black Death. A half bovate, described as 'nief land' (*terra nativa*) and lying vacant and in decay, was entered by 'freeholder' Richard Achard in 1356. He was liable to the customary services, which included the making of a stall for the collection of toll at All Saints' fair in Macclesfield.

---

[124] Possibly evolving from an infield-outfield system, Sylvester, *Open Fields of Cheshire*, pp. 17–28, and 'A Note on Medieval Three-Course Arable Systems in Cheshire', *Trans. Hist. Soc. of Lancs. and Cheshire*, 110 (1958), pp. 183–86; H. E. Hallam (ed.), *The Agrarian History of England and Wales, II 1042–1350* (Cambridge, 1988), p. 399. See also G. White, 'Open fields and rural settlement in Medieval west Cheshire' in *The Middle Ages in the North-West*, (ed.) T. Scott and P. Starkey (1995), pp. 15–35.

[125] B. K. Roberts, 'A Study of Medieval Colonisation in the Forest of Arden, Warwickshire', *Agricultural History Review*, 16 (1968), pp. 101–113; for the Yorkshire uplands see T. A. M. Bishop, 'Assarting and the Growth of the Open Fields', *Economic History Review*, 6 (1935), p. 19; and Postles, *South Yorkshire Pennines*, p. 12.

[126] These can clearly be seen in an early seventeenth century map, MR 354.

[127] P. H. W. Booth, '"Farming for Profit" in the Fourteenth Century: the Cheshire Estates of the Earldom of Chester', *Journal of the Chester Archaeological Society*, 62 (1979), p. 77; P. Morgan, *War and Society in Medieval Cheshire, 1277–1403*, Chetham Society, 3rd ser., 34 (1987), pp. 82–3.

He was later amerced, along with other tenants, for failing to make this stall – even though he had sublet the holding to Alan Pekke on entry.[128] Villein William Boyle held a messuage and four acres in Sutton, including one of new increment, around the time of the pestilence. This holding passed in the early 1350s to William son of Roger Lowe. During his tenancy it was listed with his main holding which was in the township of Rainow and, as it did not form his main tenement, was probably sublet. The land next passed to William's sister-in-law, Alice, who married Robert Dounes of Sutton after payment of a merchet in her widowhood in 1371. Robert was subsequently described in the 1383/4 rental as holding, among other lands, 1½ bovates by right of his wife. In 1377 Robert and Alice granted a croft, measuring one rood, lying by the house of another bovate holder, Alexander Gaoler, and in 1382 they were both amerced for failing to make the customary stall for toll.[129]

Those described as 'villeins' or of 'servile status' can only be identified through their payment of merchet at the manor court. This was paid on only ten occasions between 1350 and 1371, when it was last recorded, and not by any of the free or customary tenants who were now holding the bovate land; of these, eight were smallholders who paid a fine in court to espouse a widow.[130] One common factor shared by this handful of villeins was their apparent poverty, and when Robert Bargh died in 1360/1 the sale of his goods and possessions realised only 13s. 1d.[131] The remaining services continued to be exacted even though the use of the terms to describe villein status fell into disuse during the last quarter of the century. For example, in the 1390s the farmers of part of Bollington township and its mill were successful in reaffirming carting services from a tenant via a suit in the manor court.[132]

---

[128] SC 2/252/7 m. 2, SC 2/254/3 m. 4.

[129] SC 11/899 m. 3; SC 2/252/4 m. 4d.; SC 11/898 m. 3; SC 2/253/5 m. 11d.; SC 2/253/10 m. 4; SC 2/254/3 m. 4.

[130] The only villeins were Agnes daughter of Hervey Bargh and Alice Fox, in 1351; both Agnes' sister, Margaret, and Alice held nief land in Sutton, SC 2/252/3 mm. 1–2d, SC 11/899 m. 2–2d. The fine to espouse one of the lord's widows ranged from 1s. 0d., 1s. 6d., 2s. 0d., to 3s. 4d., SC 2/252/2 m. 4d, SC 2/252/15 m. 3, SC 2/253/2 m. 2, m. 3d, SC 2/253/5 m. 11d.

[131] SC 2/253/1 m. 2d.; see Table 21.

[132] SC 2/254/13 m. 4–4d. Carting services in Bollington were still owed in 1503, CHES 33/9 m. 6.

The majority of individual holdings in the manor were concentrated in one of the manor townships and only one in ten people held land in a neighbouring vill as well. The manor was roughly divided along geographical lines between the south-east, centred on Sutton, Hurdsfield and Rainow, and the north-east, centred on Whaley, Kettleshulme and Disley. In total 44 people held land in two townships, and ten in three: forester John son of Richard Sutton held land in four, and William Dounes of Shrigley held land in five. In the north-east land tended to be concentrated in larger holdings with a significant number of smallholders and undertenants. However, as commons were shared, inter-township boundaries were probably ill-defined. This rule did not, though, extend to Bosley where only one of the 35 tenants in c. 1400, Richard Hordren in neighbouring Sutton, held land elsewhere. The tenants in this township, who paid 1s. 0d. an acre, were mostly wealthy peasants with a third of tenants holding over 22 acres and only a sixth holding under nine acres.[133]

In the second half of the fourteenth century more than 80 acres of approved or assarted land, or 6% of the rented total, was let in the Macclesfield manor court. This, which attracted entry-fines of 4s. 0d. an acre and rents of 8d. an acre, changed hands in two main periods: the late 1350s and early 1360s and the 1380s and 1390s. Apart from the two larger enclosures of 20 and 16½ acres undertaken by members of two influential local families – Nicholas Dounes in Normanwood (Kettleshulme) in 1359 and William Joudrel in Disley in 1360/1 – these consisted principally of areas of under three acres with many being intakes of a quarter of an acre or less.[134] A further 45 acres of waste were sold in 1380. As by far the greater part was of township wasteland, this should not be considered in the same light as the pre-Black Death enclosure of underwood by local lords, and it may well reflect a pattern that had been established within the manor over the previous two centuries.[135]

---

[133] The size of these holdings was underestimated, M. J. Bennett *Community, Class and Careerism*, pp. 102–4.
[134] SC2 252/10 m. 5d., SC 2/254/5 m. 7; SC 2/252/12 m. 2, SC 2/252/15 m. 2.
[135] For the infield outfield system see G. C. Homans *English Villagers of the thirteenth century* (Camb. Mass. 1941) and Postan *Economy and Society*, p. 60; these small scale assarts were also a feature of the Yorkshire uplands, M. Stinson 'Assarting and Poverty in early fourteenth century western Yorkshire', *Landscape History*, 5 (1983), pp. 61–2.

The small areas were usually described as either parcels or enclosed places (*placea*), and were often situated adjacent to houses. They were enclosed by a wide range of different inhabitants including burgesses, smallholders and a forester. The parcels included: 1*d*. of yearly rent, next to a house, by Alice widow of Richard Eydale in 1360; 2*d*. by John son of William Holyncete in 1384 and 2*d*. by John son of Robert Holyncete twelve years later; ½*d*. by forester John Cresswall in 1385; and 1*d*. by Hugh Chorlegh in 1396. Other small enclosures worth between ½*d*. and 2*d*. were let in Rainow, Hurdsfield and Sutton in 1363 and 1366–8. These intakes related to the new enclosure and re-enclosing of wastes as well as the infilling of vacant areas; for example the ½ rood of new land adjacent to the mill in Sutton taken by Adam Bagylegh in 1396.[136] Some would have been temporary extensions to the arable, such as the 3½ acres of poor and stony ground approved without licence by William Joudrel which was already out of cultivation by the time his son was charged for its assarting; some sublet plots may also have been soon abandoned. Even the more substantial examples enclosing was rather limited in scope and included the 3½ acres of underwood (*in defenso*) taken by Robert son of William Dounes and John Walkedene in 1388, and the three acres of the old Midgley vaccary, by then leased out, which was taken by the aforementioned Roger Oldhed in 1390.[137] The period saw the rise of many families who were able to increase and consolidate their holdings as a result of regular acquisition and exchange of land. It has been calculated that William Joudrel (Jodrell), for instance, received five times the rent he paid himself through subletting, and this enabled him to build up a powerful land base.[138] Like William, many of those gaining lands were the inhabitants of the townships in the north-east of the manor. In Whaley Richard Whitehull increased his income from rents by £1.[139] There are other examples of this.

Firstly, William son of Roger Ashton entered two messuages and thirteen acres of land in Kettleshulme which had been his father's in 1376. When his son, another William, entered his holdings in 1387, amounting to just under 25 acres, a near doubling of their

[136] SC2 2/252/11 m. 5, SC 2/254/6 mm. 6–6d., SC 2/254/12 m. 6, SC 2/255/2 mm. 3–4d.; SC 2/252/15 m. 2, SC 2/253/2 mm. 2–3d., SC 2/253/3 m. 10d.

[137] SC 2/254/5 m. 7; SC 2/254/9 m. 4d.; SC 2/254/12 m. 5d.

[138] M. J. Bennett, *Community, Class and Careerism*, pp. 106–7.

[139] See his biography in Appendix One and, for example, SC 2/253/5 m. 10, SC 2/254/3 m. 3.

land had taken place within a decade. His elder brother Benedict, who had already entered a 8¾ acres tenement in Kettleshulme in 1361, went on to concentrate his holdings in Whaley where he paid entry-fines of £3 14s. 2d. over the next 20 years. His acquisition in this township of ten messuages of various sizes and rents included tenements of twelve and eight acres and a further eight-acre tenement in Kettleshulme. In all he acquired more than 40 acres of land, although the total acreage may have been larger as at least two of these holdings were rented at 4d. an acre. The holdings were a combination of land attached to messuages and modest enclosures like those of two, four and five acres. He leased or sold ten acres, although his actual assarting was meagre and included only one rood and fifteen perches.[140]

Secondly, the under-forester Robert Shryglegh and Thomas, his son, significantly increased their holdings in Rainow and Shrigley townships. Before acquiring the nearby tenement of Spuley, a five-acre enclosure with a house in Rainow, Robert had assarted the three acres that had separated it from his house. This later passed to his son Thomas whose other acquisitions, through purchase and leasing, included six acres, an enclosed meadow, a croft with a house and wood of around five acres, and a further ¾ of an acre in Rainow. He also granted a messuage with 9½ acres, held jointly with rent holder John Rossyndale in Sutton, and 9½ acres (Calrofold) in Rainow. His brothers Robert and John obtained Sowcar, which was a two acre enclosure in Rainow, and another three-acre enclosure in Sutton. Thomas's son John further increased the family's land by assarting small areas at the close of the century.[141]

In conclusion, the overwhelming majority of tenants of Macclesfield manor in the later fourteenth century were either free or customary tenants who were quit of labour and most other services.

---

[140] For example, William, SC 2/253/9 mm. 3–4, SC 2/254/8 m. 2d.; Benedict, SC 2/252/13 mm. 3–4, SC 2/252/14 m. 3d., SC 2/252/15 mm. 2d.–3, SC 2/253/2 m. 2d., SC 2/253/3 m. 8, SC 2/254/4 m. 4d. For a full list, see their biographies in Appendix One.

[141] SC 2/252/9 m. 5d., SC 2/252/10 m. 5d., SC 2/252/15 m. 3, SC 2/253/5 mm. 10d.–11, SC 2/253/6 m. 3d., SC 2/253/10 m. 4, SC 2/254/1 m. 12, SC 2/254/5 m. 7, SC 2/254/11 m. 6d.; SC 2/253/11 m. 3d., SC 2/253/12 m. 1d., SC 2/254/11 m. 4, SC 2/254/12 mm. 6–6d., SC 2/254/14 m. 5, SC 2/255/2 m. 4. John Shryglegh had a career as a clerk in Ireland, M. J. Bennett, 'Sources and Problems in the Study of Social Mobility: Cheshire in the Later Middle Ages', *Trans. Hist. Soc. of Lancs. and Cheshire*, 128 (1979), p. 63.

They were able to exchange and sell their land on surrender at the manor court on payment of a fine or relief of two years rent. This led, particularly after the Black Death, to the consolidation of holdings and considerable subletting. The townships with the largest number of holdings were Sutton and Rainow to the south-west and Disley and Whaley on the foothills of the Pennines to the north-east. As forest assarts the vast majority of these holdings were rented at 8*d*. an acre and had been mostly approved and enclosed on a piecemeal basis. The process created a landscape of small fields and enclosures, as well as larger more isolated farmsteads, which were extended into the wastes by small assarts or intakes that were, by this period at least, usually of less than one acre.

The exploitation of the demesne areas of the forest for grazing, fodder, fuel and carpentry was regulated by fines or amercements in the local courts. The first half of the fourteenth century had witnessed the most intensive use of the demesne and by the time of the Black Prince in the middle of the century, if not before, the demands of lordly income had already overridden those of game management. The second half of the century was characterised by the increasing leasing of revenues and the continued evolution of the demesne pastures into what became, in effect, common pastures for the tenants. The woodland of the ancient forest had been largely eroded through a combination of over-use, neglect, assarting for cultivation and over-grazing. However, both Lyme Handley and Swanscoe were later converted to parks, and some woodland remained intact until more recent times.[142]

The process of leasing concentrated wealth and power in the hands of a few local tenants and outsiders, and effectively converted some hamlets and townships into separate manors. Those who had benefited as a result of patronage, office holding and land acquisition had by the fifteenth century attained gentry status. These developments can be seen from the 1390s when the mills at Rainow, worth 16*s*. o*d*. a year, Pott, worth 5*s*. o*d*. a year, and Bollington, worth nine marks a year were leased by Geoffrey Dounes for terms of ten years in 1391/2. From 1398 the township of Sutton was leased by John Legh for £20 annually and in the following year the herbage and pasturage of Macclesfield park, including the manor-house and orchard, was let for a term of twelve years to John Macclesfield,

---

[142] See, for example, P. F. Kenworthey, 'Rural Settlement in East Cheshire' unpubl. Thesis (Manchester 1949).

senior, clerk, at ten marks a year.[143] By the mid-fifteenth century the general escapes of all pastures were similarly leased.

At the end of the fifteenth century the piecemeal enclosure of the commons and wastes by local families, who were now described as either yeomen or labourers, was still taking place.[144] In the case of yeoman Nicholas Adshead of Shrigley, for instance, his enclosure of two acres occurred a century after a Robert Addesheved, a wealthy peasant holding nearly 20 acres in the same vill, had assarted a small parcel of half a rood; a John Adshead also entered the borough in the earlier fifteenth century.[145] Other yeomen approving land at this time had ancestors of a similar status: John Brodhurst (Brocwalhurst in the fourteenth century, later Brocklehurst), Ralph Dey and Ralph Holynshed (Holyncete). The labourers were frequently women and some were building squatter cottages on the common land. Agnes Hordron approved two parcels totalling an acre in Sutton while more than a century earlier a Richard Hordren had held eight acres with a house there, while one servant Maud daughter of Thomas probably dwelt nearby. Finally, in the late thirteenth century two men had assarted an acre with two houses in Hephales in Poynton while in the fourteenth century a family of this name were established smallholding tenants in Sutton. In 1352, for instance, Margery Heppal, entered just under eight acres while a century and a half later a person of the same name built a cottage worth ½d. in Sutton common.

Table 1   *Fines Levied for Escapes on to the Demesne Pastures*

Animal	Foggage	Herbage
Horse (*Caballus*)	1½–4d.	3d.–1s.
Cattle (*Averium*)	1–2d.	3–5d.
Sheep (*Ovis*)	¼–1d. (usually ½d.)	¼–1d.

---

[143] Sutton had previously been leased to Ralph Standish before 1378, and to John Beauchamp for life in 1382, *C.P.R., 1346–99*, pp. 461, 124, 185, 216.

[144] CHES 33/9.

[145] SC 2/325/15 m. 6d.

Table 2   *Oaks Felled, c.1327–57*

Enclosure	Total	Notes
Disley Wood	12	
Dane Wood	27	4 to canon o. Rochester at 3s. 4d. (Hawksyard) 6 to earl o. Huntingdon at 10s. (Hawksyard)
Lyme Wood	100	60 at 3s. 4d., 40 for lord
Shrigley	432	40 for lord
Others	39	3 to Ad. Mottrum at 5s. (probably Lyme)
Unspecified	657	
Total	*1,267*	

Table 3   *Oaks Felled in Shrigley Wood, c.1327–1357*

Year	No. of Oaks
1327/8	76
1332/3	15 (*Shrigley Common*)
1333/4	54
1335/6	20
1336/7	2
1337/8	14
1340/1	13
1341/2	103
1342/3	6
1343/4	33
1344/5	12
1346/7	2
1347/8	2
	+ 80 (including 40 for the lord)
Total:	432

CHES 33/6 mm. 36d.–38d.

Table 4 *Wood Sold in the Forest by Ralph Carpenter, 1382/3*

Name of purchaser	O.	Wood	Value	Location
Adam Tydrynton	B	1 crop	12d.	
William Lynster	B	1 tree	2s.	
		1 crop	2d.	
Hamon Henryson		2 trees	2s.	
Richard Hubart		2 trees	12d.	
William Whitehull	T	1 tree	18d.	
		1 green tree	2s. 6d.	
		1 tree	12d.	
		1 crop	30d.	
John Kempe junior	U-T	1 tree	2s.	
		1 tree	6d.	Lyme
John *Hickesone* of Hawkhurst	U-T	1 tree	18d.	
John Davenport of Bramhall (pledge John Sherd)		1 tree	4s.	
Adam Spark	B	1 crop	2d.	
Robert Niksone		1 tree	3d.	
Robert Jonessone		1 tree	3d.	
John Nycolsone		1 tree	12d.	
Robert Brocwalhurst and Robert Jonessone	U-T	1 green oak	3s.	'Cartlach'
Richard Whitehull	T	1 crop	4s.	Swineshurstgate
		1 crop	5s.	the Longlache
Roger Turnour	T	1 tree		Knuckwood
		2 trees	20d.	Swineshurst
John Godemon and Adam Hephales	T T	5 crops	16d.	the Boothgreen
William Hayfeld	B	3 crops	6d.	Edalebrink
John Holyncete	T	1 crop	3d.	the Oakenbank
Gilbert Hulcokes	U-T	3 crops	12d.	the Oakenbank
Roger Oldhed	T	1 crop	6d.	the Oakenbank
Robert Addesheved	T	1 crop	18d.	Edale
Peter Frenche	B	1 crop	2d.	Edale

Name of purchaser	O.	Wood	Value	Location
William Hugsone		1 crop	2d.	Edalehead
		1 crop	12d.	Edalebrink
John Schagh vicar of Prestbury		2 crops	18d.	Swineshurst & Edale
William Goldesone		1 crop	2d.	Hazelhurst
Robert Hyde		1 crop	18d.	Hazel 'lak'
Adam Taillour		1 crop	6d.	Edale
Sum			47s. 1d.	

Abbreviations: O, Origin (T – tenant; U-T – under-tenant; B – burgess);
(*croppe*: cropping '*stipit*': tree)
Halmote, SC 2/254/4 m. 5d.

Table 5 *Bosley Tenants Indicted for Pasturing their Livestock in
Sutton Common, 1378/9*

Richard Peket	thirteen oxen & other animals
Adam Donelot	sixteen oxen & cows
William Hordren	sixteen oxen & heifers
Adam Huetteson	sixteen heifers & other cattle
Edmund Clewlowe	all his cattle
William Neuton	twelve heifers & other animals
Robert Perkynsone	20 heifers & other animals
John Wodecok	ten oxen, cows, & heifers
Roger Hordren	twelve oxen & heifers
Ranulph Wodecok	twelve oxen & cows
Richard Peket junior	six cattle
Jak Fylle	twelve cattle & heifers
William Swettok	six cattle & heifers
William Revesone	six cattle
Adam Bouker	twelve cattle
Peter Dobbeson	twelve cattle
John Mayoteson	sixteen cattle & heifers
Henry Shepherd	ten cattle
William Shepherd	twelve cattle & heifers
Edmund Ashton (of Sutton)	twelve cattle & four heifers
William Togod (of Sutton)	nine cattle

averiis: cattle; *bobus*: oxen; *juvencis*: heifers; *vaccis*: cows.
SC 2/254/1 m. 3d.

Table 6 *Land Rented in the Manor Townships,*
in the Later Fourteenth Century

Township	Approx. Acreage[1]	Approx. Assarts 1347–77[2]	% of Holdings with some 'new' land, 1384[3]
Sutton[4]	530	3%	
Hurdsfield	130	4%	
Rainow	240	2%	
Disley	155	10%	90%
Pott Shrigley	180	25%	
Kettleshulme[5]	126	1.5%	50%
Yeardsley/Whaley	165	2%	55%
Macclesfield Borough: Ancient Lands[6]	43½	10%	
Roughwood, Roewood	130	18%	
Offenomes	22		

[1] Based on the standard rent of 8*d.* per acre for forest assarts. Some land in Sutton, Rainow and Whaley was rented at 4*d.* an acre (or less). The rentals frequently do not refer to the actual acreage, SC 11/898–899.

[2] Described as approved or assarted either in the forest eyres, 1347–8 and 1357, or in the halmote, *c.* 1349–1377.

[3] Where calculable.

[4] Excluding Wincle, Midgley, Hollinset and other outlying areas. In neighbouring Bosley there were 702 acres in the early fifteenth century, Bruell, 'John de Macclesfield Cartulary', fo. 7.

[5] An estimate.

[6] This excludes burgages.

2 Courts and Demography

'The study ... of the family and domestic experiences of the medieval peasantry has a very bright future ... it will be full of extraordinary details about the social experiences of these people.'[1]

So concluded Judith Bennett in her introduction to the use of court rolls to reconstruct medieval village families. Modern research using these sources largely developed in the 1960s following the lead taken by Professor Raftis at Toronto.[2] He has not been alone in describing them as 'potentially the greatest source for information upon medieval social life'.[3] Britton, of the same school, later referred to them as 'magnificent sources' that enable 'the historian to go beyond superficial stereotypes'.[4] More recently, and using a different approach, Razi has stated that they are 'a unique and an excellent source for the study of rural society, economy and demography'. Likewise, Poos and Smith describe them as 'the most voluminous evidence for studying many aspects of medieval society'.[5]

This apparent recognition of their potential has not been matched by agreement on their use. The early work of the Toronto school entailed the identification of peasant families and their

[1] J. M. Bennett, 'Spouses, Siblings and Surnames: Reconstructing Families From Medieval Village Court Rolls', *Journal of British Studies*, 23 (1983), p. 46.

[2] J. A. Raftis, *Tenure and Mobility* and *The Estates of Ramsey Abbey* (Toronto 1957), and 'Social Structures in Five East Midland Villages. A Study of possibilities in the use of court roll data', *Economic History Review* 2nd ser. 18 (1965), pp. 83–99; for an overview of the historical use of court rolls see 'The Historiography of Manorial Court Rolls' in *Medieval Society and the Manor Court* (ed.) Z. Razi and R. Smith (Oxford 1996), pp. 1–35.

[3] Raftis, 'Social Structures', p. 83.

[4] E. Britton, *The Community of the Vill* (Toronto 1977), pp. 6–10.

[5] 'The Population History of Medieval English Villages: A Debate on the Use of Manor Court Rolls', L. R. Poos, Z. Razi and R. Smith in Razi and Smith (ed), *Manor Court*, p. 334.

classification according to status. This was achieved by reference to specific types of court activity with service as a pledge, juror or in local office being related to wealth, influence and social control. Razi, however, heavily criticised a methodology which relied too heavily on the linking of surnames to familial ties.[6] His work was more demographic in content as he aimed to measure population trends over a 130 year period using 'census-like enumerations' of those appearing in the first five years of each decade.[7] This, he believed, would ensure the inclusion of the majority of male tenants.

But as the enthusiasm for court roll studies blossomed so their reliability as a source material became increasingly questioned. Although Professor Hilton found 'a remarkable example of small town existence' in Halesowen's borough court, the information was 'too fragmentary' to provide evidence regarding 'general social attitudes'.[8] This, along with a sometimes suspect methodology, led Wrightson to comment that 'a shadow is cast over work which is potentially a massive contribution to the understanding of English rural society in the past'.[9] Recent publications have greatly contributed to this debate.[10] This study, it is hoped, can shed some further light on the problems and potential of these sources.

The heaviest burden facing any student beginning such research is the problem of medieval surnames. It was not until the middle of the fourteenth century for the midlands and the south, and the end of the century for the north, that hereditary surnames became common.[11] The linking of names such as cowherd, smith, John, Henry, shepherd, son, *sutor*, taylor and webster to identify successive generations of families by Raftis has rightly been considered

[6] Z. Razi, 'The Toronto School's Reconstitution of Medieval Peasant Society: a Critical View', *Past and Present*, 85 (1979), pp. 141–57.

[7] Z. Razi, *Life, Marriage and Death in a Medieval Parish* (Cambridge, 1980), p. 24.

[8] R. Hilton, 'Small Town Society in England Before the Black Death', *Past and Present*, 105 (1984), pp. 77–8.

[9] K. Wrightson, 'Medieval Villagers in Perspective', *Peasant Studies*, 7 (1978), p. 213.

[10] Razi and Smith (ed.), *Manor Court*.

[11] P. McClure, 'Patterns of Migration in the late Middle Ages: The Evidence of English Place-Name Surnames', *Economic History Review*, 2nd ser., 32 (1979), pp. 167–82.

suspect.[12] Bennett asserts that the use of multiple surnames was 'relatively rare' and largely confined to the pre-plague period, as it was clearly in the interests of the court system to discourage ambiguity. Such a hypothesis is almost impossible to test although her solution, that imprecise surnames should 'be ruthlessly eliminated from consideration', provides a useful starting point in the process of identification.[13]

Although the use of computers in the analysis of court roll material has often been suggested, and can extend the availability of socio-economic data to a wider audience, the inconsistency of surnames remains, at present, an almost insurmountable hurdle.[14] Even if the majority of post-plague surnames were in fact stable, then the variations in spelling would still present problems.[15] The only way of accurately assigning raw data to individuals is through the meticulous examination of the entries. As Raftis has rightly pointed out 'the process whereby the individual villager is discovered ... is painfully slow and tedious, yet possible'.[16] This is most effectively achieved by the use of card-indexing.[17] Razi's work, for instance, involved four stages: registration of information, spatial location, family reconstruction, and only then identification.[18] Only by following a rigorous and careful procedure can individual people emerge from the irregularities of court roll entries.

In spite of their use for demographic purposes the court rolls do not open up a clear vision of medieval society for several important reasons. Firstly, not all individuals made appearances. DeWindt, for example, found that the rolls provided only around half the total names when the study additionally made use of court books,

---

[12] J. A. Raftis, 'The Concentration of Responsibility in Five Villages', *Mediaeval Studies*, 28 (1966), pp. 94–102, and *Warboys: Two Hundred Years in the Life of an English Medieval Village* (Toronto 1974), pp. 116–21.

[13] J. M. Bennett, 'Village Court Rolls', p. 41.

[14] For a database using court rolls see, for example, 'The Dyffryn Clwyd Court Roll Project, 1340–52 and 1389–99: A Methodology and Some Preliminary Findings', A. D. M. Barrell, R. R. Davies, O. J. Badel and L. B. Smith in Razi and Smith (ed.), *Manor Court*, pp. 260–77.

[15] Razi, *Medieval Parish*, pp. 3–4; see below p. 59.

[16] Raftis, *Warboys*, p. 13.

[17] J. M. Bennett, 'Village Court Rolls', p. 36; A. Macfarlane has described this use of card-indexing as 'absolutely essential', in *Reconstructing Historical Communities* (Cambridge, 1977), pp. 102–5 and on the use of computers, pp. 209–14.

[18] Razi, *Medieval Parish*, pp. 12–24.

Hundred Rolls and accounts: an overall 20% under-enumeration was suggested, with a precise figure considered 'an exercise in futility and frustration'.[19] Britton, on the other hand, in his study of an East Midlands village, found that 90 per cent of individuals, or 95 per cent of families, listed in the lay subsidies of 1327 and 1332 also appeared in the contemporary courts.[20] Discrepancies in the numbers of those appearing could relate to differences in time, procedure or local custom.[21] Secondly, the number of appearances an individual made was for the most part dependent on such factors as sex and status, with females, smallholders and the poor irregularly occurring.[22]

Thirdly, not all people appearing were necessarily members of the jurisdictional community being studied. Raftis, for example, identified a number of individuals on the Ramsey Abbey estates who were presented in the courts of neighbouring townships for trespass and other business.[23] Hilton, in his studies of small urban centres, suggested that the proportion of residents appearing in the courts was between 40 per cent and 50 per cent, which made precise estimates, therefore, 'incalculable'.[24] Dyer believes that at least a third of those in both rural and urban areas were wage-earners.[25] The conditions of many of those people improved in the aftermath of the Black Death and those seeking short-term or seasonal work may locally have been highly mobile.[26] Finally, medieval communities were not static and cannot be viewed in isolation.[27] Hilton found 'hierarchical and interlocked' communities, and Britton discovered that the manor of Broughton, in Cambridgeshire, was 'interconnected with a surprisingly large number of communities

[19] E. B. DeWindt, *Land and People in Holywell-cum-Needingworth: Structures of Tenure and Patterns of Social Organization in an East Midlands Village, 1272–1457* (Toronto, 1972), pp. 166, 170–1 n. 3.

[20] Britton, *Community*, pp. 73–4.

[21] Poos and Smith discuss presentment juries and procedural changes in Razi and Smith (ed.), *Manor Court*, pp. 342–9.

[22] Poor peasants 'hardly appear in the post-plague court rolls', *ibid.*, pp. 336–40, 387.

[23] Raftis, 'Social Structures', pp. 88–9; also E. DeWindt, *Land and People*, p. 278.

[24] Hilton, 'Small Town Society', pp. 64–7.

[25] C. Dyer, *Standards of living in the later Middle Ages: Social change in England c. 1200–1520* (1989), p. 213.

[26] Dyer, *Standards of living*, pp. 229–231.

[27] Razi, *Medieval Parish*, pp. 118–9; E. DeWindt, *Land and People*, p. 175.

over a very wide area'.[28] Any attempts at defining a community in strictly geographical terms would be destined for failure.[29]

Most research using court rolls has attempted to classify either families or individuals along the lines of class and status. Frequently the results have divided communities into three wide-ranging social groups. Raftis identified main families, officials and tradesmen, and those on the fringe.[30] Others in the Toronto school initially followed his lead with Edwin DeWindt using the terms major, intermediate and minor.[31] Razi too used a tripartite stratification.[32] Britton, however, devised a more complex system through the division of people into four groups based around court appearances: 'A' were those holding office two or more times and serving as jurors three or more times; 'B' were those holding office once and serving as jurors under three times; 'C' were those not holding office; and 'D' were non-residents.[33] Anne DeWindt took this categorisation further by taking into account landholding: in group one were economically active families and individuals who held long established tenures and who were active in the courts; in group two were those who made fewer appearances and were less active as office-holders and in court administration; in group three were local residents who only occasionally were involved in court or community affairs; and in group four were labourers, cottagers and outsiders.[34]

The bias and recurrent unreliability of court rolls certainly calls for a cautious approach. Although used for the compiling of demographic and other statistics, precise calculations are unsuitable without careful guidelines and a recognition of potential difficiencies. The need to supplement information with reference to other sources, especially those relating to land, cannot be over-stressed.[35] Bennett lays down four criteria by which a set of rolls

---

[28] R. Hilton, *The English Peasantry in the Later Middle Ages* (Oxford, 1975), p. 54; Britton, *Community*, p. 189.

[29] Macfarlane, *Reconstructing Historical Communities*, p. 206.

[30] Raftis, *Social Structures*, p. 98.

[31] E. DeWindt, *Land and People*, p. 207.

[32] Razi, *Medieval Parish*, p. 83.

[33] Britton, *Community*, pp. 12–3. In this classification the greatest concentration of business related to families in groups 'A' and 'B'.

[34] A. DeWindt, 'Peasant Power Structures in Fourteenth Century King's Ripton', *Mediaeval Studies*, 38 (1976), pp. 258–64.

[35] This was the recent conclusion of Poos and Smith, Razi and Smith (ed.), *Manor Court*, p. 354.

can be assessed for study: firstly, that family reconstruction is based only on the largest collections of surviving rolls; secondly, that the courts should provide a high quality of entries based around several criteria; thirdly, that the manorial jurisdiction must be closely tied in with the geographical one; and fourthly, that supplementary data in the form of other extant sources is available.[36]

The Macclesfield series of court rolls is extremely valuable as both the jurisdiction and landscape differed from that found in many corresponding studies. Before going on to describe the methodology used and the problems and procedures encountered it is necessary to outline in some detail the nature of the jurisdiction and the courts. As Poos and Smith have recently concluded:

> 'the local study based upon the nominal linkage of various kinds of documentary evidence will remain the most important source for progress in the interpretation both of those communities and, importantly, the institutions generating those sources.'[37]

The court rolls of Macclesfield are now in the Special Collection: Court Rolls in the Public Record Office (SC 2) and survive in considerable numbers from the time of the Black Death.[38] The absence of only five full years of courts between 1349 and 1396 gives the opportunity for copious and in-depth research. The administration of Macclesfield Hundred during this period was not under the direct control of the sheriff of Cheshire. Although some Macclesfield business was dealt with in the Chester county court, which served in effect as a local supreme court of justice, the

---

[36] J. M. Bennett, 'Village Court Rolls', pp. 33–6. The Macclesfield material satisfies these criteria except for the third, as the (under-) tenants of four townships held by local lords – Bosley, Tytherington, Marple and Taxal – although they were within the jurisdiction of the Macclesfield halmote for some purposes, did not enter their land on payment of a fine at the manor court.

[37] Those of the Toronto school have used the evidence for the large ecclesiastical estates of the East Midlands, and Razi the West Midlands; the Dyffryn Clwyd rolls offer an interesting comparison with Macclesfield, Barrell, Davies, Badel and Smith in Razi and Smith (ed.), *Manor Court*, pp. 260–97, 354.

[38] SC 2/252. A summary list of the court rolls, with commentary, is given by Anne Curry in 'The Court Rolls of the Lordship of Macclesfield, 1345–1485', *Cheshire History* (Autumn, 1983), pp. 5–10.

Hundred owned no suitors to this court.[39] It had its own master-serjeant of the peace, an hereditary position vested in the Davenport family. After the Black Death this was held by John Davenport of Bramhall, probably by lease as a member of a junior branch of the family, and from 1385 until the end of the century it was leased to the Leghs.[40] This officer, with the aid of two under-serjeants, had the responsibility of carrying out the earl's instructions and for making arrests.[41]

The main revenue collector for the greater part of the Hundred was the poker or bailiff. The manor had its own collector, a post attached to the office of hereditary gaoler of Macclesfield, and in the mid-fourteenth century this was held by Adam Mottrum. In the later fourteenth century, as the manor administration increasingly overlapped with that of the forest, this office usually became known as the 'bailiff of the forest'.[42]

In the borough, local officials were elected yearly, namely a reeve who collected burgage rents and a catchpoll market tolls and other revenues. Lesser officials acted for the market, the pavage and the assizes of bread, meat and ale.[43] The office of mayor was reserved for those of the highest social standing and, although apparently chosen annually, only handful of men served during the second half of the fourteenth century.

Each year an eyre for the whole Hundred of Macclesfield (including the manor and borough) was held between late spring and late summer at Macclesfield by the justiciar of Chester. This heard the more serious suits and levied fines on those guilty of a variety of offences (including those against the statute of labourers). Apart from writs concerning land pleas which were issued and tried at Chester, the eyre gave the Hundred a high degree of

[39] V.C.H. Chester II, pp. 15–18. R. C. Palmer, The County Courts of Medieval England, 1150–1350 (Princeton, 1982), pp. 56–7.

[40] T. P. Highet, The Fourteenth Century Davenports, Chetham Society, 3rd ser., 9 (1960), 22, pp. 36–43.

[41] P. Hill (ed.), 'County Court of Chester Indictment Roll 1354 to 1377', Univ. of Liverpool unpubl. thesis (1996), for example, p. 172.

[42] Booth, Financial Administration, p. 93. The manor court (halmote) also increasingly took on the role of a forest court. The manor-forest describes those townships that owed suit to this court, as distinct from those which owed suit to the separate Hundred court.

[43] Those serving as custodians for the pavage were appointed in the mayor's court and were of a similar status to the other officials elected in the portmote. Birkenhead Public Library, Macclesfield Collection, B/6/19.

independence. Attached to its sitting were a number of other judicial functions which included separate indictments for the manor-forest, borough and the remainder of the Hundred. Indictments in the eyre were made by a jury of important local men which consisted, outside the borough, of four men from the township concerned together with the two adjacent ones.[44] The offences were predominantly felonies, affrays with bloodshed, the overburdening of pasture, the making of purprestures, and poaching or hunting in the forest. Filed together with these records are those relating to the forest, such as pleas or presentments of vert, presentments by the coroner or serjeant of the peace, and pleas of gaol delivery.[45] Three sessions of the Hundred court, meeting between August and November and described as sitting 'post eyre', dealt with the personal suits that had not been concluded in the eyre.[46]

The less serious cases were the responsibility of the three local courts – halmote, portmote and Hundred – held at approximately three weekly intervals. All met at Macclesfield in a new 'Mothall' erected in the town in the 1350s: the halmote served the manor (or manor-forest) and met on a Monday; the portmote served the borough and met on a Tuesday; and the Hundred court met on a Monday for the larger area not served by the other two courts.[47] Before we go on to describe these in more detail it is necessary to briefly explain their role in relation to the wider judicial system.

It has been demonstrated that government and administration within the Hundred was overhauled and improved by the Black Prince in the mid-fourteenth century. This was accompanied by the elevation of Robert Legh of Adlington to the position of earl's foremost officer in the Hundred.[48] He was rider of Macclesfield

---

[44] This was standard procedure both in the forest eyres and the forest pleas in the county court, eg. *C.C.R.*, pp. 217–8. For a general overview of the proceedings in eyres see B. Hanawalt, *Crime and Conflict in English Communities, 1300–48* (Cambridge, Mass., 1979), pp. 33–45.

[45] For example, SC 2/254/1 m. 1, CHES 25/20 m. 85, m. 95. Gaol Delivery was held during the eyre. The three coronerships in Macclesfield Hundred in the fourteenth century were the forest, the Hundred and Longdendale.

[46] These suits were probably, but not always, of a more serious nature than those in the local courts, and were also more frequently impleaded across the manor, borough and hundred boundaries.

[47] *B.P.R.*, iii, pp. 251–2; this was the re-erected hall of forester Robert Foxwist, which contained a row of shops underneath.

[48] Booth, *Financial Administration*, pp. 87–9.

Table 7 *Structure of the Macclesfield Courts*

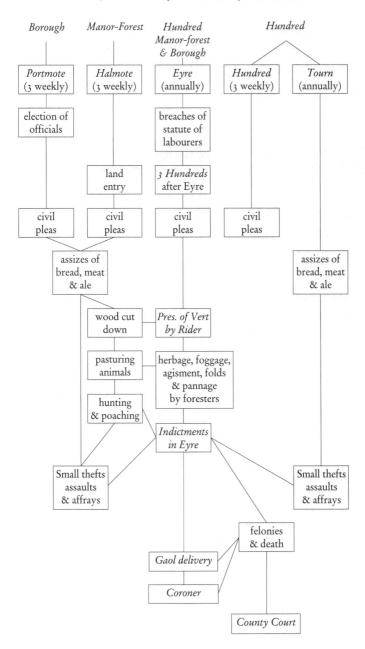

forest and as lieutenant to the steward of the manor, he had the responsibility of holding the three courts, together with a tourn and other special inquests. In the holding of inquests, separate from the yearly eyres held before the justiciar or his deputy, he oversaw the indictment of those suspected of serious felonies.[49] He was thus the most powerful of the earl's servants within the Hundred.

In both the halmote and portmote 'great courts', attended by a full body of suitors, were held at the three terms of Michaelmas, Hilary and Trinity to which presentments were made. These were mainly concerned with business associated elsewhere with a 'court leet' and were closely related to the holding of the yearly eyres into which they transferred the more serious business. Breaches of the peace or affrays (although these were also presented at other courts), offences relating to the assizes of ale, meat and bread, and occasionally small thefts and larcenies formed most of the business dealt with. For these either fines were imposed, and paid in instalments at other court sessions during the year, or suspects were mainperned for significant sums under the pledge of between one and six people. The role of the pledges was to ensure the appearance of the suspect at the following eyre under pain of forfeiting the sum and probable amercement.[50] Items relating to the forest, such as poaching or the sale of wood, were included in the manor court even though they sometimes related to the wider Hundred area; in this respect, the halmote resembled the forest attachment court held elsewhere.[51]

For the remainder of the Hundred, outside the manor and borough, Robert Legh held a 'tourn of the bailiff' to which presentments were made by a jury of four from each township and its two neighbours. It dealt, for instance, with presentments for minor felonies and assaults, and the amercement of offences against the assize of ale and bread.[52] The Hundred court also presented and

[49] These were held mainly after Michaelmas although others may have corresponded to the customary terms of Hilary and Trinity.

[50] Mainprise is discussed by D. J. Clayton in 'Peace Bonds and the Maintenance of Law and Order in Late Medieval England: the example of Cheshire', *Bulletin of the Institute of Hist. Res.*, 58 (1985), pp. 133–48.

[51] G. J. Turner, *Select Pleas of the Forest*, Selden Society (1901), p. xxxix.

[52] There is no resemblance between the Macclesfield tourn and that held by the sheriff elsewhere in Cheshire. P. H. W. Booth, 'The Sheriff of Cheshire and Wirral Hundred,' Univ. of Liverpool Dept. of Continuing Education unpubl. booklet. A closer parallel is with the tourn held by the steward of the manor of Wakefield; see M. O'Regan, *The Medieval Manor Court of Wakefield* (Leeds, 1994).

convicted those guilty of affrays, and fines were sometimes levied following indictments, such as those for theft, in the tourn. Another 'bailiff's tourn' within the halmote and portmote, mentioned only periodically but which may have been held annually, dealt solely with the assizes of weights and measures (not presentments for ale or bread which were presented in the 'great courts').

The local courts, therefore, convicted and fined those guilty of breaches of the peace, and either made attachments or allowed bail for those suspected of more serious crimes. They were courts at the lower end of the judicial system whose records included people of all social ranks and which recorded the transfer and improvement of manor land. As was customary in Cheshire courts, judgements were made by a body of doomsmen ('judicatores'), which was an office attached to landholding. They made judgments in civil pleas, except those involving trespass or land by writ of right, which were decided by a jury, and affixed damages where money or goods were owed or detained. They may additionally have had a role in the assessment of fines and amercements, which could also be set by the bailiff or steward, although on two occasions two affeerers ('taxatores') were named.[53]

The presentment juries, made up of four men from three town-ships, were part of the procedure of the 'great courts' and of the courts at other times when affrays had been committed. Additionally they were sworn in when suits were brought over the breaking of service agreements against the statute of labourers in the halmote. A township might be amerced for failing to present an affray and for not attending, by some or all of its men, the appropriate inquest into its conclusion. At the three terms amercements were levied for common suit and these were almost invariably imposed upon non-resident rent holders; in the portmote, for example, the vicar of Sandbach was amerced for non-attendance on four occasions and the abbot of Chester on seven. Otherwise the courts would have been attended only by those who had been personally summoned.

Constables were appointed for townships throughout the Hun-dred after the Black Death. Their earliest mention in the manor was in 1360/1 when those of both Kettleshulme and Pott were fined for refusing to act. This suggests that the office was an innovation;

---

[53] The affeerers included forester John Cresswall, SC 2/254/7 m. 5, SC 2/254/3 m. 5d. For an example of doomsmen assessing damages in a civil action, see SC 2/254/12 m. 7.

a few months earlier one of them, Richard Dausone of Shrigley, had been fined for not wishing to serve William Dounes. It was the constables who initiated personal criminal suits by bringing a complaint ('billam') before the court. In 1377, for example, the two constables of Sutton were amerced for failing to present an action taken by a Sutton man against another from Marple.[54]

The greater part of the business of the three courts concerned civil pleas brought by local residents. By their charter burgesses of Macclesfield could not be impleaded in other local courts, so actions against them by outsiders, including manor tenants, were generally brought in the portmote. Some residents of the manor also prosecuted pleas in the portmote against outsiders, presumably over a trade or a market agreement. Suits involving people from different areas of the Hundred were more frequently prosecuted in the eyre and the 'post-eyre' Hundred court; the local courts, however, might have offered a more speedy conclusion. In the last quarter of the century the proceedings of the Macclesfield fair courts, held after the All Saints and Barnaby fairs, were included in the portmote. In the civil actions brought in these fair courts both parties were sometimes non-residents; these suits, however, were not always successful.[55] Mayor's courts were also held during this time and leading burgesses surreptitiously encouraged their use.[56]

In this study I shall concentrate on two of the three courts – the halmote and portmote. They were held between eighteen and 23 times a year with the first of the year, the 'great court' after Michaelmas, being by far the most important. In the borough this was the time when the assize was set and the reeve, catchpoll, and custodians of the assizes were elected. Convictions at the Michaelmas halmote were often not fully recorded and instead were

[54] SC 2/252/13 m. 4d., SC 2/252/14 m. 3d., SC 2/253/2 m. 2.

[55] In the fair court in June 1384, for example, John Harstoneslegh of Macclesfield made a false claim in his suit of debt against William Broun of Derby. In a portmote of the same month, John Sherd of Disley brought an unspecified civil action against Robert Walker of Stockport, who was distrained after failing to attend for the second time. Chester City Record Office, Earwaker MSS CR 63/2/339 rot. 1, m. 2–2d.

[56] For examples of the mayor's court, see SC 2/315/15–16, Chester City Record Office, Earwaker MSS CR 63/2/338 mm. 8–9, and the Macclesfield Collection in Birkenhead Public Library. See the Chapter on crime below, p. 144, for an attempt by the burgesses to divert money to the common chest.

listed as fines in subsequent courts; this is indicative of their financial role. Throughout the year the entries were generally formalised and abbreviated and closely integrated with the workings of the other courts. A summary of their types of business can be found in Table 8.

As well as personal suits, both courts had other distinctive and important functions. The portmote's foremost concern was with the regulation of the assizes of bread, meat and ale as well as the control of breaches of the peace. The halmote's was the record of the transfer of land through the procedures of surrender and entry and exchange which was accompanied by the customary relief of two years rent. However the entry into land in the townships that were not part of the demesne – Bosley, Tytherington, Marple and Taxal – was excluded even though these presented affrays and other offences to the court. Although the assarting or enclosing of waste was properly entered with a fine in the halmote it can also be found in the Ministers' Accounts or sometimes amongst other business in the records of other courts.[57] The Ministers' Accounts also record heriots which were only usually mentioned in the halmote on their sale.

An additional function of the halmote was the recording of minor infringements of forest law. Fines were mainly levied against local residents when only a small amount of wood was taken and this was probably equivalent to its value. The only items of the third session of the halmote held after All Saints in 1367–8, for example, were fifteen cases of trespass which followed convictions at the inquest at Michaelmas; those fined included two burgesses, two men from Poynton and a man from Bramhall. Those attached on suspicion of minor trespasses, such as illegal fishing, were mostly outsiders. Sales of wood, waifs and the like seem to have been entered at the end of the halmote roll simply for convenience, and sometimes appear on separate membranes.[58]

The halmote was by far the most profitable of the three local courts even though the Hundred court had jurisdiction over a more populous area. The usual annual figure of under £5 for the portmote was between a third and half that of the halmote. There was a general rise in the levels of business in all three courts as the century progressed (with the portmote continuing to rise at the expense of

[57] SC 6/803–4, or filed, for example, amongst the palatinate records, e.g. CHES 25/20 m. 87.
[58] SC 2/253/3 m. 10. For example, SC 2/253/12 m. 1d., SC 2/254/3 m. 4d.

Table 8 *Types of Business in the Macclesfield Courts, 1349–96*

	%	
	Halmote	*Portmote*
Civil Pleas	21.6	36.1
Affrays and Hues	15.5	27.4
Land Transfer	21.	1.
Assizes (ale, bread & meat)	1.7	13.2
Forest Business	16.8	2.4
Manor Court Business	6.5	
Common Suit	3.8	3.9
Borough Court Business	3.1	
Pasturing Livestock	2.5	
Service Fines	2.4	1.3
Heriots Sold	2.0	
Pledge Amercements	0.75	1.9
Scolds	0.1	2.2
Taking Turves & Hedgerows	0.01	2.2
Trespass Fines	0.8	1.4
Theft	0.5	0.8
Pannage	0.5	0.5
Marriage Fines (merchet)	0.4	
Debts / Recognizance	0.75	
Bail (for Eyre)	0.4	
Animal Forfeits Sold	0.3	0.2
Other	1.6	2.4
	100.00	100.00

SC 2/252/2–15, SC 2/253/1–12, SC 2/254/1–15, SC 2/255/1–2;
Chester City Record Office, Earwaker MSS CR 63/2/338–339.

the halmote in the closing decade). Profits of the halmote, however, were largely a result of levels of land entry, and to a lesser extent wood sales, and the revenue from this court peaked in the years following the plague – the early years of the 1350s and 1360s. Before going on to describe how the court records can be used to estimate population, a brief overview of the debate on national demographic trends is needed.

It is now generally held that the population of England grew substantially in the 200 years or so after the Domesday survey, and by the end of the thirteenth century it had reached between two and four times that of 1086.[59] The rate of growth varied between regions and was affected by availability of land, as under-developed areas, such as those in the north and west, experienced a more dynamic expansion. In the woodlands of Arden a four-fold increase had occurred by 1279 while in the Lincolnshire fenland another dramatic rise, between the Conquest and the early fourteenth century, followed the colonisation of new land for cultivation.[60]

The theory that the population of England reached its medieval peak in the early years of the fourteenth century, and then went into decline, has been fiercely debated. The occurrence of a 'Malthusian' population crisis, in which rising mortality was linked to over-population, land exhaustion and falling yields, has been posited.[61] This, combined with the famine years of 1294, 1314–5 and 1321, and the drought of 1326, produced an alleged downward spiral. The second decade of the fourteenth century has generally be seen as the turning point, and this was most evident in the intensively farmed three-field region of the Midlands; two studies, for instance, have put the fall there at around 15 per cent.[62] A more extreme deterioration occurred on some Worcestershire estates where a 42% decline in population occurred between 1299 and 1349. A parallel decline within some urban centres before the pestilence has been attributable to economic factors.[63] However, in marginal areas,

---

[59] E. Miller and J. Hatcher, *Medieval England: Rural Society and Economic Change, 1066–1348* (1977), pp. 28–33; J. C. Russell, *British Medieval Population* (Albuquerque, 1948), p. 366; R. Smith, 'Human Resources' in Astill and Grant (ed.), *Countryside of Medieval England*, pp. 189–96.

[60] Miller and Hatcher, *Medieval England*, pp. 31–2; J. B. Harley, 'Population trends and agricultural developments from the Warwickshire Hundred Rolls of 1279', *Economic History Review* 2nd ser., 11 (1958), pp. 8–18.

[61] Postan, *Economy and Society*, pp. 38–9; Russell, *British Medieval Population*, pp. 232–4; and disputed by, for instance, B. F. Harvey, 'The Population Trend in England Between 1300 and 1348', *Royal Hist. Soc.*, 5th ser., 16 (1966), pp. 23–42.

[62] Razi, *Medieval Parish*, pp. 39–40, and L. Poos, 'The Rural Population of Essex in the Later Middle Ages', *Economic History Review* 2nd ser., 38 (1985), pp. 515–30.

[63] Dyer, *Lords and Peasants*, pp. 237–9. R. Britnell, 'The Black Death in English Towns', *Urban History*, 21 (1994), pp. 195–210. The Black Death was still 'a turning point in urban history', p. 210.

including the Cheshire forests, land colonisation and its associated rise in population continued until the eve of the Black Death.[64]

By the time the plague reached England in the summer of 1348 a watershed in British demographic history had been reached.[65] Estimates of mortality have been in the region of 30–50 per cent, with the higher figure generally being accepted.[66] In the short term its effects were compounded by harvest failure in 1351 and high prices in the following year.[67] The resulting high level of vacancies in peasant holdings, it has been believed, ultimately benefited some members of society who had previously been landless or had shared family holdings. This view is supported by the speed in which they were filled and in Halesowen, for instance, over 80% of vacant holdings were entered within one year; on the Crowland Abbey estates few new names could be found amongst the takers.[68] The fact that a proportion remained vacant over a longer period of time has been used to indicate a continuing stagnation. One component in this was a change in land use, and recent work by Titow has shown that these holdings were not necessarily unexploited and that vacancies do not represent 'a valid measure of the true extent of the peasants' withdrawal from agriculture'.[69] The conversion to pastoral farming was more evident in some regions, although it was not always profitable.[70]

The further outbreaks of plague between 1360 and 1362, along with those in 1369 and 1375, are believed by some historians to have prevented any long term recovery of the population. Their effects,

[64] Morgan, *War and Society*, pp. 80–1.

[65] Described as 'the longest period of declining and stagnant population in recorded history', in Miller and Hatcher, *Medieval England*, p. 11.

[66] Postan, *Economy and Society*, p. 33, and Razi, using court rolls, *Medieval Parish*, pp. 106–7. Russell, *British Medieval Population*, pp. 214–17, advocates a lower figure.

[67] A. R. Bridbury, 'The Black Death', *Economic History Review* 2nd ser., 16 (1973), p. 584; R. H. Britnell, 'Agricultural Technology and the Margin of Cultivation in the Fourteenth Century', *Economic History Review* 2nd ser., 30 (1977), pp. 53–65.

[68] Razi, *Medieval Parish*, p. 110; F. M. Page, *The Estates of Crowland Abbey* (Cambridge, 1934), pp. 123–4.

[69] J. Z. Titow, 'Lost Rents, Vacant Holdings and the Contraction of Peasant Cultivation after the Black Death', *Agricultural History Review*, 42 (1994), p. 97.

[70] For a discussion on Cheshire see Booth, 'Farming for Profit', pp. 73–89.

unlike those of the Black Death, were more regionalised. Hatcher found the 1360–2 death-rates to be two-thirds of 1349 in Cornwall, yet followed by a rapid recovery, and Bridbury that famine prices, higher than those in 1352, continued until 1365.[71] Courts rolls have offered contrasting results: Razi found 1369 to have been the worst year in Halesowen, while Raftis suggested a short-term recovery to 1340 numbers by 1370 in the manors he studied.[72] Overall, however, pre-plague population levels are not now believed to have returned in England until the sixteenth century.[73]

The debate on the socio-economic results of the Black Death and other later fourteenth century plagues has continued to flourish. That long-term improvements were brought to the lives of many peasants has generally been accepted although the time and scale of such changes has been disputed.[74] A combination of increasing availability of land, the decline in labour services, the shortage of labour, and the rise in wages resulted in a shift in the balance of power. A symptom of this was the passing of the statute of labourers which both sought to limit wages to their pre-1349 levels and limit migration through the enforcement of long rather than short-term contracts. The initial gains of wage-earners may have been limited, or even non-existent, as consistent high food prices before the late 1370s cancelled out a corresponding rise in wage levels.[75] On the other hand, improvements could have been made as a result of extra food allowances and payments in kind.[76]

[71] Bridbury, 'Black Death', p. 584; J. Hatcher, *Plague, Population and the English Economy, 1348–1530* (1973), pp. 128–9.

[72] See also A. E. Nash, 'The mortality pattern of the Wiltshire lords of the manor, 1242–1377', *Southern History*, 2 (1980), pp. 31–43; Poos, for example, found a 'temporary recovery in the generation after the Black Death' but this was followed by 'prolonged decline and stagnation', *Rural Population of Essex*, p. 529.

[73] J. M. W. Bean, 'Plague, Population and Economic Decline in England in the Later Middle Ages', *Economic History Review* 2nd ser., 15 (1962/3), pp. 425–37; Hatcher, *English Economy*, pp. 63–7; Dyer, *Lords and Peasants*, pp. 218–35.

[74] R. Hilton, *English Peasantry*, p. 38; J. Hatcher, 'England in the Aftermath of the Black Death', *Past and Present*, 144 (1994), pp. 3–35; Dyer, *Standards of living*, pp. 140–50.

[75] Bridbury, 'Black Death', pp. 583–4.

[76] J. Hatcher, *Black Death*, pp. 22–5; see also C. Dyer, 'Changes in Diet in the Late Middle Ages: The Case of Harvest Workers', *Agricultural History Review*, 36 (1988), pp. 21–37.

The effects of the second wave of plagues combined with economic decline resulted, it has been argued, in the population falling below an 'optimum level'.[77] Court rolls have played an important role in furthering this demographic debate. In Razi's opinion there was a 6 per cent reduction of population in Halesowen in the early 1360s, a 13 per cent increase in the 1370s, and a 7 per cent fall in the 1380s and 1390s.[78] Raftis saw a 'drastic depression' on the estates of Ramsey Abbey in the 1390s, following an earlier and swift recovery.[79] Overall, Edwin DeWindt calculated a 52 per cent drop of population between 1300 and 1450.[80]

Such regional studies can, therefore, greatly contribute to our understanding of demographic trends. Cheshire has tended to be neglected as the county did not pay royal taxation after the thirteenth century. In the Domesday survey of 1086 it was characterised, like much of the North-West, by substantial levels of waste, and the 5.4 people per square mile was fewer than 60 per cent that of the neighbouring counties of Derbyshire and Staffordshire.[81] Although this figure equates with Yorkshire and Lancashire these, according to Russell, experienced a far higher rise in the following three centuries.[82] In the past the county has been considered backward, poor and for the most part empty of people.[83] The evidence, however, does not support the view of such a desolate region.

There was a greater diversity in landscape than in most other counties, with the cultivated land being heavily concentrated towards the centre and west of the county. In the twelfth and thirteenth centuries population expansion in Cheshire meant that some areas were beginning to show signs of land pressure on available land, and by the early fourteenth a contraction in growth may have begun to occur.[84] Of the forests, land clearance in Wirral,

---

[77] Postan, *Economy and Society*, p. 43; M. Mate, 'Agrarian Economy after the Black Death: the manors of Canterbury Cathedral Priory, 1348–91', *Economic History Review* 2nd ser., 37 (1984), pp. 341–54.

[78] Razi, *Medieval Parish*, p. 117.

[79] Raftis, *Ramsey Abbey*, p. 265.

[80] E. DeWindt, *Land and People*, pp. 167–8.

[81] *V.C.H. Chester, II*, p. 247.

[82] The rise attributable to these two counties was at least double that given for Cheshire, Russell, *British Medieval Population*, p. 313.

[83] H. J. Hewitt, *Medieval Cheshire*, Chetham Society, New Series, 88 (1929), and *Cheshire Under the Three Edwards*, p. 12.

[84] Booth, 'Farming for Profit', p. 79; Hallam (ed.), *Agrarian History*, p. 535.

which was already well-settled in the eleventh century, was largely complete by the end of the thirteenth century. The forest of Mondrem too had lost most of its woodland by the earlier fourteenth century, while much of the landscape of Delamere, its twin, was poorly drained and infertile. In Macclesfield forest, as we have seen, the first half of the fourteenth century was crucial in the extensive clearing of woodland around the perimeter of the forest for arable cultivation. A great deal of assarting, though, had taken place during the late twelfth and thirteenth centuries, with clearance of the manor-forest being largely complete by the start of the fourteenth century.[85]

In the absence of the records of taxation for elsewhere in England it has proved particularly difficult to provide accurate estimates of Cheshire's later medieval population. Dorothy Sylvester, considering an average township as containing only around ten families, thought there was a maximum of around 12,000 in the eleventh century, while Hewitt's pre-Black Death estimate of 20,000 people is certainly too low.[86] Finally, Russell's calculation of 15,500 in 1377 is based on the assumption that Cheshire's population density was identical with that of Lancashire.[87]

Before going on to discuss the data contained in the Macclesfield court rolls, and the contribution it can make to the local demographic debate, it is necessary to briefly refer to the problem of households. Russell based his calculations on the twin notions of a medieval nuclear family and under-tenants living in separate dwellings, and thought that a multiplier of 3.5 was sufficient for extents and poll-tax records.[88] Hilton, however, has indicated that a household might contain both family members as well as live-in servants (*famuli*).[89] Krause believed that a multiplier of 4.5 or even

---

[85] Assarting continued in Macclesfield manor-forest, at a greatly reduced rate, until the eve of the Black Death; see above pp. 6–7.

[86] Sylvester estimated a density of only ten per square mile in 1086, which had risen to 20 per square mile in 1300, 'Rural Settlement', p. 10; Hewitt, *Medieval Cheshire*, pp. 146–7.

[87] Russell, *British Medieval Population*, pp. 44–5. According to M. J. Bennett the poll-tax figures for Lancashire on which Russell based his Cheshire figures do not allow for an under-enumeration of at least 25%, *Community, Class and Careerism*, p. 240.

[88] *ibid.*, pp. 64, 259.

[89] Hilton, *English Peasantry*, pp. 27–36.

5 would be more appropriate.[90] As such differences can radically effect our estimates of the population, the number of wage-earners, servants and family members who did not hold tenancies are crucial to our understanding of medieval society.[91]

The process whereby individuals were identified from the Macclesfield court rolls was both laborious and slow. The use of a hand-written card index system was essential, as it allowed for additions and alterations to be made and for new information to be inserted. The amount of data that can be obtained on certain individuals from a good series of rolls led to six by four inch cards being chosen. The sheer number of names also meant that it was more practical to form a separate index system for each court. It was important that a full transcription / translation of the records was made to enable the card entries to be summarised and abbreviated where possible.

A card was headed by the full name and any other information crucial to a person's identity, such as a place of origin or family ties. Data on that individual was then entered in chronological order under a reference number for the year and court. As this was primarily in note form it was easy for the cards to be updated or altered and compared or re-filed if necessary. From a period of 46 years around 4,000 cards on more than 3,000 individuals appearing in the halmote and portmote courts were made (see Table 9). The vast majority of these contained only one or two entries although a handful of individuals needed as many as ten cards. It is evident that this process of identification is on-going and as new evidence is examined hidden links between individuals might still be revealed; in another one or two cases links are suspected but impossible to prove. The difficulties surrounding surnames, the deficiencies in the entries and occasional illegibility all combine to make some inaccuracy inevitable. There has been no attempt to claim a statistical precision which is not supported by the records.[92]

---

[90] J. Krause, 'The Medieval Household: Large or Small?', *Economic History Review* 2nd ser., 9 (1956/7), pp. 420–32.

[91] A 150% variation in the Domesday population would result from using 3.5 or 5. multipliers, Postan, *Economy and Society*, pp. 31–4.

[92] Inaccuracy caused by the problems of identification set out above has been estimated to be in the region of 2.5% and 4% of the people in the halmote and portmote respectively; see G. Ohlin, 'No Safety in Numbers: Some Pitfalls of Historical Statistics' in R. Floud, *Essays in Quantitative Economic History* (Oxford 1974), pp. 59–78.

It was particularly difficult to assign entries to cards when common name elements were used. Most problems related to surnames prefixed by 'le' to denote a trade and 'de' to denote place-name origin. Two writs under the names 'le Gaoler' and 'de Morton', for instance, were disallowed by the doomsmen as 'there were many under this name'. There were also several tailors, shepherds, walkers, 'turnours', Worths, Suttons, Tydryntons, and Lowes. In the case of the latter there were three Roger Lowes in neighbouring townships and five William Lowes encountered during the period. It was easy to distinguish between them when a time of death was known, when the township was specified, or when a relationship was given. However it was impossible to classify a random entry – other than noting it on all the relevant cards – which introduces a further element of statistical inaccuracy. Those who can be identified as appearing under different names include: John son of Agnes Starky as John Falyngbrom; John Frisby as 'le Heuster'; Richard Hockerley as 'le Swordsliper'; Hervey Sewall as 'le Bagger'; Benedict and his brother John Hancokeson as 'del Persones'; David Golbourn as 'le Walsh'; William son of William son of Adam Balle as 'de Hephales'; Richard Crouther as 'de Barthomley'; and John son of Henry Mulnere as John Hannesone of Pott.

Table 9   *An Example of an Index Card*

Kynder, Robert

o. Sutton.

H252/5 (13)

10s. – Enters with Marion his wife a tenement called 'le Sparhaukesert' in Sutton; formerly of ... Holyncete; R. - 5s.; Pl. Robert Holyncete; & afterwards gave the lord 2s. for licence to enfeoff Marion for the rest of her life. F. - 2s.

H252/15(3)

2d. – by licence acquires small 'place' of land in Sutton; formerly of Robert Holyncete; R. – 1d.

H253/2(10)

Juror, p.land.

H253/3(6)

Juror, p.land (Sutton).

H254/5(12)

M. – 4*d.* for digging turves in 'les Coombs' this year without licence, as pres. by the rider.

H254/6(14)

Tenant of Sutton, died this year.
Marion his widow, for a draught animal of his heriot, sold to her – 12*s.* 0*d.*

Kynder, Marion wife of Robert

H252/5 (13)

Enters with Robert tenement called 'le Sparhaukesert'; Robert enfeoffs her for life (see Rob.).

H252/6(1)

M. – 6*d.* for ale.

H252/15(1)

M. – 6*d.* for ale.

H254/6(14).

12*s.* 0*d.* - for a draught animal of Robert's heriot, sold to her; Pl. John Leversegge.

H254/13(10)

Robert her son enters all land & tens. formerly of her in Sutton (R. – 5*s.* 1*d.*).

Abbreviations

F.: fine; M.: amercement; o.: of; p.: plea; Pl.: pledge; pres.: presented; R.: rent; tens.: tenements.

These cases represent a very small percentage of those appearing in the courts. Family surnames represented fewer than 10 per cent of the total surnames occurring in the manor (excluding those connected with place) and 15 per cent of those in the borough. In the halmote just under half of surnames had a place-name origin, including some relating to families, and around 13 per cent had one relating to trade. In comparison only 35 per cent of those in the portmote had a place-name origin while more than 20 per cent were connected to trade. By far the greater problem encountered was when sons took the same name as their fathers. Although 'junior' and 'senior' were often used it was not always apparent which generation the court roll referred to.

At the outset of the research it was useful to obtain landholding data for the area from the two fourteenth-century rentals. When the first of 1352 was compared with the land entry data in the halmote very little initial correlation was found: 43 per cent of landholders appeared only in the courts and 30 per cent appeared only in the rentals. However this rental, compiled in the aftermath of the Black Death, appears to be unreliable. It is probable that many of the holdings listed in the rental were, in fact, sublet and many of the names of tenants which appear in it, although present within the manor prior to the plague, do not appear subsequently. The correlation of the court roll evidence is was much greater with the rental of 1383/4. Of those tenants mentioned in both rentals only 8% did not also appear in the courts; these were predominantly non-resident tenants.

An appearance in the court rolls, however, is not indicative of residence. Of the 1,921 people appearing in the halmote only a quarter can be directly related to landholdings. If we leave aside the 493 (26 per cent) females then we are left with 422 (30 per cent) out of a total of 1,428 males who were tenants. This low figure is in part the result of deficiencies in the procedure, as land entry by undertenants to local lords was not enrolled for the townships held as sub-manors: Bosley, Marple, Tytherington, and Taxal.[93] These four townships were on the periphery of the manor and generally contributed less business to the halmote; only 22.5 per cent of affrays, for example, took place there.[94] Contrast this with their contribution to the mize (tax to the earl of Chester in

[93] Bollington was included in the second rental only: all the 24 recorded tenants in 1383/4, of whom three were women, appeared in the courts as well as a further two whose land was in decay. (SC 11/898 m. 5).

[94] 28 in Marple, 20 in Tytherington, 14 in Bosley, and 7 in Taxal.

1405) which a very significant part (42 per cent) of the manor-forest total.[95]

There were some disparities in the nature and tenancies of these vills. In the manor of Bosley in 1400, for instance, there were 34 tenants including four women. Here, though, land was rented at 1s. 0d. an acre rather than the customary 8d. (or 4d.) prevalent elsewhere in the manor-forest and only one of the tenants held land in other townships. This is surprising considering its proximity to common land bordering that of both Sutton and Macclesfield. Only four of these tenants appeared in the halmote before this time, and only fourteen affrays were presented compared to 74 for neighbouring Sutton.[96]

In the absence of information about landholding it was harder to identify those belonging to the other vills while at the same time, like Bosley, some under-enumeration may have occurred as a result of fewer court appearances. In total the 7% of the males who can be associated with all four of these townships must surely be an underestimate. It was deemed necessary, therefore, to exclude them from general calculations of the overall population.

Even if we assume that tenants from Tytherington, Marple and Taxal appeared regularly in the courts, unlike those of Bosley, then this could still not explain the origin of the 70 per cent of male surname entries who cannot be identified as tenants. Several of the studies already referred to have not only indicated the impossibility of identifying all those appearing in court but also the unrewarding nature of the task. Yet a meticulous examination can disclose an abundant amount of information and, at the same time, can pose important questions about the reliability of court-roll evidence and the structure of medieval society.

[95] Bosley at 30s. 5d. and Marple at 29s. 4d. were second and third behind the most populous township of Sutton at 31s. 9d., followed by Bollington at 15s. 2d., Tytherington at 14s. 2d., Rainow at 13s. 3d. and Whaley at 12s. 5d. with the remainder paying below 10s. (John Rylands University Library of Manchester, Tatton MS, 345). These payments cannot readily be linked to either land value or tenants in the 1383/4 rental: Shrigley, with land rented at 119s. 6d., paid 6s. 8d. compared with 7s. 0d. by Kettleshulme, with land rented at only 84s. 6d., and 9s. 9d. by Disley, with land rented at 103s. 10d.

[96] 'John de Macclesfield Cartulary', f7: using a multiplier of 3.5 this would give another 119 people (rising to 170 with multiplier of 5). The overall rental value was just under £35 which was £8 10s. more than Sutton which contained nearly three times as many holdings.

It would have been in the interests of both the courts and the attenders that a high degree of clarity was employed in the compilation of the rolls. This would have prevented confusion over summonses and the levying of fines and amercements. It was possible, though, that their financial function precluded this as business tended to be entered in relation to payments due rather than simple chronology. Only rarely was the status of outsiders specified by reference to their place of origin (usually by 'de' and occasionally by the phrase 'manens in'). In total only 1 per cent of males were said to belong to local townships within the Hundred and another 2 per cent from those outside it. For a few more their origin was easy to determine as they were involved in associated business; Adam Okes, for example, appeared once as a pledge for Richard Okes of Eaton.[97]

So who were all these non-tenants who where recorded on the court rolls, and were they well enough known to the Macclesfield authorities to make reference to their place of dwelling unnecessary? We have already mentioned the frequent duplication of surnames; Richard Blagge of Adlington, for instance, shared his with two burgesses as well as with tenants from Bosley and Sutton. Another explanation lies in the number of relatives dwelling in nearby townships – some may also have been young or servants and may have shared households (I shall return to this shortly).

The advantage of using the evidence from two connected courts was that known residents could be cross referenced between them. Approximately 6 per cent of the halmote males were burgesses or borough residents, which was the same proportion as manorial males appearing in the portmote. This, like the figure for Bosley, is again rather low given their close proximity and sharing of common and forest rights and suggests a certain exclusiveness between the rural and urban populations. It is further evidence that those from nearby settlements only infrequently appeared in the courts of neighbouring jurisdictions. The core of the problem of identification appears to lie not so much with tenants from other townships but with those that cannot readily be associated with any particular place.

It was much harder to assign residence or status to those who made occasional appearances in both courts. For example, in 1354 Richard Heeth was pledged by John Judkyn after he failed to prosecute a plea of debt against Richard Wambok. These are the

[97] SC 2/253/3 m. 8d.

only references to any of them in the borough court.[98] In the halmote Richard Heeth appeared four times between 1359 and 1366 during which time he was twice pledged by a Richard Janny of Bosley.[99] He could, then, have originated from this vill as an associate or undertenant of Richard Janny.[100] On another occasion Richard Heeth pledged Robert Dounes of nearby Sutton (a holder of nief land), and Robert stood pledge when Richard's daughter Marion first appeared in 1356. This was for breaking and burning hedges, an offence often linked to poverty or absence of land. Ten years later, in 1365, Adam Brocwalhurst purchased a messuage and enclosure of land in Hurdsfield that had previously been held by Marion, perhaps through marriage; he also successfully sued her for either this or some other land.[101] It seems reasonably certain, therefore, that this Richard Heeth and his family lived in the manor.

The same is not true of John Judkyn or Richard Wambok. John was presented in a halmote of 1354 for unlawfully pannaging his pigs in the forest after Easter, and he too may have been an undertenant, servant or temporary resident.[102] In the absence of further evidence, though, he has been categorised as an 'isolated individual' – or a local person for whom it is impossible to determine precise residence. Richard Wambok, on the other hand, was classed as a probable outsider: a solitary reference in a borough suit of debt cannot be used to indicate any permanence of association with the area.

[98] SC 2/252/6 m. 1.

[99] SC 2/252/11 m. 5, SC 2/252/15 m. 2d., SC 2/253/1 m. 3, SC 2/253/2 m. 2d.

[100] There was no Richard Janny in Bosley in 1400, although an extensive holding of John Jauny included fields and enclosures, at least two messuages, a croft and the watermill; another Richard Janny lived in nearby Bollington. (M. J. Bennett, *Community, Class and Careerism*, p. 102).

[101] SC 2/252/7 m. 2, SC 2/253/1 mm. 2d.–3, SC 2/253/2 m. 2.

[102] SC 2/252/6 m. 3.

Table 10   *The Number of Appearances made by Males in each Court*

No. of Apps.	Halmote (%)	Portmote (%)
1	42.2%	46.8%
2	18.8%	14.8%
3–4	14.8%	11.3%
5–9	12.6%	11.7%
10–14	3.9%	5.2%
15–19	2.9%	3.8%
20–29	2.2%	2.1%
30–49	1.7%	3.5%
50–99	0.7%	0.7%
100 & over	0.2%	0.1%

Table 11   *The Number of Appearances made by Females in each Court*

No. of Apps.	Halmote (%)	Portmote (%)
1	65.9%	44.5%
2	21.2%	14.1%
3–4	10.5%	10.9%
5–9	2.0%	14.8%
10–14	0.4%	5.7%
15–19		4.9%
20–29		2.6%
30–49		1.6%
50–99		0.8%

To avoid repetition I will refer to five more examples of those appearing in both courts. Firstly Thomas Kyrkehouses was amerced in the portmote with leading burgess John Boyle – possibly his employer – for failing to prosecute their plea of trespass against John Tyllesone le Jayler (another unknown man). As he was further mentioned when eleven of his geese were said to have been stolen, it is reasonable to assume that he was a local man bringing produce to sell at the market. This is confirmed by his appearance in the halmote for pasturing twelve sheep on Rainow common, and he also lawfully pannaged his pigs in the forest. His wife Margery was

Table 12   *A Summary of the Identification of Males Appearing in the Courts*

	Total	Male	Fem.	T.
Halmote	1,921	1,428	493	422
		(74%)	(26%)	(30%)
Portmote	1,712	1,122	590	
		(65.4%)	(34.5%)	

Abbreviations
Fem.: female;
T.: tenants;
Res.: probable residents;
Vil : townships held by lords as tenants of the earl (Bosley, Tytherington, Taxal and Marple);

amerced once for selling ale.[103] Secondly, John Mustardmon appeared in the portmote for breaking the assize of bread (a commodity which was sometimes sold by outsiders), and is recorded as a co-defendant with burgess cloth-worker Richard Burelles in an unspecified plea of trespass brought by an outsider. His only appearance in the halmote was for cutting holly without licence, an offence committed by many burgesses which was related to the feeding of cattle.[104] He may have thus been a short-term borough resident and a servant of Richard Burelles.

The third example is William Bolywod who was mentioned in the portmote following an assault by Geoffrey Dounes (a local man of near gentry status), and once in the halmote when acting as a pledge for a Hugh Buttelegh. A reference in a forest pannage roll (see below) reveals that William was from the nearby township of Butley.[105] Fourthly, William Etkus, a chaplain, appeared once in the portmote as the victim of an assault, by Roger Barker, and once in the halmote when he sued John Rouland, a chaplain of Bosley, for a debt of 2s. 0d. William was an inhabitant of Etchells, within the Hundred.[106] Fifthly, William Vesty served as a pledge in the halmote for Margaret daughter of Richard Harfot over a service

---

[103] SC 2/253/2 m. 2; SC 2/253/5 m. 8, m. 10; SC 2/253/7 m. 2.
[104] SC 2/254/7 m. 2; SC 2/254/8 m. 2; SC 2/254/12 m. 9d.
[105] SC 2/253/5 m. 5; SC 2/253/11 m. 1; SC 2/254/5 m. 7; SC 2/254/4 m. 13.
[106] SC 2/254/12 m. 7, SC 2/254/13 m. 7d. He was described, during the 1380s, as of Etchels (or Eccles), when taking one oak from the forest, and of Stockport, where he assaulted John Clerk. He was also accused, with

Table 12 continued

Res.	Vil.	Burg.	Man.	Is.I.	Out. H.
447 (31%)	(7%+)	(6%)		(20%)	(2%)
(40%+)			(6%)	(40%+)	(4.5%)

Burg.: burgesses appearing in the halmote;
Man.: manor tenants appearing in the portmote;
Is. I.: isolated individuals;
Out. H.: those from outside Macclesfield Hundred.
(SC 2/252/2–15, SC 2/253/1–12, SC 2/254/1–15, SC 2/255/1–2;
Chester City Record Office, Earwaker MSS CR 63/2/338–339).

fine. In a portmote nine years later he was described as coming from Adlington, when he was amerced for an affray.[107]

Of these examples, then, Thomas and John will be included in our list of probable residents and at least two of the three Williams in that for outsiders. Without referring to other documents these random court roll appearances can be rendered almost meaningless for demographic study. It would be tedious, though, to refer to many more of these examples so we can summarise the status and identity of the males appearing in the halmote as follows. Approximately half the total cannot be defined as manor tenants, burgesses or likely residents of the four sub-infeudated townships. However, nearly a third (31 per cent) of these apparent non-residents, that is 447 males, made a sufficient number of court appearances to denote a close association with the manor-forest: they were in service or involved in local trade, they pastured their animals on the commons, and their wives (especially as ale- sellers) or other family members were also mentioned.

The residence of some of these can be clearly demonstrated. Those dwelling in Disley, for example, included William Holynworth who

ten others, of throwing down a house and abducting timber (CHES 25/21 m. 9, m. 18, CHES 25/8 m. 23d). At the end of the 1380s he was indicted, as a chaplain of Robert, son of Robert Legh, dean of Macclesfield, for the extortionate collection of toll at Prestbury (CHES 25/22 m. 10). In the mid-1360s, a William, son of John Etkus of Poynton, was indicted for an affray in Poynton (CHES 25/20 m. 23).
[107] SC 2/252/8 m. 5d., SC 2/253/1 m. 4d.

served as constable, and William Hode who appeared on sixteen different occasions.[108] The explanation must lie, for the most part, in the widespread subletting of tenancies. This is supported by the number of multiple holdings and the smaller number of tenants who held land yet did not reside within the township; the latter registered no court appearances nor were they presented for common suit. A tenant such as William Dounes was practically a manorial lord in his own right. The identification of undertenants does require the careful analysis of their court roll entries, and cannot be based solely on the number of their court appearances. A concise reference to a few of these will suffice.

Firstly, William son of Richard Prounyng made five court appearances of which four related to affrays in Sutton. As a resident he grazed cattle and pigs within the forest. His father appeared in the courts for two pleas, served as a pledge and was amerced for ale along with his wife. Richard also took wood from the Coombs and pannaged his pigs in Lyme.[109] Secondly, Hamon Lyncrofte made four appearances in the halmote between 1352 and 1355, of which two were for pasturing in Rainow common, one was for a hue in Bollington and one was for pledging a Richard Lyncrofte for another hue in the same township.[110] This Richard Lyncrofte was a smallholder who held 2½ acres with Ellen, his wife, in Rainow, which he entered shortly after the plague in January 1350, together with another messuage and over 3½ acres which he and his son later alienated by charter, in August 1363. His court appearances amounted to one plea and standing three times as a pledge: for the daughters of John son of William, the former holder of the land he entered in 1350, for a hue in Bollington and for his own son, Richard, concerning a hue in Rainow.[111] This family, then, were residents of Rainow and / or Bollington, where it is possible that they shared the same household or tenement.

[108] Holynworth, c. 1384–1387: SC 2/254/5 m. 8d., SC 2/254/6 m. 6d., SC 2/254/8 mm. 3–3d. Hode, from 1375: SC 2/253/8 m. 3d. – SC 2/255/2 m. 4d.

[109] William, c. 1372–1387: his affrays SC 2/253/6 m. 3d., SC 2/254/3 m. 4, SC 2/254/8 m. 3, SC 2/254/9 m. 4, and pannage, for example, SC 2/254/4 m. 13. His father, c. 1368–1389: SC 2/253/3 m. 10d., SC 2/253/8 m. 3, SC 2/253/12 m. 1d., SC 2/253/6 m. 3, SC 2/254/2 m. 3, SC 2/254/11 m. 4.

[110] SC 2/252/4 mm. 4–4d., SC 2/252/5 m. 5, SC 2/252/6 m. 3.

[111] Richard c. 1349–1367: SC 2/252/2 m. 4, SC 2/252/6 m. 3, SC 2/252/10 m. 5, SC 2/252/13 m. 3d., SC 2/252/14 m. 3d., SC 2/252/15 m. 2, SC 2/253/1 m. 3, SC 2/253/2 m. 3d.

Thirdly, Adam Boterale and his wife were both amerced on four
different occasions for breaches of the assize of ale, which were the
only references to them in the courts.[112] Henry Boterale, who may
have been related to Adam, and his wife were amerced similarly
on another five occasions and, although he made no further appearances, Henry was, on one occasion, described as working for the
lord in the Oakenbank.[113] Such a presentment for the assize of ale
in the halmote can often be used to denote residence, as brewing
was associated with the ownership of surplus grain and involvement
in the supply of the local market. It appears to have been more
prevalent amongst manorial smallholders situated furthest from the
borough, such as in Whaley and Marple.

Resident status as a long-term undertenant cannot, though, be
assigned to the majority of those who made occasional appearances
in the court records. For many, their relationship with the manor
was probably less enduring. The example of William Pay was hard
to determine as his wife's single amercement for ale came eight
years after his own for wounding.[114] The taking of short-term leases
and service contracts may have been responsible for the existence
of large numbers of temporary residents who had migrated a short
distance across local boundaries.

For nearly 300 males, or 20 per cent of the total who appeared
in the halmote, precise identification thus remained impossible.
These, termed 'isolated individuals', represent a mixture of labourers
and servants, temporary residents, those dwelling in the surrounding
vicinity, and outsiders passing through the jurisdiction. Unfortunately, even after much painstaking work, at this stage conclusions
must be tentative. In summary, around a third of males recorded
in the halmote records were tenants, another third were undertenants, workers or temporary residents, and a final third were
outsiders from the neighbouring locality, who either shared the
forest resources or were linked to residents through family ties or
employment.

The portmote records present even greater challenges of identification. One immediate difference is the larger proportion of
females recorded who, out of a total of 1,712 surname entries,
constitute 590 individuals (34.5 per cent). Although there is no full
list of burgage holders, the rentals include other land that came

---

[112] c. 1363–1389: SC 2/252/15 m. 2 – SC 2/254/11 m. 4.

[113] c. 1371–1389: SC 2/253/6 m. 3 – SC 2/254/11 m. 4; SC 2/254/1 m. 12.

[114] c. 1354–1362, SC 2/252/6 m. 3, SC 2/252/14 m. 3.

within the borough's territories (namely offenomes, ancient lands and the Roewood). Unfortunately, there is no close correlation between those listed as paying these rents and those most frequently appearing in the portmote. It seems, therefore, that there was some distinction between the most active trading burgesses and those holding land or rents on the periphery of the borough. By the end of the century the burgages themselves were concentrated in the hands of a small group of people, many of whom were chaplains or outsiders: for example, the abbot of Chester and the vicar of Prestbury.[115] It was necessary, therefore, to try and categorise the 1,122 portmote names almost entirely on their court appearances.

Identification of the leading burgesses could be completed with confidence as the court business readily equates with trading activity and the names of jurors is more frequently recorded. For example, William Dale, mercer, made over 50 appearances and regularly served as a juror and in office; his wife was also periodically amerced for ale.[116] Although less active, Hugh Pulton made seven appearances and his wife, Alice, was amerced fifteen times for brewing; he was involved in two suits, two affrays and served as a juror.[117] Such individuals however, comprised only a quarter of all portmote males.

---

[115] SC 2/255/1 m. 5d. John Macclesfield, senior, clerk, in particular was acquiring large numbers of burgages, 'John de Macclesfield Cartulary', for example, fo. 196–201; A. F. Butcher, 'Rent and the Urban Economy', *Southern History*, 1 (1979), p. 18.

[116] William Dale appeared in the records throughout the period, SC 2/252/2 m. 3 – SC 2/255/2 m. 5d. It is probable, however, that this refers to more than one person. He was the former holder of a burgage in Chestergate, the street where his wife unlawfully raised the hue, SC 2/252/15 m. 4. William was a custodian of ale in 1374/5, catchpoll in 1382/3 and a custodian of bread and meat in 1393/4, SC 2/253/8 m. 5, SC 2/254/4 m. 6, SC 2/254/15 m. 5. He failed to produced his weights for the tourn in 1387, SC 2/254/9 m. 6. Alice, wife of William Dale, appeared for one unlawful hue and for ale between 1359 and 1364, SC 2/252/10 m. 4d., SC 2/252/13 m. 5d., SC 2/252/15 m. 4d. Margery, wife of William Dale, appeared for one affray and for ale between 1370 and 1372, SC 2/253/4 m. 3d. - SC 2/253/6 m. 5d. William Dale of Stockport held a tenement in the borough c. 1369/70–1, when he was amerced for common suit, SC 2/253/4 m. 3d. – SC 2/253/5 m. 8.

[117] Hugh, c. 1370–1386: SC 2/253/4 m. 3d., SC 2/253/7 m. 2d., SC 2/253/8 m. 5d., SC 2/253/9 m. 5d., SC 2/253/12 m. 2, SC 2/254/4 m. 6, SC 2/254/8 m. 1. His wife Alice, c. 1367–1383: SC 2/253/2 m. 4 – SC 2/254/4 m. 6, m. 7d.

As in the halmote, more than half of those mentioned remained initially unidentified. One example is Robert Bagylegh who appeared for two assaults, as a defendant in a plea of trespass and for not coming to an inquest. His wife, apart from one assault, appeared five times for baking.[118] Another is Hugh Lether who was amerced twice for common suit in 1369 and 1384. In 1375 Annabel Lether made the first of her seven appearances, which included four for ale, and was probably Hugh's wife or relative.[119] A third is Richard Neuton who appeared four times for assaults as well as once in a suit between 1376 and 1387. His son, Richard, was a defendant in a suit of debt in 1388 but did not appear subsequently.[120] Of these, Robert can be included as a resident along with Annabel although Hugh is less certain, while no firm residential status can attributed to Richard.

A medieval borough's role as a trading centre meant that there were always some temporary residents, most of whom were work-men or servants. In 1378, for instance, John Prestall was amerced for an offence against the statute of labourers and his wife was amerced for the assize of ale.[121] Likewise Adam Kent appeared twice in pleas of debt, and his wife was amerced once for the assize of ale, between 1352 and 1358.[122] Through careful analysis another 15 per cent were included as residents on either a temporary basis or of a status below that of full burgess, giving an initial proportion of residents of around 41 per cent.

As a borough was at the hub of local trade its court would have attracted a larger number of outsiders than that of a manor. Suits involving offences against the statute were brought against servants, many of whom were the offspring of local residents. In 1373, for instance, forester John son of Richard Sutton, who held land in

[118] Robert, c. 1389–1395: SC 2/254/10 m. 8, SC 2/254/12 m. 9, SC 2/254/15 m. 5d., SC 2/255/1 m. 6d. His wife Margery, c. 1387–1395: SC 2/254/9 mm. 6–6d. – SC 2/255/1 mm. 5–5d.

[119] Hugh, SC 2/253/4 m. 3, Chester City Record Office, Earwaker MSS CR 63/2/339 rot. 1, m. 1. Annabel, c. 1375–1388: SC 2/253/8 m. 5d., SC 2/253/9 m. 5, SC 2/254/3 mm. 5–5d., SC 2/254/4 m. 6d., m. 7d., SC 2/254/1 m. 9.

[120] Richard, SC 2/253/9 m. 5d., SC 2/254/3 m. 5d., SC 2/254/4 mm. 6–6d., SC 2/254/8 m. 1. His son, SC 2/254/9 m. 6d.

[121] John was probably in service to resident Roger Bedulf during this year. SC 2/253/12 m. 2d., SC 2/254/2 m. 4d.

[122] SC 2/252/5 m. 4, SC 2/252/9 m. 7, SC 2/252/10 m. 4.

four townships as well as in the borough, used the portmote to prosecute John son of Adam Brocwalhurst. Three years later he brought the first of two pleas in one year against Richard Bole of Bosley, with one further plea being introduced by Adam Huetteson of Bosley; these were the only references in either court to Richard.[123] Similarly both William and Geoffrey Dounes brought a number of suits in the portmote against the sons and daughters of manor tenants and smallholders.[124] Clearly none of these people were actual residents of the borough.

The association of life-cycle servants and labourers with the borough may have extended little beyond their hiring and their visits to the local market and fairs. It is only in the cases of those who made regular or occasional appearances in court over a substantial period of time that any degree of permanency of residence can be assumed. As in the manor a few employees would have dwelt in the households of their hirers. In 1383 John Leversegge, a manor and borough tenant who was active as a burgess and in both courts, had two *famuli*: the aforementioned Hugh Lether and John Hobbeson (who does not appear in either court).[125]

Suits of debt frequently involved outsiders, especially at the time of the fairs. The origin of around 9 per cent of this class was specified of whom half came from outside the Hundred. As we have seen, another 6 per cent of the same type were manor tenants. In summary, then, between 40–50 per cent of males appearing in the portmote can be classed as residents, with a similar number of isolated individuals who were, for the most part, servants, labourers and local residents who appeared in relation to trade or service. The remainder, between 10 per cent and a maximum of 20 per cent, were outsiders who were mostly from Macclesfield's surrounding rural hinterland and left isolated references in the court records.

To a partial degree it is possible to test the accuracy of the court roll evidence by employing the separate rolls of the forest pannage and pastures. Each year between 89 and 154 people paid fines, or

---

[123] Both references to Richard Bole concerned service agreements, SC 2/253/7 m. 2d., SC 2/253/10 m. 5.

[124] William, for example, against Maud Kys of Rainow over a service agreement, SC 2/253/6 m. 5, and Geoffrey, for example, against John Brocwalhurst, SC 2/253/12 m. 2d.

[125] SC 2/254/4 m. 6d. See n. 119 above.

received licences, to graze their pigs in Lyme.[126] Although the rolls listing such payments survive for only twelve years (just over a quarter of the total), if we compare the names with those in the courts we find an under-enumeration of up to 20 per cent. It is impossible to estimate how many of those were residents, and at least a tenth of the total appear to have belonged to the neighbouring township of Butley. Another seven or eight men were close relatives of those appearing in the courts, and included people of high status such as John and Robert, the sons of Robert Worth of Tytherington. Only ten males who, in this short sample, appear in three or more years could be added to our list of permanent or established residents.[127]

Taking these lists at face-value, another 65 males would have to included amongst our isolated individuals category. For example, although Benedict Lucas was not mentioned in the courts, his son Robert was one of those who made random appearances; he was involved in a plea and was amerced once in the halmote for the assize of ale.[128] Secondly, Thomas Hyne was a servant of burgess Richard Rowe, whose only reference in the courts was for an assault over his fellow-servant with a knife in the borough; this was eight years after his pannage payment.[129] Thirdly, William Roper was a labourer at the time of pannage and did not appear in the courts for another thirteen years when he too was guilty of an assault in the borough.[130] Fourthly, Hugh Cordys' only appearance in the portmote, which was again for an affray, was four years after his pannage fine.[131]

An examination of the escape fines is singularly useful as prefixes sometimes denoted a person's origin: 'f' for the forest, 'b' for the

---

[126] SC 2/253/4 mm. 9–10, SC 2/253/5 m. 5, SC 2/253/8 m. 9, SC 2/253/9 mm. 11–12, SC 2/253/10 m. 6, SC 2/253/12 m. 5, SC 2/254/1 m. 9, SC 2/254/2 m. 5, SC 2/254/3 m. 8, SC 2/254/4 m. 13, SC 2/254/5 m. 4, SC 2/254/8 mm. 5–7.

[127] For example, 'Honde Plont' three times, Richard Oldefeld (possibly the father of John, who appeared in the courts) four, Robert Feket, William Cloppespoke and William Powroner five, and Hugh Honde six times.

[128] SC 2/254/4 mm. 4–4d.

[129] SC 2/254/1 m. 9d., SC 2/254/11 m. 9.

[130] His pannage payment was in 1378/9. He drew his knife in the assault in 1391, while his wife, Isabel, was herself the victim of an assault in the borough in 1382. SC 2/254/2 m. 5d., SC 2/254/4 m. 6, SC 2/254/12 m. 10.

[131] His affray was upon Richard Bolynton in 1374, SC 2/253/5 m. 5, SC 2/253/8 m. 5.

borough and 'h' for the Hundred. These confirm the residence of some of those in the pannage lists, such as Richard Oldefeld, Honde Plonte and Fylle Grene. The number appearing under the surname 'le Herdmon' and 'le Shepherd' adds to our list of wage-earners, although some of these may have appeared in the courts with a different name. From a sample of thirteen years twelve individuals shared surnames with other manor residents and *may* have been relatives, while of the ten listed more than once at least six were from Bosley. Overall the pasture lists might add another 50 or 60 people to those in the 'isolated individuals' category.[132]

These additional rolls, therefore, shed further light on the complexities of the communities being studied. They augment the court evidence on the strata of society, usually hidden from official documents, that lay beneath that of the manorial or borough tenant, for whom life cycle service, migration, and temporary residence were probably important features of their existence. Although statistically they would make little difference to the number of confirmed residents, they would nevertheless have been a crucial factor in the wider demographic trend.

So, how far does the court-roll evidence reflect short-term trends in population? The inconsistencies in the appearances of many individuals would clearly exclude them from numeration.[133] At the beginning of the study it was hoped that a count of people appearing in five-year periods might reasonably reflect the population in the second half of the century.[134] In spite of the deficiencies noted above, these five year periods were indeed fairly accurate in recording the more wealthy and influential male members of the communities, with the majority of identified residents appearing in

[132] SC 2/253/4 m. 8, SC 2/253/5 m. 4, SC 2/253/7 m. 8, SC 2/253/8 m. 8, SC 2/253/9 m. 10, SC 2/253/10 m. 7, SC 2/253/12 mm. 8–9, SC 2/254/1 m. 3, m. 6, m. 8, m. 11, SC 2/254/2 m. 10, SC 2/254/4 mm. 14–16, SC 2/254/5 m. 5, SC 2/254/9 mm. 7–8, Chester City Record Office, Earwaker MSS CR 63/2/338 m. 5.

[133] This is one of the main criticisms levelled by Poos and Smith in their criticisms of Razi's work, in Razi and Smith (ed.), *Manor Court*, p. 338.

[134] As the rolls are incomplete, nine periods between 1349 and 1396 were selected: six five-year and three four-year ones for the halmote, and five five-year and four four-year ones for the portmote. See Table 13. To estimate the inaccuracy of using four rather than five year periods, the number of 'new' individuals appearing for the first time in the fifth year, where the period was complete, was found to be approximately 7.5% of the total in the portmote and fewer than 10% in the halmote.

successive periods. There were, however, some notable exceptions.[135] Some of these discrepancies might be be explained by age and life-cycle changes or even absence from the community (such as for military or other service). The appearance of between 250 and 400 known male residents, both urban and rural, in each period is summarised in Table 13 and analysed below. Court rolls display, it seems, wide variations in function and custom and there will thus be inconsistencies in their suitability for different areas of research. In this respect although those for Macclesfield, which had a peculiarly financial purpose, are not well adapted for the measurement of precise trends in population they are useful indicators of the general picture.

Table 13   *Summary of Males Appearing by Period*

				Periods					
Halmote	*(1)**	*(2)*	*(3)*	*(4)*	*(5)**	*(6)*	*(7)**	*(8)*	*(9)*
	1349	1354	1359	1365	1370	1375	1381	1386	1391
	1353	1359	1364	1370	1375	1380	1385	1391	1396
Total	180	224	322	311	273	264	271	288	239
Residents	153	167	230	230	194	194	194	219	152
Portmote	*(1)**	*(2)*	*(3)*	*(4)*	*(5)**	*(6)***	*(7)**	*(8)*	*(9)*
	1349	1354	1359	1365	1370	1375	1381	1386	1391
	1353	1359	1364	1370	1375	1380	1385	1391	1396
Total	147	190	209	202	265	186	222	237	287
Residents	103	128	157	132	155	116	121	121	124

* four year period;
** approx., 3½ year period only.
(1): SC 2/252/2–5; (2): SC 2/252/6–10; (3): SC 2/252/11–15; (4): SC 2/253/1–4, Chester City Record Office, Earwaker MSS CR 63/2/338; (5): SC 2/253/5–8; (6): SC 2/253/9 – SC 2/254/2; (7): SC 2/254/3–6, Chester City Record Office, Earwaker MSS CR 63/2/339 rot. 1; (8): SC 2/254/8–12; (9): SC 2/254/13 – SC 2/255/2, Chester City Record Office, Earwaker MSS CR 63/2/339 rot. 2.

[135] For example: Roger son of William Barker was present in periods one, four, five, six, seven, eight, and nine; John Bentelegh of Whaley in periods three, four, five and seven; John son of Edmund Bosedon in periods two, three, five, six, seven and eight; and John son of Adam Brocwalhurst in all periods except for the eighth.

That a high death resulted from the Black Death is evident in the number of vacant holdings. The Ministers' Accounts record a rise of such holdings in the manor from six to 46 between 1348 and 1349, and state that heriots were due from 66 tenants. The immediate administrative effect on the manor-forest has been described as 'severe' with some rents being taken from crops and goods.[136] In 1354 an order of the Black Prince administration allowed decayed holdings, described as 'ruinous', to be placed with tenants without the payment of reliefs or arrears of rent.[137] The halmote record contains 28 land entries in each of the first two years following the Black Death and a further fourteen and eight entries in the subsequent two. This gives a total of 78 entries in the first four years after the plague (the roll for 1353/4 is missing). As the contemporary rental contained an approximate 258 holdings this would suggest a tenant death rate of at least 30 per cent.[138]

Although the new rental, made in the spring of 1352, lists the tenants in each township, some of these tenants did not formally enter their holdings in the halmote court until a later date. One explanation for this is age. For example, when Roger Barker entered his father's tenement in September 1350 the relief was pledged by John Cloghes who was granted the land in Roger's minority.[139] In the rental this holding was marked by the letters *va*.[140] Another

---

[136] Booth, *Financial Administration*, pp. 89–91.

[137] B.P.R., iii, p. 166.

[138] This is based on their grouping in the 1352 rental, with some individuals holding more than one tenement. The proportion of tenancies that were transferred in each township in the halmote between 1349 and 1353 are: Sutton 48%; Eddisbury 100% (two holdings only); Rainow 62%; Upton 0% (only four holdings); Hurdsfield 56%; Pott Shrigley 14%; Stanley 40%; Disley 80%; Yeardsley and Whaley 44%; and Kettleshulme 45%. While in the borough, excluding burgages, it was was 39% (SC 2/252/2–5, SC 11/899).

[139] SC 2/252/2 m. 4d.

[140] As these letters were written in different ink from the main text of the rental, they must have been added at some unknown later date. Half the male tenants and four times as many female tenants had 'va' written alongside their names. Of the male tenants more than three-times as many did not make any appearances in the halmote. It is possible that 'va' was an abbreviation for 'vacans' – in this sense, probably referring to land, tenements or cottages that were sublet. Although more than half of the tenancies were marked in this way, 'va' was sometimes written against only

factor may have been the large amount of subletting that was taking place. Robert Grosvenour, for instance, was a non-resident who did not pay the £1 3s. 2d. relief for his father's tenement until July 1356, even though he was listed as the tenant in the 1352 rental.[141]

The fact that land was not immediately taken up after the Black Death does not mean that it was left unused.[142] In the halmote of February 1355, for example, 41 people were amerced for pasturing on land that had been taken into the lord's hands: of these, this was the only court appearance for Richard Halyloft, William son of Henry, John Morlegh, Walter Homeldon, John Knotte (who was said to have been the former holder of land rented at 1s. 9d. in Rainow in 1370) and Roger Gerveyne.[143] The land remaining out of cultivation for longer was probably more marginal or more suited to grazing. The hamlet of Eddisbury in Rainow, for instance, which had previously been held by two tenants, was in decay for sixteen years before being entered at a reduced rent and without relief in 1374/5.[144]

part of the holding. An alternative explanation is that 'va' is an abbreviation for 'viva averia', and thus indicated those tenants who owed heriots at their death; it was decided that liability to heriot was to be determined on that basis in the 1355 eyre, SC 6/802/11 m. 1. The sale of animals taken as heriots was recorded in the halmote courts, but an analysis of the tenants and their landholdings does not reveal any close link with those marked by 'va' in the rental.

[141] This holding again had 'va' written alongside it in the rental. Apart from this land entry, SC 2/252/7 m. 2d, the only references to him in the courts were 20 amercements in different years for common suit, SC 2/252/5 m. 5 – SC 2/254/14 m. 4.

[142] J. Titow, 'Lost Rents', pp. 97–114.

[143] SC 2/252/6 m. 3.

[144] In the 1352 rental there were two holdings in Eddisbury (both of ancient land, with 'va' written alongside). The first, consisting of a messuage and carucate rented at 11s. 4d., is left blank and presumably had no tenant. It had formerly been held by Hugh Foxwyst, and his brother, William Trevyn, a chaplain, entered it in 1354 at the rent of 11s. 4d. The rent was in arrears by the time Richard Crouther of Barthomley entered it in 1363, and was again in arrears from 1365. Both William and Richard were amerced for common suit prior to the public proclamation of the arrears. When Henry Mareschall entered Foxwyst's holding in 1374, at a reduced rent of 5s. 0d., it was said to have been in decay for the previous sixteen years. Henry let it to John Cresswall, at 5s. 0d. rent, in 1384/5. John was the first manor resident to hold it since Black Death. SC 11/899 m. 3, SC 2/252/6 m. 3, SC 2/252/12 m. 2, SC 2/252/14 m. 3d.–4, SC 2/252/15 m. 2,

A comparison between the names listed in the 1352 rental and those recorded in the court rolls establishes the length of time after the Black Death before holdings were fully entered by the tenant. For example: William Balle succeeded to his father's tenement in December 1350; Nicholas son of Henry Dounes entered his father's small parcel of land, rented at 4d., in January 1351; John Fall entered his father's tenement in Whaley in October 1352; John Shydyort entered his father's land in July 1355; and land in Disley listed under the heir or heiress of William Haldene and 'now' in decay, was entered in late December 1355.[145] It was not until 1359/60 that the number of entries to land fell to their average for the remainder of the century.

It has been claimed that the new outbreaks of plague in the 1360s may have been instrumental in preventing a full recovery in the post-Black Death population. In the Macclesfield halmote there were 23 entries to land in the two years between 1361–63 and another five in the following year. If all these were the result of death this would suggest deaths in the region of 40 per cent of those in the three years after 1349. When another outbreak hit the region in the winter of 1369 there were 20 land-entries, which was the highest number for any year except for the period 1349–51. The death of at least 20 tenants in 1361/2 and another 30 in 1369 (between 8 per cent and 12 per cent) is suggested. However these

---

SC 2/253/1 m. 2d, SC 2/253/8 m. 3, SC 2/254/6 m. 6d. The other messuage, of five acres, which included an acre of increment, was rented at 3s. 4d. and entered by Roger son of John Halle of Somerford in 1349. It passed to William Croumon in 1359, and was also later acquired by John Cresswall (again the first time by a resident) in 1394, by grant of William son of William Birchels, at a rent of 3s. 0d. John let this to his servant, Adam, in 1396 (SC 2/252/2 m. 4, SC 2/252/11 m. 5, SC 2/255/1 m. 7, SC 2/255/2 m. 3d).

[145] SC 2/252/3 m. 2d., SC 2/252/5 m. 5, SC 2/252/6 m. 3d and SC 2/252/7 m. 2 (all these had 'va' written in the rental, SC 11/899). Haldene's land, rented at 3s. 1d. in Stanley, consisted of two messuages with adjacent land and a house approved in the early fourteenth century, SC 11/899 m. 3d. In 1360 it was acquired by Adam Stafford who died two years later (SC 2/252/11 m. 5d., SC 2/252/14 m. 3d). It passed to Adam's daughter, Joyce, who made no court appearances, and the next mention of it was nearly 25 years later when it was 'in decay' and was taken by forester John Sherd, (SC 2/254/4 m. 4). It is listed under John Sherd's holdings in the rental the following year (SC 6/806/6 m. 3).

figures reveal two important differences. Firstly the number of entries quickly returned to normal, and secondly the entries reveal a growing market in land rather than actual succession amongst peasant families. The tenancies were rapidly filled and there is evidence relating to the consolidation of holdings by some wealthy or rising tenants. The effects that these outbreaks had on the undertenant population must have been significant yet impossible to quantify. There is no evidence of an increase in tenant deaths in 1375 when plague again visited England: there were no land-entries in 1374/5 and only four in 1376/7. The only other year of high mortality was 1383/4 when eleven entries were recorded, with no abnormalities in the subsequent years.

If we compare the rental of 1352 with that of 1383/4, we find that the land of the manor was divided at the later date into a smaller number of holdings held by fewer people. This holds true for all townships except Rainow, with the greatest consolidation taking place, in the north-east of the manor, in Disley and Whaley.[146] In addition, there was little evidence of land being left in decay.[147] There is generally insufficient data in the rolls to address the problem of replacement rates.[148]

To summarise, the halmote records show a substantial increase in the numbers of identified residents between the later 1350s and the later 1360s. This was the decade of recovery of population levels and the consolidation of holdings, when a large number of land acquisitions and exchanges were recorded in the manor court.[149] In

[146] The number of holdings in 1383–4 is: Sutton 96; Rainow 32; Hurdsfield 10; Shrigley 7; Stanley 4; Disley 10; Whaley 15; and Kettleshulme 12; the north-east may have been the area best suited to pasture.

[147] Only Sutton (7%), with seven holdings partly in decay, showed a significant number. Of the other townships Rainow had two holdings (6%) and Disley one (10%), while Kettleshulme's one holding (12%) was an assart of the late 1350s, SC 2/252/10 m. 5d. An earlier list of land in decay can be found, for example, in the account for 1371/2, SC 6/804/4 m. 2d.

[148] See S. Thrupp, 'The Problem of Replacement Rates in the Late Medieval English Population', *English Hist. Rev.*, 2nd ser., 18 (1965), pp. 101–199; the thriving land market and the increasing number of small-scale intakes or assarts may also have accommodated family members.

[149] There were 131 land entries, grants, assarts and approvements in the halmote between 1360/1 and 1368/9. There were 21 entries the following year as a result of the outbreak of plague, SC 2/252/12–15, SC 2/253/1–4, Chester City Record Office, Earwaker MSS CR 63/2/338 m. 7. See also Hatcher, *English Economy*, p. 32.

the 1370s a decline in those appearing in the courts followed the plague of the previous decade, and then numbers rose slightly during the late 1380s. The beginning of the 1390s witnessed a further decline which resulted in numbers falling below those of the early 1350s. Overall the picture is one of prolonged population decline following an initial recovery from the mid-1350s to the mid-1360s, the result of growth checked by the re-emergence of plague.

The portmote records also show a substantial rise in the population of the borough after the Black Death until the middle of the 1360s, when the further outbreaks of plague again precipitated a fall. The downturn began in the later 1370s and continued into the 1380s. Unlike the manor the numbers of both isolated individuals and outsiders in the borough remained high and this may be indicative of an upturn in the local economy during the later years of the century. However, the overall resident borough population at this time could barely have been above the level of the 1350s.

What, therefore, can be concluded about the use of this court-roll evidence to estimate local populations? Firstly, it seems there was probably a higher proportion of 'outsiders' appearing in the Macclesfield manor court records than in many other series of rolls on account of the manor's relationship with the forest. This means that barely a third of males who occur in the halmote records either entered land officially in the court or were included in the rentals. In the portmote, parallel to the situation found elsewhere, the proportion of residents referred to in the courts was, at best, only around a half. It is thus not possible to view rural or urban societies as static, closed or isolated from their wider communities. Secondly, only a small fraction of the total populations of manor and borough made regular and frequent appearances, and these names were of those of higher status and influence. In this respect the courts provided a useful index of both their presence and behaviour. However, the much larger numbers who made occasional and random appearances means that it is impossible to use the documents to determine accurate levels of population. Thirdly, a significant proportion of those making few appearances were in fact resident undertenants, servants and wage earners. Any estimate of the population would need to embrace these, although inaccuracies would occur as a result of the irregularity of their appearances. This is partly explained by the temporary nature of their residence. Court rolls, on the other hand, can greatly illuminate our knowledge of medieval society as they are the only sources in which people of this social level are consistently mentioned.

In conclusion, the evidence suggests that the manor townships had at least 600 to 700 hundred residents in the twenty-year period following the Black Death, which fell to between 500 and 600 by the turn of the century. However, this needs to be revised upwardly to take into account the number of undertenants and short-term residents, and a cautious estimate of between 800 and 900, at the end of the century, is possible. The 1350 rental lists 240 messuages or tenements for the seven demesne townships.[150] The highest numbers were in the south-east at Sutton (and neighbouring Bosley, not included in the above figures), at Rainow and in Whaley, (together with Marple, also not included) to the north-east. There must have been some seasonal variation in the numbers and it must be stressed, until further evidence is available, that these are cautious estimates. If we were to include people in Marple, Bosley, Tytherington and Taxal, and then add these to the more populous hundred, then the region must have supported a substantial pre-Black Death population.[151]

Macclesfield borough was probably comparable in size with many other market towns of the period, and an estimate of the stable population of between 350 and 400, which declined to around 300 in the last quarter of the century, seems acceptable.[152] If we were to include temporary residents and servants and those entering the town for leisure or trade, then at specific times during the summer or autumn months the population may have risen to over 500.

So what significance do these estimates have for Macclesfield Hundred and Cheshire as a whole ? If we take the Hundred first. Although a third of the hundred townships were included as part of the wider forest in the mid-fourteenth century forest eyre, by

[150] With a minimum 3.5 multiplier this would give a population of 840 (the figure of 1200 with one of 5 appears too high). Many of these holdings, however, were beginning to be transformed into multiple holdings or consolidated farms.

[151] For a comparison, see for example R. Hilton, 'Low-level Urbanization: The Seigneurial Borough Of Thornbury in the Middle Ages' in Razi and Smith (ed.), *Manor Court*, pp. 490–1; he stressed the greater danger of under- rather than over- estimating the population using court rolls.

[152] Further research estimating the population in these areas, as well as the townships such as Adlington which were experiencing significant land clearance just prior to the Black Death, would be of great interest.

the start of the fifteenth century the forest was limited to those townships which owed suit to the manor-court. In the Cheshire Mize Book of 1405 only a quarter of the townships were part of the manor-forest, and these paid only a quarter of the Macclesfield Hundred tax.[153] Even if we take a conservative estimate of the manor and borough populations in the second half of the fourteenth century, then Macclesfield Hundred must have supported a minimum of 3,500 people at this time. This assumes an even population density although, as we have seen, the manor-forest included large areas of commons and wastes. The maximum post-Black Death figure is unlikely to have risen above 5,000 people.

Not only is this sufficient to dispel any lingering impressions of an area empty of people, but it has important implications for the population of the county as a whole. It is particularly difficult to estimate Cheshire's population, given the wide variation in its landscape. However, in using Macclesfield we are dealing with a region associated with late clearance which had, at least in parts, a very low density of settlement.[154] Macclesfield hundred, for example, contributed only 10% of the total mize paid by the county in 1405 and the manor-forest, alone, only 2%.

In the light of the evidence provided by the Macclesfield court-rolls, therefore, the county's population in the late fourteenth century must have been in the region of 25,000 to 30,000. This means a significant revision of Russell's estimate, of 15,500 for Cheshire in 1377, which can now be seen as an under-estimate of at least 50%, and possibly as high as 100%. But this is only conjecture, and a significantly higher population density in parts of western and central Cheshire would result in a higher estimate still. More work is needed in this area. Ultimately the figure rests on the percentage of under-tenants, temporary residents and those in each household. The court rolls offer us a tantalising glimpse of their lives but, unfortunately, no conclusive proof of their numbers.

---

[153] Although the mize payments in the manor-forest cannot readily be linked to either the rent paid or the number of holdings in the rentals, the most populous townships, like Sutton and Bosley, paid the highest amounts; see n. 95 above (John Rylands University Library of Manchester, Tatton MS, 345).

[154] Dodd, 'Domesday Cheshire', pp. 15–20; Sylvester, 'Rural Settlement', pp. 1–4, 7–10; Dodd, 'Clearance of the Medieval Waste', pp. 21–6.

3 Economy, Society and Social Structure

Court rolls contain a great deal of evidence regarding the medieval economy and society. As we have seen in the last chapter this has been employed in the reconstruction of social and family groups. In particular, a person's service as either a pledge or a juror has important implications for their status and influence within the community. This categorisation has been most successful when related to landholding. In Macclesfield manor five clearly defined groups or categories of tenants can be distinguished, based upon the standard rent of 8*d.* an acre which was charged for the vast majority of holdings. These, and the approximate acreages they equated to, were:

1	30*s.* 0*d.* and over	(44 acres and over).
2	15*s.* 0*d.* to 29*s.* 11*d.*	(22 to 44 acres).
3	6*s.* 0*d.* to 14*s.* 11*d.*	(9 to 22 acres).
4	2*s.* 0*d.* to 5*s.* 11*d.*	(3 to 9 acres).
5	below 1*s.* 11*d.*	(3 acres and below).

In this chapter, then, I will examine the nature and content of an individual's court appearances in the light of these land-holdings, before attempting a thorough summary of the social structure.[1] I will begin by looking at the local economy and secondly at involvement in the process of the courts.

The local courts had an important role in the settling of disputes. The extent of a person's involvement in debt and detinue litigation was indicative of their wealth and trading interests. These must be treated with caution as more substantial suits could be impleaded in the Hundred eyre; these, as we have noted, were primarily between residents of the Hundred. In addition burgesses might bring suits in the mayor's court.

In the halmote the majority of suits related to the breaking of service contracts, as wage earners were employed from townships throughout the manor-forest. The sixteen people involved as either plaintiffs or defendants in ten or more civil actions during the period

[1] See pp. 110–18 below.

represented fewer than 0.1 per cent of all those appearing in the courts (1.5 per cent of the resident males) and included no women. Of these sixteen, six (37.5 per cent) were jurors on five or more occasions and ten (62.5 per cent) were pledges on five or more times. Only four people were involved in 20 or more suits, and of these three were members of the Downes family: Geoffrey (55) William (46) and Reginald (20). The Downes family were of gentry status but the fourth in this group, Adam Cok (30), was a wealthy peasant who held at least three messuages in Sutton.

In the portmote only 32 of those appearing (2 per cent) were involved as plaintiffs or defendants in ten or more suits. Most suits were for minor debts of under five and, rarely, above 10 shillings. Of these 32, a quarter were women of whom six brewed ale and twelve held land either in the borough fields or in the manor. Of the 24 men, half were pledges on five or more occasions, 14 (58 per cent) were office-holders; and seven (29 per cent) were jurors five or more times. The person involved in the largest number of lawsuits was William Bullynche, a fuller, who also brought eleven actions in the halmote.[2]

The portmote records occasionally include suits brought follow-ing the All Saints and Barnaby fairs, and these help to provide a cross-section of the people, including tradesmen, who visited Macclesfield.[3] The borough attracted small numbers across a wide area in spite of the competition from Stockport market.[4] The boroughs of Knutsford and Congleton and the markets of Alderley, Wilmslow and Sandbach (dealing in local cloth) were also within easy reach. These must have attracted Macclesfield people and there is evidence to suggest that some nearby boroughs were dealing with

---

[2] See Bullynche's biography in Appendix One.

[3] For example SC 2/254/10 m. 9d., SC 2/254/11 m. 9, SC 2/254/12 m. 8; Chester City Record Office, Earwaker MSS CR 63/2/339 rot. 1, m. 2. The business of these fair courts increased in the last quarter of the century. Those mentioned include: William Baker of Cubley (Derbyshire); Richard Glover, a mercer of Manchester; John Potter of Burwardsley; Thomas Sheter of Sheffield; Thomas Spycer of Northwich; a salter from Fairfield; a man from Nottingham who dealt in pottery and woollen cloth; and people from Preston, Burton (Cheshire *or* Staffordshire), Wilmslow, Congleton, Adlington, Knutsford, Mobberley, Mottram St. Andrew, Dukinfield and Butley.

[4] It led, in the later thirteenth century, to the burgesses' exaggerated claim that it caused Macclesfield to be 'devastata et destructa', *C.C.R.*, p. 215.

a greater quantity of trade.[5] The apparent scarcity of visitors to Macclesfield from the east of the region was a consequence of both the landscape and the dominance of a number of small market-centres within Peak forest in Derbyshire.[6] Overall trade appears to have come from an area of around 30 miles to the north and west.[7]

The number of suits for debt brought in the portmote suggests that local trade was small-scale. The average of ten debts a year in the 1360s increased to a peak of around fifteen in some years during the 1380s and 1390s. In the halmote an annual average of fewer than five debts increased to double that figure from the later 1360s. However, as suits could also be brought in the eyre and the three Hundreds after the eyre, we should be cautious when dealing with these numbers, and there is nothing to indicate that debt litigation in Macclesfield was not comparable with that found in other small urban centres throughout the country.[8] Those for 3s. 0d., 3s. 6d., and 3s. 10d., with 6d. damages, were common, and burgess Adam Clokspoke, for instance, owed 1s. 1d., 1s. 2d., 2s. and 2s. 7d.[9]

[5] M. J. Bennett, *Community, Class and Careerism*, pp. 115–7; Hewitt, *Medieval Cheshire*, p. 68.

[6] The markets of Glossop and Charlesworth were in easy reach, as were those close to the Staffordshire border such as Cubley, Hartington, Monyash and Tideswell. Coates 'Derbyshire Markets and Fairs', *Derbyshire Archaeological Journal*, 85 (1965), pp. 91–111.

[7] Although people from the rural hinterland would have brought their produce to market, many of their purchases would probably have been of limited value. As well as visiting traders from Macclesfield and elsewhere, local villages contained their own shops and suppliers. As Dyer said 'internal exchanges that went on between townspeople … must account for a great deal of urban commercial activity', C. Dyer, 'The consumer and the market in the later middle ages', *Economic History Review*, 2nd ser., 42 (1989), pp. 321–2.

[8] Hilton found that 40% of pleas of debt in court rolls, were for between 1s. 0d. and 5s. 0d. (*English Peasantry*, pp. 46–7). Over 70% were within the range 1s. 0d. to 10s. 0d., E. Clark, 'Debt Litigation in a Late Medieval English Vill' in *Pathways to the Medieval Peasant*, J. A. Raftis (ed.) (Toronto, 1981), p. 252. There were up to 40 or more suits for debt a year in one small Gloucestershire borough, Hilton, 'The Seigneurial Borough of Thornbury', p. 503.

[9] SC 2/252/11 m. 3d., SC 2/253/1 m. 4d., Chester City Record Office, Earwaker MSS CR 63/2/338 m. 1. Although Adam's trade is unknown, his wife was a weaver, SC 2/252/12 m. 8. Their son, John, was guilty of three affrays in 1366–67, but was not subsequently mentioned in the local courts, SC 2/253/1 m. 4d., SC 2/253/2 m. 4d.

The more substantial debts generally involved either chaplains or executors of wills, and were thus not necessarily related to trade. Other debts related to those of a high status and may have involved money loans, while the farmers of the stallage also brought actions to recover their revenues. Other debts were acknowledged and enrolled using the phrase '*cognovit se debere*'; these were debt recognizances which listed the terms when payments were due.[10] Robert Worth of Tytherington, along with three burgesses, for instance, acknowledged a debt of £4 5s. 4d. in the halmote to the chaplain of Prestbury for (tithe) sheaves of corn in nearby Upton, Tytherington and Fallibroome.[11] Adam Kyngeslegh, clerk and escheator of the county, was owed the largest sums although some of these were recovered in suits.[12] The halmote records show that four men – William Blag, William Huntte, Macclesfield burgess Robert Hasty, and Henry Lyster of Stockport – were liable for debts of £6 of silver, £4, and £2 to Adam, servant of William Hulm.[13] As none of these men originated in the manor it is interesting to note a further function of the court. The largest debt

---

[10] For the different types of recognizances, see D. Clayton, 'Peace Bonds', p. 142. For example (forester) John Shert (*sic.*) owed 36s. 8d. to Robert Legh in the portmote, SC 2/254/3 m. 5d, and Gilbert Hulcokes 21s. 8d. to chaplain Robert Buckard in the halmote, SC 2/254/8 m. 3.

[11] SC 2/253/3 m. 8. Thomas Oselcok and Hervey Sewall, both butchers, and Alan Joneson. Sewall was a custodian of bread and meat in 1355/6, and Oselcok a catchpoll in 1354/5 SC 2/252/7 m. 3, SC2/252/6m. 1.

[12] The debts owed to Adam included: 36s. 8½d. for the sale of an ox, lamb and calf. 22s. 8½d., 21s. 8d., 20s. 0d. jointly by three men and by one other man. 19s. 5½d., 17s. 4d., 17s. 3d., 13s. 4d. (on three occasions), 12s. 0d. (twice) jointly by two and three men. 11s. 8d., 10s. 0d., (twice), by a man from Staffordshire and one from Sutton. 9s. 7d., 9s. 3d., 6s. 8d., and several of 5s. 0d. and below. The total sum was £15 17s. 0d. recovered in the halmote, and a further £1 0s. 0d. from a single debt in the portmote (SC 2/254/6 m. 6d., SC 2/254/9 m. 4, SC 2/254/10 mm. 6–7d., SC 2/254/12 mm. 6–8d., SC 2/254/13 m. 4–4d., SC 2/254/15 m. 4). See his biography in *Ch.Acc.* (2), pp. 152–53.

[13] SC 2/254/14 m. 4. William Hulm was one of fourteen men who made a recognizance to the prince of £1066 13s. 4d. at the Chester exchequer in 1363, cancelling a conditional sum of £1,000 owed by John Mascy, parson of Sefton, his brother, Sir Richard Mascy, and others, following threats and other wrongdoings, *B.P.R., iii*, pp. 421, 455.

in a suit was the £40 John Rossyndale, knight, and John Hephales, chaplain, recovered against four local men.[14]

As by custom burgesses could not be impleaded in outside courts, suits had to be brought by manor-tenants in the portmote. These are useful as they can illustrate trading links between the two communities. Forester Edmund Dounes, for example, sued Richard Walker for the detention of woollen cloth and Adam Aleyn of Sutton sued tanner Richard Spencer for a debt of 20s. 0d.[15] Burgesses likewise sued manor tenants in the halmote, and Richard Burelles, for instance, brought two actions against men of Bollington. As we have already seen outsiders could appear as defendants and plaintiffs in both courts. In the halmote at the end of November 1377, for example, Roger Lighthaseles of Marple failed in his suit of debt against John Cowdrey of Prestbury, and Richard of Marple was amerced in a suit of trespass against John son of Richard of Sutton.[16]

In actions of detinue, when the goods are specified, they are usually of small value and indicate the importance of the hire and sale of animals. The halmote records, for instance, list the detention of a cow, a calf, a bullock and an ox. The parties indicate the movement of livestock between townships: smallholder Adam Wodecok, for example, detained a cow of William and Roger, sons of burgess William Bullynche. William Smyth of Sutton brought an action for a bullock against smallholder Adam Haregreve of Bollington, and John Oldefeld of Sutton brought actions for cattle and sheep against several local men.[17] The suits in the borough court more frequently related to the detention of grain: an outsider,

---

[14] SC 2/254/1 m. 12. John Bosedon (category one) and John Shryglegh (category two), William Lowe and Robert Byran, were burgess tenants who both held land in the manor-forest. As ancient demesne of the earls of Cheshire, Macclesfield was exempt from the 40s. 0d. limit that could be impleaded within local courts established under the statute of Gloucester, Clark, 'Debt Litigation', p. 252.

[15] SC 2/254/11 m. 9, SC 2/254/12 m. 10d.

[16] Burelles in 1390–92, SC 2/254/12 m. 5d., SC 2/254/13 m. 5d. The halmote in 1377, SC 2/253/12 m. 1.

[17] SC 2/253/6 m. 3, SC 2/252/7 m. 2d. John Oldefeld owed debts of 29s. 7d. to two men and recovered debts of 26s. 7d. against two other men between 1388 and 1391. He also sued, for example, John Scorgell (unident-ified) for the detention of eight oxen and four sheep, worth 12s. 4d. In 1390/1 he leased the escapes upon the Minns (Sutton common) for a three year term, SC 2/254/9 m. 4, SC 2/254/11 mm. 5d.–6, SC 2/254/12 m. 7d.

for example, brought an action for a bushel of rye, against a man
from Mottram St. Andrew. Burgess William Bullynche, a fuller,
detained 2½ bushels of rye against Alice, the widow of Thomas
Clogh. William Stubbes, a burgess, and manor tenant William Lowe
of Rainow sued each other for the detention of a horse and
foal.[18] The goods detained were frequently brass pots, mazer bowls,
cloth or small items of clothing.

Table 14   *Resident Families with Trade Surnames*

Surname[1]	Borough	Manor[2]
Cloth Workers:		
Blanket-maker (Chaloner)	1	
Fullers (Walkers)	7	2
Glovers	3	
Linen draper	1	
Tailors		9
Tanners (Barkers)	3	
Shepherds		9
Herders		2
Shearers		1
Victuals:		
Bakers	3	
Cooks	2	2
Salters	3	2
Wood Workers:		
Cartwrights (Wrights & Wood turners)	4	14
Coopers	2	2
Others:		
Carters	1	2
Chapmen	2	
Fletchers	3	5
Gardeners		2
Goldsmiths	1	
Harpers	3	1
Horner		1

[18] SC 2/255/2 m. 6, SC 2/253/8 m. 5d., SC 2/253/9 m. 5.

Surname[1]	Borough	Manor[2]
Marler	1	
Mason		3
Millers	2	7
Mustard (sellers)	1	
Paver	1	
Painter	1	
Saddlers	1	
Smiths	2	5
Tinkers	1	1

[1] male surnames only.
[2] including Bosley, Tytherington, Marple and Taxal.
(SC 2/252/2–15, SC 2/253/1–12, SC 2/254/1–15, SC 2/255/1–2;
Chester City Record Office, Earwaker MSS CR 63/2/338–339).

As the majority of the leading burgess tradesmen were not referred to by names denoting their occupation, surnames can denote relatively little about the actual crafts and trades being carried on in the town (Table 14). Evidence of craft or industrial activity is contained either in the infrequent references to the regulatory assizes or in the fines, in eyre, for breaches in the statute of Labourers. Of the four people amerced for false grain measures in 1363 two, Richard Rowe and Richard Kenworthey, were leading burgesses, one was a wife of a burgess, and one man, with the surname of Bollington, cannot be identified. In 1376 three burgesses and one apprentice broke the assize of craftsmen by selling leather at an excessive price. A tourn of weights and measures held in the portmote after All Saints in 1387 found the following were at fault: one gallon ale-pot; one dry grain measure; six merchants with stone weights to sell wax, pepper and other goods; four with stone weights to sell wool; two with sticks to sell cloth; and two butchers who refused to swear their oath.[19] From these examples, Macclesfield again appears similar to other small urban centres.[20]

The brewing of ale was common in medieval households, and was carried out primarily by women as a part-time occupation.[21]

[19] SC 2/252/14 m. 5, SC 2/253/9 m. 5, SC 2/254/9 m. 6.
[20] R. Hilton, 'Lords, Burgesses and Hucksters', *Past and Present*, 97 (1983), pp. 3–15; and *English Peasantry*, pp. 80–9.
[21] Hilton, *Small Town Society*, p. 60.

Although the necessary materials were easy to come by, the process involved a significant input of both time and labour.[22] Two strengths of ale could be brewed and it was necessary to offer for sale any surplus. Dyer, though, has refuted the traditional view of brewing ale as being intrinsic to a peasant's diet, as it was unlikely that much grain would be left over.[23] In rural areas it was largely 'a sporadic and discontinuous trade' and one divided between a small group of 'professionals' and the majority who sold irregularly and occasionally.[24]

In the Macclesfield portmote the ale statute was set by the jury at the Michaelmas court who elected two custodians or tasters. The price was fixed for the best ale ('bona' or 'optima') which was sold both within the borough and in the surrounding area ('in patria'). The burgesses were involved, then, in the supply of the local market and not merely brewing for their their own consumption. The prices of the ale obviously fluctuated according to grain prices.[25] The two custodians were drawn from the burgess trading-community and included the husbands of ale-wives; on one occasion they were amerced for failing to carry out their office. The presentments for infringements against the assize were generally made at the three great courts of the year, and the measures were presented at a yearly tourn after Michaelmas.[26]

These presentments have long been considered to have been a form of disguised licensing and to have been 'among the business

---

[22] J. M. Bennett, 'The Village Ale-Wife' in B. Hanawalt (ed.), *Women and Work in Preindustrial Europe* (Indiana, 1986), p. 21. Several houses contained brewing equipment in seventeenth century Rainow. Laughton, *Rainow*, p. 35.

[23] A group of at least nine women, indicted for taking excessive salary, were described as carriers of water within the borough, CHES 25/19 m. 4d. C. Dyer, 'English Diet in the Later Middle Ages' in T. H. Ashton, P. R. Coss, C. Dyer and J. Thirsk (eds.), *Social Relations and Ideas: Essays in Honour of R. H. Hilton* (1983), pp. 191–214.

[24] Dyer, *Lords and Peasants*, pp. 346–8; J. M. Bennett, 'Village Ale-Wife', pp. 23–4.

[25] In 1349/50 at ½d. a gallon for ale within and at 1d. for three gallons outside; and from the mid-1370s at 1d. a gallon inside and ½d. or ¾d. outside (SC 2/252/2 m. 3, SC 2/253/10 m. 5, SC 2/253/12 m. 2, SC 2/254/4 m. 6, SC 2/254/9 m. 6).

[26] SC 2/252/8 m. 4d. The words 'galonem' and 'lagena' were both used to describe the ale measures; the grain measure was the 'hopa'.

expenses of small commercial concerns'.[27] Those frequently amerced, therefore, should not be seen as ordinary household brewers, but as those engaged in a commercial activity for the supply of the local market. Within this 'licensing' system there may have additionally operated some real attempt to regulate and control the trade.[28] This is reflected in the range of different infringements for which the brewers were amerced.[29]

In total 285 people were presented for breaches of the assize of ale in the portmote, of whom 92 per cent were female – this represents 45 per cent of the total females appearing.[30] Of the 22 men amerced, seventeen belonged to a brewing household. The scale of the trade at any one time is illustrated by the number using unsealed measures. Between 1362 and 1372 an average of 34 were amerced for this offence each year, and in 1363/4 47 payed £1 6s. 3d. in amercements. In the first half of the 1390s, between 32 and 36 were amerced each year for breaking the assize. Those involved could represent up to 10 per cent of the overall population. Ale would have been sold from houses, established ale-houses or by street vendors. A woman who sold from her house was sometimes referred to as a 'brasiatrix' (with one also called a 'pandoxatrix').[31] There was considerable

---

[27] J. B. Post, 'Manorial Amercements and Peasant Poverty', *Economic History Review* 2nd ser., 28 (1975), pp. 308–10.

[28] A borough ordinance of 1404 stated that all outside brewers should pay stallage of 12d., that all ale-sellers should pay the same amount, and that all brewers, butchers and bakers should observe the assizes regarding quality under pain of 6d. to be paid to the common chest (Birkenhead Public Library, Macclesfield Collection, MA B/2/1).

[29] These were: simply breaking the assize, between 3d. and 6d. (maximum 18d.); selling weak ale, usually 3d. (maximum 12d.); selling with a false measure or one that was not marked or signed, usually 3d. (maximum 6d.); refusing to sell to neighbours or a specific person when a person had ale available, 3d. (maximum 12d.); not displaying a sign in the market or outside the brewer's house, 3d. or 6d.; refusing to allow measures to be tested, between 3d. and 12d.; selling at a higher price than that set by the assize, between 1d. and 6d.; selling ale that was unfit, 3d.; selling bad ale (a few amercements), 3d. or 4d.; and using a false grain measure, 6d.

[30] Compared with around 31% in rural Wakefield. H. Jewell, 'Women at the Courts of the Manor of Wakefield, 1348–1350', *Northern History*, 26 (1990), p. 61; and a quarter in rural Brigstock, J. M. Bennett, 'Village Ale-Wife', p. 23.

[31] Amice Fletcher (see Appendix One), was described as a tranter when amerced, for failing to display her seal, in 1375, SC 2/253/9 m. 5.

variation in the frequency with which individual brewers were amerced. These penalties must have added to their costs and the most regular sellers could be charged between once and three times per year. To a certain extent this may have protected 'professionals' from the small-scale sporadic brewer with little capital.

For example, over a period of 33 years Margery, wife of Richard Kenworthey, paid at least 18s. 7d. for brewing amercements. Although she began to brew in 1359 she did not take it up seriously until 1371/2, the year her husband farmed the common oven, after which she was amerced in all but three of the 20 years following. In 1372/3 she was presented on five occasions and amerced a total of 5s. 6d.: of this, 2s. 6d. for refusing to sell ale, 6d. was for selling at the sum of 3d. a gallon, and another 2s. od. amercement (the highest recorded for ale) was unspecified. In total, she paid at least 11s. 5d. for refusing to sell, for selling in an unmarked measure and for refusing to have her ale-pan tested.[32]

Her refusal to be tested is indicative of both regulation and attempts at evasion, while the example of Alice, wife of William Sparky, also suggests an element of resentment. Alice began brewing in 1352 and continued to do so regularly until 1389, when she was an old woman, and resumed again in 1395. In 1355 she was amerced 1s. od. for a tumult in court, and at the following session another 6d. for breaking the assize of ale. At the same time her husband was amerced the high sum of 3s. 4d. for accusing the custodians of making a false and malicious presentment of her; later in the year she was amerced another 2s. od. for a dispute (the usual term for being a scold). After this she was consistently presented between one and three times in most years, and her amercements for ale between 1352 and 1389 amounted to more than 12s. od. (with another 6d. in 1395–6). Unlike Margery, however, she was never charged for refusing to sell ale, and was amerced only 1s. 3d. for selling with an unmarked measure. In addition, she was fined another 9d. for breaking the assize of bread on three occasions.[33]

It was common for women to have breaks in their brewing careers. This may have been the result of lack of capital or because

[32] SC 2/252/10 m. 4d. – SC 2/252/15 m. 5d., SC 2/253/6 mm. 5–5d., SC 2/253/7 mm. 2–3 – SC 2/254/13 m. 6d., m. 8d.

[33] SC 2/252/4 mm. 6–6d. – SC 2/254/10 m. 9d., SC 2/255/1 m. 6d. – SC 2/255/2 mm. 5–6. SC 2/252/7 mm. 3–3d. William was amerced for his false grain and gallon measures in 1349, SC 2/252/2 m. 3. The amercements after 1389 may have referred to a daughter or relative.

of a concentration upon other activities. Margery, wife of Richard Kenworthey, for instance, stopped brewing for seven years between 1364 and 1371. During this time, from 1367/8, Richard employed a maid who was amerced four times in three years for ale offences. This maid was also amerced once, in 1367, for selling bread that was not baked in the common oven; this was three years before Richard leased the common oven.[34] As Roger Falybron apparently remained single, his maid carried out the task of brewing and was amerced on fifteen occasions.[35]

Although brewing was widespread amongst all social groups, the actual supply of ale was dominated by the wives of a small group of leading burgesses. If we analyse the presentment data by social status we find that 58 per cent were wives of the established burgess families, 33 per cent were isolated or unknown women, 7 per cent were specified servants, and 2 per cent were isolated men. More than half the amercements related to a small group of brewing households and the contribution to the local supply by those brewing occasionally or on a small-scale could not have been significant. Many of this dominant group may have sold from ale-houses (see Table 16). Another characteristic of the leading brewers was that their households were more likely to sell bread; in this instance, though, it was the husbands who were more frequently amerced. Of the 49 women who were presented on ten or more occasions 41 per cent were also amerced for bread, compared with around 25 per cent overall and only 13 per cent of isolated individuals.

The leading ale suppliers, therefore, were predominately the wives of established burgess tradesmen (at least half of whom were office holders). Their households included a fuller, a tailor, a leather craftsman, a cloth-seller, a wool merchant, a smith, a mercer and several butchers. Many of the leading burgesses appear to have been general mercers or traders to the businesses of whom the selling of

[34] SC 2/252/10 m. 4d. – SC 2/252/15 m. 5d., SC 2/253/6 mm. 5–5d. – SC 2/254/13 m. 6d., m. 8d. Richard's maid, SC 2/253/3 m. 9 – SC 2/253/5 mm. 8–8d. Richard leased the common oven in 1371/2, SC 2/253/6 m. 7.
[35] Roger's maid, Agnes Starky, was amerced ten times for ale between 1362 and 1376, and another six times between 1387 and 1396, SC 2/252/14 m. 5 – SC 2/253/9 m. 5d., SC 2/254/8 m. 2 – SC 2/255/2 m. 6. Roger's other maid, Maud, was not involved in brewing, and was convicted five times for carrying off turves and once for trespassing in the park, SC 2/252/13 m. 5 – SC 2/253/6 m. 5.

ale and bread must have made a significant contribution. Only six out of the 49 women appear to have acted alone and independent of other trades. In contrast, the activity of a large number of women who brewed intermittently must have related, at least in part, to ownership of surplus grain.

As the borough contributed to the supply of its surrounding hinterland, brewing in the manor was of a rather different nature. The presentments in the halmote were made at the Michaelmas court which amerced those for brewing over the previous year (in a manner similar to that of the tourn held in the Hundred townships). Those amerced were usually said to have brewed only once, and a frequent woman offender was referred to as an 'ale-wife' ('brasiatrix'). Unlike those in the portmote, these presentments more closely resembled a licensing system, rather than any attempt at regulation, and the actual offence was merely that of offering ale for sale.

As indicated by other studies, the brewing of ale in rural areas was more intermittent. Out of the 248 people presented in the halmote only eighteen households were amerced between five and nine times and only one person more than ten. The manor trade was almost equally divided between men (48 per cent) and women (52 per cent).[36] From the mid-1360s as many as 20 people were amerced each year and this rose to a peak of 52 in 1389 when the resultant revenues were 17s. 8d. This was exceptional, and those amerced were middling to poorer peasants, of category three or less, of whom only four were women.[37] The greatest number of offenders was in the township of Sutton, followed by Marple, Shrigley, Disley, Whaley, Kettleshulme and Rainow. As many brewers were undertenants, their places of origin are not always known. The majority of the nineteen presented on five or more occasions appear to have been from the more outlying townships, such as Marple and Whaley, which were thus furthest from the urban trade. Those amerced three times included a butcher, John

[36] There could be considerable variation in the sex ratio, Hilton, *English Peasantry*, pp. 45–6, 104, and *Small Town Society*, p. 60; J. M. Bennett, 'Village Ale-Wife', pp. 22–26.

[37] SC 2/254/11 m. 4. Long-term residence could be an important factor in brewing, J. M. Bennett, 'Village Ale-Wife', p. 24. Up to half of tenant families were involved in three villages of the bishopric of Worcester in the late fourteenth and early fifteenth centuries, Dyer, *Lords and Peasants*, p. 348.

Robynsone of Whaley, John Forster of Saltersford and Robert Jackson of Taxal. Ale-selling was also an activity that involved both husbands and wives and this was the case in sixteen of these nineteen households. Brewing in the manor, therefore, was a peasant activity which was probably connected to periodic surpluses of grain and undertaken for the supply of the local market.

The two officials of the assize of bread and meat were elected, along with those for ale, at the Michaelmas portmote. Of the 136 people amerced for offences in this area, more than 90 per cent were involved in the selling of bread. Baking was an irregular activity that, unlike brewing, was not dominated by a small group of sellers. Of those presented, two-thirds were amerced on only one occasion and only fifteen individuals were presented more than twice. This activity was associated either with burgess households, who also sold ale and meat, or with a large number of small traders and hucksters. As the offence was usually baking against the assize it was probably, again, a form of licensing. On one occasion, though, Cecily, wife of Ranulph Upton, was amerced 4d. for selling bread made with poor and unsuitable flour. The most likely form of regulation would have involved weight, and people sometimes refused to have their loaves tested. The amercements were consistently assessed at 3d. or multiples of 3d. The burgesses involved often sold better quality bread, such as wastel and simnel ('artocopes').[38]

The resident with the largest number of amercements (seven) was the wife of Robert Blagge whose bread included wastel. Robert also sold wax and pepper and was presumably related to innkeeper Stephen Blagge. Others selling bread included the salter, Thomas Spycer, and John Mustardmon. Several outside tradesmen were amongst those most frequently amerced: Thomas Baxster of Prestbury (seven times), Robert Baxster of Congleton (three times), and two men called Henry Baxster from Congleton and Knutsford, who were both amerced twice. Only a quarter of those presented were in households amerced on five or more occasions (compared to 13 per cent of individuals) and of them half were also important suppliers of ale. In 1386/7 six leading butchers and bakers were indicted for withdrawing suit to the common oven: Robert Heye,

[38] SC 2/255/1 m. 6d. There were only around about four or five full-time bakers in Halesowen before the Black Death, all of whom were male, Hilton, *Small Town Society*, p. 60. 'Many of those in service occupations or the food trades relied for their living mainly on satisfying urban demand.' Dyer, *Consumer and Market*, p. 322.

Robert Blagge, William Pemberton, Ranulph Upton (whose household had the highest number of amercements), John Oselcok and Margery Baxster. Here again the borough seems to have had a role in supplying the rural area, and there were no presentments for baking offences in the halmote.[39]

In contrast a small and influential group of butchers appear to have been at the forefront of the economic life of the town (see Table 17). Their trade was sometimes linked with stock rearing in the manor-forest and was often combined with the selling of fish as well as ale by their wives. The fact that most, if not all, held office as custodian of the assize must have led to the inspection of fellow butchers and associates. This may not always have been welcome, and in one year two tradesmen were presented for failing to perform their duties.[40] The variation in frequency amongst the amercements, which ranged from 3*d*., 6*d*., and 8*d*. to 12*d*., again reveals a system that sought to control and regulate as well as license. There were regular attempts at evasion: some butchers, for instance, obstructed the custodians by refusing either to observe the assize (6*d*., 9*d*. or 12*d*.), or by being unwilling to have their meat tested (3*d*., 4*d*. or 6*d*.).

They may have had good reason to conceal their meat.[41] Edmund Hayneson, for example, was one of four people amerced in 1370 for relinquishing their oath to the trade of butchers. In 1388 he was also amerced 3*d*. for selling a calf or deer calf ('vitulum') to fellow butcher Robert Heye and for then being reluctant to take the assize. His total amercements were 7*s*. 8*d*. over a period of a quarter of a century (1356–1389), and he was presented on eighteen occasions in fourteen separate years. Three of these amercements were for

---

[39] Thomas Baxster of Prestbury, *c*. 1382–92, SC 2/254/4 m. 7d. – SC 2/254/13 m. 8; Robert and Henry Baxster of Congleton, SC 2/253/1 m. 4, SC 2/253/8 m. 5, SC 2/254/9 m. 6d.; Henry Baxster of Knutsford, SC 2/252/4 m. 6d., SC 2/252/5 m. 4d.; Spycer, SC 2/254/3 m. 5; and Mustardmon, SC 2/254/8 m. 2. Of those withdrawing suit, SC 2/254/12 m. 9, Oselcok was a custodian of ale in 1382/3 and a custodian of bread and meat in 1383/4; SC 2/254/4 m. 6, Chester City Record Office, Earwaker MSS CR 63/2/339 rot. 1, m. 1. See Blagge's biography in Appendix One, and Alan Pierson below.

[40] Robert Heye and William Hayfeld were amerced 2*d*. each for not attending court to make their presentments, SC 2/253/12 m. 2d. Robert, a butcher, was also amerced 1*s*. 0*d*. for the assize of meat.

[41] P. W. Hammond, *Food and Feast in Medieval England* (1993), pp. 84–90.

selling bad or diseased meat. His wife, Agnes, was fined 3s. 10d. for breaches of the assize of ale between 1370 and 1386.[42]

Robert Heye's amercements amounted to more than £1 in the closing quarter of the century (1374–1396) and included 4s. 0d. for refusing to take the assize on at least seven different occasions. In the same period his wife, Joan, paid over 5s. 0d. for ale and 6d. for bread. As well as the case with Edmund Hayneson, he was amerced 7d. for the cost of a calf on another occasion and paid the highest single amercement of 2s. 0d. for selling (horse) meat with murrain. In addition, he was amerced 1d. for not making his presentment while serving as a custodian for the assize of ale. His disagreement or rivalry with fellow butcher, Reginald Cook, led him to draw his knife and both men were also unjustly accused of involvement in an affray.[43] Reginald paid amercements of more than 12s. 0d. over a thirteen year period (1383–1396) of which 3s. 6d. was the result of his unwillingness to take the assize on at least seven occasions, once while serving in the office of the custodian of ale (he also served as reeve). His association with the manor brought him to the aid of William Slegh (who was later mayor), when he was assaulted at Rainow in 1388, and in 1396 a tenant shot arrows at him in Hurdsfield.[44]

William Pemberton sold pork and fish as well as, on occasion, good quality bread. His amercements over a fifteen-year period (1381–1396) totalled 7s. 8d., including two for diseased meat ('leprosas') and 9d. for bread. His possessions included a bow, which he used to assault ale-wife Amice Fletcher, and which he may have used for hunting. In c. 1377, helped by three others, he killed a hind at Tegg's Nose Brook, and later he purchased in the halmote a colt and a cow from the heriots of two tenants. He also

<hr />

[42] SC 2/252/7 m. 3d. – SC 2/254/10 m. 8. SC 2/253/5 m. 8, SC 2/254/11 m. 9. Agnes, SC 2/253/5 m. 8 – SC 2/254/8 m. 1.

[43] Robert, SC 2/253/8 m. 5 – SC 2/255/2 m. 6. SC 2/253/8 m. 5d., SC 2/253/12 mm. 2–2d., SC 2/254/4 m. 7, SC 2/254/11 m. 7. He was a custodian of ale in 1377/8 and catchpoll in 1388/9, SC 2/253/12 m. 2, SC 2/254/10 m. 8. See his biography in Appendix One. Joan, SC 2/254/4 m. 7 – SC 2/255/2 mm. 5–6.

[44] SC 2/254/4 mm. 6d. –7 – SC 2/255/2 mm. 4–6. He was custodian of ale in 1387/8 and 1391/2, and borough reeve in 1395/6. SC 2/254/9 m. 6, SC 2/254/13 m. 6, SC 2/255/2 m. 5, SC 2/254/9 m. 5. His wife, Amice, was fined 2s. 1d. for ale and 4d. for bread during this time, SC 2/254/3 m. 5 – SC 2/255/2 m. 6.

held small amounts of land in Bollington and a man was amerced for trespassing in his corn there, and for detaining his axe. In 1386 William was in gaol for a trespass.[45]

In 1392 these three butchers – Robert, Reginald and William – were described as regrators of meat and fish, including mullet and ray, which had been purchased from Adam Fyssher over a two year period. Three years later two other men, butcher Robert Thorbald and William French, were accused of selling wine purchased at Chester by false and untested measures.[46] William French also held a small holding in Sutton and pastured sheep, draught-beasts and pigs in the forest. As all five of them paid fines or purchased wood from the forest they may have been involved in stock-keeping to a minor and varying degree.[47]

In contrast with fish, meat was only rarely brought in and sold by outsiders. William Cain le Flesschewer of Knutsford, for example, was amerced three times in the portmote. In the rural area peasants must largely have supplied themselves although, as with baking, supplies from the town's market played a supplementary part. There were only two butchers resident in the manor, as far as the evidence shows, and both were undertenants in Whaley. As in the borough these had a wider role in the selling of victuals. John Robynsone held a messuage and an acre for a term of years and was presented three times for meat.[48] William Menerell was presented twice for meat and once for ale.[49]

[45] SC 2/254/3 m. 5–SC 2/255/2 mm. 5–6. SC 2/254/10 m. 8, SC 2/253/10 m. 1, SC 2/254/4 m. 4d., SC 2/255/2 m. 3, SC 2/254/11 m. 5d., SC 2/254/7 m. 2. He was fined 2s. 0d. for wounding Amice Fletcher in 1386, SC 2/254/8 m. 1.

[46] SC 2/254/13 m. 8. One 'pipe' had been bought at Chester for 43s. 4d. and cost 5s. 0d. to carry to Macclesfield; they sold it there at 6d. a gallon rather than a reasonable 8d., to the great harm of the neighbourhood and community, CHES 25/22 m. 47d.

[47] French held a messuage at Wincle, at 1s. 0d. rent, SC 11/898 m. 2d. He was catchpoll in 1375/6, a custodian of ale in 1374/5 and bread and meat in 1372/3 and 1376/7(SC 2/253/9 m. 5, SC 2/253/7 m. 2, SC 2/253/8 m. 5, SC 2/253/10 m. 5). He pastured at least three horses and 30 sheep. Thorbald was a custodian of bread and meat in 1382/3 and ale in 1395/6. (SC 2/254/1 m. 6, m. 11, SC 2/254/2 m. 10, SC 2/254/4 m. 6, m. 8, SC 2/254/5 m. 5, m. 10, SC 2/255/2 m. 5).

[48] SC 2/254/3 m. 3d., SC 2/252/10 m. 5, SC 2/253/1 m. 2. A man of this name was amerced thirty years later for ale, SC 2/255/2 m. 3.

[49] SC 2/252/10 m. 5, SC 2/252/11 m. 5, SC 2/254/3 m. 3. His wife also regularly sold ale, SC 2/252/5 m. 5 – SC 2/252/12 m. 2.

Cloth-making was another trade organised and geared towards the local market. The early stages of the process involved a very small outlay and used tools that were produced locally. This led to the widespread use of women, who were employed on a piece-rate basis, to do the tasks of spinning, carding, combing and, to a lesser extent, weaving. Spinning made a vital contribution to the income and economy of both urban and rural households.[50] In our period it is perhaps too early to detect the specialisation in cloth production that was later prevalent in the Pennines. The fines for labour offences, though, reveal a concentration of cloth producers in the more upland areas in the north-east of Macclesfield Hundred. In 1361, for example, 32 weavers and nine spinners were fined.[51] These were all women, with the exception of Roger Wodecok, who was also a fuller.[52] The two fulling-mills in the manor-forest, however, which were located at Macclesfield and Whaley, were not at this time very profitable.[53]

The evidence from items recorded as stolen or detained in the portmote reveals a small-scale local textile industry similar to that found in other small towns.[54] Wool was sold, for instance, by Adam Kyngeslegh, John Leversegge and Nicholas Upton: all of them held substantial landholdings in the manor while both Adam and John were also burgesses. Those involved in the selling of cloth appear generally to have been mercers, such as Richard Burelles and William Sparky, and the widow of butcher, office-holder and former mayor Alan Pierson.[55] Sparky also held land in the borough

[50] A. R. Bridbury, *Medieval English Clothmaking: An Economic Survey* (1982), pp. 9–10; Dyer, *Standards of living*, pp. 132 and 172.

[51] SC 2/252/12 m. 8. These were quite high numbers compared, for instance, with Wiltshire. E. M. Thompson, 'Offenders Against the Statute of Labourers in Wiltshire, 1349', *Wilts. Arch. and Nat. Hist. Magazine*, 33 (1904), pp. 384–409.

[52] Women were mostly spinners in some areas, Hanawalt (ed.), *Women and Work*, p. 11; and also weavers in others, S. A. C. Penn, 'Female Wage-Earners in Late Fourteenth-Century England', *Agricultural History Review*, 35 (1987), p. 6.

[53] Booth, *Financial Administration*, p. 98.

[54] Hilton, *English Peasantry*, p. 80; Dyer, *Consumer and Market*, p. 322.

[55] Bailiff's tourn held within the portmote, SC 2/254/9 m. 6. Kyngeslegh, SC 2/252/14 m. 3d., SC 2/252/15 m. 2d., SC 2/253/2 mm. 2d.–3, SC 2/253/3 m. 10d.; see n. 12 above for his debts. Upton, SC 2/253/5 m. 10d.–11, SC 2/254/9 m. 4. See the biographies of Leversegge and Burelles in Appendix One.

fields.[56] The finishing of cloth was done by burgesses such as William Bullynche, Thomas and Robert Walker, who were fullers, Richard Knyght and Roger Balleson who were tailors, and William Nog who was a blanket maker. The wife of labourer Richard Charge was a weaver.

In the manor-forest textile-workers were concentrated to a certain extent in the townships of Rainow, Disley, Whaley, and especially Marple. Those involved were for the most part wealthy peasants holding between nine and 22 customary acres (category three), and who were also engaged in agrarian activities. The most prominent of these were the tailors. The spinning and weaving was mainly carried out by their wives and daughters, although female under-tenants and wage earners were also involved. The women also operated on a part-time basis and continued the work alongside other economic activities.[57] In the case of some smallholders the business appears to have involved the whole family or household: for example, William Fall, a category five tenant of Whaley, Robert Falle, an undertenant of Disley, and (undertenant) Thomas Falle. Information about textile-workers is summarised in Table 18.

The person who best epitomises the relationship between the manor-forest and trade in the borough was Alan Pierson, who was mayor in 1376–7 and a farmer of the borough stallage.[58] He was almost certainly related to John Pereson, a category four landholder from Rainow, who he employed, along with his son Thomas, as a servant. As a burgess and butcher he was presented on at least nine occasions for the assize of meat and amerced a total of 5s. 4½d. He was amerced six times between 1350 and 1355, and then three times between 1361 and 1366; his servant John was

[56] SC 2/253/7 m. 1, SC 2/253/9 mm. 3–4, SC 2/254/12 m. 6. SC 11/899 m. 1d., SC 11/898 m. 1d., mm. 3–3d. He granted, for instance, two burgages, a barn, and a close with a marsh adjacent to it in 1383, Chester City Record Office, Earwaker MSS CR 63/2/339 rot. 1, m. 1. He was a custodian of bread and meat in 1355/6 and 1372/3, and a custodian of ale in 1376/7, SC 2/252/7 m. 3, SC 2/253/7 m. 2, SC 2/253/10 m. 5.

[57] In two Worcestershire villages only two tailors were manorial tenants while most cloth-workers were probably labourers or cottagers, Dyer, *Lords and Peasants*, pp. 345–6. For those involved, see, for example, the fines for offences against the statute of labourers in the eyre, SC 2/252/12 m. 8, CHES 25/19 m. 4d.

[58] See *Ch.Acc.* (2), p. 166. He was catchpoll in 1349/50 and reeve in 1352/3, SC 2/252/2 m. 3, SC 2/252/5 m. 4.; 'John de Macclesfield Cartulary', fos. 48, 138–9.

amerced once in 1355/6. His livestock included cattle and pigs, as well as several score of sheep which he pastured throughout the manor commons.[59] His widow, Maud, later had stone weights for selling wool and it is likely that both her trade and Alan's butchering were linked to his stock rearing.[60] He is the most successful local example of a new breed of butcher-graziers who were also a feature of some other post-Black Death communities.[61] Such trade marks, perhaps, the beginnings of an exploitation of the upland pastures of the forest for stock-rearing alongside the operation of a local wool trade.

This economic exploitation of the manor-forest replaced an earlier one which utilised the woodlands for iron-working. Although there was a drastic reduction in the number of forges after the Black Death, a small group remained established within the borough. Roger Barker, for example, held three in the market place in addition to his substantial borough and forest holdings. In 1383 the purchase of the right to dig coal by six men was enrolled in a halmote court. These included burgess smith Nicholas Jolynet, Richard (son of burgess smith William) Botfysh, John Smyth of Macclesfield, and Robert Smyth of Stanley.[62]

To turn to the operation of the courts, we can see that the existence of a local elite, who were associated with office-holding and other types of decision making, has become widely accepted.[63] One important feature of this was the role of the jurors acting in the local court. Hilton, referring to their 'crucial importance', has

---

[59] SC 2/252/3 m. 4 – SC 2/252/6 m. 1d., SC 2/252/13 m. 5 – SC 2/253/1 m. 4d. SC 2/252/7 m. 3d., SC 2/253/4 m. 5, m. 8. SC 2/253/12 mm. 8–9, SC 2/254/1 m. 6, m. 8, m. 11, SC 2/254/2 m. 10.

[60] This is Maud's only appearance, SC 2/254/9 m. 6. Alan's first wife, Alice, sold ale between c. 1351 and 1364, SC 2/252/4 m. 6 – SC 2/252/15 m. 4d. John Pereson, SC 2/252/13 m. 4d., SC 2/254/4 m. 5, SC 2/254/15 m. 3d., SC 11/898 m. 3d., and his stock SC 2/254/2 m. 10.

[61] C. Dyer, *Warwickshire Farming, 1349-c. 1520. Preparations for Agricultural Revolution*, Dugdale Soc. Occasional Papers, 27 (Oxford 1981).

[62] SC 11/899 m. 1, SC 11/898 m. 1, SC 2/254/4 m. 5d. William Botfysh and John Smyth served as custodians of bread and meat in 1350/1 and 1383/4 respectively, SC 2/252/3 m. 4, Chester City Record Office, Earwaker MSS CR 63/2/339 rot. 1, m. 1. See the biographies of Barker and Jolynet in Appendix One.

[63] C. Dyer, 'Power and Conflict in the Medieval Village', in D. Hooke (ed.), *Medieval Villages* (Oxford) 1985, pp. 27–32.

described their 'de facto control of village affairs'.[64] By examining those serving, and their family relationships, over long periods of time Britton has referred to the 'heritability of jurorships'.[65] In practice, unlike the judgers or doomsmen, they were sworn from the main body of suitors. Unfortunately in the Macclesfield courts their names are not consistently recorded although they appear more regularly in the portmote records. It is only possible, therefore, to draw broad conclusions regarding their role.

In the manor at least a fifth of those who can be positively identified as male residents served in the halmote juries. Of these nearly 80 per cent were mentioned between one and four times, and only 1 per cent between ten and fifteen times. Of the eighteen referred to more than five times three were foresters, three were farmers of the forest revenues, two were members of branches of the Downes family, and one, Benedict Ashton, obtained the largest amount of land through transfer in the halmote. However they also included the wealthy peasants of category three. These, holding between nine and 22 customary acres, obtained income and influence through subletting: Benedict Norman, for instance, held three messuages including an enclosed farmstead in Sutton; Nicholas Stones held at least five messuages in Whaley; carpenter Edmund Juddesone held four messuages in Rainow; while William son of John Lowe was purchasing woodland and waste in Rainow.[66]

Many of those serving as jurors in the halmote can also be found as jurors for the manor-forest in the yearly Hundred eyre. Those individuals who were responsible for indicting other members of the community were a combination of the foresters and their officials, the most wealthy in terms of landholdings (categories one and two), and the most active peasant farmers (category three) who were either subletting or acquiring land.

In the borough, for which there is more evidence, over a quarter of those who can be positively identified as male residents acted as jurors. In contrast with the manor, the portmote juries were concentrated in the hands of a much smaller group, chosen, admittedly,

[64] Hilton, *Small Town Society*, p. 68 and *English Peasantry*, p. 54.

[65] Britton, *Community*, pp. 19, 45–7, 102.

[66] SC 11/898 m. 2d., m. 3d., m. 4d., Lowe, SC 2/253/8 m. 3, SC 2/253/11 m. 3d., SC 2/254/3 m. 4, SC 2/254/11 m. 4, CHES 25/20 m. 87. Lowe pastured many animals and may also have served as an under-forester, SC 2/253/9 m. 10. Juddesone, SC 2/254/5 m. 8. See the biographies of the Ashton and Juddesone families in Appendix One.

from a smaller community (see Table 19). Although 70 per cent were mentioned between one and four times, this time 9 per cent served between ten and nineteen times and 5 per cent between 20 and 23 times. One of the responsibilities of the borough juries was the election of the borough officials, and of the 30 who served on five or more occasions at least 27 were elected to office.[67] If we compare them to the jurors serving in the Hundred eyre, the significance of landholding again becomes apparent. Over a ten-year period just under half of those who served on the eyre juries also held land within the manor, and a quarter held significant or substantial holdings (of category three and above) in their own right. This does not, however, equate with large scale agrarian activity, as most held either just a few acres or were wealthy tenants who sublet their land. The majority of jurors, therefore, were active trading burgesses who were very likely to be elected to local office. However, there was some variation and in a single portmote jury a wide cross-section of the burgess community was usually represented.

Table 15 *Number and Frequency of Pledges in Each Court,*
c. 1349–96

No. People		No. of Times Served							
	Total	1–4	5–9	10–19	20–9	30–9	40–9	50–9	60–9
Portmote:	225	175	26	19	2	2			1
(%)	(100)	(78%)	(12%)	(8%)	(0.8%)	(0.8%)			(0.4%)
Halmote:	397	341	36	12	5	1	2		
(%)	(100)	(86%)	(9%)	(3%)	(1.3%)	(0.3%)	(0.5%)		

(SC 2/252/2–15, 2/253/1–12, 2/254/1–15, 2/255/1–2;
Chester City Record Office, Earwaker MSS CR 63/2/338–339).

The other role for which the court records provide evidence ample evidence is that of pledging. Those who did this frequently were often professionals who were, in effect, local officials appointed by the court.[68] It would not be surprising, therefore, to see a link between these and 'those of major standing in the community'.[69]

[67] For a link between jurors and village office holding, see S. Olson, 'Jurors of the Village Court: Local Leadership Before and After the Plague in Ellington, Huntingdonshire', *Journal of British Studies*, 30 (1991), p. 252.
[68] Hilton, *The Seigneurial Borough of Thornbury*, pp. 504–5. In the Macclesfield portmote the bailiff, or catchpoll, was often recorded as the pledge.
[69] E. DeWindt, *Land and People*, pp. 245–6.

According to Razi there was 'a direct relationship between the socio-economic status of a villager and the number of times he served as a surety; the wealthier he was the more he served as a pledge'.[70]

Over the period nearly 400 people served as pledges in the halmote. The vast majority, 86 per cent, served between one and four times. Most of these acted for family or neighbours while many can be identified as outsiders or are isolated individuals. No one group of people dominated any of the townships. However, there was a direct link between status and pledging amongst those who served most frequently (see Table 20). If we examine those who acted five or more times, at least 85 per cent can be associated with the subletting of land, and only two held fewer than nine customary acres; one of these, Richard Grene, held at least two messuages, while the other, William French, was a burgess.[71] Of the eight who acted on 20 or more occasions, three were members of the Downes family, one, John Cresswall, was a forester, and another, Roger Ashton, was the father of the person who made the largest land acquisitions.

In the portmote a total of 225 individuals served as pledges. The vast majority of these, 78 per cent, served between one and four times with only 10 per cent serving on ten or more occasions. As in the halmote many were outsiders who acted for neighbours or associates. Of the 50 (22 per cent) who served five or more times at least 34 (68 per cent) were office-holders. The most active belonged either to one of the two leading families, of Slegh and Rowe, who had a near monopoly of the office of mayor, or were farmers of the market revenues (see Table 21).

If we examine the pledge relationship we find that no obvious pattern emerges. Many occasional pledges acted for their sons, daughters, wives, families or servants. Thomas Walker, for example, stood pledge for his wife, two of his maid-servants, and for Amice daughter of Thomas Barker on seven different occasions. The wide variety of people served by those acting most frequently is indicative of their professional role within the court. Richard Slegh, for example, acted for over 80 per cent of people on only one occasion, while acting for burgesses, maids and those of high status, such as

[70] Z. Razi, 'Family, Land and the Village Community in Later Medieval England', *Past and Present*, 93 (1981), p. 12.
[71] Grene, *c.* 1355–1375, SC 2/252/7 m. 2d. – SC 2/253/8 m. 3. French, *c.* 1375–1395, SC 2/253/9 mm. 3–4 – SC 2/255/1 m. 7d. See n. 47 above.

William Dounes and John Macclesfield. Although his son, William, also became mayor he did not continue this active role. Similarly in the manor the most active pledges did not always closely follow township boundaries. John Cresswall, for instance, served people in Bollington and Kettleshulme as well as Sutton and Rainow where he held land. William Dounes stood for those in Bollington, Kettleshulme, Rainow, Shrigley and Poynton. Outsiders, though, frequently brought their own pledges; when a burgess appeared in the manor court, for instance, he would usually be accompanied by a fellow-burgess.[72]

If an individual was unable to find a pledge, the word 'pauper' was entered alongside his name. In such cases the bailiff (catchpoll) acted instead, and this might explain both the regularity and variation in some of those serving. It might have been necessary to pay someone to act as a pledge, and this is a view supported by Pimsler who has described the process as the 'acceptance of money for service'.[73] Although both pledges and jurors were drawn from the same strata of society there was, it seems, no clear relationship between them. An individual might serve several times in both activities but the most active pledges operated via the courts in a professional manner. In the portmote only a third of the most active pledges, who served on nineteen or more occasions, also served as frequently as jurors. In the halmote, in which fewer names were recorded, only 7 (12 per cent) of the 56 who acted as pledges five or more times were mentioned with equal parity as jurors. Both activities, though, were connected with status and those with landed wealth or in office had a greater disposition to appear repeatedly.[74]

One further indicator of court activity is the presence of those who witnessed land transfers. The majority of people in this group

---

[72] Walker, portmote c.1350–58 (he died c.1363/4, SC 2/252/15 m. 5), SC 2/252/6 m. 1d. – SC 2/252/9 m. 7. Slegh, portmote c.1351–1373, SC 2/252/4 m. 6 – SC 2/253/7 m. 2d. Cresswall, halmote c.1363–1383, SC 2/252/14 m. 3d. – SC 2/254/4 m. 4d. Dounes, halmote c.1351–1377 (he died in 1388/89, SC 2/254/10 m. 7d.), SC 2/252/4 m. 4 – SC 2/253/11 m. 3d.

[73] M. Pimsler, 'Solidarity in the Medieval Village ? The Evidence of Personal Pledging at Elton, Huntingdonshire', *Journal of British Studies*, 17 (1977), pp. 1–11. Pledges were frequently amerced in civil actions in the Macclesfield courts.

[74] Olson, *Jurors of the Village Court*, pp. 246–7.

were referred to only once or twice and they were, presumably, associates and neighbours who were specific to an individual grant. In the portmote 45 people were mentioned as witnesses, of whom 80 per cent acted on a single occasion and nine (20 per cent) five or more times. In the halmote 64 people are mentioned of whom 63 per cent acted between one and four times, and 24 (37 per cent) on five or more occasions. There is a good correlation between those mostly frequently serving as both witnesses and pledges in the two courts. In the halmote these were of the highest social standing within the manor: Robert son of William Dounes 47 times, John Cresswall 38, Geoffrey Dounes 25, John son of Richard Sutton nineteen, William Dounes eighteen; Reginald Dounes sixteen and Thomas Shryglegh thirteen times. In the portmote all were either office-holders or served as mayor: Richard Rowe nine times; William Slegh nine, Roger Barker six, Richard Slegh six and John Leversegge five times.

By the later fourteenth century the office of mayor of Macclesfield was well established, and by the end of the century there were deputies to assist the mayors. During our period, after the period of Jordan Macclesfield's dominance, the two families of Rowe and Slegh predominated. In 1354 it was claimed that William Rowe had withdrawn from the manor, as bondman of the prince in the forest, and that his son, Richard, had become a burgess by lapse of time. By this date Richard was already serving as borough-reeve and became mayor for the first time in 1369.[75] In c. 1409–10 Reginald Dounes was mayor and, as relative of Geoffrey of Shrigley, was thus a member of the most influential family in the manor. In the later fourteenth century Reginald served as parker of Macclesfield and, together with John Legh, assarted over twelve acres of waste in Sutton. In the early fifteenth century Lawrence Savage paid a 3s. 4d. entry fine, apparently in the same year he served as serving as mayor; this family were later important landholders in the town, although there is no earlier reference to

[75] B.P.R., iii, pp. 162–3. Richard served as mayor 1369–73, 1375–6, 1378–83, 1385–89, SC 2/253/9 m. 5, SC 2/254/13 m. 6d, 'John de Macclesfield's Cartulary', fos. 38–9, 41–3, 46–9, 60–3, 91, 94, 136–7. He had been a custodian of ale in 1349/50, catchpoll in 1350/1, and reeve in 1354/5, SC 2/252/2 m. 3, SC 2/252/3 m. 4, SC 2/252/6 m. 1. He rented shops in the town, SC 11/898 m. 1d. Stephen Rowe held the office c. 1427–30, SC 2/315/16.

them.[76] The office of mayor, therefore, was open to those who may not have had a long pedigree in the town. In the second half of the fourteenth century only seven mayors are mentioned by name: John Macclesfield, John Bernewell, Richard Rowe, Richard Slegh and William his son, Roger Alcok, and Alan Pierson.[77]

The minor officials of the borough were elected at the Michaelmas portmote court. As the collectors of revenues, the reeve and the catchpoll had greater responsibility than the custodians of the assizes, who had the largest turnover of officers. There was no difference, however, in the status of those serving nor was there any apparent progression through the offices to that of mayor. Of those who can be identified as resident male burgesses in the period at least one fifth were elected to office. As we have already seen juror Richard Kenworthey, for instance, helped elect himself as custodian of bread and meat and served on the two other 'great portmote' juries during the year. He continued to trade while serving in office, and was amerced for brewing whilst a custodian of bread and meat, and for baking whilst a custodian of ale. In addition he was amerced for bread while farming the common oven. There are no examples of custodians presenting their wives, although they did present those serving in other offices. A high frequency of serving in office was, like that of juror, the prerogative of a small group of tradesmen burgesses.[78]

Before going on to analyse the social structures of the two communities, it is first necessary to identify in brief those who were

---

[76] Dounes, SC 2/315/16, SC 6/804/3 m. 4, SC 2/254/1 m. 7d. In 1394 Reginald purchased all the lands of Robert Kynder after his execution, SC 2/254/15 m. 4. He was farmer of the stallage with Roger Alcok in 1383/4, SC 2/254/5 m. 7. Geoffrey was serving as custodian of Macclesfield gaol in 1384/5, CHES 25/21 m. 20. Savage, SC 2/315/16 m. 2.

[77] Jordan Macclesfield, c. 1348; John Bernewell, 1357; John Macclesfield, 1359; Richard Slegh, c. 1359–63, 1366, 1369; Richard Rowe, c. 1369–73, 1375–6, 1378–83, 1385–89; Alan Pierson, 1376–7; William Slegh, c. 1375, 1390–1, 1396–8; Roger Alcok, 1391–3, 1395–6, 1399–1402, 1404–7; Reginald Dounes, c. 1409–10, 1412–16. See British Library, Cotton Cleopatra DVI, John de Macclesfield Cartulary, and Bruel, 'John de Macclesfield Cartulary'. See also SC 2/315/15–6, and the Macclesfield Collection housed in Birkenhead Public Library. Occasional references are made in the later fourteenth century court rolls, SC 2/252–255.

[78] Hilton, *The Seigneurial Borough of Thornbury*, pp. 506–7, 516.

at the forefront of regional society.[79] Jordan Macclesfield had been the keeper of the manor, park and forest *c.* 1325–31, and had held extensive lands in Shrigley (where he had assarted 10 acres in 1341/2), Hurdsfield and Upton. In the borough his rents included that of the principal messuage.[80] His son, John, maintained these holdings, although he was not as influential as his namesake. Another prominent tenant was John Macclesfield, senior, who was probably the son of manorial stock-keeper John Alcok ('le Deye'), and was a clerk of considerable wealth and standing.[81] As a result of service to Richard II, his wealth from rents included the principal messuage of the borough which was crenellated with stone in 1398, the manor of Bosley, as well as other manors in Cheshire, Middlesex, Hertfordshire and Essex and some ecclesiastical revenues. In 1399 he entertained the king in his home town of Macclesfield. Following the king's deposition, John consolidated his landed power in east Cheshire, and became the main tenant in the borough and also extended his manor-forest holdings. In many instances he was the partner of other powerful people of the locality: Peter Legh and his son John, Adam Kyngeslegh and his daughter, Katherine, who was John's concubine, Roger Alock, the mayor of Macclesfield, John Macclesfield, parson (a probable relative of John) and William Wylot of Clayton in Derbyshire.[82]

[79] For a discussion see M. J. Bennett, 'Sources and Problems', pp. 59–95. I am particular grateful to Paul Booth for allowing me to refer to his data on individuals from the Ministers' Accounts (SC 6 804–808). These have partly been used in the biographical notes in *Ch.Acc.* (2), pp. 118–191; see also Ormerod, *History of Cheshire*, vol IV, pp. 661, 676, 700, 748–9, 761, 775, 781, 786.

[80] He was the son of Thomas Macclesfield (CHES 29/21 m. 27. SC 6/1090/15, SC 6/802/1, SC 6/1277/2, SC 6/1297/2). For his lands, see CHES 33/5, SC 11/899 m. 1–1d, m. 3d. He served as mayor in 1337/8 and 1348, Birkenhead Public Library, Macclesfield Collection, MA B/6/19, John de Macclesfield Cartulary, fo. 126. Ormerod, *History of Cheshire*, pp. 745–49. He died in about 1359, *B.P.R., iii*, p. 342.

[81] D. K. Maxfield, 'Pardoners and Property: John Macclesfield, 1351–1422, Builder of Macclesfield Castle', *Journal of the Chester Archaeological Society*, LXIX (1988 for 1986), pp. 79–80; *Ch.Acc.* (2), pp. 118–19; M. J. Bennett, *Community, Class and Careerism*, p. 150.

[82] Maxfield, 'Pardoners and Property', pp. 79–95; his total income from rents was around £70 a year and added to those from his ecclesiastical holdings resulted in a yearly sum of more than £250, *ibid.*, p. 86. See also 'Was John Macclesfield a Scoundrel ?', *Cheshire History*, 28 (1991), pp. 19–20.

The Leghs of Adlington were the most influential family in the wider forest area. We have already met Robert Legh, the elder, who died about 1370, having served as rider of the forest, justice of labourers for Macclesfield Hundred, and deputy steward or bailiff of the manor and Hundred (with responsibility for holding the courts). In the manor of Adlington he had overseen the assarting of more than 350 acres in the 1330s and 1340s.[83] His son, Robert Legh the younger, continued to hold the local courts, as deputy steward or bailiff of the manor, from 1371 to 1377, and just before his death in 1382 leased the herbage of Lyme Handley, with William Dounes, from 1372 to 1376.[84] Arguments over the wardship of lands led to what amounted to local warfare between Robert and his half brothers, Peter and John; this resulted in disorder and eventual murder. Peter and John were joint deputy stewards of the manor, as well as farmers of the Handley herbage, from 1383. Peter, steward from 1386 and a justice of eyre and rider of the forest from 1394, was a man of considerable social standing, with an annual income of over £42 from his rents in Cheshire. By the time of his execution for rebellion in 1399, he was the sole holder of the Handley pasture. Robert, son of Robert Legh the younger, was the first of his family line to be knighted, and served as sheriff of the county and master-forester of the Cheshire forests. He died in 1408.[85]

The Downes family were of gentry status and were largely resident within the manor. One branch held, as foresters, the manors of Downes in Sutton and Taxal from the later thirteenth century, and in our period the income of Edmund son of Edmund Dounes, who died before 1400, was £5 13s. 4d. a year.[86] His brother, Reginald, was parker of Macclesfield in the late fourteenth century and mayor of Macclesfield in the early fifteenth. Another branch of the family became established at Shrigley at the early part of

---

[83] CHES 33/6 m. 41. *Ch.Acc.* (2), pp. lxi–lxii, 155–6.

[84] The younger Robert also served the Black Prince in France, *Ch.Acc.* (2), pp. lxii–lxiii, 157–8. William Legh acted as deputy steward between 1377 and 1380, SC 2/253/11–12, SC 2/254/1–2.

[85] *Ch.Acc.* (2), p. lxii; Ormerod, *History of Cheshire*, pp. 661, 671–3. See P. McNiven, 'The Men of Cheshire and the Rebellion of 1403', *Trans. Hist. Soc. of Lancs. and Cheshire*, 129 (1979), pp. 1–29. Robert, son of Robert, Legh was acting steward at the end of 1386, SC 2/254/7 m. 2–3. Peter held the local courts at Macclesfield from 1387 to 1394/5, SC 2/254/8 – SC 2/255/1.

[86] Ormerod, *History of Cheshire*, pp. 777–82.

the fourteenth century, and in 1341/2 William Dounes asserted 24 acres there. After the Black Death William, this William's son, was a verderer and agister of the forest and possessed land-holdings in five of the manor townships. In 1380 he was Robert Legh's partner in a twelve-year lease of part of the manor of Bollington with its mill. His son, Robert, was a justice in eyre and deputy steward of Macclesfield manor in 1400, and had acquired lands in Worth (as forester) and Upton by marriage, and also asserted two acres of underwood in 1388. He leased, with his brother Geoffrey, and others, the mills of Bollington, Rainow and Shrigley, and part of the manor of Bollington, for ten years in 1391. Geoffrey also purchased the right to mine coal in the forest for 6s. 8d. in 1371/2.[87]

As the Legh family were responsible for holding the local courts, they had to be brought before the county court of Chester to be indicted for crimes. As verderer and agister, William Dounes was active in the administration of justice by making forest presentments, by serving on the indictment juries in eyre, and by regularly acting as a pledge. He was, in effect, the lord of the 'manor' of Shrigley who sublet tenancies and, judging by his involvement in lawsuits, employed a significant number of people.[88] In contrast neither John son of Jordan, or John Macclesfield, senior, who travelled abroad and spent much of his life in London, were as actively involved in local power-broking and affairs.

Fourteen men paid rents of over 30s. 0d. for land in the manor-forest, or held more than 44 Cheshire acres, during the period.[89]

---

[87] Reginald, SC 6/804/8 m. 4; he (or another of this name) was serving as mayor in 1409–10, 1412–16, John de Macclesfield Cartulary, fos. 91–2, 120–21, 123, 140, 145–6, 160, 188–9, 216. William, CHES 33/5, CHES 33/6 m. 40d. For William son of William, see CHES 33/6 m. 36, SC 11/899 m. 1d, m. 2d., m. 3–3d, SC 2/253/5 m. 10, SC 2/254/2 m. 4, SC 2/254/11 m. 4, B.P.R., iii, pp. 335, 338, SC 6/802/17 m. 1, SC 6/802/15 m. 4, SC 6/803/13 m. 1, SC 2/253/8 m. 4. Robert, SC 6/804/6 m. 4, SC 2/254/9 m. 5, SC 2/254/13 m. 4. Geoffrey, SC 2/253/6 m. 3. Ormerod, History of Cheshire, pp. 772–76.

[88] William appeared in the halmote from 1349 until his death in 1388/9, SC 2/252/2 m. 4 – SC 2/254/10 m. 7d. He sought the service, for example, of Margaret daughter of Richard Alot and Richard Dausone, in Bollington and Shrigley, and Amice Fletcher and Maud Kys of Rainow in the borough, SC 2/252/6 m. 1d., SC 2/252/13 m. 3d, SC 2/253/6 m. 5.

[89] All these categories are only approximate, because of subletting; many of those in category one, for instance, appear to have held far more than

They included John Macclesfield senior, clerk, John son of Jordan Macclesfield, William Dounes and the foresters John (son of Richard) Sutton and John Cresswall. As indicated above not all were actively involved in the local courts. Their business in the halmote can be summarised as follows: 38 per cent were involved in five or more pleas; 77 per cent in three or more land transactions; 54 per cent acted as pledges on five or more occasions; and at least 46 per cent served as jurors. They were particularly to be found in the indictment juries in the Hundred eyre, where a higher proportion of this group served than in that of the manor court.

John Cresswall, for instance, increased his manor landholding by 21s. 0d., acquired Eddisbury which had been in decay, made two small assarts and leased forest waifs and escapes. He served as a pledge on 50 occasions in the halmote, was frequently a witness to land transactions, and regularly served on indictment and manor-court juries.[90] William Joudrel (Jodrell) established a power base in the north-east of the manor as a result of his service to the Black Prince in Gascony. He acquired over 60 acres of land, including an assart of 16½ acres, for which his son Roger later paid an entry-fine. He acted as a pledge in the halmote on nineteen occasions, and served on indictment and manor-court juries.[91] In

is indicated in the rentals. For a comparison with elsewhere in Cheshire, including Bosley, see M. J. Bennett, *Community, Class and Careerism*, pp. 97–104.

[90] SC 2/252/6 m. 3 – SC 2/255/2 m. 4d. His land transactions, SC 2/252/14 m. 3d., SC 2/253/2 m. 3d., SC 2/253/5 m. 10d., SC 2/253/8 m. 3d., SC 2/254/1 m. 7d., SC 2/254/2 m. 4, SC 2/254/6 m. 6d., SC 2/255/1 m. 7, SC 2/255/2 m. 3d. As a forester he presented a theft to the halmote in 1373, and he also served on an indictment jury in eyre, for example, in 1382/3. SC 2/253/7 m. 1d., SC 2/254/4 m. 8. He leased, along with others, the waifs and abstracts between 1374/5 and 1382/3, the escapes of Midgley and Dane(wood) in 1382, those of 'Warrilowside' in 1388, and those of Coombs for the winter of 1389. He was coroner of the forest in 1390/1, CHES 25/22 m. 10d. SC 2/253/8 m. 4, SC 2/253/9 mm. 3–4, SC 2/253/10 m. 4, SC 2/253/12 m. 1, SC 2/254/2 m. 4, SC 2/254/3 m. 4d., SC 2/254/4 m. 5d., SC 2/254/9 m. 4d., SC 2/254/10 m. 7d.

[91] 1350–1376, SC 2/252/2 m. 4d. – SC 2/253/10 m. 4. His land transactions, SC 2/252/3 m. 1, SC 2/252/10 m. 5d., SC 2/252/12 m. 2, SC 2/252/13 m. 4d., SC 2/252/14 m. 3–4, SC 2/252/15 m. 2d., m. 3d., SC 2/253/1 m. 2, SC 2/253/2 m. 3d., SC 2/253/8 m. 3d., SC 2/254/5 m. 7, CHES 25/20 m. 87. He was an indictment juror in the eyres of 1374 and 1375, SC 2/253/8 m. 7–8, SC 2/253/9 m. 14. M. J. Bennett *Community, Class and Careerism*, p. 106.

contrast, John son of Edmund Bosedon, who held great Hurdsfield, and the Upton family played little part in the business of the manor courts.[92]

The land-holdings of those belonging to this category of manorial tenants were mainly close to Macclesfield borough, particularly in the townships of Sutton, Hurdsfield and Rainow. Only William Joudrel was active in the approving of the forest commons and wastes, whereas Robert son of William Dounes grubbed up a mere two acres and John Cresswall took fewer than four acres. Their own holdings were the size of small manors and contained substantial pasture, and they were also extended through the leasing of other properties, including the forest pastures. As they are rarely mentioned, therefore, in the forest records for infringements of the commons and pastures, we know little of their livestock numbers. For the men in this category the farming of revenues, such as the forest pastures, together with office holding, helped to generate their wealth and influence. Most appear to have been successful in increasing their landholdings, although not dramatically, in the aftermath of the Black Death. Approximately half were not resident in the manor.

Category two contained 39 men who held land paying rent between 15s. 0d. and 29s. 11d., or around 22 to 44 long acres in the manor. They included several of similar status to those in category one, who either lived or received their rents outside the manor. The most notable of this group was Adam Kyngeslegh who also held substantial land in partnership with Robert Legh.[93] Members of this category regularly served as jurors in both the local courts and in the eyres, although fewer were also active as pledges. Their business in the halmote can be summarised in this way: 16 per cent were involved in five or more pleas; 55 per cent were involved in three or more land transactions; 32 per cent were pledges on five or more occasions; at least 45 per cent were jurors; and 13 per cent of their households sold ale. Approximately a fifth, the smallest proportion of any category, were non-residents.

They were a combination of old-established families, including foresters like Roger son of John Dycon of Sutton, and rising individuals such as Benedict Ashton. In terms of office-holding

[92] SC 11/899 m. 3–3d., SC 11/898 m. 3d., CHES 25/20 m. 87. Bosedon, however, regularly appeared on the indictment juries in the eyre, SC 2/254/4 m. 8, SC 2/254/5 m. 10.

[93] See Adam's biography, Ch.Acc. (2), pp. 152–3.

they included under-bailiff of the manor Nicholas Byran, and future mayors Roger Alcok and (parker) Reginald Dounes. Their wealth was in part associated with subletting. This was the group that can most readily be shown to have increased their landholdings during the period. This was possible through the availability of existing land rather than through assarting which was generally confined to very small parcels. Although evidence of their ownership of livestock is not forthcoming, many of their holdings must have included a significant proportion of pasture. Three of them pannaged more than six pigs.

John Leversegge, for instance, was really a burgess who held both burgage plots and land in the borough fields. In the manor-forest his holding included a bovate in Hurdsfield which he sublet, and he grazed more than 20 draught animals on the pastures. He was actively involved in the portmote where he was a juror on at least 27 occasions, and a pledge on at least fourteen. In the halmote he served as a pledge on eleven occasions.[94]

Thomas, son of under-forester Robert Shryglegh, increased his landholding by around 20 acres in Shrigley and Rainow. In addition he leased the Woodhouse in Hurdsfield, and Ingersley in Rainow which included a house with a croft and meadow and the wood which grew there. He also held some borough land, and pastured more than 60 sheep and 20 draught-beasts. In the halmote he acted as a pledge on 30 occasions and served on indictment juries.[95] As a burgess, Roger Alcok served as mayor in most years between 1390 and 1407, and increased his landholding by nearly 40 acres in Sutton. Benedict Ashton's acquisitions in the Whaley / Kettleshulme area were the largest of any individual in this period and have

---

[94] c.1381–1396, SC 2/254/3 m. 4d.–5 – SC 2/255/2 m. 5–6. See his biography in Appendix One.

[95] He appeared in the halmote from 1361 until his death 1390/1, SC 2/252/13 m. 3 – SC 2/254/12 m. 6. His land transactions, SC 2/253/5 m. 11, SC 2/253/6 m. 3d., SC 2/253/10 m. 4, SC 2/254/1 m. 7d., m. 12, SC 2/254/5 m. 7, SC 2/254/11 m. 6d. He owed common suit to the portmote in 1369, Chester City Record Office, Earwaker MSS CR 63/2/338 m. 1. He was a serving under-forester, SC 2/253/9 m. 10. His stock and service as an indictment juror, for example, SC 2/254/1 m. 3d., m. 11. He was the custodian of the goods of the chantry of the Holy Trinity in Macclesfield in 1388, SC 2/254/10 m. 6. See Robert's biography in *Ch.Acc.* (2), pp. 172–3; a John Shryglegh was a clerk in Ireland, M. J. Bennett, 'Sources and Problems', p. 63.

already been referred to. He sat regularly on the jury in the halmote and for the indictments in eyre.[96]

Those in category two, therefore, were relatively wealthy individuals who had risen above peasant status yet were below the local gentry such as William Dounes. They were often people of ambition, and some improved their income markedly in the aftermath of the Black Death and through the leasing of local revenues. Their influence over their undertenants was reinforced through their regular appearance on indictment juries. Of all the categories they had the largest proportion (40 per cent) of those presented for assaults and affrays in the local courts.[97]

In category three were were 154 male landholders who represented the upper strata of peasant society. They held land rented at 6s. 0d. and 14s. 11d. or between ten and 20 customary acres. Their contribution to the running of the courts was less apparent: only 14 per cent were involved in five or more pleas, 35 per cent in three or more land transactions, 18 per cent served as pledges on five or more occasions, at least 30 per cent as jurors, and 26 per cent of their households sold ale. The most successful families of this group would rise to category two within a generation – for example, the fathers of Benedict Ashton and Roger Batemon. The more influential served on indictment juries, leased revenues or held local offices. John Oldefeld, for example, leased the escapes of the forest, and Roger Oldhed acted as an agister and under-forester.[98] Unlike those in category two, though, fewer of them were able either to increase their land holdings significantly or to acquire income through subletting. Although they made the largest number of assarts in the manor, the total area was small. Five people, for instance, approved between one and four acres, and five others parcels of under one rood. They were preeminently the category of tenants most closely associated with both the exploitation of the forest pastures for livestock as well as with the cloth trade. The proportion of non-residents was between a quarter and a fifth.

[96] Alcok was also borough reeve in 1383/4, Chester City Record Office, Earwaker MSS CR 63/2/339 rot. 1, m. 1; see n. 77 above. His land, SC 2/254/3 m. 3d., SC 2/254/4 m. 4d., SC 2/254/5 m. 8, SC 2/254/10 m. 7, SC 2/255/2 m. 3. He farmed the stallage with Geoffrey Dounes in 1383/4, SC 2/254/5 m. 7. See Ashton's biography in Appendix One.

[97] See Chapter Four, pp. 155–59.

[98] Oldefeld leased the escapes for a three year term from 1390, SC 2/254/12 m. 7d., SC 2/254/13 m. 5. Oldhed, CHES 33/6 m. 36.

John Brocwalhurst from Kettleshulme, for instance, increased his holding by around ten acres. His court appearances included serving as a pledge on ten occasions and also as constable of the township. He regularly purchased, or paid fines for, woodland fodder and grazed the largest number of animals of any tenant on the forest pastures. They amounted to more than 100 sheep and over 20 cattle, as well as horses, and pigs. Others involved in keeping sheep included Richard Hordren of Sutton who had over 40 as well as a small number of horses, oxen and pigs.[99]

The grazing of livestock may have been linked, in some instances, with the production of woollen cloth. John Cok managed to acquire around nine customary acres of land in Sutton. His stock included a small number of sheep and his wife was a weaver. His son, Adam, pastured various animals, including horses, sheep and pigs.[100] The stock of two tailors from Rainow, though, may not have included sheep: both Richard Tyllesone and John Dykeson grazed animals, including horses, oxen, and pigs. Carpenter Edmund Juddesone, who served on indictment juries, grazed sheep, horses and oxen, and kept a pig, while his son, Thomas, grazed over 40 sheep and a working horse.[101]

A considerable drop in status is involved when we move from category three to four. Of the 155 men in this latter group, who held land rented at between 2s. 0d. and 5s. 11d., or three to nine customary acres, very few individuals apparently made any significant land acquisitions in the aftermath of the Black Death. This, however, is misleading as some sublet land on short-term leases, while several were the sons of those in category three who were thus able to acquire land away from family holdings. Many also belonged to established local families such as the Achards and

[99] See Brocwalhurst's biography in Appendix One. Hordren, SC 2/254/1 m. 11, SC 2/254/2 m. 10, SC 2/254/3 m. 8.

[100] John, c. 1349–1367: SC 2/252/3 m. 1, SC 2/252/7 m. 2, SC 2/253/2 m. 3d. John's wife, SC 2/252/12 m. 8. Adam entered his father's holding in 1369 and assarted ¼ rood of waste in Sutton in 1392. He owed substantial debts, with others, to Richard Rode and Adam Kyngeslegh in 1391, and was amerced for digging turves and fishing in the forest in 1384. SC 2/253/4 m. 1, SC 2/254/5 m. 7, SC 2/254/12 m. 6, SC 2/254/13 m. 4–5. His stock, SC 2/254/1 mm. 6, m. 9, m. 11, SC 2/254/2 m. 5, m. 10, SC 2/254/3 m. 6, m. 8

[101] SC 2/254/1 m. 6, m. 9, m. 11, SC 2/254/2 m. 5, m. 10, SC 2/254/3 m. 6, m. 8, SC 2/254/4 m. 13–16. See Juddesone's biography in Appendix One.

Eydales. Up to a third may have been non-residents, and seven were burgesses of the highest standing.[102]

The assarts by the three people in this group amounted to a mere one acre, a single rood and a small parcel adjacent to a house worth 1*d*. In terms of court activity members of this category generally made few appearances: 8 per cent were involved in five or more pleas, 16 per cent in three or more land transactions, 1 per cent, or 3 per cent if we include two burgesses, served as pledges on five or more occasions, at least 10 per cent were jurors, and 15 per cent of their households sold ale. Of the resident members none was able to lease forest revenues, while the only office-holder was the constable, William Archer, of Sutton.

Although they did not obviously exploit the pastures as much as those in category three, several possessed a significant number of livestock. The animals of John Boller of Bollington included, like many others, both horses and oxen while he also made hafts using the local woodland. Those with sheep included William Archer, who pastured flocks of 40 and 62 in addition to his other animals.[103] Roger Lowe and William, his son, pastured between 40 and 60 sheep, together with cattle and horses, and cows and pigs.[104]

[102] Richard Eydale and Richard, his son, were listed as cobblers from the borough when fined for offences against the statute of labourers in 1351–2, SC 2/252/3 m. 5, SC 2/252/4 m. 1d. Richard, senior, held 'Draycote Styns', a 4¾ acre close in Sutton, between 1352 and 1356, SC 2/252/5 m. 5, SC 2/252/8 m. 5. Richard Eydale junior was a reeve of the Blessed Mary chantry, c. 1372–79, SC 2/253/7 m. 1, SC 2/254/2 m. 3–3d., and served on an indictment jury relating to various thefts (including by Richard Eydale) in the eyre in 1390 (see Table 28), CHES 25/22 m. 19. The other burgesses included mayor Richard Rowe, John Slegh, fuller William Bullynche, William Kenworthey, butcher and farmer of the stallage Henry Dyot, and wealthy tenant Roger Falybron.

[103] Archer, SC 2/254/1 m. 6, m. 9, m. 11, SC 2/254/4 m. 14–16. He was constable in 1377/8, SC 2/253/12 m. 1. John and Nicholas Boller were indicted and fined 6s. 8d. for making hafts, and John was later indicted for over-pasturing with one working horse and two other draught-beasts. SC 2/253/9 m. 14, SC 2/253/11 m. 5, SC 2/254/5 m. 10.

[104] This or another William son of Roger Lowe was a burgess from the late 1380s (he was reeve in 1390/1). He was granted extensive properties in the town and in Hurdsfield in 1391 (SC 2/254/12 m. 8, SC 2/254/13 m. 7). A William Lowe was also an under- forester or servant of the foresters who made presentments of the escapes (SC 2/253/9 m. 10, m. 14, SC 2/253/10 m. 7, SC 2/253/11 m. 5, SC 2/253/12 m. 5, SC 2/254/1 m. 11, SC 2/254/4 m. 14–16, SC 2/254/5 m. 10).

In category five there were 60 male tenant-smallholders with land rented at below 1*s*. 11*d*. or fewer than three customary acres. These smallholders made few court appearances: none were involved in five or more pleas, only 6 per cent were involved in three or more land transactions, none served as jurors, but 22 per cent of their households sold ale – the largest proportion of all categories. Only two served more than five times as pledges and these were the burgess William French and John Holyncete (there were several men of this name), who both acted on seven occasions. Although some may have additionally sublet land it would have been necessary for many of them to have supplemented their income through working for others. Several of their wives were weavers or brewers of ale. Richard Alcok, for instance, was a carpenter with tuppence-worth of land in Bollington. Those who had the capital to approve land were often burgesses. For example, harper Richard Clyve, who was soon to marry Alice Slegh and acquire several burgages, approved two parcels of a rood each, and William Bullynche's son approved wasteland that was rented at only 2*d*.[105]

A couple of them were more wealthy than the rest, and of a higher social standing than their land-holdings suggest. John Werynton of Kettleshulme, for example, asserted two acres and was an inquest juror, and his livestock included horses, oxen, and pigs.[106] A substantial number, more than a third and possibly as many as a half of this category, of whom six were burgesses, may have been non-resident.

As we have already seen, because a large proportion of the land of the manor was sublet, about 30 per cent of those appearing in the halmote were undertenants. These were little involved in running the courts and few made more than five appearances during their lifetime. Although they might occasionally act as pledges, no undertenants served as jurors. Their place of residence has to be established by indirect means. For example, other members of their families appeared in the courts, or the undertenants belonged to a household which brewed and sold ale. In addition, they might be amerced for labour offences, or graze their animals on the forest pastures.

The majority, if not all, of this group must have supplemented their income through work for others. Brewing would have been

---

[105] SC 11/898 m. 5; SC 2/254/12 m. 5d., SC 2/253/2 m. 3.
[106] Werynton, SC 2/254/1 m. 3, m. 6, m. 8, m. 9, m. 11, SC 2/254/4 m. 14, SC 2/254/5 m. 5, m. 7, SC 2/254/12 m. 5.

important, and 40 people appeared in the courts solely on this account, several of whom were from Marple or Whaley. Richard Carleton appeared once for ale and was a servant of burgess fuller William Bullynche. Others in service would have included shepherds and herdsmen. Agriculture was carried out alongside crafts, and Richard Cooper of Kettleshulme, for instance, also kept both cattle and pigs.[107] Of the eleven who had livestock, seven had a working horse and four belonged to households which sold ale.

The difference between such people and those described in this monograph as 'isolated individuals' was the permanence of residence or association with the manor exhibited by the former. The latter made only one or two court appearances and were labourers, migrants, the poor, and those from the neighbouring areas. Five men, including John Raynald of Norbury, for instance, sought work elsewhere in the autumn of 1393 after working for forester John Sherd.[108] The final group, who constituted fewer than 5 per cent of the total, are the known outsiders who either originated from further afield or were locals passing through the jurisdiction. The townships of origin were mostly within a short walk of the manor townships, such as Adlington, Prestbury, Bramhall, Marton and Stockport. Only 2 per cent were from the nearby counties of Staffordshire, Lancashire or Derbyshire. The appearances of these 'outsiders' in the courts relate to pleas, trade, affrays and the use of the forest resources (including poaching).[109]

In the absence of a detailed burgage rental it was at first more difficult to categorise tenants of the borough. However as burghal wealth was rarely dependent upon land or rent holdings, the evidence for both trade and court activity discussed in this Chapter provided a good indicator of status. Although fewer than half of all portmote males could be identified as residents, an even smaller proportion – one in ten – made regular appearances in the court. This group, made up of around 100 men during the second half of the fourteenth century, supplied the majority of the jurors and

---

[107] SC 2/254/11 m. 4. Cooper, SC 2/254/3 m. 8, SC 2/254/4 m. 14–16.
[108] SC 2/254/15 m. 3.
[109] Those taking wood from the forest included Richard Mason of Stockport, Richard Torkynton of Bramhall, Robert Denys of Alderley and William Serle of Prestbury. Those who pastured their animals included John Dyconsone of Gawsworth and William Henreson of Rode, SC 2/253/1 m. 2, SC 2/253/9 m. 3–4, SC 2/254/2 m. 9–10d.

office-holders, the regular pledges, and those most frequently involved in lawsuits. They were the active trading burgesses who
dominated the market-place. In total they constituted only 9 per
cent of all males appearing, although up to a quarter of the long-term
resident male population. As they were not a homogenous group
they will be divided them into two categories: 'A', of around 40
individuals (3.5% of the total), and category 'B', of around 60
(5.5%).

Category 'A' were the most influential within the burgess community, and most closely resemble an 'elite' group. All were
office-holders and all but four were mentioned as portmote jurors
more than once; 26 (67 per cent) served on five or more occasions,
and nineteen, or (49 per cent) on more than nine occasions; in
addition they formed the bulk of all indictment juries. 30 acted as
pledges on at least five occasions, 22 on more than nine and ten
on nineteen or more. Those operating in a 'professional' capacity
were largely drawn from this group; for instance, Henry Dyot,
Roger Falybron, Richard Kenworthey, Richard Rowe and Richard
Slegh.[110]

Over half were involved in five or more portmote suits, with
seven in more than fifteen and two, William Bullynche (who was
also involved in nine in the halmote) and Richard Kenworthey,
in more than 30. Their trades were dominated by victuals, cloth-
working, and leather crafts and many appear to have been general
mercers.[111] The majority of households were involved in the supply
of ale, with over half of the wives amerced for ale on five or more

[110] Dyot c. 1350–1370: SC 2/252/2 m. 3 – SC 2/253/4 m. 3; Henry died
in 1382, SC 2/254/3 m. 5. Falybron, c. 1355–1367: SC 2/252/6 m. 1 –
SC 2/253/3 m. 9. He served as a pledge only once after this, in 1383, and
died in 1390/1, SC 2/254/4 m. 7, SC 2/254/12 m. 9d. Kenworthey,
c. 1358–1394: SC 2/252/9 m. 7d. – SC 2/254/15 m. 5d. Rowe, c. 1350–1383:
SC 2/252/3 m. 4 – SC 2/254/4 m. 6–6d. Slegh, c. 1352–1370: SC 2/252/4
m. 6 – SC 2/253/4 m. 3.

[111] Butchers (Robert Heye, Henry Dyot, John Heppal, Thomas Oselcok
and Alan Pierson); cloth (Richard Burelles and William Sparky) and wool
sellers (John Leversegge, Nicholas Upton and the widow of Alan Pierson);
cloth-workers (fuller(s) William Bullynche and probably John Walker, and
tailor Richard Knyght); leather craftsmen or cobblers (William Lynster and
Thomas Daukynsone); smiths (William Botfysh and probably Roger Barker
who held several forges); and mercers (Robert Blagge, Stephen Blagge, who
held a cellar tavern in the early fifteenth century, and William Dale who
was also a miller).

occasions, and eighteen (46 per cent) amerced on ten or more. The six most prolific brewers, who were amerced nineteen or more times included two, the wives of William Sparky and Richard Kenworthey (who farmed the common oven), amerced over 30 times.[112]

The land or rent holding of some of this group must have been substantial. It includes Roger Barker, whose annual income from sublet holdings in Macclesfield and Sutton totalled £5, Henry Dyot, who also farmed the stallage, Roger Falybron, William Lynster and Ranulph Whytlof.[113] At least a third of the group held land in the borough fields and a quarter were also manor tenants. Three men, two of whom held the office of mayor, asserted small parcels of land within the manor.[114] The holdings of burgesses outside the town were nearby, in the townships of Hurdsfield, Sutton, Rainow and, in one instance, Shrigley.

In the second half of the fourteenth century, then, the borough was dominated by a handful of burgess families. The two most influential were the Sleghs and the Rowes, who monopolised the office of mayor for at least 29 of these years. Other important families, such as Falybrom and Upton, also possessed land in the manor-forest.[115] The majority of the elite, however, do not appear to have held land outside the town, and few seem to have maintained their influence beyond a generation. The younger sons of fuller William Bullynche for example, were smallholders in Hurdsfield, where William also held a tenement with buildings and 8½ acres.

---

[112] See pp. 92–3.

[113] See 'John de Macclesfield Cartulary', fos. 38–42, 47–50, 59–63, 66–8, 79–80. Dyot, a butcher, was a custodian of bread and meat in 1349/50, reeve in 1351/2, and farmer of the stallage in 1351, SC 2/252/2 m. 3, SC 2/252/4 m. 6, SC 6/802/7 m. 1d. Lynster was a custodian of ale in 1369/70, 1370/1, 1383/4 and 1388/9, and a custodian of bread and meat in 1375/6 and 1381/2, SC 2/253/4 m. 3d., SC 2/253/5 m. 8, SC 2/253/9 m. 5, SC 2/254/3 m. 5, SC 2/254/10 m. 8, Chester City Record Office, Earwaker MSS CR 63/2/339 rot. 1, m. 1.

[114] William Slegh, two acres, with an entry-fine of 8s. 0d., and ¼ rood in Hurdsfield, in 1379 and 1393, SC 2/254/1 m. 12, SC 2/254/14 m. 4d.; Roger Alcok, a small parcel next to a house at the Ridge in Sutton in 1384, SC 2/254/5 m. 8; John Walkedene, 1½ acres of underwood (in Hurdsfield) in 1388, SC 2/254/9 m. 4d.; and Richard, son of William Bullynche, who asserted a small enclosure worth 2d. in Hurdsfield in 1367, SC 2/253/2 m. 3.

[115] SC 11/899 m. 3d.–4, SC 11/898 m. 3d.

Category 'B' can be defined as the less influential of the resident trading burgesses. Nearly half, at least 44%, were office-holders and at least a similar number were jurors. Unlike those in category 'A', though, they did not dominate the juries of indictment. Only 13, or just over a fifth, were significant pledges and only three acted on nine or more occasions. They made, on average, between six and 20 appearances. Their trades were indistinguishable from those in category 'A' and many households were again involved in commercial brewing.[116] Nearly half had wives who regularly brewed ale, of whom a third were amerced on ten or more occasions. Six (10 per cent) were leading brewers, including four who were amerced more than 20 times: Alice wife of Geoffrey Burgeys, Maud wife of Hervey Sewall Bagger, Agnes wife of Robert Carles, Agnes wife of Robert Parmonter and the wives of Peter Stare and William Pemberton.[117]

Around one in six of this category held land in the borough fields and five (8 per cent) held land in the manor, in the townships of Sutton and Hurdsfield. Some of these may have derived a considerable proportion of their income through rural or urban rents: for example, John son of Henry Sydsworth in Sutton, William Sondebache who held land in the borough fields and in Hurdsfield, Roger Astbury who held land in the fields and in both townships, and John Boyle and John Falyngbrom Starky, both of whom held several burgages.[118] Many of the burgesses included in categories 'A' and 'B' kept livestock, and the keeping of swine was almost universal amongst them.[119]

[116] Butchers (Reginald Cook, William Pemberton, John Maykyn and John Oldefeld); tailors (Roger Balleson and Robert Carles); leather craftsmen (William Kenworthey, William Snowball and cobbler Richard Prestbury); smiths (Hugh Lauton and John Somerford); and a baker (Thomas Kenwrek).

[117] Alice Burgeys, c. 1370–1392, SC 2/253/4 m. 3d. – SC 2/254/13 m. 6d., m. 8d. Agnes Carles, c. 1352–1396, SC 2/252/4 m. 6 – SC 2/255/2 m. 5–6. Agnes Parmonter, c. 1357–1377, SC 2/252/9 m. 7 – SC 2/253/12 m. 2. Peter Stare's wife, c. 1357–1383, SC 2/252/8 m. 4d. -SC 2/254/4 m. 6, m. 7d.

[118] SC 11/899 m. 1d.–3d, SC 2/254/13 m. 6d; 'John de Macclesfield Cartulary', fo. 49–56, 117–8, 122–3, 137.

[119] For pigs, see the pannage of the borough, SC 2/253/9 m. 11. Apart from Alan Pierson and William French, whose large flocks of sheep have already been referred to, those who pastured cattle in the forest included mayor Richard Rowe, William Sondebache, Roger Barker, John Sydsworth, Robert Thorbald and John Boyle. Those with working horses included Richard Walker, William Stubbes, Roger Brounhull, William Bullynche

There were another 120 males resident in the borough who, for the most part, made fewer than ten appearances in court and will be included within a category 'C'.[120] Many of them were the sons of burgesses and had, still to establish themselves. Only around 20 (16 per cent) served as portmote jurors and none were recorded on more than five occasions. Of the three who acted as more than an occasional pledge only one, John Knokeden (six occasions) was a burgess. Robert Worth of Tytherington and hereditary gaoler of the lordship of Macclesfield, Adam Mottrum, were of a higher status and should be classified as external landholders. Those that would fall within this group who also had manor holdings, such as Robert and Thomas Shryglegh, were, in effect, wealthy tenants who also received rents from sub-let burgages.[121] Fewer than 10 per cent had enclosures or holdings in the borough fields. Around eighteen, (10 per cent) of households, had wives amerced for ale on several occasions with twelve important brewers being presented ten or more times. They included Isabel wife of John Lymnour and the wives of Robert Hasty, John Hayne, William Wynge, Adam Swordsliper, Hugh Pulton, Richard Mulnere and Nicholas Ravenowe.[122] Another 60 individuals were non-resident burgage-holders, whose court 'appearances' were limited to their amercements for common suit. Some of them were men of standing who held burgage-rents throughout the period while the

and William Sparky (SC 2/253/12 m. 5, m. 8–9, SC 2/254/1 m. 6, m. 11, SC 2/254/2 m. 10, SC 2/254/4 m. 14–16. Some burgesses, like William Lynster and William Sondebache, were also presented for taking holly and other greenwood as fodder; for example, SC 2/253/10 m. 2, SC 2/254/1 m. 11, SC 2/254/3 m. 6).

[120] They include butchers (Hugh Cook, Richard Bagger and Henry Gaoler); a carpenter (Richard Egge); cloth-workers (chaloner William Nog, and fuller Robert Walker who farmed the manor fulling mill, SC 6/803/13 m. 1).

[121] See their biographies Ch.Acc. (2), pp. 160–3, 172–3, 190.

[122] Isabel Lymnour, c. 1352–1377, SC 2/252/4 m. 6 – SC 2/253/12 m. 2. Hasty's wife, c. 1363–1378, SC 2/252/14 m. 5 – SC 2/253/12 m. 2d. Hayne's wife, c. 1373–1396, SC 2/253/7 m. 3 – SC 2/255/2 m. 5–6. Margery Wynge, c. 1374–1391, SC 2/253/8 m. 5 – SC 2/254/13 m. 6d. Alice Swordsliper, c. 1360–1382, SC 2/252/11 m. 3d. – SC 2/254/4 m. 6. Alice Pulton, c. 1367–1383, SC 2/253/2 m. 4 – SC 2/254/4 m. 6, m. 7d. Cecily Mulnere, c. 1367–83, SC 2/253/2 m. 4 – SC 2/254/4 m. 6–7, and once in 1390, SC 2/254/11 m. 8. Ravenowe's wife, c. 1386–1396, SC 2/254/7 m. 3 – SC 2/255/2 m. 6.

holdings of others were the result of short-term legal transactions, and several were clergymen.[123]

Around 170 individuals, or 15 per cent of all males, form a fourth category, 'D'. They were short-term residents or wage-earners in the borough, of whom 28, described as 'servants of ...', did not appear under their own names. Members of this group rarely made more than five court appearances and cannot be associated with land or rent holding. Around 50 can be included because of their trade, or on account of the selling of ale by their wives, such as Hugh Salter, cobbler John Cayrugge and his son, and butcher Richard Napton.[124] Another 40 had wives or other members of their family who were referred to in other business in the borough court.

A final category would need to include the 40 per cent or more of 'isolated individuals'. They made between one and three appearances and nearly a quarter were amerced solely because of their involvement in affrays. Of these, 122 were amerced on one occasion, twelve on two and six on three. They can be summed up as traders, labourers, non-residents from the locality and those travelling through the borough. Of those specified as non-residents around half originated from outside the Hundred.[125]

Women made up a quarter of those appearing in the courts, but they constituted only 13 per cent of the total landholders (excluding those who held jointly with their husbands). Of the 61 females holding land, 49 (80 per cent) were described as daughters, and the

[123] Those from nearby included John Glover of Butley, Thomas Fitton of Gawsworth, and John Ibot draper of Offerton. From slightly further afield were Thomas Snelleston of Snelston, Thomas Swetenham of Swettenham, Robert Taillour of Chorley, William Dale of Stockport, Roger Juddesone of Chelford and Richard Burdon of Fairfield. The clergymen included: John Caton parson of Gawsworth, the abbot of Chester, Richard Pygot, vicar of Prestbury, and John Tydrynton, vicar of Sandbach. The chaplains included John Brounhull and Stephen Leve.

[124] SC 2/252/7 m. 3–3d, SC 2/253/6 m. 5d, Chester City Record Office, Earwaker MSS CR 63/2/338 m. 1, SC 2/253/7 m. 3.

[125] The places most frequently referred to were: Congleton, Prestbury, Adlington, Alderley, Dukinfield, Eccles *or* Etchels, Knutsford, Mottram St. Andrew, Mobberley, Stockport, Swettenham, Wilmslow and the counties of Lancashire and Derbyshire in general. In addition the small number of traders who travelled from farther afield included Richard Glover, a mercer from Manchester, John Etwell of Nottingham, who traded woollen cloth and pottery, and others from the towns of Burton and Newcastle.

majority of them would have subsequently married. In the categories of manorial tenants women were: 7 per cent (one person) of category one; 9 per cent (four holdings) of category two; 13 per cent (23 holdings) of category three; 10 per cent (17 holdings) of category four; and 20 per cent (14 holdings) of category five.

The most economically active females were the heiresses of wealthy families who maintained their income through subletting. In categories one and two were the daughters of leading families. They included Isabel, heiress of John son of Jordan Macclesfield, with more than 60 acres in Hurdsfield and Shrigley, Isabel daughter of Thomas Fitton, lord of Gawsworth, and Margery daughter of Roger Joudrel. Of a lesser status, were Margaret, daughter of Richard Anker, a member of an established family from Disley-Stanley. On the borderline with category three was Ellen, daughter of Roger Oldhed, who benefited from her father's office-holding and assarting. Margaret, daughter of Hugh Dounes, and Margaret, daughter of William Sutton, jointly held over 20 acres, including four messuages and a cottage, in Sutton in 1352. By 1384, though, Margaret Dounes was left with only three messuages and under five acres of land. Margaret Sutton had alienated two acres to Thomas Cloghes, and a messuage and 9½ acres to wealthy tenants Thomas Shryglegh and chaplain John Rossyndale.[126]

The largest number of properties held by women in the manor came within category three, of those holding between nine and 22 customary acres. It is difficult to determine the precise nature of many of these holdings as they were held at reduced rents or jointly with co-parceners. Margery, daughter of Ralph Wilcok, for example, held over 12 acres and 3½ messuages in Whaley at only 3s. 7d. rent, and the 6s. 6d. holding of Thomas Potte was shared amongst his six daughters. One of these daughters, Emma, left the manor to work prior to her marriage.[127] The majority of women's holdings, though, were clearly below ten acres and the highest proportion

---

[126] SC 11/899 mm. 2–3d., SC 11/898 m. 2, m. 4. Macclesfield, SC 2/253/10 m. 4; Fitton, SC 2/252/2 m. 4, SC 2/252/9 m. 5. Joudrel, SC 2/252/2 m. 4. Oldhed, SC 2/252/14 m. 4, SC 2/253/9 mm. 3–4. Sutton, SC 2/252/3 m. 2d., SC 2/253/8 m. 3d., SC 2/254/3 m. 3d.

[127] SC 11/899 mm. 3d.–4. Potte's daughters entered the land in 1381, SC 2/254/3 m. 3. Emma left to work in Adlington in the autumn of 1388, SC 2/254/10 m. 6, and married John son of John Togod c. 1393, when two of her sisters (Margaret and Ellen) granted their portion, worth 1s. 1d., to her husband, SC 2/254/14 m. 5.

were smallholdings of under three acres. Only three women were referred to by a surname.[128] Joan Calverhale held between two and 4½ acres in Rainow and was later indicted for a number of felonies. Alice Fox was the joint holder of two messuages and 1¼ bovates of nief land in Sutton (rented at 4s. 4d.). Only one other female land-holder, Margaret wife of Richard Smyth of Bollington, was mentioned in relation to the assize of ale.[129]

Although a higher proportion of those appearing in the portmote were women they were more likely to be referred to as anonymous wives or daughters. The majority appeared either as ale-wives or as a result of their life-cycle service. There is evidence to suggest that a small group of largely independent women were poor and on the fringe of borough society. They frequently appeared for taking wood and turves for fuel, which was either broken from the town's hedgerows or collected from the park, as well as for having committed affrays or for being scolds. In a handful of cases women, such as Amice Fletcher, were engaged in a combination of petty larcenies and acts of violence. Amice, however, was unusual in that she held a burgage and was the wife of butcher, John Oldefeld.[130] The single most important determining factor in the lives of townswomen at this time was their access to burgage or other land, which would have brought both income and common rights, such as those relating to woodland and pasture.

Finally, research has shown that medieval houses could be substantial structures. Inside they could be cleaned and well cared for yet there are few archaeological remains of the furniture or chattels inside them.[131] Occasional references to thefts in the courts or the items forfeited in gaol delivery are, therefore, very important in extending our knowledge of household possessions. The normal cottage in fourteenth-century England may have contained little apart from a few items of clothing, a working tool, a spinning distaff

---

[128] Maud Stubbes, who held an acre in Sutton, may have been related to William Stubbes who held over eight acres of land in the same township, SC 11/898 m. 2–2d. For a later Maud, see p. 170 n. 106 below.

[129] SC 11/899 m. 2–2d., SC 11/898 m. 2d.–3d., m. 5. Smyth, SC 2/254/2 m. 3. For Joan Calverhale, see the biography of Thomas Stanystrete in Appendix One.

[130] See Amice's biography in Appendix One.

[131] Dyer, *English Peasant Buildings*, pp. 18–45. M. Beresford and J. Hurst, *Wharram Percy Deserted Medieval Village* (1990), pp. 41–4.

or wheel, and a brass pot or pan.[132] In a wooded area of East Anglia in the early fourteenth century, for instance, the theft of a brass pan, a hood, and a woodhook were recorded.[133] The most important possessions would have been the land, croft and house, the livestock and some basic furniture and pottery; only the wealthy peasantry and burgesses probably had more.

In the Macclesfield courts the main references to possessions are in the pleas of detinue, many of which related to the executors of wills. The most elaborate possessions belonged to the clergy and included the set of velvet bed-hangings and with woollen and linen cloth worth 40s. 0d. stolen from John Caton of Gawsworth. The 'treasure' detained by chaplain Richard Brounhull and the widow of under-forester Richard Chaumpayn from Thomas son of Thomas Cheadle consisted of: six spoons, worth 16s. 0d.; two silver vessels, worth 16s. 8d.; bed-clothes without hangings, 6s. 8d.; and two buckles, worth 3s. 4d.[134] The use of this word, however, suggests that these were unusually valuable and the most expensive item most commonly referred to was a mazer bowl. These ranged in value between 4s. 2d. and 10s. 0d., and were owned by burgesses such as Roger Falybron, Jordan Macclesfield and butcher Thomas Oselcok.[135]

The item most frequently detained was the brass pot.[136] Its value varied considerably and some were worth more than mazers. In 1363, for instance, there were two worth 5s. 0d. and 8s. 0d., one of which belonged to borough resident Sibyl Janny, who had two more taken as distraints three years later. They could have been used for brewing, such as that of Cecily widow of Peter Neuton. The only one of fuller William Bullynche's 33 suits that also included

[132] R. K. Field, 'Worcestershire peasant buildings, household goods, and farming equipment in the later Middle Ages', *Medieval Archaeology*, 9 (1965), pp. 105–45; Dyer, *Standards of living*, pp. 170–7; J. Langdon, 'Agricultural Equipment' in Astill and Grant (ed.), *Countryside of Medieval England*, pp. 86–107.

[133] B. Hanawalt, *Crime in East Anglia in the Fourteenth Century. Norfolk Gaol Delivery Rolls 1307–16*, Norfolk Record Society, 44 (1976).

[134] CHES 25/20 m. 61; SC 2/253/9 m. 5.

[135] Falybron recovered his in the portmote against butcher Hervey Sewall, and Macclesfield recovered his in the Hundred after eyre court against John Slegh, SC 2/253/2 m. 2, SC 2/252/3 m. 8. Oselcok had his, said to be worth 10s. 0d., stolen, CHES 25/20 m. 31.

[136] They held between one and six gallons, and virtually all peasants had them by the 1380s, Dyer, *English Diet*, p. 204.

Margery, his wife, concerned the detention of an ell of woollen cloth and a brass pot. The case was brought by fellow-burgess, William Sondebache.[137] Other household goods included a leaden vessel and a tripod, and small items which were usually dry grain measures. The most frequent possessions that were either stolen or detained were cloth or small items of clothing.[138] Personal suits were brought in the portmote, for instance, over a cap, a hat, and a brooch.[139]

The implements used in affrays are good indicators of weapons that were carried and of tools that lay close at hand. The most common weapon was the stick or staff, followed by knives or baslards which were owned by people of all social groups: burgesses, chaplains, external traders, and labourers. Swords were restricted to the more wealthy burgesses and were sometimes carried by outsiders. The tools most commonly referred to were the pole-axe, the pikel (pitchfork) and turf spade, while others included a hook, a flail, a hoe and a small hammer. The possession of a chest indicates the presence of items of higher personal value. Ellen, daughter of John Batemon of Sutton, (category three), had a brass pot worth 5s. 0d., and a chest worth 3s. 4d.[140] A summary of the goods of local men in the later fourteenth century is contained in Tables 22 and 23.

[137] SC 2/252/14 m. 4, SC 2/253/1 m. 3. Bullynche, SC 2/253/1 m. 4d. Three years earlier, before her husband died, Cecily Neuton was amerced for selling ale with an unsealed measure, SC 2/253/3 m. 9, SC 2/253/5 m. 8d.
[138] In the borough, thefts from burgesses included: two sheets, two pairs of woollen cloths, two shirts and two breeches, worth 3s. 4d., from John Leversegge; a linen sheet with lambs' fur worth 8s. 0d. from Robert Parmonter; and a garment worth 3d., two towels worth 4d. (and a peck worth 1d.) which were taken from leather craftsman William Lynster. CHES 25/22 m. 40, CHES 25/20 m. 37, CHES 25/21 m. 4.
[139] SC 2/252/8 m. 4, SC 2/252/9 m. 7d, SC 2/252/10 m. 4, SC 2/252/11 m. 3.
[140] SC 2/253/7 m. 1.

Table 16   *Borough Ale-Wives and their Households c. 1349–96*

This table shows the number of amercements for the assizes of ale and bread (*ale . bread*), of 'ale-wives' women, in relation to their husbands' trade (where applicable) (*ale . bread & meat*).

Name	No.	Off.	House.	Trades
Lowe, w. Wll.	42.5	*	.3	
Walker, Alc., w. Wll.	40.0	*		
Sparky, Alc. w. Wll.	38.4	*	.1	
Kenworthey, Mrgy. w. Rch.	36.3	*	1.5	
Hurdesfeld, Agn. w. Rg.	35.		2.	
Burgeys, Alc. w. Gff.	32.4	*		
Carles, Agn. w. Rb.	30.	*		Tailor
Hayfeld, Ell. w. Wll.	27.3	*	.1	
Stare, w. Pet.	27.			
Spark, Agn. w. Ad.	27.4	*		
Upton, Ell. w. Nch.	26.4		1.1	(wool merchant)
Astbury, Agn. (d. Th.)	25.1			
Lymnour, Isb. w. Jn.	23.			
Botfysh, Alc. w. Wll.	21.4	*	.2	Smith
Parmonter, Agn. w. Rb.	21.			
Slegh, Alc. w. Wll.	20.3	*	.1	
French, Alc. w. Wll.	20.	*	1.	(Merchant)
Starky, Joan	19.			
Heye, Joan w. Rb.	19.2	*	.40	Butcher
Wynge, Mrgy. w. Wll.	18.2			
Hayne, w. Jn.	17.1	*		
Swordsliper, Alc. w. Ad.	16.5			
Starky, Agn., serv. Rg. o. Falybron	16.	*		
Hasty, w. Rb.	15.			
Oselcok, Agn. w. Th.	15.	*	4.30	Butcher
Pulton, Alc. w. Hgh.	15.			
Stubbes, Mrgy. w. Wll.	15.	*	.1	
Jolion, Amc. w. Jn.	14.1	*	.1	Smith
Mulnere, Cec. w. Rch.	14.1		1.	

Name	No.	Off.	House.	Trades
Brounhull, Agn.	14.			
Bulkylegh, Luc. w. Rnph.	14.			
Foliot, Edth. w. Gff.	14.	*		
Jolynet, Isb. w. Nch.	14.	*	1.	Smith
Rowe, Alc. w. Rch.	14.	*	2.	
Ravenowe, Mrgy. w. Nch.	13.	*		
Amice Fletcher w. o. Jn. Oldefeld	12.		.12	Butcher
Turnour, w. Wll.	12.5	*		
Brounhull, Joan w. Rg.	12.	*		
Sewall, Maud w. Herv.	11.	*	1.34	Butcher
Carter, Alyn. w. Th.	11.	*		
Hayneson, Agn. w. Edm.	11.		1.18	Butcher
London, Alc.	11.			
Maykyn, Isb. w. Jn.	11.	*	.16	Butcher
Smyth, Alc. w. Jn.	11.	*		
Barker, Amice d. Th.	10.1			
Fecheler, Mrgt., w. Jn.	10.			
Skot, w. Rg.	10.			
Pemberton, (Ell.)w. Wll.	9.2		.27	Butcher
Cook, Amc. w. Reg.	9.1	*	.30	Butcher

Abbreviations

No.: the number of times amerced for the assizes of ale, bread and meat.

Off.: indicates that their husband held office within the borough.

House.: the number of amercements within their household, i.e., by their husbands (where applicable).

Trades: refers to any other known trades in their households, i.e., normally by their husbands.

Table 17   *Portmote Butchers and Bakers, c. 1349–96*

This table records those individuals regularly amerced for the assizes of bread and meat (*ale . bread & meat*).

Name	No	Off.	Ale-Wife	Notes
Heye, Rb.	.40	*	*	
Sewall, Herv.	1.34	*	*	
Oselcok, Th.	4.30	*	*	
Cook, Reg.	.30	*	*	
Pemberton, Wll.	.27		*	
Hayneson, Edm.	1.18		*	
Cook, Hgh.	.17			
Maykyn, Jn.	.16	*	*	
Heppal, Jn.	.14	*	(*)	
Oldefeld, Jn.	.12		*	
Dyot, Hen.	.9	*	*	farmer o. stallage
Pierson, Al.	.9	*	(*)	mayor
Bagger, Rch.	.7			
Symeson, Jn., Baker	.7	*		

Table 18   *Manor Residents Involved in the Cloth-Trade*

Name	Cat	Vill	Trade	Livestock
John Dykeson	3	Rainow	tailor	many draught-beasts & pig(s)
Robert Jackson	3	Whaley & Disley	tailor	pig(s)
Benedict Persones	4	Disley	tailor	pig(s)
Richard Tyllesone	3	Rainow	tailor	draught-beasts, & pigs
William Benet	3	*Sutton*	tailor	
Roger Bugge	U-T	*Kettleshulme*	tailor	
Roger Wodecok		*unknown*	weaver & fuller	
Wife of Roger Wodecok			weaver & ale-wife	
Agnes wife of John Cok	3	Sutton	weaver	

Name	Cat	Vill	Trade	Livestock
Ellen wife of William Olyver	5	Whaley	weaver	several sheep, draught-beasts & pigs
Sarah wife of John Olerenshawe	3	Whaley	weaver	
Wife of James Pymyng	4	Kettleshulme	weaver	
Wife of Richard Stanlegh	5	Disley	weaver	
Margery wife of Gilbert Maggeson			weaver	
Daughter of Nicholas Stones	3	Whaley	weaver	draught-beasts & pigs

Cat: land / rent holding categories; U–T: under-tenant.

Table 19 *Portmote Jurors, c.1349–96*

Name	No	Pl.	Off.	Land	Notes
Kenworthey, Rch.	29	31.7	*	5	farmer o. stallage deputy serjeant peace
Byran, Rb.	29	5.4	*	3	deputy mayor
Leversegge, Jn.	27	8.8		2	(wool trade)
Hayfeld, Wll.	27	1.2	*	4	wright
Knyght, Rch.	23	9	*		tailor
Dale, Wll.	21	8.5	*		mercer
Rode, Rch.	20	3.3	*	5	
French, Wll.	19	3.3	*	5	(merchant)
Slegh, Wll.	18	14.2	*	3	mayor
Lynster, Wll.	18	16.4	*		leather craftsman
Upton, Nch.	15	2.1		1	(wool merchant)
Spencer, Rch.	14	5.10	*		
Stubbes, Wll.	14	7	*	3	
Barker, Rg.	13	5.7	*	2	(holder of forges)
Turnour, Wll.	12.	0.3	*		
Prestbury, Hen.	10.	0	*		
Blagge, Stph.	9.	0.1	*		mercer & baker
Brounhull, Rg.	9.	11.6	*		
Bullynche, Wll.	9.	6.6	*	4	fuller

Name	No	Pl.	Off.	Land	Notes
Heppal, Jn.	9.	1.1	*		butcher
Rowe, Rch.	9.	31.2	*	4	mayor
Slegh, Jn.	9.	2.1	*	4	
Sparky, Wll.	9.	2.2	*	5	cloth-seller
Blagge, Rb.	8.	0.5	*		mercer
Tydrynton, Ad.	7.	1.	*	3	
Burelles, Rch.	6.	4.3	*		cloth-seller
Burgeys, Gff.	6.	3.	*		
Heye, Rb.	5.	1.3	*		butcher
Lowe, Wll.	5.	0.1	*	?	
Walkedene, Jn.	5.	1.8	*	5	

Abbreviations and Key
Pl. the number of times served as a pledge. number of times amerced;
Jur. serving as a juror;
Off. serving in borough office;
Land land / rent holding categories.

Table 20 *Halmote Pledges, c.1349–96*

Name	No	Jur.	Township	Land	Notes.
Dounes, Gff.	43.16	5	Shrigley/B'ton	(3)	farmer o. stallage
Cresswall, Jn.	44.6	9	Sutton/Rainow	1	forester, farmer o. mill
Dounes, Wll.	39.1		Shrigley	1	forester, verderer & agister
Batemon, Jn.	29.2	3	Sutton	3	
Grene, Rch.	27.3		Rainow	4	
Ashton, Rg.	23		Whaley/K'hulme	3	
Shryglegh, Th.	25.5	8	Shrigley/Rainow	2	
Dounes, Reg.	20.4	1	Sutton	2	parker, farmer o. mill
Joudrel, Wll.	19.	2	Disley/Whaley	1	
Shryglegh, Rb.	17.2	2	Rainow/Shrigley	3	under-forester
Gaoler, Hen.	17.		Sutton	3	
Byran, Nch.	15.2	1	Hurdsfield	2	under-bailiff
Holyncete, Rb.	15.	2	Sutton	2	

Name	No	Jur.	Township	Land	Notes.
Sherd, Jn.	12.4	5	Stanley/Disley	2	forester
Oldefeld, Jn.	11.4	2	Sutton	3	
Mottrum, Ad.	11.1			-	bailiff & gaoler
Sutton, Jn., sen.	11.		Sutton	1	forester
Gardener, Rb.	10.3	1	Rainow/Sutton	3	
Leversegge, Jn.	9.2		H'field/Maccl.	2	(wool trade)
Brocwalhurst, Jn.	9.1	1	Kettleshulme	3	constable
French, Wll.	9.1		Burgess	5	(merchant)
Janny, Rch.	9.1		Bollington	(4)	under-forester
Dounes, Hgh.	9.		Sutton/Rainow	(3)	farmer of stallage & mills
Homeldon, Edm.	9.	3	Sutton	3	under-forester
Hulcokes, Glb.	9.		Sutton/o. Hollinset	-	
Byran, Rb.	8.3	1	Burgess/H'field	3	deputy mayor
Gardener, Nch.	8.		Rainow/Sutton	2	farmer o. escapes
Coton, Jn.	7.2		Sutton	2	
Batemon, Rb.	7.2	1	Sutton	3	
Schore, Wll.	7.2		Whaley/Disley	-	
Oldhed, Rg.	7.1	1	Sutton	3	agister
Stanlegh, Rch.	7.		Disley	5	
Bagylegh, Rch.	7.			-	*unknown*
Barker, Rg.	7.		Sutton/Maccl.	2	
Henreson, Th.	7	4	Whaley/K'hulme	3	
Holyncete, Jn.	7.		Sutton	2	
Dounes, Rb. s. o. Wll.	6.2	1	Shrigley	1	forester
Slegh, Wll.	6.1		Burgess/H'field	3	mayor
Bosedon, Th.	6.1		Sutton/H'field	3	
Neuton, Nch.	6.1		Sutton/Upton	3	
Persones, Rb.	6.1		Whaley	3	
Heppal, Wll.	6		Sutton	3	
Hyde, Th.	6.		Whaley	(3)	
Mottrum, Rg.	6.	4	Stanley	(5)	forester
Pierson, Al.	6.		Burgess	-	

Name	No	Jur.	Township	Land	Notes.
Shydyort, Jn.	5.4	11	Sutton	3	
Mottrum, Jn. s. o. Ad.	5.2		Sutton	3/2	bailiff
Alcok, Jn.	5.1		Rainow	(4)	stockman
Shryglegh, Jn.	4.2	3	Shrigley/Sutton	2	

Table 21 *Portmote Pledges, c.1349–96*

Name	No	Jur.	Off.	Land	Notes
Slegh, Rch.	57.7	2	*		mayor
Rowe, Rch.	31.2	9	*	4	mayor
Kenworthey, Rch.	31.7	29	*	5	farmer o. stallage
Falybron, Rg.	23.1	1		4	
Dyot, Hen.	20.1	3	*	4	farmer o. stallage, butcher
Pierson, Al.	19.1	2	*		farmer o. stallage, butcher
Lynster, Wll.	16.4	18	*		leather craftsman
Walker, Wll.	17.2	1	*		
Whytlof, Rnph.	17.2	o	*		
Slegh, Wll.	14.2	18	*	3	mayor
Botfysh, Wll.	13.2	2	*	5	smith
Brounhull, Rg.	11.6	9	*		
Clyf, Jn.	11.3	o		3	
Walker, Jn.	11.2	2	*		fuller
Daukynson, Th.	11.1	2	*		cobbler
Oselcok, Th.	11	.3	*		butcher
Dale, Wll.	9.4	19	*		mercer
Parmonter, Rb.	9.1	4			
Sewall, Hervey	9.1	o	*	4	butcher
Mottrum, Ad.	9.	o			bailiff & gaoler
Knyght, Rch.	9	23	*		tailor
Leversegge, Jn.	8.8	27		2	(wool trade)
Neuton, Nch.	8.	o	*	3	under bailiff
Walker, Th.	8.	o	*		

Name	No	Jur.	Off.	Land	Notes
Helegh, Th.	7.1	1	*	4	chaplain
Balleson, Rg.	7.	1	*		tailor
Stubbes, Wll.	7	14	*	3	
Bullynche, Wll.	6.6	9	*	4	fuller
Neuton, Pet.	6.2	1		3	
Prestbury, Rch.	6.2	1	*		cobbler
Macclesfield, Jn.	6.1	0		1	mayor
Caton, Wll.	6.	1			
Knokeden, Jn.	6.	0	*		farmer o. oven
Worth, Rb.	6.	1		(3)	o. Tytherington
Spencer, Rch.	5.14	14	*		
Barker, Rg.	5.7	13	*	2	smith
Rossyndale, Jn.	5.6	0		(3)	knight
Byran, Rb.	5.4	29	*	3	deputy mayor
Vernon, Rb.	5.2	0			
Bosedon, Th.	5.1	0		3	
Foliot, Gff.	5.	0	*		
Hayneson, Edm.	5.	0			butcher
Maykyn, Jn.	5.	1	*		butcher
Bower, Rg.	4.1	0			
Boyle, Jn.	4.1	2	*		
Burelles, Rch.	4.3	6	*		cloth-seller (& baker)
Grene, Rch.	3.3	0		4	
Rode, Rch.	3.3	20	*	5	
Bedulf, Rg.	3.2	3	*		

Table 22 *The Livestock and Chattels of some Manor Residents*

Name	Land	Vill	Stock	Other Chattels.
Joan d. o. Wll. Calverhale[1]	2–4½ acres	Rainow	3 cows, 5s. 0d., 2 bullocks, 6s. 0d., 5 yearling calves, 1s. 4d.	*unknown*
Wll. Shoteswall[2]	10 acres	Whaley	6 sheep, 2 lambs, and wool at 6d.	*unknown*
Robert Bargh[3]	Villein		2 sheep, 2s. 6d.	russet cloth, 8d., 1 coat, 6d., 1 overcoat, 12d., 1 bowl, 4d., 2 oat baskets, 3d.
Robert Smale[4]	Under-Tenant	Rainow	4 cows, 8s. 9d., 4 calves, 7s. 0d., 1 pig, 13d., 7 sheep, 12d., 1 colt, 5s. 0d.	10s. corn in barn, wheat & rye growing, 1 brass pot, 2s. 4d., a wooden & iron chest, 14d.
William Dunbull[5]	8 acres with house	Sutton	beasts incl. horses, and a pig.	overcoat with hood of dark cloth, short jacket of green cloth, bow & eight arrows, pair of shoes, pair of gloves, & pair of stockings.
(Edmund Homeldon)[6]				1 brass pot, 10s. 0d., 1 mazer bowl, 5s. 0d., a sword, 3s. 4d., 1 table & cloth, 10s. 0d., iron chimney, 6s. 8d., 1 wain, at 10s. 0d., iron brooch & 1 'cobbard', 2s. 6d., a leaden vessel, 8s. 0d., a trough, 2s. 0d., & mixed cloth, 3s. 4d.

[1] Goods taken and sold after her felony, SC 2/254/5 m. 8. Evidence from the escapes shows that she sometimes grazed more animals.
[2] Goods taken after a felony, CHES 25/20 m. 43.
[3] Goods sold at his death, totalling 13s. 1d., SC 2/253/1 m. 2d.
[4] Goods, in the hands of Edmund Smale, after a felony, SC 2/253/8 m. 8.

⁵ Goods stolen, totalling 3s. 4d., CHES 25/19 m. 11.

⁶ 'broche de ferro et 1 coubart', and a 'wortrogh', SC 2/253/1 m. 2. These appear to be the principal goods of John Dycon, forester, which were claimed by his son, Roger Dycon, in a civil action in 1365 against Edmund Homeldon, a reeve of the chantry of the Blessed Mary. In an earlier plea, successfully brought by William Motlowe in 1357 over 35s. 0d. rent, Homeldon denied he was the executor of Dycon's will but later agreed that he was the administrator. In the later case Dycon was amerced for his false claim. SC 2/252/8 m. 5, SC 2/252/15 m. 5d.

Table 23   *Examples of Goods and Chattels Forfeited by Felons*

Name	Vill	Goods	Value
Richard Burelles	Burgess	corn in grange	60s. 0d.
		2 horses	18d.
		1 'Sheldemare'	10s. 0d.
		1 calf	3s. 0d.
		1 brass pot	3s. 0d.
		2 sheep	3s. 0d.
		other	½ mark
Thomas Walker	Macclesfield	1 grey horse	20s. 0d.
	& Prestbury	1 bay horse	½ mark
		1 red horse	6s. 0d.
		corn	40s. (& 14s.?)
		1 brass pot ...	40d.
		1 posnet	18d.
		another posnet	10d.
		1 fur (*sic.*)	4d.
		4 weak chests	2s. 0d.
		mazer	½ mark
Amice Fletcher	Burgess	1 brass pot	6s. 8d.
		4 pigs	...
		1 stirk	3s. 4d.
William Bedenhale servant	Borough	corn, wheat & oats	5s. 0d.
		5 lambs & 1 sheep	2s. 6d.
John Lovell	Gawsworth	3 heifers (o. Wll. Nedham o. Derbyshire)	12s. 0d.

Name	Vill	Goods	Value
		1 colt	2s. od.
		1 cow & 1 heifer	10s. od.
		1 brass pot	15d.
		sheaves in field	12d.
		hay in grange	12d.
Robert Hargreve	Hundred	1 horse	10s. od.
		3 colts	6s. od.
		3 oxen	30s. od.
		3 cows	20s. od.
		3 heifers	18s. od.
		5 twinters	25s. od.
		1 stirk	40d.
		2 calves	2s. od.
		1 piglet	8d.
		41 sheep	37s. od.
		2 brass pots	4s. 6d.

CHES 25/20 m. 27, m. 35, m. 85; CHES 25/22 m. 7, m. 18, m. 41d.

4 *Crime and Patterns of Conflict*

'Only detailed, village by village studies co-ordinating criminal and manorial evidence will indicate the social status of those who turned to crime'.[1]

Cheshire has long been accepted as 'one of the least law-abiding parts of the country'.[2] Its association with the Black Prince's campaigns, for instance, have led to descriptions of an area where disorder was rife and hardened soldiers resorted to petty violence to solve their disputes. The county's archers regularly provided a significant proportion of the men in the Black Prince's campaigns and in the 1380s they constituted up to 20 per cent of those serving in France.[3] The number of longbows found in the heriots of those in the west of Cheshire has been used to illustrate the importance, in this area at least, of part-time soldiering amongst a wide range of tenants below gentry status.[4] However it is Morgan's view that military service in the County was largely confined to those of gentry status and the link between violence, disorder and warfare went far deeper than the supply of men for the earl's campaigns. The practice of livery and maintenance formed irresistible ties between gentry and peasants and as there was 'seldom any separation' between the domestic and military retinue, the 'boundary between public and private warfare was ill-drawn'.[5]

The links between military service, patronage and office holding

[1] B. Hanawalt, 'Economic Influences on the Pattern of Crime in England, 1300–1348', *American Journal of Legal History*, 18 (1974), p. 297.

[2] Hewitt, *Cheshire Under the Three Edwards*, pp. 105–7; M. McKisack, *The Fourteenth Century, 1307–99* (Oxford 1959), p. 204.

[3] *V.C.H. Chester, II*, p. 33. For a possible link between soldiering and disorder in the south-east of England, see E. Searle and R. Burghart 'The Defence of England and the Peasants' Revolt', *Viator* 3 (1972), pp. 375–6.

[4] M. J. Bennett, 'Sources and Problems', p. 79; J. L. Gillespie, 'Richard II's Cheshire Archers', *Trans. Hist. Soc. of Lancs. and Cheshire*, 125 (1974), pp. 1–39.

[5] Morgan, *War and Society*, pp. 55–6, 226–7.

were, therefore, very firm indeed.[6] In the absence of any resident nobility the gentry of Cheshire were not subject to control and became locked into a struggle for power, prestige and landed wealth. The long history of the county in supplying the military needs of the crown led to an over dependence on certain individuals and the need to balance competing interests with service, of which the practice of granting criminal immunity was merely one manifestation. A man, whether experienced in foreign warfare or in local criminal activity, could be welcomed if useful.[7]

During the time of the Black Prince there appears to have been a widening of this power base as a result of an attempt to expand revenue via the leasing of land and office, and this further led to 'a breakdown in relationships between the most powerful' and the rest of society.[8] In the trailbaston proceedings of 1353 substantial monetary fines were paid following serious accusations involving assault, bribery and corruption by many gentry and officials.[9] Those most hostile to the removal of Richard II and most active in the ensuing rebellion, such as Peter Legh, who was executed for his disloyalty, were those with the most to lose.[10] As Powell had said:

> 'the explanation for the prevalence of corruption and judicial malpractice lies in the nature of the social and political structure of medieval England. The law ... reflected the character and needs of society itself.' [11]

There is a great deal of evidence for the disorder that took place within Cheshire during the second half of the fourteenth century. In 1357, gangs of men entering Peak forest were accused of woundings, driving people from their lands, and abduction with

[6] P. H. W. Booth, 'Taxation and Public Order: Cheshire in 1353', *Northern History*, 12 (1976), pp. 16–31.

[7] M. J. Bennett, *Community, Class and Careerism*, pp. 94–106. Purchasing a pardon could be 'a routine pecuniary transaction for many offences and offenders' J. G. Bellamy, *Crime and Public Order in England in the later Middle Ages* (1973), p. 194.

[8] Booth, 'Taxation and Public Order', p. 28. For example *B.P.R., iii,* pp. 251, 258, 290. For benefits of membership of retinues, see E. Powell, *Kingship, Law and Society. Criminal Justice in the Reign of Henry V* (Oxford 1989), p. 90, and Bellamy, *Crime and Public Order*, pp. 23, 71.

[9] John Legh, for instance paid £20, P. H. W. Booth, 'Calendar of the Cheshire Trailbaston Proceedings 1353', *Cheshire History*, 11 (1983), p. 43.

[10] McNiven, 'Rebellion of 1403'.

[11] Powell, *Kingship, Law and Society*, pp. 111–2.

ransom. In 1360 an order was made to prevent large assemblies in the county, following the abbot of Combermere's complaint that a 'great number' had crossed the border into Shropshire. Two years later a further order prohibiting the riding of armed men claimed that 'some persons of the county have ridden and still ride in warlike pride'.[12] Such actions also arose in neighbouring Lancashire where, in a field near Liverpool in 1345, a local dispute led to the murder of 27 men for which 175 people were pardoned, largely on account of their service in Gascony.[13]

The most influential members of the gentry within Macclesfield Hundred were the Legh of Adlington family. In the forest eyre of 1357 Robert Legh the elder was fined over £88 for forest offences, most notably for the expansion of the cultivated area of his manor of Adlington prior to the Black Death. Under the Black Prince, Robert became the single most powerful individual within the area as the rider and keeper of the forest, as well as deputy steward of the manor. In 1351 he was accused of withholding money which was due to the earl from a fine.[14]

Following his death about 1370, a feud broke out between the two branches of his family. Robert the younger, his son from his first marriage, paid a fine of 500 marks to purchase the wardship of James son of John Legh, with all the lands that belonged to his father and mother.[15] Peter and John Legh, his sons from his second marriage, and Maud their mother, with others such as Richard and Robert Middelton, sought to recover those lands through a campaign of forgery, violence, intimidation and murder. In 1376 Peter Legh and Richard Middelton, with the aid of more than 50 armed retainers (from as far away as Lancashire, as well as Knutsford, Tatton, Sale, Etchels, Mobberley and Rostherne), ejected Robert from his lands in Adlington, maimed his bailiff, killed his cattle, damaged his

---

[12] *B.P.R., iii*, pp. 178, 267, 383–4 and 442–3; a number of other complaints and petitions were raised against Cheshire men. For example, *Rotuli Parliamentorum, ii*, p. 352.

[13] These included Robert son of John Legh and several other Cheshire men, G. Barraclough, 'Two Liverpool Medieval Affrays', *Trans. Hist. Soc. of Lancs. and Cheshire*, 85 (1933), pp. 74–81.

[14] *Ch.Acc.* (1), pp. 248–9 and CHES 33/6 m. 41; also £20 for acquiring the manor from his mother, Ellen, in 1352 without fine, *B.P.R., iii*, pp. 53, 66, 90. For biographies, see *Ch.Acc.* (2), pp. 155–8.

[15] I am indebted to Phyllis Hill for permission to refer to her unpubl. thesis, 'Chester County Court Indictment Roll', pp. 870–76, 578, 946.

harrows and ploughs, and put his manor-house in a state of defence 'as if for war'. John Legh was rescued from Chester Castle and with Peter and Robert Middelton and others lay in wait to kill Robert. When this failed they rode to Whaley where they murdered the wealthy forest tenant, William Joudrel, another man who had served in Gascony and who was an ally and servant of Robert Legh. In addition they sent out others to eject Robert's tenants from Poynton. These events were a violent response to an order for arbitration between the parties from the Black Prince himself.

After Robert's death in about 1382, the office of steward of Macclesfield passed to Peter and John Legh. However, in 1386–7, Robert, son of Robert Legh, and Thomas Arden were indicted for occupying the office of steward of the Hundred. Robert held sessions of the halmote, portmote and Hundred court between September and January, although local officials, namely the catchpoll and bailiffs, failed to attend. By February, however, Peter Legh had been appointed as steward of the manor. In the same year both Robert and Thomas were accused of taking wood and game from the forest, although the jurors were unwilling to indict them.[16] In local feuds, however, 'the fight for dominance was a violent one in which crime might be used as well as the court system'.[17]

This apparent failure by the Black Prince to prevent bloodshed and disorder was not all it seems. A degree of violence was tolerated by all orders of medieval society and served many uses. The king and the earl relied on powerful men and their retainers while peasants would call on them for protection. It has been argued that 'aggressive behaviour was common in defence of one's honour and rights' and would have been, therefore, treated sympathetically in many circumstances.[18] Although the conviction rate was probably very low, the consequences of finding a suspect guilty of felony was too severe in a society where close day-to-day bonds and contacts were made with one's neighbours.[19] An indictment was punishment in itself as it involved the taking of goods and chattels on arrest and the payment of the accused's expenses, not to mention the possibility of a dangerous and uncomfortable stay in gaol.

---

[16] CHES 25/21 m. 22, m. 29; SC 2/254/7 m. 1–6, SC 2/254/8 m. 1–3. Further accusations and indictments were made regarding Robert's servants, CHES 25/22 m. 8, m. 10.

[17] Hanawalt, *Crime and Conflict*, pp. 49, 63.

[18] Hanawalt, *Crime and Conflict*, pp. 61, 45.

[19] *ibid.*, p. 57.

Officials, too, had to find their own expenses and widespread corruption and extortion could only be reduced to an acceptable level. Jurors were also reluctant to convict those whom they either knew or feared and the payment of substantial fines by the wealthy, along with service, could excuse many different crimes and misdemeanours. Furthermore an accusation should not be simply equated with a crime as the 'criminal law was frequently used as a weapon of social conflict'.[20]

The nature of such corruption can easily be demonstrated within the county. It is evident that not only could very serious charges be levelled against leading members of the county society but that these same people played an important role in the administration of its justice. The decentralised and ineffective judicial system, coupled with the earl's use of pardons, resulted in blatant abuses of power and the escape of many from punishment.[21] Even for those brought to justice and found guilty, there was no reason why crime should limit a future career or social advancement. The rise of a tenant at Frodsham, for instance, was not hindered by a fine of over £26 for the abduction and rape of a wife and the theft of a husband's goods.[22] Sir John Hyde, the leader of the archers from Macclesfield Hundred on the Crécy campaign, for example, was accused of taking bribes.[23]

In the 1353 trailbaston sessions Adam Mottrum, the hereditary gaoler and manorial rent-collector of Macclesfield, was accused of the largest number of offences within the county. These ranged from the illegal taking of excessive money from prisoners, making profit from Black Death heriots, collusion with criminals, as well as theft and abduction.[24] In 1355 he was accused of wearing armour in court before Robert Legh, the steward of the manor when Robert called him a liar after he had released a prisoner. Although Adam was pursued by Robert, Robert's son, William Dounes, John Coton, John Fitton of Gawsworth and John Norlegh with knives and

---

[20] Hanawalt, *Crime and Conflict*, p. 273. The indictment was a 'particularly effective method of harassing an opponent', Powell, *Kingship, Law and Society*, p. 95.

[21] P. H. W. Booth, 'Calendar of the Cheshire Trailbaston Proceedings 1353', *Cheshire History*, 11 (1983), pp. 39–51, *Cheshire History*, 13 (1984), pp. 22–8.

[22] J. P. Dodd, 'The Growth of a Middle Class in Frodsham Manor, 1300–60', *Journal of Chester Arch. Soc.*, 64 (1981), pp. 38–9.

[23] Booth, 'Calendar of Trailbaston Proceedings', pp. 43–5.

[24] *ibid.*, pp. 27–8; *B.P.R., iii*, pp. 335, 338.

swords drawn, he was later pardoned by the Black Prince.[25] The prince's protection was insufficient for an adversary of Adam, forester Robert Foxwist, who had appealed to the earl in 1352 following threats made to him. Robert was fined for an unlicensed alienation and forfeited his lands on killing William Asthull, who had been sent to arrest him.[26] In the borough, the mayor and local officials were accused at the start of Richard II's reign of conspiring to get all suits, except for those involving land, impleaded within the mayor's own court so that the revenues might be transferred to the common chest. The earl lost out further when they created burgesses from various counties in order to withdraw and withhold his toll. When a leading burgess, Roger Bedulf, was accused of murder in 1379 the catchpoll arrested his goods which were then, by agreement of the mayor and others, received by a butcher, who was his brother, and others unknown, before they and Roger were taken from the vill.[27]

Another hereditary official, John Davenport, the master serjeant of the peace of the Hundred, was accused of a number of extortions. When Robert Legh, the younger, had tried to arrest Peter Legh and others in 1375, John was accused of not only refusing to help in the arrest but with assisting Peter to lead them to safety.[28] In addition John took a party of 46 men to Yorkshire in the 1360s where they entered the house of Elizabeth, widow of Nicholas Worteley, assaulted her servants, tore her deeds, and carried away her goods, so that she fled in terror.[29] In 1378 John Davenport, John Grene and Philip Sondebache – serjeants of the peace of the Hundred – together with William Wylot, Hugh Dounes, William Bradley of Lostock and Robert Mascy were accused of feloniously killing a man at Macclesfield.[30] The under-serjeants of the peace were themselves accused of extortionate behaviour at markets and fairs at Macclesfield, Stockport and elsewhere. They were involved, for instance, in a serious affray at Macclesfield fair in 1372.

Crime was, therefore, an endemic feature of medieval as of modern

---

[25] This presumably took place in the Macclesfield eyre, 'County Court Indictment Roll', p. 30; B.P.R., iii, pp. 258, 347.
[26] Those responsible may have included Adam Mottrum, B.P.R., iii, pp. 15, 145 and 317, and Ch.Acc. (2), pp. 143–4.
[27] County court, CHES 25/8 m. 5.
[28] 'County Court Indictment Roll', pp. 838–40.
[29] C.P.R., 1364–7, p. 140.
[30] CHES 25/8 m. 1d.; for an earlier offence, see CHES 25/20 m. 34d.

society. It is not clear, though, how far the behaviour outlined above affected individual peasants or their communities. Several studies, have highlighted the role played by the 'grasping and aggressive' wealthier members of village society in promoting social conflict.[31] Closely related to this has been the debate about whether or not the rise in disorder in the post-Black Death period was a result of conflict between newcomers and established families.[32] Hanawalt's work has demonstrated that peasants were most likely to victimise those of a similar or slightly higher status to themselves, while those at the bottom or margins of society could be easily controlled or punished through court rather than criminal action.[33]

One final possible factor that might have increased the incidence of crime in the Macclesfield area was the nature of the landscape and the operation of forest law. Such marginal and border areas were often attractive both for those who wished to commit crimes such as poaching and robbery, and for outlaws seeking a secure refuge. In 1352, for example, three brothers indicted for murder in the West Riding of Yorkshire fled to Cheshire, while in 1354 other criminals were reported to have successfully found hiding-places in the woods around Chester.[34] The story of Robin Hood may not have been entirely relevant to fourteenth century England but it was well-known and ingrained within popular culture. The east Cheshire upland landscape of woodland, heath and moorland may have given more opportunity for crime and encouraged the carrying of weapons for protection. Furthermore, as a pastoral area sharing borders with two other counties, it could have been attractive to thieves as animals were frequently pastured and driven over a wide area.

Before we use the courts to examine local crime and conflict in detail it is necessary to make a few important points. When referring to crime we are primarily concerned with theft of goods. Larceny, burglary and robbery were capital felonies, provided the goods involved were valued at one shilling or more. In Cheshire, however, a fine rather than hanging was often acceptable to the judges. If

---

[31] Razi, *Medieval Parish*, p. 77; Page, *Estates of Crowland Abbey*, p. 140.
[32] See, for example, J. A. Raftis, 'Changes in an English Village after the Black Death', *Medieval Studies* 29 (1967), p. 164; for a contrary view see Razi, *Medieval Parish*, pp. 122–4.
[33] Hanawalt, *Crime and Conflict*, pp. 158–68.
[34] *B.P.R., iii*, pp. 52, 161.

the value of the property was below one shilling then minor punishments could be applied, and if the victim was primarily determined to recover the goods then it was probably more practical to bring suits over the detention of chattels in the local courts. Petty larceny is, therefore, under-represented in the records, and an indictment was probably a last resort. It was not unusual for those so accused to be referred to as 'common' takers or thieves on their first recorded offence. Likewise, Macclesfield criminals might be convicted for 'many felonies'.

I shall deal first with crimes such as affrays and hues, which were not felonies and were generally, therefore, dealt with and punished with fines in the local courts. More serious cases, often involving bloodshed, led to indictments, although some of the perpetrators were later fined in the same way.

I.   AFFRAYS

A significant proportion of the business of the local courts was taken up with the recording of fines and amercements for affrays and assaults.[35] These could involve an assault with or without violence, a dispute leading to the drawing of weapons, or an outright brawl between two or more people. All of them, in response, might conclude with the raising of the hue and cry. The vast majority, more than four-fifths, did not involve the spilling of blood, woundings or serious injury and around two-thirds of the total were committed within the borough.

Before the the early 1360s it was customary for both the halmote and portmote courts to list offences under the general term 'hue', with no description of the time, place, background or people involved. After this time more detailed information was usually given, including the names of both parties, the date and location, with most being described as either assaults or affrays. Hues were only subsequently referred to when raised unjustly or in the course of an assault. More serious cases led to indictment at the yearly

[35] 'affraia pacis.' As they constituted nearly 90 per cent of all court presentments their financial nature, along with the probable ease of their concealment, should not be underestimated. The brevity of this type of presentment, however, disguises a wide variety of motives and actions, and no distinction has been made between the affray and the crime described as 'insultum fecit', which involved similar levels of violence.

eyre although there was some overlap in the recording of offences between the courts.

The frequency of presentment for affray was not high considering the size of the area and its population. However it is not apparent how far the halmote and portmote reflect the true extent of this type of behaviour as, in some years, a significant number of indictments were made in the eyre. I shall, therefore, use the fines made in the two courts for statistical analysis and refer to the eyre indictments for further evidence of individuals.

In the halmote there was on average one affray prosecuted for which a fine was levied every six weeks. The frequency was lowest in the early 1350s, and it rose to a peak in the mid to later 1360s, when there was about one a month. In the borough there was approximately one affray presented every three weeks. As with the manor, the frequency increased during the 1360s and then remained consistently high for the rest of the century before rising again towards its close. During the 1390s there was approximately one recorded every two and a half weeks. It is not clear how far affrays recorded in the local courts represent the true level of violent conflict, since at least twelve of them were reported as concealed, six in the borough and seven in the manor townships. The indictments of the yearly eyre do not provide significant additional numbers of these offences, although those recorded there can sometimes give more details of what actually happened.[36]

Affrays did not occur evenly throughout the week or year. Sunday – 'the day of murder in medieval society' – was by far the most frequent day in both areas, followed by Monday and Thursday in the borough and Thursday and Tuesday in the manor.[37] (Table 24).

[36] Around two every three weeks in 1394/5, SC 2/254/12–15, SC 2/255/1–2. Although it was customary for the townships to present an affray at the next court, this was not always the case. In 1384, for instance, the borough was fined 12d. after it failed to report Thomas Grene's wounding of Richard Henneschagh, with a sword on his head, after Easter (Chester City Record Office, Earwaker MSS CR 63/2/339 rot. 1, m. 2). However, Alan Wrught's assault of Adam Haregreve with a sword in Bollington, in May 1391, was not presented in the halmote until the following February – the accounting year following (SC 2/254/13 m. 4d).

[37] B. Hanawalt, 'Violent Death in Fourteenth and Early Fifteenth Century England', *Journal of Comparative Studies in Society and History*, 18 (1976), p. 305. The accuracy of the Macclesfield rolls in recording the precise day is questionable, as the day given in the courts was occasionally different to that given in the indictment.

Sunday was the medieval community's one regular day of leisure and, although no time of day was recorded in the Macclesfield courts, those in other areas have demonstrated that twilight and night were the hours when unlawful killing was most likely to occur. Assaults and violent disputes, like homicides, were seasonal and affected by the movement of people such as at harvest time. Patterns of work and leisure were also important. In general, the greatest number of affrays in Macclesfield manor and borough took place in May. In the borough significant numbers also occurred during August, September, March and June. Macclesfield borough, in this respect, has similarities to the general pattern found within rural society, where a high frequency of such crimes occurred during the autumn months and the lowest during the winter.[38] Unfortunately precise locations are not given in the rolls and, except for a handful of cases said to have taken place inside a house, those in the borough were usually described as having taken place in one of the three main streets, the representatives of which made the presentments. Wallgate recorded the highest number, followed by Jordangate and Chestergate. In the manor they were concentrated in the population centres of Sutton and Bollington, and there were also a significant number in the north-east.

There was some difference in the way that affrays and hues both affected, and were dealt with, by the two jurisdictions. Although there was a tendency for fines to diminish as the century progressed, particularly after the mid-1370s, the assessed amount was consistently lower in the portmote. Although 6d. was the most frequent fine relating to the unlawful raising of the hue in both courts, 3d. was imposed in a third of all borough affrays compared with only 4 per cent of those in the manor. Likewise, more than double the number of manor hues incurred a fine of 1s. 0d. This probably reflects the greater disruption that an unnecessary or malicious hue and cry would have caused in a rural township. A similar picture emerges with affrays, where 3d. was once again most frequently imposed as a fine in the portmote, whereas 1s. 0d. occurs in only 18 per cent of cases, compared with 30 per cent in the halmote. The drawing of a knife, a not uncommon event in the borough, usually led to a fine of 3d. in the last quarter of the century whereas in the manor 3d., 6d. or even 1s. 0d. could be levied.

[38] Homicide numbers rose in rural areas between March and September, peaking in the latter month, while London showed little variation, Hanawalt, *Crime and Conflict*, p. 99.

Table 24 *The Seasonal Nature of Hues and Affrays, c.1349–96*
(Fines in the Halmote and Portmote Courts)

Month	Manor	Borough
January	7	18
February	17	19
March	6	39
April	12	11
May	22	47
June	16	33
July	12	26
August	12	41
September	18	39
October	11	16
November	14	21
December	7	19

Day	Manor	Borough
Sunday	51	124
Monday	17	73
Tuesday	21	31
Wednesday	13	19
Thursday	27	45
Friday	5	2
Saturday	13	24

SC 2/252/2–15, SC 2/253/1–12, SC 2/254/1–15,
SC 2/255/1–2;
Chester City Record Office, Earwaker MSS
CR 63/2/338–339.

The abbreviated and formulaic court-roll entry reveals little about a dispute's origin. Many undoubtedly began on the spur of the moment, and in the course of people's everyday lives, although the level of violence that was characteristic of some medieval disputes often suggests a more deep-rooted and bitter conflict. In Bollington, for example, an incident between two women was sparked by the throwing of a stone at a trespassing pig and its subsequent unjust impounding, while in the borough a visiting man from Etchels threw a stone at a cat that was sitting in a window; he missed and hit a woman, injuring her.[39] In 1355 a personal lawsuit between Roger Skot and Richard Fletcher later escalated into a brawl after Roger defaulted in an agreement to sell Richard turves. In the suit Roger was amerced 3d. with 2d. damages, while in the affray which followed fines of 1s. 0d. with 1s. 0d. damages for Roger, and 1s. 0d. with 6d. damages for Richard were imposed. Robert Fox 'of Blythe', who only appears in the portmote records between March and May 1384, had a dispute with Robert Hasty, a burgess and mercer. A few weeks after Hasty had drawn his knife in an affray, they were both amerced after failing in civil actions for trespass against each other.[40]

Table 25   *Weapons Mentioned in Portmote Affrays*

Weapon	No. Drawn	No. Hit	No. Bl.	No. Death	Total
Sticks	19	60	51		135
Knives	40	6	18	3	65
Fists / Hands	1	58	6		64
Stones		7	5		11
Swords	4		6	1	10
Bows		5	3		8
Pole-axes		2	2		4
Pikels	1		1		2
Arrows (Bow-shot)		1	1		2
Stools		1	1		2

The following were all referred to once: spade; small hammer; hoe; cambrel; harp; trough; pair of tongs; pair of iron 'lignarum'; 'pykreneld'; 'tribula'; 'bateldour'; 'carde'; 'yevele'; and 'vuginibus sine baculo'.

Long-standing conflict is shown in at least eight disputes which led to two or more affrays and involved both revenge attacks and repeated assaults. On consecutive days in January 1390, for instance, Ellen Slak struck Ellen Hobler in Chestergate and drew blood: on

[39] SC 2/255/1 m. 7d.; SC 2/254/11 m. 9.
[40] Roger was thus 1s. 11d. worse off and Richard 4d.; at the next two courts Roger was amerced 1s. 3d. for defaulting and then losing a civil action brought by another man over an 8s. 0d. debt (SC 2/252/7 m. 3. Fox, Chester City Record Office, Earwaker MSS CR 63/2/339 rot. 1, m. 1d.–2).

a Saturday she struck her with her fist and threw her to the ground, and on the following day Hobler hit her with a stick. Likewise, Alice, widow of Roger Balleson, twice assaulted Maud Glover in Easter week 1384, and wounded her once. In May 1393 outsider John Plesyngton had the hue unjustly raised against him and on the following day was assaulted by a travelling female harpist, Margaret Symphaner, who struck him with her instrument. As these were his only appearances it is likely that they were connected.[41]

Table 26 *Weapons Mentioned in Halmote Affrays*

Weapon	No. Drawn	No. Hit	No. Bl.	No. Death	Total
Sticks	4	23	14		42
Knives	15	4	4		23
Bows	4	5	7		16
Arrows (Bow-shot)		9	4		13
Swords	3	1	6		10
Fists / Hands		4	1		5
Stones		2	1		3
Pole-axes			2		2
Pikels	1	1			2
Turf Spades		1	1		2

The following were all referred to once: axe; working hook; 'clatro'; 'goode'; and 'formulam'.
Abbreviations
No.: the number of times they were drawn, used to hit with, drew blood (Bl.) and death.
SC 2/252/2–15, SC 2/253/1–12, SC 2/254/1–15, SC 2/255/1–2;
Chester City Record Office, Earwaker MSS CR 63/2/338–339.

Although a person's hands and fists – which were used to hit, push or scratch – were most frequently mentioned in both courts, sticks or staves were the most common weapon.[42] The widespread carrying of arms might have been for personal protection, as well as for criminal activity, and knives and baslards were certainly carried by many outsiders travelling through or to Macclesfield, as

[41] SC 2/254/11 m. 7d–8; Chester City Record Office, Earwaker MSS CR 63/2/339 rot. 1, m. 2, rot. 2, m. 2.
[42] Hanawalt found that cutting implements were most frequently used in Northamptonshire, Oxford and London, 'Violent Death', pp. 10–11.

well as by a few established tenants and burgesses. (Table 26). The fear of ambush or robbery, for instance, was probably more prevalent when travelling through an upland forest landscape. Swords were used by those of category two status (Nicholas Gardener, Robert son of John Holyncete and John Leversegge) with the remainder probably being carried by outsiders, including at least three men from Wales. In addition, arms might also be carried by the servants and retainers of local families, particularly those embroiled in bitter disputes, and, at times, by those in military service. The servants of Robert, son of Robert Legh, for example, were accused in 1389/90 of abducting a woman, hunting, cutting wood and probably of carrying arms.[43]

The carrying of longbows was far more common in the manor. Although it was illegal to travel with their strings attached they were occasionally fired; more frequently, though, they were used as sticks for hitting people.[44] They were carried by sons, servants, burgesses (John Falyngbrom, William Pemberton and Stephen Blagge), outsiders, those of indeterminate status but not, it seems, by any established tenants. In 1385/6 a public proclamation made in the Macclesfield eyre forbidding the carrying of swords, sticks and other weapons in the borough led to the arrest of five men.[45]

As far as actual bloodshed and woundings were concerned, the most dangerous weapon was the stick. These were occasionally described as cudgels and one was said to have been spiked.[46] They caused, for example, blood to flow violently and the breaking of an arm, although the blows were rarely fatal. Bows were used similarly and those wielding them were held responsible for breaking a head, a hand and drawing blood. If they were the rarest instrument of death in medieval England, it was not uncommon for them to be carried in the vicinity of Macclesfield forest and occasionally fired; most arrows, though, either missed their target or caused

[43] CHES 25/22 m. 8, m. 10, CHES 25/8 m. 26d. One servant of Robert Legh (the younger ?) killed tenant Richard Hurtheven at Bollington in 1381, CHES 25/21 m. 9.

[44] By law bows could only be carried on the highway with their cords detached, *B.P.R., iii*, p. 15.

[45] These included William Kenworthey, who was also accused of seizing, as escapes, the animals of six tenants in Coombs, and John Strynger, of Adlington (CHES 25/21 m. 23).

[46] 'tarynga baculi', SC 2/254/11 m. 6.

non-fatal injuries. Richard Mere, for instance, was amerced only 4*d*. for firing an arrow at Roger Byran's wife at Bollington in 1383, while Roger was amerced 10*d*. for drawing blood after retaliating with a stick. In another incident in 1382, John son of William Honford was fined 1*s*. 0*d*. for striking and wounding William Grene in the leg at Kettleshulme.[47]

Bows were more a feature of premeditated ambush, and the spontaneity of many affrays made them unsuitable for use. Henry son of William Wynge (chaplain) of Macclesfield, for instance, fired at wealthy tenants John Rossyndale, knight, and Thomas son of Roger Mulnere at Sutton in 1392. In the borough outsiders John and Thomas Caws both struck William Fourbour of Knutsford, with an arrow, in 1395 and John Jayler fired at two further outsiders, who both returned fire, in Chestergate in 1390.[48]

Swords were usually employed by outsiders and in most instances they were merely drawn. Actual sword-fights were rare although one occurred in Jordangate in 1394 after the aforementioned Henry Wynge, chaplain, assaulted John Saillour. In the manor, Robert Holand wounded another outsider at 'le Coldoke' in Disley, in 1381. More frequently they were used in self-defence or to threaten. In 1393, for instance, Robert Holyncete placed his sword over Richard Sherd's leg in an incident that also involved Richard's son, John (see below).[49]

If we now relate the number of affrays to the status of the parties we find further differences between the rural and urban communities. In the borough only around 40 per cent of those involved were actual male burgesses, whereas between a third and a half were outsiders. In the manor just over a third of those involved were tenants, while just under a third were probably residents, which left the proportion of possible outsiders in the region of 25 to 30 per cent. As the number of outsiders identified in the rolls is so small – only between 5 and 10 per cent in both areas – it is likely that a large proportion of those of unknown origin were labourers,

---

[47] SC 2/254/4 m. 5; SC 2/254/3 m. 4.

[48] SC 2/254/13 m. 5d., SC 2/254/15 m. 6d., SC 2/255/1 m. 6.

[49] SC 2/254/3 m. 3; SC 2/254/15 m. 4, m. 6. In the indictment Wynge's assault was said to have taken place on a Friday rather than on Wednesday, and John Saillour was described as dangerously ill as a result of an injury to his right fore-arm, CHES 25/22 m. 29.

servants, temporary residents or those from the surrounding hinterland; a smaller number would have been travellers or tradesmen. In terms of actual numbers both rural and urban affrays were concentrated amongst those of a lower or indeterminate status.[50] Only a quarter of Macclesfield tenants were actually involved in affrays with only a fifth being the guilty party. Some of the more serious cases involved a handful of well-armed people originating from across a wide area: these, as has already been suggested, may have involved retainers and have been related to politically motivated conflicts within the county.

In the summer of 1391 Robert Cotrell of Derbyshire, with others, ambushed Ralph Turnour at night-time in Marple and left him wounded. In November of the same year three outsiders made two attempts to harm John Hyde at Whaley; firstly by wounding him on the head with a knife after lying in wait, and, on the following night, by ambushing him again and ill-treating him as they attempted to break into his house. Other incidents in the manor involved attacks by men from both Derbyshire and Staffordshire. In the borough knives were carried and sometimes drawn by people such as John Potter of Burwardsley, in west Cheshire, who assaulted a burgess tradesman on a Monday in May 1392. In all these cases the cause of the affray is unknown although it was more frequent for an outsider to assault another outsider than a local resident.[51]

One of the most serious incidents of the period occurred at the Barnaby fair on a Saturday in June 1372. Although the portmote records the fines imposed on some people, the indictments in both the eyre and the county court give further information and suggest a more complex and prolonged event.[52] It appears initially to have involved up to a dozen men and may have started when John Echeles attacked Roger Hurdesfeld and his wife, John Yrish, and Agnes Stele with a stick. Robert Dounes (a customary tenant who was required to provide a stall for the collection of toll) was then attacked with a sword and sticks by three men including Philip Sondebache and John Grene, under-serjeants of the peace. These,

---

[50] In London up to a quarter of homicides involved servants, Hanawalt, *Crime and Conflict*, p. 136.

[51] SC 2/254/13 mm. 4–4d., m. 8, SC 2/254/9 m. 4, SC 2/254/15 m. 3, SC 2/255/2 m. 4, SC 2/255/1 m. 8d.

[52] 'County Court Indictment Roll', p. 662; SC 2/253/7 m. 3; CHES 25/2c m. 65–67.

Bosley) in 1367 (he was fined for another affray at the same court), and William Oldefeld (category three, Sutton) in 1379.[67]

William Taillour of Hockerley in Whaley, an undertenant, was involved in at least six instances of affray between 1392 and 1396. He was assaulted by a man from Mobberley, who drew his knife on him, and by Benedict Turnour (probably of Marple) who struck him with a stick. In return he assaulted Richard Tyllesone (category three, Rainow) and John Clerk (servant of Thomas Falle) with a stick, undertenant William Hode of Disley, and drew his knife upon William Dande (unidentified).[68]

More than half of all men (around 54 per cent) identified as resident in the borough during this period were presented as the instigators of affrays. This was particularly the case amongst the more active burgesses (at around 58 per cent) although the leading members of the community appeared less frequently. If we take the examples of those serving as mayor, Richard Rowe was assaulted in 1371/2 by (office-holder) Roger Brounhull, while in execution of his office, and by Roger Stoke. Roger Bedulf, a borough reeve, was also fined for unjustly raising the hue against Rowe in 1376.[69] Before he came mayor, Stephen Rowe assaulted at least five people between 1391 and 1396.[70]

Young William Slegh was fined 1s. 0d. for an affray in 1362, his first court appearance. In 1388 Griffith the Welshman raised a stick to strike William in Rainow; in this, he was aided by fellow-burgess, Reginald Cook, who struck Griffith with a stick.[71] William's brother, Richard Slegh, was not involved in any affrays, but paid a fine of

---

[67] He was also indicted for pasturing sixteen cattle in Sutton common in 1380, and was fined 2s. 0d. for a rescue over an unnamed forester in 1362 (SC 2/252/13 m. 4, SC 2/253/2 m. 3d., SC 2/254/1 m. 10d., m. 12).

[68] SC 2/254/14 m. 4d., m. 5d., SC 2/254/15 m. 4, SC 2/255/1 mm. 8–8d., SC 2/255/2 m. 4.

[69] SC 2/253/6 m. 5, m. 7, SC 2/253/9 m. 5. Bedulf was a custodian of ale in 1369/70, 1370/1 and 1372/3, bread and meat in 1377/8 and reeve in 1375/6, SC 2/253/4 m. 3d., SC 2/253/5 m. 8, SC 2/253/7 m. 2, SC 2/253/12 m. 2 SC 2/253/9 m. 5. See Brounhull's and Stoke's biographies in Appendix One.

[70] These were: Robert Byran, the fellow executor of Richard Rowe's will, John Hurdesfeld, Richard Burelles, Joyce Brounhull, Henry Haynesone, at whom he threw a knife, and Geoffrey Ludlow. Stephen was catchpoll in 1395/6, custodian of ale in 1400/1, and served as a portmote juror during this time (SC 2/254/13 m. 6d., m. 8, SC 2/254/15 mm. 5–6, SC 2/255/1 m. 6, SC 2/255/2 mm. 5–6, SC 2/255/4 m. 5.

[71] SC 2/252/13 m. 6d., SC 2/253/7 m. 3; SC 2/254/9 m. 5.

Table 27   *The Hues and Affrays of Thomas son of William Spycer, c.1369–96*

Year	Incid.	Other Person	Bl	F.	Weapon(s)	Location
1361	Hue			3d.		Jordangate
	Aff.		bl	6d.		Jordangate
1363	Aff.		bl	6d.		Hurdsfield
1370	Ass.	Ellen Bromyleghs	bl	6d.	fists	*borough*
	Vict.	John Cartwright				Tytherington
1371	Aff.	Margery Deye		3d.		*borough*
	Vict.	Robert Coleman (Welshman)			drew knife	Wallgate
1372/3	Vict.	Thomas Rousthorn chaplain				*borough*
	Vict.	Richard Stele				*borough*
1382	Ass.	Isabel w. Will. Roper		6d.	hands ov. back	*borough*
1384	Vict.	John Wodehous				*borough*
	Vict.	Robert Hullesone				*borough*
	Ass.	Thomas Cokshutte of Swettenham		3d.	drew knife	*borough*
1387	Vict.	Reginald Cook	bl.		cambrel	Chestergate
1389	Vict.	Richard Wryght			baslard	Wallgate
1390	Ass.	Philip Forde		6d.	stick ov. arm	Wallgate
1394	Vict.	John Leversegge			threw to ground struck with stick	Wallgate
1395	Ass.	Richard Turnour, wright		6d.		Chestergate

Abbreviations

Incid.: Incident (Ass. - Assaulted; Vict. - Victim; Aff.-Affray);
Bl.: drew blood; F.: Fine.
SC 2/252/13 mm. 5–6, SC 2/252/15 m. 3d., SC 2/253/4 m. 2, m. 3d.,
SC 2/253/5 m. 8d., SC 2/253/7 m. 3, SC 2/253/8 m. 5, SC 2/254/4 m. 6,
SC 2/254/9 m. 6d., SC 2/254/10 m. 9, SC 2/254/12 m. 9, SC 2/255/1 m. 5,
SC 2/255/2 m. 5d.; Chester City Record Office, Earwaker MSS CR 63/2/339
rot. 1.

3*d.* in 1370 for unjustly presenting a hue between a man and his wife.[72]

Those involved in the largest number of offences were burgesses such as the fuller, William Bullynche, and the baker, Thomas Spycer.[73] William was involved in more than ten incidents in and around the borough.[74] In total, he was fined 5*s.* 1*d.* for hues and affrays and another 3*d.* for one that was falsely presented. The involvement of Thomas Spycer in hues and affrays during the reigns of Edward and Richard, led to amercements of more than 3*s.* 9*d.*[75] In contrast, the butcher John Oldefeld was the victim of assaults on at least five different occasions.[76]

William Lounesdale appeared in the portmote in connection with several serious acts of violence and affray in the 1380s. In December 1384, in an incident which may have intended to harm or intimidate him, Ranulph Fletcher hit Lounesdale on his fingers with a stick, and drew blood. In May 1385 this developed further when he was attacked by Ranulph and three other men, including Thomas the servant of Alan Pierson, who together used two bows, a knife and

[72] SC 2/252/12 m. 3d., SC 2/253/4 m. 3d.

[73] See the biographies of Bullynche and Leversegge in Appendix One.

[74] These took place between 1357 and 1372. In the borough these were against his son, resident Hugh Pulton, when he drew his knife, burgess William Stubbes and William Somerbache; and in Hurdsfield he made an affray against Henry Wode and unjustly raised the hue on another occasion. He was wounded by Roger Barker, with a knife, and by John Barker, with a stick, in the borough between 1378 and 1381. He also unjustly raised the hue in Hurdsfield in 1357 (SC 2/252/9 m. 5, SC 2/252/12 m. 3, SC 2/252/13 m. 5, SC 2/253/1 m. 4, SC 2/253/2 m. 4, SC 2/253/4 m. 1, m. 3d., SC 2/253/7 m. 2, SC 2/253/12 m. 2d., SC 2/254/3 m. 5).

[75] See Table 27. His assault upon Ellen Bromyleghs was shortly before her indictment for being a nuisance, as a scold, to Thomas' wife, SC 2/253/4 m. 3d., SC 2/253/5 m. 3. John Wodehous failed to appear against him, in a civil action of trespass, at the same time as Wodehous's amercement for affray (Chester City Record Office, Earwaker MSS CR 63/2/339 rot. 1, m. 1d). Spycer paid a further 2*s.* 0*d.* for breaches of the assize of bread and for his failure to either prosecute suits or appear in court.

[76] Those who assaulted him, included: Amice Fletcher, his future wife, in 1367; John Fecheler (resident), who drew a knife on him in 1370; burgess William Hayfeld, in 1371; burgess John Sydsworth, who struck him with a stick in 1383; and burgess Richard Spencer, in 1396. SC 2/253/3 m. 9d., SC 2/253/5 m. 8d., SC 2/253/6 m. 5d., SC 2/254/4 m. 7d., SC 2/255/2 m. 6. He also had the hue unlawfully raised against him in 1387, SC 2/254/8 m. 1d.

a baslard to injure him. In April 1388 burgess John Walkedene struck him on the head with a stick, and once again blood was drawn. In Whit week of the same year he was at the centre of an affray that involved five people in Wallgate, who fought with sticks while one threw a knife at him. In March the following year six people again fought with sticks in Wallgate, and this time William was on the same side as John Walkedene in attacking, along with two others, his former adversary Thomas son of John Pierson. It is worth noting that William was serving as a borough official at the turn of the century.[77]

As in the manor several people of a similar status became embroiled in a number of related and overlapping disputes, several of whom were either cobblers or leather workers. Between them Robert Maykyn and Denise, his wife, were involved in at least nine affrays as well as being indicted for a number of small larcenies.[78] Robert made an affray upon Roger Hurdesfeld in 1372, drew his knife on John Gumbeltoth in 1377, and assaulted John Ferour of Macclesfield with a stick in 1389, who struck back and stabbed him with a knife. Further blood was spilled in 1385 when Thomas Sherd hit Robert with a stick, he retaliated, and the servant of burgess William Lynster, a cobbler, also struck Robert again with a stick.[79]

On Michaelmas day 1370, which was a Sunday, Richard Stele attacked John Wosewale with a pair of tongs and Maud his wife responded by wounding Richard and drawing blood. In the same incident, which took place in Wallgate, John Jolion attacked John Wosewall, who had assaulted him a few months earlier, and John Wosewall himself struck John Gumbeltoth. Shortly afterwards John Wosewale failed to prosecute a plea of debt against both Richard Stele, and John Jolion, who was a leather craftsman. In 1375 John Wosewale assaulted burgess William Snowball, another

---

[77] SC 2/254/6 mm. 5–5d., SC 2/254/8 m. 1d., SC 2/254/10 m. 9. He was a custodian of bread and meat in 1400, SC 2/255/4 m. 5.

[78] Robert's indictments were for taking a saddle from the house of Nicholas Upton in 1384, and for entering a barn, at night-time, between 1391 and 1393, to take oats, two capons, and woollen cloth and clothes worth 3s. 4d. Denise was also indicted for taking a cord rope, worth 2d., and for being a scold (SC 2/254/13 m. 6d., CHES 25/21 m. 24, m. 32, CHES 25/22 m. 5, m. 40).

[79] SC 2/253/3 m. 9, SC 2/253/6 m. 5d., m. 7, SC 2/253/10 m. 5d., SC 2/254/6 m. 5d., SC 2/254/8 mm. 1–1d., SC 2/254/9 m. 6, SC 2/254/10 m. 8, SC 2/254/11 m. 8, SC 2/254/13 m. 8d.

leather craftsman, and Hugh Barker, servant of cobbler, William Lynster, in Hurdsfield. John's wife, Maud, also assaulted Richard Stele in a separate affray.[80]

Those referred to as chaplains might include men from quite a wide range of the social spectrum. They were, as Hanawalt asserts, 'criminous out of proportion to their numbers'.[81] The local examples come predominantly from the borough where Thomas Helegh, for instance, was responsible for three unlawful hues while a fourth was said to have taken place within his house.[82] A number of chaplains appear to have carried knives, and John Hayfeld drew his on three occasions in the borough during 1389 and 1390.[83] In Sutton John Rouland drew his knife on fellow-chaplain, Henry Cotes, on the Monday after Christmas in 1389.[84] Swords, as we have seen, were also carried by some chaplains.[85] Chaplains who made affrays against women included John Reys and William, chaplain of Wilmslow, in 1370/1.[86] An affray by John Schagh, the vicar of Prestbury, against William Snowball was initially concealed before being presented in the portmote.[87]

On a Thursday in June 1394 Thomas Worth first obstructed then

[80] SC 2/253/5 mm. 8–8d., SC 2/253/4 m. 3d., SC 2/253/12 m. 2, SC 2/253/9 mm. 3–4. Although a leather craftsman, John Jolion may be considered to have been of a higher status as he served as a juror, as an affeerer at court, as borough reeve in 1382/3 and as a custodian of ale in 1390/1 and 1394/5, SC 2/253/9 m. 5, SC 2/254/3 m. 5d., SC 2/254/4 m. 6, 2/254/12 m. 8, SC 2/255/1 m. 5. This group were also involved in other incidents.

[81] Hanawalt, *Crime and Conflict*, p. 264. There were 30 indictments against beneficed clergy in the Chester county court, 1354–77, including ten for assault and three for homicide, 'County Court Indictment Roll', pp. lxviii–ix and 324–6. For an example of homicide see CHES 25/8 m. 3d., m. 40d.

[82] SC 2/252/2 m. 3, SC 2/252/4 m. 6, SC 2/252/5 m. 4, SC 2/252/10 m. 4.

[83] Against a fellow chaplain, Margery Alcok and John Saillour, SC 2/254/10 m. 9, SC 2/254/11 mm. 7–7d. In 1392 he was amerced 12d. for the theft of a gate (or part of a gate) from Macclesfield church and was further accused of stealing two stirks from Gawsworth SC 2/254/14 m. 4.

[84] SC 2/254/11 m. 5d. Other chaplains that behaved in the same way include John Rose, SC 2/253/4 m. 3d., Geoffrey Halghes, Chester City Record Office, Earwaker MSS CR 63/2/339 rot. 2, m. 2, and John Rossyndale, SC 2/255/2 m. 6.

[85] SC 2/254/15 m. 6; see Henry Wynge p. 153 above.

[86] SC 2/253/5 mm. 8–8d.

[87] Jordangate was fined 2s. od. and John Schagh 1s. od. at consecutive courts in 1363, SC 2/252/14 m. 5d.

threw to the ground by their vestments and threatened 'horribly' two chaplains, William Bannebury and Thomas Tervyn (the latter with a knife), while in All Saints chapel in Macclesfield. Although the records do not elaborate, this was presumably a long standing dispute which was later settled by a love-day at Swettenham Green between the mayor and Worth.[88] Some clergy, such as Robert Buckard of Northenden and Stockport, had an important political position in the conflicts taking place within the Hundred.

One of the main differences at this time between the rural and urban areas was the extent of the involvement of women in crime. In the manor they participated in just over a fifth of hues and affrays compared with a third of those in the borough. They were, however, actually responsible for instigating a much smaller number of cases – about 8 per cent in the manor and around 9 per cent in the borough – which is comparable with the 11 per cent found in the manor of Wakefield.[89] In both the borough and manor of Macclesfield women were more frequently involved in raising the hue and cry, particularly in those instances when it was raised unlawfully. They were responsible for sixteen of the 25 occasions in the manor, and at least fifteen of the 27 cases in the borough. In terms of affrays females in the manor were nine times more likely to be assaulted by a male than vice versa although this is reduced to only three times more likely in the borough.[90] In the latter women were more likely to be involved in an affray with another female; in the manor, there were 2½ times more affrays involving both men and women than those involving only females.

The apparent infrequency of the involvement of women in affrays masks the significant role played by a few townswomen. In fact a quarter of all female affrays involved just ten women: Amice Fletcher, the wife of John Oldefeld, nineteen or more; Denise widow of Peter Brounhull, at least ten; Alice wife of William Botfysh, Maud Stubbes and Marion Pevere, nine; Ellen Slak, seven; Alice Taillour, six; and Denise wife of Robert Maykyn, Ellen Achard and

---

[88] CHES 25/22 m. 38.

[89] Hanawalt, *Crime and Conflict*, p. 123.

[90] The ratio of victims to indictments in different parts of the country was a constant 1:9, Hanawalt, 'The Female Felon in Fourteenth Century England', *Viator* 5 (1974), p. 254.

Alice Balleson, all five.[91] The majority of these women were seemingly independent, some were clearly poor, and six were also presented as scolds. Although the majority of women were far less likely to commit assault than were their male counterparts, these ten were clearly an exception to Hanawalt's assertion that women were 'less physically aggressive'.[92] In the borough around 80 per cent of the women who took part in such crimes can be identified as residents compared with around two thirds in the manor. The wives of established burgesses were more likely to be involved than manorial tenants although in both areas those of the highest social status were excluded.

The way in which a female assaulted was also different, as women generally used their hands, fists or nails rather than objects. When they did use weapons, as with men, sticks were used most frequently although stones or tools were often used in all-female assaults. Only twice was a knife raised against a woman, once in self-defence and once by a chaplain, and on no occasions by a woman herself.[93] When assaulting men they used only their hands, a stick or a stone. Nearly all female affrays involved individuals rather than groups.

Examples of women involved in such actions include Ellen Achard, who was the servant of burgess John Boyle in 1381/2, and was probably the daughter of Richard Achard (category four) of Sutton. In 1378 she was convicted of carrying off timber from the property of burgess John Walker and burning it. She was assaulted by several established burgess residents, between 1383 and 1394, including William Pemberton and John Hayne, tradesmen, and the wives of Stephen Blagge and William Botfysh. She also assaulted the aforementioned Denise wife of Robert Maykyn in 1390.[94]

Ellen Slak's appearances in the portmote related to affrays (in Chestergate) between 1390 and 1392. Her only assault was upon Ellen Hobler, whom she struck with her fists and threw to the ground. Hobler retaliated with a stick. She was assaulted herself by

---

[91] No widows were found to be involved in assaults or hues in some areas, P. Franklin, 'Peasant Widows' "Liberation" and Remarriage before the Black Death', *Economic History Review* 2nd ser., 39 (1986), p. 196.

[92] Hanawalt, *Crime and Conflict*, p. 123.

[93] SC 2/254/10 m. 8, SC 2/254/11 m. 7. As with men, women used knives and hatchets most often to kill, Hanawalt, *Crime and Conflict*, p. 124.

[94] SC 2/253/12 m. 2, SC 2/254/3 m. 5d., SC 2/254/4 m. 7, SC 2/254/11 m. 9, SC 2/254/10 m. 9d., SC 2/254/11 mm. 7d.–8d., SC 2/255/1 m. 5.

John Smyth junior with a stick, Isabel daughter of burgess John Souter, who threw a stone at her, and Lucy maid of burgess William Dale who wounded her with a stick.[95] Marion Pevere's involvement in theft, arguments and disputes is summarised in Table 28. Many of the women most frequently involved in affrays appear to have been independent – either widows or unmarried – or appear to have been poor. One indictment, for instance, refers to Margaret 'le Comyn Wymmon'.[96]

Table 28   *The Court Appearances of Marion Pevere*

Year	Am./F.	Court Appearances
1350/1	:	6*d.* for carrying off turves from her neighbours
1351/2	:	3*d.* for bread
		3*d.* for ale
		3*d.* for carrying off turves and burning hedges
1352/3	:	3*d.* for ale
1354/5	:	3*d.* for quarrelling with her neighbours
1355/6	:	40*d.* for divers thefts
1357/8	:	12*d.* for quarrelling (twice)
1359/60	:	12*d.* for quarrelling
1360/1	:	12*d.* for quarrelling
1363/4	:	12*d.* for an affray in Jordangate
1363/4	:	12*d.* for an affray in Jordangate (x2)
1365/6	:	6*d.* for hue in Jordangate
		12*d.* for trespass made in gaol ('pauper') Richard Janny fails to prosecute in a plea of debt
1366/7	:	6*d.* for licence to agree with Adam Swordsliper and his wife in pleas of debt and trespass
1367/8	:	3*d.* for licence to agree with Denise Brounhull in a plea of debt

[95] She also took a 'cane' from Robert son of William Dale and threw it to the ground (SC 2/254/11 mm. 7d.–8, SC 2/254/12 m. 10, SC 2/254/13 m. 6d., m. 7d).

[96] CHES 25/22 m. 60. Other examples of female violence include Christine, wife of Thomas Rowe, who hit Rose Rossyndale, with a stool, in Jordangate in 1392, SC 2/254/13 m. 8, and Alice, wife of Thomas Sherd who assaulted two women in separate affrays in 1395/6, SC 2/255/2 mm. 5–6.

Year	Am./F.	Court Appearances
1370/1	:	15d. for ale. William chaplain of Wilmslow made an affray over her in Jordangate
1371/2	:	3d. for ale. Roger Bedulf fails to prosecute in a plea of debt
1372/3	:	3d. for ale
		3d. for refusing to sell ale
		12d. for an affray over Ellen wife of William Hayfeld in Jordangate who she struck with a wheel (rota) and drew blood
1374/5	:	John Wryght indicted for breaking her finger with a stick
1375/6	:	Robert Tydrynton fails to prosecute in a plea of trespass. Amice Fletcher fails to prosecute against her and Joan her daughter
1377/8	:	Marion Chaumpayn made an affray over her and struck her with a stone
		Letitia Sclatere made an affray over her and struck her with her hands in an affray in Chestergate
Total	15s. 4d.	

Am./F. (amercement or fine).
SC 2/252/3 m. 4 – SC 2/253/12 mm. 2–2d.

The related presentment of women as scolds was largely confined to the borough. The offence was usually described in terms of a woman quarrelling with her neighbours. These were presumably the accusers, who were not themselves amerced, and were mostly the wives of other burgesses; in one instance, the mayor himself was involved. The substance of this crime may have involved accusations, slander or insults, and amercements could be higher than for affrays, with 6d. and 1s. 0d. being common.[97] The penalty could be even higher for those who were repeatedly presented and in 1358, for example, the wife of Thomas Walker was bound over on pain of half a mark to keep the peace after being presented three times.[98]

If we look at those amerced we find quite a close correlation with

---

[97] The women were described as either a 'litigatrix' or 'obiurgatrix', and the offence was usually 'litigavit cum vicinis'.

[98] SC 2/252/9 m. 7d.

the names of those presented for affrays. In the borough around two thirds were independent women (or daughters) while the wives tended to belong to middle-ranking burgess families, including office-holders, and not those amongst the burgess elite. Ellen daughter of Maud Bromyleghs, for example, was both convicted and indicted for being a scold.[99] Her daughter was assaulted twice by Denise Maykyn between 1387 and 1388, and was presented as a scold along with Amice Fletcher.[100] Of the four presentments in the halmote, two were of women from the borough while the remaining two were of Alina wife of Roger Hokerlegh (category three) from nearby Bollington.[101] Poverty appears to have been a factor in the behaviour of some of these independent townswomen. For them presentation for taking firewood, punishment for being a scold, violence and sometimes theft became a normal feature of their lives.

II. FELONIES

The most serious crimes of all that were committed in the area were felonies which resulted in indictments. An indictment itself is merely an accusation, and does not necessarily imply guilt. The proportion of those accused in this way who were hanged in the later middle ages was unusually low, and one reason for this might have been the reluctance of jurors to bring about the death of those who were neighbours or familiar to them.[102] By concentrating on the manor-forest and borough this study is dealing with a relatively small number of cases. Although it is not possible, therefore, to

[99] In 1356 and 1371, SC 2/252/7 m. 3, SC 2/253/5 m. 3. One of her accusers was the wife of burgess Thomas Spycer whose husband assaulted her prior to her indictment in 1370, SC 2/253/4 m. 3d.

[100] SC 2/254/8 m. 1d., SC 2/254/9 m. 6, SC 2/254/11 m. 9, SC 2/255/1 m. 6d.

[101] SC 2/254/5 m. 7, SC 2/254/11 m. 4. Alina and Roger were involved in a small number of affrays, SC 2/254/3 m. 3, SC 2/254/6 m. 6, while Roger was presented for over-pasturing in Bollington or neighbouring Rainow, SC 2/253/5 m. 10, SC 2/253/12 m. 1. The others were: Margery, wife of Robert Vernon, and Ellen, wife of Richard Mere, SC 2/253/9 mm. 3–4, SC 2/254/4 m. 4.

[102] Conviction rates were generally higher in England for outsiders, Hanawalt, *Crime and Conflict*, pp. 53–62. In the Chester county court half of the indictments had no outcome, 'County Court Indictment Roll', p. lxxxii.

analyse the data statistically, some conclusions regarding the nature of the crimes and those involved can be drawn.

a) Homicide

The killing of another person might come about in a variety of ways. In a society where carrying of weapons was commonplace, and violent attacks by one person on another were frequent, it is not surprising find injury, bloodshed or death resulting from such behaviour. The perpetrators of such killings were mainperned in the local court, usually at the rate of 13*s*. 4*d*., to appear at the following eyre. However, a subsequent indictment did not necessarily mean any further punishment, and two of those killed had themselves previously been accused of homicide. John Haywod of Over Alderley, for example, was a smallholder in Sutton who was killed at Macclesfield by wealthy burgess Roger Barker in 1382. Just over two years earlier John had himself been indicted for the death of Thomas Lynford (unidentified) whom he had shot with an arrow in Bosley.[103]

However, homicides were markedly different from affrays in that a higher proportion of non-residents were involved in the former, which suggests that death was not usually the consequence of a brawl or dispute between neighbours. The fact that nearly three quarters of those involved were sons, servants, outsiders or simply unidentified suggests a predominance of young or temporary residents.[104] Apart from the John Haywod case, no other indictment for homicide involved parties both of whom were tenants of either the borough or the same manor township. In the borough, for example, two of the homicides involved Welshmen while in another instance the servant of Thomas Rowe killed the servant of Richard Rowe with a spade in 1391.[105] No women were either victims or suspects during the period although one woman, Maud Stubbes, was

---

[103] SC 2/254/4 mm. 6–7; SC 2/254/2 m. 9. John Leversegge was said to have abetted Barker, and was found not guilty in the county court, CHES 25/8 m. 15.

[104] This conflicts with Hanawalt's findings, namely that 46 per cent were from the same village, *Crime and Conflict*, p. 171.

[105] Ellis of Flintshire killed David ap Gron in 1371 and Arthur Wodehale killed William Walsh in 1380 (CHES 25/20 m. 56; CHES 25/22 m. 5, m. 7; SC 2/254/1 m. 5.

severely beaten by another woman in the borough in 1400.[106] In the majority of cases only one person was accused and in fewer than a quarter was another person said to have helped the perpetrator.

It is not easy to estimate the number of violent deaths, as the majority of indictments in the Macclesfield eyre related to the wider Hundred area. In total there were more than 20 in a period of just over 40 years, half in the manor and half in the borough. As there could be as many as two or even three in a particular year, this implies an annual homicide rate of very high proportions.[107] Unlike the affrays no obvious chronological pattern emerges and they were, for the most part, spread evenly throughout the year. There were, it is true, fewer during the mid-winter, and on some days such as Tuesday, Wednesday and Friday. Where the weapon used was specified, a knife or a sword was used in seven cases, an arrow shot from a bow twice, and a stick and spade once each.

The political murder of William Joudrel, and the ability of local gentry such as the Leghs of Adlington to employ armed retainers to execute their orders, might be the reason behind a number of similar attacks or attempts to intimidate. There does appear to have been a greater degree of planning behind some homicides and the accused was sometimes said to have lain in wait for his victim in a premeditated fashion. Adam son of Adam Balle, for example, was abducted to his father's fields in Bosley in November 1368 where he was struck down by Thomas Eydale and John son of Thomas Holyncete. The violence demonstrated in other cases indicated either a clear intention to kill or at least a reckless disregard for life. In June 1391 two men, led by Reginald the Welshman of Haddon, lay

[106] Maud was the daughter of William and Margery Stubbes. William, or another of the same name, was custodian of bread and meat in 1370/1, a custodian of ale in 1372/3 and 1387/8, and catchpoll in 1377/8 (SC 2/253/5 m. 8, SC 2/253/7 m. 2, SC 2/254/9 m. 6, SC 2/253/12 m. 2). His wife, Margery, was an ale-seller who was amerced fifteen times (4s. 0d.) between 1368–1396, SC 2/253/3 m. 9 – SC 2/255/2 m. 5d. Maud was amerced as a scold, was involved in a number of affrays and thefts, and was indicted, for instance, along with her mother, for taking eight stakes from the park in 1384/5 (SC 2/254/12 m. 10, SC 2/254/15 m. 6., CHES 25/21 m. 15, CHES 25/22 m. 50). In 1401/2 she was seriously wounded by Ellen, wife of John Massy, after which she was said to be in peril of death, although she had recovered sufficiently to strike Alice Taillour with her fists a few weeks later (SC 2/255/4 m. 5d).

[107] The record of indictments is incomplete. For London Hanawalt has estimated between 5.2 and 3.6 deaths per 10,000, 'Violent Death', p. 302.

in wait for Richard Hubart at Marple, wounded him on his head with a sword and then mutilated all his limbs.[108]

Robbery may have been a either motive or a consequence of homicide in other cases. In 1379, for instance, undertenant John Dande of Disley killed John Shotelsworth the younger with an arrow shot from his bow before fleeing across the border to Derbyshire. The accused man's possessions included a colt (stag), worth 4s. od., a 'Doustagg', 3s. od., and a 'Brounstagg', 8d., which had been been taken from his victim in Disley common. Whatever the motivation, death or serious injury were frequently inevitable given the number and range of weapons available. In the spring of 1398, for instance, two men, led by James of Woodford, armed with bows, swords and daggers, murdered Thomas Roket, an undertenant, with a sword.[109]

Finally, it is clear that in some cases of homicide the judicial process was ineffectual. On a Saturday in early spring, 1353, Robert son of Hugh Holt and John son of Jordan Macclesfield, with the aid of Richard Strangeways, killed William son of John Hervy (an undertenant of Sutton) at Hurdsfield. The process whereby Robert and John were to be outlawed was started in the next eyre. It was claimed, however, that under-forester Richard Janny not only aided Robert's escape but also carried off his goods while receiving Richard Strangeways in his house. The chattels, including a cart, ended up in the hands of the accused's brother who, with his associates, were subsequently accused of theft.[110]

b) Theft

The medieval crime of theft really refers to two felonies – that of grand larceny (using the verb 'furo') and robbery. Larceny, or stealing goods and chattels, overwhelmingly predominated in Macclesfield and there were very few indictments for actual robbery. Those convicted of minor offences paid a fine at the local courts, of at least 2s. od., although many victims of petty larceny, where the value of the goods did not exceed 12d., would have sought to recover them through civil action. In one instance the low fine of 5s. od. was recorded in the portmote for house-breaking, and the theft of iron goods, at the manor of Downes.

[108] CHES 25/20 m. 36; CHES 25/22 m. 1od.
[109] SC 2/254/1 m. 3, m. 5; CHES 25/22 m. 56.
[110] SC 2/252/5 m. 6.

In the majority of cases sureties were agreed and the accused were bailed until the next eyre. It is again worth noting that an indictment does not necessarily prove guilt and those levelled by three men against Amice Fletcher, the local inhabitant most noticeably associated with crime, were withdrawn.[111]

An analysis of both the local courts and the indictments in eyre reveals no obvious seasonal pattern to the crimes, although we are dealing, in comparison to assaults and affrays, with a far smaller sample of cases. Monday was the most significant day for thefts and this was followed by Thursday, Sunday and Tuesday, with Friday again having the least.[112] If we examine the property that was supposed to have been stolen we find that livestock was most frequently recorded, with cattle, sheep and horses recorded in around 41 per cent of cases. Those involving small animals, capons, geese and piglets, amounted to another 5 per cent although this was almost certainly an underestimate, as petty larceny was far less likely to lead to an indictment; when it did those presented were often referred to as 'common thieves'.

Cloth or clothes were the next most frequently taken goods and were recorded in nearly a quarter of the cases. Of the remaining items only household goods (including timber), at around 12 per cent, made up a significant number of cases: corn, baskets and food were recorded in around 6 per cent; carts and related items in around 5 per cent; and money in around 3 per cent. The figure for money is perhaps misleading as a number of additional cases, mostly recorded in the county court, involved the taking of money by extortion and threats – often as a result of the extortionate behaviour of office-holders.[113] The description of goods being stolen or carried away suggests that actual house-breaking, whether literal

---

[111] The goods taken at Downes included a hoe and weathercock, SC 2/252/9 m. 7d.; CHES 25/20 m. 72.

[112] Hanawalt found that September to November was the most important period for larceny with May to August also being high; that burglary was often higher in the long winter nights, and that robbery was not seasonal, Hanawalt, *Crime and Conflict*, pp. 68, 85, 112. A high number of incidents appear to have taken place in Macclesfield in 1383/4.

[113] Hanawalt found that cattle were taken in two-thirds of larcenies, with cloth being the most common household goods, *Crime and Conflict*, pp. 72–3; cattle were also most frequently taken within Cheshire, 'County Court Indictment Roll', pp. xxx–xxxiii.

or involving some form of forced entry, was surprisingly rare within the manor and borough at this time.[114] Goods, it seems, were most frequently taken from outside.[115]

More than eight out of ten of those indicted were male. If we exclude one large gang – consisting of twelve men from Lancashire – we find that only around one third of the men involved can be identified as residents of the manor or borough, with another third being from the adjoining region or townships, leaving the remaining third, who cannot be identified, as being probable outsiders. The role of women was somewhat different as approximately two-thirds can be identified as resident tenants or servants. The nature of the theft also showed the now well-established differentiation between the sexes, with female crime primarily related to either petty larceny, or items that could be easily carried away, in which they usually acted alone or with the aid of one other person. Men, on the other hand, were more frequently involved in small groups or gangs and their thefts, often involving animals, were carried out over a wider area. In terms of the bringing of cases before the courts, therefore, females were more heavily represented in the local rather than eyre or county court jurisdictions.

The most serious thefts of all involved taking goods from houses. In 1383, for example, Roger son of burgess Thomas Daukyn(sone) was indicted for the burglary of William Smale's house at Sutton; he took a blanket worth 2s. 0d., while those with him took other goods. Later in the year his wife, Milicent, with others, burgled the house a second time and this time took silver worth 5s. 6d. and woollen and linen cloth worth half a mark. The goods taken from barns and out-houses, which were even more rarely entered, included grain, sheaves, hay and a blanket.[116]

The property most commonly stolen from houses was cloth and this presumably included both clothes and cloth which had been made for sale. Those with the most access to household goods were maids and servants who had the added advantage of not needing

---

[114] For the period c. 1354–96, only around four instances of burglary and seven of house-breaking have been found; they were more commonly recorded in the county as a whole, 'County Court Indictment Roll', pp. xxviii–ix.

[115] Hanawalt found that most larcenies took place in either streets or fields with fewer than 20% inside dwellings, *Crime and Conflict*, p. 76.

[116] CHES 25/21 m. 6, m. 8; SC 2/254/4 m. 7. For example, CHES 25/21 m. 32.

to resort to entry by violence or stealth. Almeria Alte, for instance, was accused of the theft of wool and cloth on leaving the service of John Walker in 1379. Agatha, servant of burgess Richard Rode, was accused and cleared of taking an ell of red cloth, from fuller William Bullynche, at Macclesfield in 1385. Although such thefts could be opportunistic others were no doubt planned and suggest that there was a market in stolen cloth. Isabel, servant of John Caton the parson of Gawsworth, for instance, was indicted in 1373 for the theft of valuable cloth in collusion with tailor Henry Peronell. Alice, wife of Richard Unwyn, was similarly indicted in 1382 for the theft of woollen and linen cloth worth 41s. 8d. at Marple which were received by John Elcok at Stockport. The act of receiving stolen goods was rarely recorded in the courts.[117]

Indictments involving theft of livestock can generally be divided into two categories: disputes between tenants, and crimes committed by those operating, usually in a gang, over a wide area. The large number of animals being pastured within the forest must have inevitably contributed to the former. Some indictments clearly had their origin in shepherding. Thomas Shepherd, for example, was indicted for taking two sheep from Rainow and over 40 from Downes. Alan Joneson was also indicted for the theft of 33 sheep from three tenants in Rainow in 1379. The impounding of animals was clearly another important issue of contention and the folds of both the lord, for animals classified as escapes or those impounded as distraints, and those of his tenants were broken, generally at night-time. As we have seen, some inter-tenant disputes spilled over into affrays.[118]

The number of casual thefts of animals is not easily quantifiable. William Shoteswall (category three), for instance, was accused of

---

[117] SC 2/254/1 m. 1d.–2d. Isabel took woollen cloth, worth 40s. 0d., table-clothes and towels, worth 13s. 4d., and other goods, worth 6s. 8d., which were taken out of the parish, CHES 25/20 m. 59, m. 61; CHES 25/21 m. 8, m. 22.

[118] Shepherd, in his first court appearance, entered just over two acres of land at Hordern in Rainow in 1355. He served as a pledge for Marion, wife of Roger Stopenhull, a few weeks later. He was indicted for felony the following year, when he was fined 40d., for bail until the eyre, and seven months later, in June 1357, William son of Roger Stopenhull entered his landholding. This was the last reference to him in the halmote records. SC 2/252/7 m. 2, SC 2/252/8 m. 5–5d., CHES 25/19 m. 13, m. 18. Jonesone, SC 2/254/2 m. 9. For the breaking of folds, see CHES 25/20 m. 62, CHES 25/21 m. 6d.

taking three heifers and one cow from William Joudrel and John Bentelegh (both category two) at Disley, and nine sheep from his son Richard at Norbury, between 1355 and 1368. When William Bouker (category four) and his son, John, were suspected in 1383 of taking a cow, worth 6s. 8d., at Disley they were described as common and notorious thieves, even though this was seemingly their first indictment. John Serle, of Disley (category three), was similarly accused of taking many animals in the township from various tenants over a period of six years as well as depasturing their corn.[119]

A number of cases hint at the patterns of movement of cattle and sheep throughout the forest, Hundred and neighbouring counties. Adam Taillour of Eccles (*or* Etchels), for instance, was accused in 1382 of stealing a cow, a heifer and two bullocks from Lancashire, while Richard Emmesson of Middleton in Lancashire was similarly indicted in 1352 for taking a foal, worth 13s. 4d., and two sheep, worth 40d., at Disley. Other outsiders, who apparently acted alone, included John son of William Bate of Staffordshire, accused of the theft of two ewes worth 3s. 0d. from a tenant at Rainow, and John son of John Pillesworth of Stockport, suspected of the theft of a mare worth 20s. 0d. at Disley, both in 1383.

Macclesfield borough was a centre for the sale of stolen animals, as the case in 1359 of a horse, worth 3s. 4d., stolen by Robert Younge at Chapel-en-le Frith, and then sold on to a burgess, shows.[120] This practice is further illustrated by the role played by two residents of the borough and their relatives, Richard son of John Fecheler and Richard son of Richard Fecheler, in the thefts committed by Thomas Clowes and Richard his son in 1383, when the animals stolen were taken to Macclesfield.[121]

---

[119] CHES 25/20, m. 11, m. 30, m. 39d., CHES 25/21 m. 1, m. 6, SC 2/254/4 m. 8d. This period culminated with John Serle's re-entry to land in the township. At this time, with two others, he was also accused of the theft of two oxen, two cows and a horse at Bramhall; the indictment, therefore, could represent a last resort by local tenants or an example of their reluctance to indict until accused of a theft elsewhere. See Serle's biography in Appendix One.

[120] CHES 25/19 m. 1, m. 24; CHES 25/21 m. 3, m. 8d, m. 14.

[121] Their combined indictments included: three cows and two heifers from Hervey Mabbeson of Sutton (by Thomas Clowes); two bullocks from Derbyshire (by Richard Fecheler); two cows from Bowdon (by Thomas with Richard's help); and one cow from another Derbyshire man

The indictments relating to the large-scale theft of livestock concerned gangs working across the region. One such associated group were based on Gawsworth and included some tenants from neighbouring Sutton (and probably elsewhere). Their thefts, which included house-breaking and the occasional stealing of cloth, extended throughout the Hundred and to Buxton in Derbyshire. They did not work within a strictly confined group as the contribution of individuals varied. Some committed theft, while others received or sold the stolen goods. Thefts of animals even took place within the group itself. One temporary member, William Standene, was received at Sutton for three weeks after he had stolen a mare, and during his stay here he took money and goods by extortion from a smallholding tenant, and on separate occasions burgled and robbed (at night-time) a tenant's house and beat his wife with a sword until she promised him 100s. 0d.[122]

One feature of this group is that they appeared to victimise certain individuals, such as Richard Eydale of Sutton, who had himself been indicted for robbery and extortion.[123] Richard Hervy was another man similarly treated, and on another occasion two men, Benedict Flynt and Richard Flynt the younger, held him, with bows and knives drawn, at the Minns (Bosley or Sutton) and threatened to kill him unless he paid them 40s. 0d. on the following Saturday, before withdrawing to Staffordshire.[124] In the most serious incident of cattle theft during the period, a gang of nine men from Lancashire,

---

(by Richard with Richard Fycheler). Richard Clowes was another person described as a notorious thief in his indictment the following year when he was accused of taking two cows, worth 16s. 0d., and 2 heifers, worth 8s. 0d., at Taxal. Thomas Clowes was a category three tenant of Sutton, while Richard, his son, was described 'de Astle' in the indictments. CHES 25/21 m. 9, m. 13.

[122] CHES 25/22 m. 11, mm. 13–14, mm. 17–19. See Table 29.

[123] The same (or different) Richard Eydale was a juror on the indictment inquest, and was a reeve of the Blessed Mary Chantry of Macclesfield, and thus possibly immune from conviction (CHES 25/22 m. 13, mm. 18–19). See p. 116 n. 102 above.

[124] CHES 25/22 m. 38. This, significantly, was presented as an affray in the halmote in which Benedict and Richard were amerced 6d. In this they were described as holding their bows over him with no mention of the threats being made, SC 2/254/15 m. 4d. Richard Flynt had earlier been indicted for firing his bow at another tenant, SC 2/254/1 m. 10d.

aided by three others, took and drove nearly 50 cattle at night-time from the demesne pasture of Blakeden in Rainow, in November 1391.[125]

Female felons were more frequently involved in small-scale thefts in which they aided, or were accompanied by, other family members. Alice, daughter of John Fouler of Woodford, for example, was helped by her two brothers and sister in carrying off goods from local townships in 1353–4.[126] The theft of small livestock and goods appears to have been more prevalent amongst women and as the value of the goods – such as capons, geese, grain measures or small garments – rarely exceeded 12d. then these would not generally lead to indictments. As maids or daughters were often referred to, then poverty was probably a significant factor in such offences. Poverty, however, was not the only motive, and Isabel, daughter of stock-keeper John Deye, was accused and found guilty of the stealing of a hoop-measure and other small items from Nicholas Upton in Macclesfield at the end of 1382.[127]

The receiving of stolen goods must have been more widespread than indicated by the legal records, and many residents may have been involved, either knowingly or unwittingly, at some stage in their lives. When Geoffrey Mascy (unidentified) paid a fine of 5s. 0d. for his theft in 1358, for example, John Holyncete paid another 1s. 6d. for having the goods in his possession. However, with the

---

[125] CHES 25/22 m. 20. Sixteen oxen, cows, steers and heifers belonging to Peter Legh; eighteen cows, steers and heifers belonging to John son of Robert Legh; two steers from Alice Longeworth; five cows and bullocks from Richard Whitlegh; and seven cows, steers and heifers from Edmund Juddesone and his son Thomas.

[126] Alice was accused of the following: with John, her brother, a theft from a house in Macclesfield; with Cecily, her sister, of taking wool and linen cloth, worth 6s. 4d. from William Walker's in Macclesfield to Woodford where, on another occasion, they were accused of stealing two measures of malted oats; and with Thomas, her brother, of taking two heifers at Hurdsfield; and leaving the parish to work in the harvest. CHES 25/19 m. 2, m. 6, m. 11.

[127] John Alcok Deye was stock-keeper of the manor. As the value of the items stolen from a burgess by Agnes daughter of William Proudeglove (unidentified), amounted to 13d., she was indicted and then convicted of theft. The goods were a kerchief, two towels, a capon and a peck-measure (CHES 25/21 m. 4).

exception of the group involved in cattle thefts, conviction for receiving was probably rare.[128]

III. INFRINGEMENTS OF FOREST LAW

Such infringements were of a rather different nature from many of the crimes already considered, as they frequently amounted to nothing more than the licensing and exploitation of forest resources by the earl of Chester's officials. Common economic and social practices included taking wood, pasturing animals and the organised hunting excursions of the gentry and clergy. Here, therefore, only the indictments for the more serious offences of poaching and hunting will be dealt with.[129] They can be divided into two basic categories: the more random taking of game or fish as a food supplement, and hunting by organised groups.[130]

The fact that the evidence for the former is rather limited should not disguise the opportunity that poaching gave to peasants to supplement a meagre diet and income. In the later thirteenth century, for instance, five men were accused of sharing the meat, hides and horns from two hinds and a stag from Macclesfield forest amongst their relatives.[131] The legal records of the second half of the fourteenth century, however, furnish only meagre evidence for such activities. In the 1357 forest eyre, a total of 92 local people from throughout Macclesfield forest were presented for failing to have their greyhound dogs lawed, and a further 29 failed to appear in connection with this. As the majority of these were dwelling within the townships around the forest periphery, such as Poynton, there is little indication that hunting dogs were common in either the manor itself or the borough.[132] Hunting with dogs was carried out by some burgesses, such as William Bullynche, who was indicted for killing a hind near

[128] SC 2/252/9 m. 7d. For another example, see SC 2/253/12 m. 10.
[129] The cutting of wood, the taking of greenwood for fodder and the use of the demesne pastures have already been dealt with in Chapter One.
[130] C. R. Young suggests that there were probably an equal number of offences for food and sport, *The Royal Forests of England* (Leicester, 1979), p. 108.
[131] *C.C.R.*, pp. 222–3.
[132] CHES 33/6 m. 37. The numbers within each township were: Sutton fourteen men, Rainow ten, Bollington at least seven, Whaley six, Disley four (including William Joudrel), Taxal three, and Kettleshulme and Hurdsfield two; in Bosley seventeen people failed to attend.

the park in 1382/3, and William Kenworthey, who with two others and a servant was suspected of killing a doe at Tegg's Nose Brook in 1377.[133]

Poachers may have frequently taken smaller animals rather than the more risky deer, and William Kenworthey was again indicted for taking three hares using nets and snares in the spring of 1384. Birds such as woodcocks and a sparrow-hawk, and a badger at Rainow on one occasion, were also taken. Fox-hunting and hare-coursing, for which Robert Harper (unidentified) and Roger Barker (a wealthy burgess) were both indicted in 1385, may well have been a pastime for those below gentry status. These two men were both described as common hunters, with Robert operating in Bosley and Gawsworth woods and Roger with dogs and greyhounds at the Minns (Sutton common).[134] In addition Robert, who seems to have hunted alone, was indicted for taking a stag in the Coombs, and on another occasion of shooting a doe with an arrow, and setting his dog on to another doe after it had been wounded with an arrow and chased from the enclosure called the Fence. Roger Herdmon, the servant of John Alcok (the manorial stock-keeper), may have worked as a guide and is described in the records as a common associate and harbourer of thieves when he was prosecuted, with others, for killing two hinds.[135]

The overwhelming majority of indictments for forest offences relate to the organised hunting parties of the gentry and clergy. This had a social as well as culinary function and appears to have had a long historical tradition.[136] In the forests of Dean and Lancashire, as elsewhere, those indicted included foresters, knights, clergy, abbots, and burgesses.[137] In the later thirteenth century those entering Macclesfield forest to hunt illegally included those from the adjacent

[133] SC 2/254/1 m. 11d. Those accompanying William Kenworthey were all burgesses: William Pemberton, a butcher, John Sydsworth, and the servant of John Clyf, SC 2/253/10 m. 1.

[134] SC 2/253/2 m. 3; CHES 33/6 m. 39; CHES 25/21 m. 25. For a brief description see Cummins, *Hound and Hawk*, pp. 110–19, 141–6.

[135] SC 2/253/10 m. 1, SC 2/254/3 m. 6, CHES 25/20 m. 14.

[136] Birrell describes it as 'one manifestation of their normal social life', J. Birrell, 'Who Poached the King's Deer? A Study in Thirteenth Century Crime' *Midland History*, 7 (1982), pp. 9–23.

[137] Hart, *Royal Forest*, p. 42; Cunliffe Shaw, *Royal Forest of Lancaster*, p. 172. Between 200 and 300 people were reported each year in the large forests of the later thirteenth century, Birrell, 'Study in Thirteenth Century Crime', pp. 11–12.

Peak forest in Derbyshire, with others such as twelve men from Buxton, and those from Staffordshire, such as the man from Alstonefield who returned with a stag. A commission set up under the sheriffs of Derbyshire and Staffordshire in 1281 to deal with the problem could not have found a lasting solution as men from those counties continued to hunt regularly in Macclesfield forest in the later fourteenth century.[138] The parties, usually consisting of between four and ten men, generally counted one or more chaplains and servants amongst their numbers. Not surprisingly those from Peak forest far outnumbered those from elsewhere, with clergy from Buxton, Fairfield, Chelmorton, Hartington, Chapel-en-le Frith, Tideswell and Wardlow all being implicated. Ecclesiastical institutions long associated with hunting were Dieulacres and Combermere abbeys, while the abbot of Chester also hunted periodically. From within Cheshire the parson of Brereton was one of the most frequent offenders as was (chaplain) Richard Redych.[139]

The actual numbers of deer reported taken by these parties – between five and ten per year – were very small indeed considering the size and area of the forest. In some of the larger forests such as Rockingham in the fifteenth century, the figure was nearer 100 a year.[140] Although it is difficult to estimate the total number of deer present within the park and forest at any one time it was unlikely to have been more than 300.[141] In 1381 eight men from Derbyshire drove 40 red deer across the county border into Peak forest, yet indictments often suggest that hunting parties were unsuccessful. The foresters' control of hunting may not have been very successful and in the the summer of 1377 indictments claimed that they had been twice assaulted: by eight men with their bows and arrows, and by eight men from Staffordshire, also with their bows, after they had killed a deer near Shutlingsloe.[142]

One explanation for the apparent fewness of the deer taken in Macclesfield forest compared with elsewhere is the conspicuous

---

[138] *C.P.R., 1272–81*, p. 475; *B.P.R., iii*, p. 407.

[139] For example, SC 2/253/9 m. 8, CHES 25/20 m. 41, m. 46, m. 57.

[140] Rockingham forest was hunted by people across the social spectrum including knights and squires, Cox, *Royal Forests*, pp. 248–9.

[141] J. Birrell, 'Deer and Deer Farming in Medieval England, *Agricultural History Review*, 40 (1992), pp. 123–4.

[142] SC 2/253/10 m. 1. Foresters both hunted themselves and were attacked by others, Birrell, 'Deer Farming'; for other examples of them being attacked with bows, see Cox, *Royal Forests*, p. 81 and *V.C.H. Stafford, II*, p. 341.

absence of local gentry and officials in most of the eyre indictments. Alexander Attecross, parker of Macclesfield, was indicted with another man for taking a doe, without licence, in the Coombs in the 1350s, while a jury in 1386 was unwilling to indict Robert son of Robert Legh of various offences, including hunting with dogs in Harrop, in William Dounes' enclosure at Shrigley and at Handley.[143]

However a county court session at the beginning of Richard II's reign might give a more accurate picture of the significance and extent of hunting by powerful local officials. William Legh, with others, was said to have hunted with dogs and greyhounds on a regular, or possibly weekly, basis between the spring and autumn of 1377, taking over 50 deer throughout the forest, at least five of which had been captured by foresters Roger Mottrum and John Sutton on Legh's orders.[144]

The examples given above enable us to draw some general conclusions about crime and conflict in the area. Although affrays were a relatively common feature of life in the two communities, the majority did not involve excessive acts of violence. They occurred in greater numbers in the borough, where the local portmote generally imposed lesser fines, than was the case in the halmote. The causes were diverse and most frequently lay in the everyday disputes relating to trespass, the taking or detaining of goods, work, services and leisure. How far the reported actions disguised more serious criminal activity, such as attempted robbery or intimidation and threats as part of ongoing disputes or rivalries, is unclear. The use of weapons – of which the sticks, knives and swords were the most common – was a more serious issue and led to a proclamation prohibiting them from being carried in the borough. The regular use of the stick in assaults is largely indicative of unplanned violence, threatening behaviour and a general desire for self-protection rather than premeditated attempts to cause serious injury or death.

The distribution of affrays closely follows the agricultural year, being concentrated within the months of spring and autumn, when social interaction was at its height. In the borough Sunday was a common day for affrays, when people were carrying out their leisure

[143] CHES 25/19 m. 10; CHES 25/21 m. 29.
[144] Over 50 red deer, including two calves, and four fallow deer (two bucks and two does – one pregnant, the other with a calf). These were taken at Blakeden, Broomycroft, Longlachemoor, Marple wood, Midgley, Oaken-clough, Saltersford, Tods Cliff and Worth (CHES 25/8 m. 3d).

pursuits, and when there may have been an influx of outsiders. Macclesfield women were more liable to commit this type of violent crime than others, although their involvement was confined to a few individuals in the borough.[145] In the manor-forest the majority of incidents involved smallholders and undertenants, although some substantial landholders (i.e. those in category two) were involved. In Macclesfield borough servants, temporary residents and those who remain simply unidentified were responsible for more than half of all affrays. Overall only one-fifth of manor tenants were fined in the local court for this offence compared with more than half of those identified as borough residents.[146] The causes of such incidents were, again, probably diverse and no definable pattern of conflict emerges from this study. It seems that a person was more likely to cause, or be the victim of, an assault with his or her neighbour or someone of a similar status. There is thus insufficient evidence from our communities to support the 'friction between the haves and have nots' noticed in some post-Black Death studies, and the picture appears closer to that described by Hilton where conflict was primarily between individuals rather than different social groups.[147]

Of the felonies, grand larceny was by far the most common and the surviving indictments suggest that the more serious cases of robbery, house-breaking or burglary were somewhat rare. The taking of small livestock and chattels whose value was below 12d. may have occurred more often and have been disguised within civil actions of detinue between neighbours and tenants. Although the age of the accused was never specified, many of those involved in crime were referred to as 'sons' or 'daughters' and this is indicative of a certain degree of youth. The indictment of maids and servants supports this, yet their actions may equally have related to poverty. Economic circumstances appear to have been important to the small group of women in the borough whose court appearances were characterised by a combination of breaking fences and hedges for fuel, petty larceny and affrays. Unlike affrays larcenies were more evenly spread throughout the year.

Geographical mobility was a factor in the more serious crimes and those leaving service agreements, for instance, were sometimes

[145] Hilton, *Small Town Society*, p. 71; Hanawalt, 'Economic Influences on Crime', pp. 261–3.

[146] The indictments make little difference in this respect.

[147] Hilton, *English Peasantry*, p. 55.

accused of taking goods with them as they moved on to townships a few miles apart. Organised gangs of horse and cattle thieves preferred areas where they were less well-known, which meant that township, Hundred and county boundaries were no obstacles to their activities.[148] Membership of the Gawsworth gang (Table 29) appears to have been flexible and changing. Wealthy landholders were able to reach over an even wider area with the aid of groups of armed retainers, and to pursue their power struggles by engaging in local internecine warfare.

We should be wary, however, of taking the court evidence at face value. Medieval records are as biased as they are incomplete, and we should be cautious of equating the pitifully low conviction rate with failure of the judicial system.[149] Although it is certainly true that a murderer might fall victim to his own violent death before being dealt with by the courts, and pardons could be effectively bought by the gentry for service and fines, the punishment of death for a felony was not sought by neighbours and friends lightly. The conviction of tenants and borough residents, therefore, was often accompanied by the words 'common' or 'many'. An accusation was in itself a punishment, and could lead to the confiscation of goods and chattels, the finding of a substantial bail, or a short spell of imprisonment. There were many options to resolve disputes and conflict between individuals and they might involve different courts and stages of the judicial system. Personal suits, threats and intimidation, and accusations which did not result in convictions might all play their part.

Closely related to this was the way in which communities used the courts to define and control behaviour. Individuals who regularly served as jurors presented those cases they deemed important and had, to a certain extent, the opportunity to punish those actions they considered most worthy of condemnation. This might account for the almost total absence of forest poaching by local residents, and the fact that offences committed by the gentry and officials had to be brought to the attention of the earl via the county court and not the local tribunals. It is possible, therefore, that the suspiciously frequent amercement of servants and those of lower status for affrays was the result of a concerted effort by jurors to control those of

---

[148] Such gangs were 'biggest danger to public order' Bellamy, *Crime and Public Order*, pp. 69–88.

[149] Powell, *Kingship, Law and Society*, pp. 91, 106.

lower status.[150] However, the evidence provided by this study lends little to support this thesis. Although some perversion of the local judicial system was likely, the presentment of those of varying status for affrays does appear to represent a real attempt to maintain public order. It is not clear, though, how far the general fine for failure to present, which was imposed upon a township (in the manor) or street (in the borough), was a factor in reducing concealment.

Finally, the fact that the majority of tenants of the manor were not involved in affrays, coupled with the comparative rarity of robbery, woundings and homicide, cautions us against exaggeration when dealing with contemporary crime and conflict. However the potential for violence may have been all too familiar to local residents, and we can only speculate as to whether a relatively small number of very serious incidents had a disproportionate influence given the size of the local population. It appears to have been common, for instance, for those travelling through Macclesfield to be armed, often with daggers or knives, and residents were soon able lay their hands on sticks and other weapons when needed. When two outsiders shot arrows at each other in one of Macclesfield's three main streets, an enduring impression of violence and danger must have been given. Its root cause must surely lie more with the nature of medieval society, and its system of patronage and service, rather than involvement of the men of east Cheshire in military service overseas.

Table 29   *Indictments of an Associated Group, c.1388–91*

	Name of Those Involved	Goods Taken	Location (Victim)
1	Th. s. Rch. Grene	...	Henbury and Pexhill
	Rch. s. Sim. Cokke	4 linen sheets, 4s.	(Rb. Addesheved)
	Bend. Annottessone	3 blankets, 6d.;	
	... Shepherd		
2	Edm. s. Rch. Symkynson	robbed 14½d.	hospital at Prestbury
			(Ad. Haregreve)
3	Edm. s. Jn. Mottrum	(cloth), 4s. &	Macclesfield
	Edm. s. Rch.	corn,	
	Symkynson,		
	Ad. s. Rch. Symkynson,		
	Th. s. Wll. Rowe, &	2 cows, 13s. 4d.	
	Edm. s. Th. Peddeley	5 calves;	

[150] *ibid.*, p. 273. See also R. C. Palmer, *English Law in the Age of the Black Death 1348–1381: A Transformation of Governance and Law* (1993).

Name of Those Involved	Goods Taken	Location (Victim)
4 Rg. s. Jn. Godemon, Jn. s. Wll. Holynsheved, Rb. Kynder o. Sutton	2 oxen, 1 cow & 1 heifer, 30s. 0d.	Buxton and led to Gawsworth & sold by Rb. Roulegh;
5 Rb. Kynder	1 ox	Sutton (of Jn. Holynsheved)
6 Jn. Holynsheved	1 ox, 10s.	Rode (of Rb. Roulegh)
7 Jn. Lovell	2 oxen, 32s.	Stockport (from John Batiller of Eaton)
8 Rb. Kynder & Rb. s. Jn. Holynsheved Simon Belot o. Gawsworth,	1 bullock & 3 heifers, 20s.	house at Buxton, received by Rb. Roulegh
9 Jn. s. Wll. Holynsheved & Rb. Kynder, Aided by: Rg. Cokke, Rb. Roulegh, Sim. Belot, & Jn. Lovell (all of Gawsworth)	2 oxen, 26s. 8d.	Gawsworth
10 Jn. s. Wll. Holynsheved & Rb. Kynder, Sim. Belot & others	1 bullock, 3 heifers, 16s.	Gawsworth received & sold by Rg. Cokke o. Gawsworth
Thefts from Adam Bouker		
11 Rg. Joneson Godemon	1 horse, 20s.	
12 Rg. s. Jn. Godemon	1 mare	Bosley
13 Wll. Standene Nch. Amot	1 mare, 26s. 8d.	Bosley Rg. s. Jn. Godemon sen. of Sutton aided; Jn. Godemon received them at Sutton for 3 weeks, &
Thefts from Richard Hervy of Sutton		
14 Wll. Standene	cloth, pot, oats, hay & other goods, took by extortion, & rode his horse;	during above 3 weeks
15 Wll. Blakeburn o. Derbyshire	1 horse, 8s. 6d.	broke house

Name of Those Involved	Goods Taken	Location (Victim)
Thefts from Thomas Wattesone of Sutton		
16 Wll. Standene (ex. serv. Nch. Olyston knight) & Nch. Amot (dec.)	money, 33s. 4d.	burgled house at Sutton (& beat wife with sword) (William broke gaol, 1392)
17		beat wife with sword until promised 100s. 0d.
18 & with others unknown		robbed house at night
19 Rch. Eydale	cloth, 2s., 2 linen sheets	threatened & detained until promised 10s. 0d.
Thefts from Richard Eydale of Sutton		
20 Wll. Blakeburn o. Derbyshire	2 blankets, red & white linen cloth & other garments, 26s. 8d. 2 bed-clothes & (buckle), 40d. & other goods;	
21	(white) cloth & blanket, 40s.	broke house at night
22 Jn. Holynsheved & Rb. Kynder	1 cow, 7s.	broke house at night at Kettleshulme
	1 ox, 10s.	broke house at Whaley, Rb. Roulegh received Jn.
23 Jn. Holynsheved & Rb. Kynder	2 oxen	Gawsworth, received by Rb. Roulegh

bos : ox; *juvenca* : heifer; *boviculus* : bullock or steer; *vacca* : cow; *jumentum*: mare.
CHES 25/22 m. 7, m. 11, mm. 13–4, mm. 17–20.

5 *Conclusion*

The first point to make about the the Macclesfield court rolls is that they cannot be used to produce precise figures for the later medieval population of the borough and manor. Although the majority of tenants appeared in the courts over a short period, in a sample of four or five years for example, their numbers are not an accurate index of levels of population. The financial nature of the rolls should not be underestimated, while the attraction of both the local market and the forest resources resulted in a large cross-section of people making irregular court appearances. It was these, constituting well over half of the total, that provide the greatest problems of indentification.

The importance of referring to other sources, in which the courts can be seen in relation to other aspects of the legal and administrative process, cannot be over-emphasised. By using the court rolls in combination with the rentals of 1352 and 1383/4 it can be shown that the subletting of land was widespread, and that holding a tenancy did not indicate that a person necessarily lived within that township. In the manor under-tenants made up a significant proportion of those who appeared in the courts, and were associated with certain types as well as frequency of appearances.

Residence could not be determined for as many as half of the people mentioned in the records. These, primarily, were the wage-earners who came from a large number of settlements across the local area. Many of them had relatives dwelling nearby and were engaged in life-cycle service. Those leaving Pott Shrigley, for instance, to work at Adlington in the autumn of 1388, included Emma, one of six daughters of Thomas Potte. John Raynald of Norbury, the former servant of forester John Sherd, similarly sought work elsewhere in 1393.[1]

As some wealthy and influential people of the locality had extensive regional landholdings, especially the foresters and a handful of other families, this meant that service was not restricted by

---

[1] SC 2/254/10 m. 8, SC 2/254/15 m. 3.

jurisdictional boundaries. Court rolls, however, are the only source that allows us glimpses into the lives of these people, and it is in the borough court, the portmote, that they are most visible.

From an early period in the history of the lordship of Macclesfield there had been a conflict in the forest between the roles of game preserve and livestock pasture. In the first half of the fourteenth century, complaints referred to the neglect and over-exploitation of the woodland, during which time large numbers of timber trees were felled and several iron-forges were in operation. The period of the Black Prince (1347–76) saw livestock rearing and revenues increase. The day-to-day administration of the forest was in the hands of the foresters and their officials. The records relating to the escapes and pleas of vert suggest a policy of exploitation of the forest in the second half of the fourteenth century that was more akin to a form of licensing to maximise revenue, rather than conservation and control. During this period some of the pastures, as well as other manorial enterprises, were leased out, which provided opportunities for local tenants. The extensive area that had made up the forest in the thirteenth century had, by the end of the fourteenth century, been reduced to that included within the jurisdiction of the manor court.

The high death-rates associated with the Black Death led to the consolidation of tenancies. Some individuals, especially those in the north-east of the manor, were able to improve substantially both their revenues and landed power-base. This, combined with the opportunity to lease sources of revenue and with military service to the Black Prince, led people such as the Jodrells and Downes to attaining gentry status. The most powerful regional family were undoubtedly the Leghs of Adlington, who were at the forefront of local public office and had a key role in the administration of the courts and in the collection of revenues. The importance of land as both a symbol and instrument of power was evident and made for feuds between servants and retainers as well as within families. The result was the growth of local conflict and violent crime which, in the case of Peter Legh, extended beyond regional political boundaries.

Beneath families such as the Leghs were those of relatively high social standing who maintained their position, at least in part, through their role within the courts. Although serving as a juror in the halmote and portmote was open to a large number of tenants and burgesses, only a small proportion of the eligible population acted frequently. A glance at the juries of indictment in the eyres, for example, quickly reveals the names of the most influential people in the communities. Another indicator of wealth is the practice of serving as a pledge for others in a 'professional' manner. However, those serving the most regularly as jurors and pledges were generally exclusive of one another. Another powerful group can be found in the borough, where those most often elected to office were drawn from a small core of active trading-burgesses.

The local peasantry exploited the forest as a source of both wood and pasture. Some of those holding between ten and 20 acres of land were significantly involved in stock-keeping and paid fines or purchased green foliage for their animals, in addition to grazing them over a wide area. Pigs were pannaged in Lyme, including those from nearby townships, but nobody paid for more than five or six at a time. Some local smallholders worked as shepherds and cowmen and this enabled some tenants from outside the manor to pasture their animals. The main draught-beasts were oxen, although working horses, used for carting, were also common, and one or two sheep were probably kept by most residents. Larger flocks were uncommon although wealthy peasants like John Brocwalhurst had 100 or more. With burgesses such as Alan Pierson stock-keeping was associated with his trade as a butcher. At the same time a local woollen cloth industry was beginning to emerge. There was a small number of tailors amongst the better-off peasants, and weaving and spinning was carried out by many households. Other smallholders supplemented their income with woodland crafts. Poaching, surprisingly, was an activity rarely mentioned in the courts.

An indication of one way in which contemporaries perceived the area lies in the relatively common practice of people travelling armed. This was usually with a small knife, dagger or baslard, with swords for those of a higher status. There may have been a greater prevalence of bows and arrows, which were occasionally fired at someone. More often, though, they were used with their cords detached for striking, as were a variety of sticks or staves, which were the most common item carried. The most serious conflict arose out of local political and familial warfare, when retainers were sent to harm and intimidate by those who considered themselves exempt from prosecution. The majority of disputes, however, were not 'inter-class' but between individuals of similar status, and they had a variety of causes. Most appear to have taken place in the borough where amercements and fines in the local courts suggest they were dealt with more leniently than in the manor. Violence or the threat of violence must have been widespread, and the prohibition of the carrying of weapons suggests a real attempt by the authorities to deal with this problem. Affrays were seasonal with the highest proportion involving local wage-earners who gathered in the borough during the summer and autumn – for service or for leisure.

The manor and borough communities had important links with people from across the region and should not be viewed in isolation. Only a small proportion of the individuals who appear in the manor court can be tied to a single township. This fact, together with the temporary nature of many wage earners' places of residence, makes it difficult to measure either demographic numbers or trends. Macclesfield borough appears to have been a typical small urban centre, with local trade based around victuals, cloth and leather crafts which supplied a local market. The town attracted people to its courts and acted as a draw to those seeking work, service or leisure. Its population, at its fourteenth-century peak, is unlikely to have reached much above 500. The figures for those appearing in the manor court, on the other hand, can lead to significantly differing estimates of the community's population, and it is necessary to be cautious. However if a post Black Death population for the manor of between 800 and 900 hundred was representative of the whole region, then this would imply a population for the whole of Macclesfield Hundred which must lead to a re-evaluation of the county figures as suggested, for example, by J. C. Russell.[2] Two factors need to be borne in mind: firstly that the manor-forest must have had a lower density of population in comparison with lowland Cheshire because of its landscape, and, secondly, that it is easier to under-rather than over-estimate the numbers of servants, wage-earners and household residents mentioned in the court rolls. The evidence for Macclesfield might indeed suggest a region that was somewhat backward, economically, but certainly one that was neither isolated nor inhabited by only a few people.[3]

---

[2] Russell, *British Medieval Population*, pp. 44–5.

[3] Population stagnation, largely as a result of the Black Death and other plagues, might explain why the business of the halmote declined in the fifteenth century, Curry, 'Court Rolls of Macclesfield', p. 9.

Appendix One: Select Biographies

THE ASHTON FAMILY

Roger Ashton of Kettleshulme and Whaley appeared in the halmote from 1351 until 1375. His service as a pledge on more than 20 occasions was comparable with the role played by some clerks within the portmote itself. He made few other appearances and did not bring any suits in the local courts; he was referred to once as a juror, and was responsible for one serious hue or affray, in Whaley in 1362. He leased a small enclosure to Adam Kyngeslegh, along with William Seynsbury and his wife, and acquired a tenement of just over seven acres in Kettleshulme.[1]

His wife, Margery, was amerced four times for breaches of the assize of ale between 1351 and 1357, and his family were one of the few who were regular brewers during the period. In 1361 Roger was convicted with other members of his family – his sons Benedict and Robert, and Robert senior – and one other man of breaking the newly erected fence around Harrop.[2]

Benedict made the largest land acquisitions of any individual within the manor-forest, and paid entry-fines of £3 14s. 2d. between 1361 and 1383. After entering just under nine acres of land in Kettleshulme he went on to acquire over 40 acres more, including tenements of twelve and eight acres in Whaley; some of this land was contained in smaller enclosures such as those of two, four and five acres.[3] Apart from his land acquisitions entries in the halmote

---

[1] SC 2/252/4 m. 4 – SC 2/253/9 m. 3–4. His land, SC 2/252/5 m. 5, SC 2/252/15 m. 2d., SC 2/253/2 m. 2, SC 2/253/3 m. 10d. As a pledge, c. 1352–1368, SC 2/252/4 m. 4d. – SC 2/253/3 m. 10d. As a juror, SC 2/253/9 m. 3; and his affray, SC 2/252/11 m. 5.

[2] SC 2/252/13 m. 3. He also purchased wood in 1367, SC 2/253/2 m. 3. Margery, SC 2/252/4 m. 4 – SC 2/252/9 m. 5.

[3] SC 2/252/13 m. 3–4, SC 2/252/14 m. 3d., SC 2/252/15 m. 2d.–3, SC 2/253/2 m. 2d., SC 2/253/3 m. 8, SC 2/253/6 m. 3d., SC 2/253/7 m. 1d., SC 2/253/8 m. 3, SC 2/253/12 m. 1d., SC 2/254/4 m. 4d., SC 2/254/14 m. 4, SC 11/898 m. 4d.

Family Tree of the Ashton Family

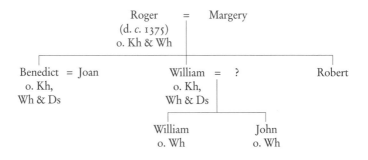

Roger   =   Margery
(d. *c.* 1375)
o. Kh & Wh

Benedict = Joan   William = ?   Robert
o. Kh,   o. Kh,
Wh & Ds   Wh & Ds

William   John
o. Wh   o. Wh

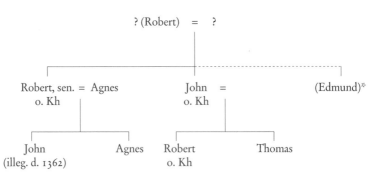

? (Robert)   =   ?

Robert, sen. = Agnes   John =   (Edmund)*
o. Kh   o. Kh

John   Agnes   Robert   Thomas
(illeg. d. 1362)   o. Kh

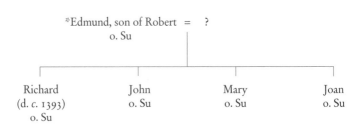

*Edmund, son of Robert   =   ?
o. Su

Richard   John   Mary   Joan
(d. *c.* 1393)   o. Su   o. Su   o. Su
o. Su

Benedict regularly served as a juror (and on the indictment juries in the eyre), as well as a witness to land entries in the halmote from the mid-1380s, while only occasionally acting as a pledge. When he was younger, between 1361 and 1367, he committed an affray in Whaley and two in Macclesfield town, in Wallgate (of which one was with his father). He was also accused of other offences and was indicted for an assault upon a woman in Whaley, and for aiding two further assaults, one with his father, in the borough between 1362 and 1365. In addition, he (or another man of this name) was one of the more than 50 armed retainers of John and Peter Legh who ejected Robert Legh, the younger, from his lands in 1376. He did not proceed with the two civil actions he brought in the halmote and portmote: one concerned the service of a maid, and the other the alleged debt of three burgesses.[4] His wife, Joan, was amerced in the three years between 1367 and 1370 for breaches of the assize of ale, as was Benedict himself in 1377.[5]

His brother, William Ashton, was amerced for a wrongful hue in Whaley in 1362. He made few other appearances in court apart from land entries and several fines for common suit, which were the only references to him between 1366 and his death which probably occurred in c. 1386/7. He may have been a non-resident although William Joudrel brought an inconclusive suit of trespass against him, and John Brocwalhurst was convicted of depasturing his corn and hay. Over 24 acres of land in Whaley passed to his son, William, in 1387.[6]

Robert Ashton's small tenement, of under six acres, in Kettle-shulme was entered by his son, John, in 1355 after having been held for a short time by James Pymyng. Around this time a burgage-holder by the name of Robert Ashton was elected custodian of the assize of ale. John was, however, illegitimate and the holding was taken into the lord's hands in 1362 and sold, presumably because

[4] c. 1361–1395, SC 2/252/13 m. 3 – SC 2/255/2 m. 3. SC 2/252/15 m. 2d., SC 2/252/13 m. 5, SC 2/253/2 m. 4; CHES 25/20 m. 19, m. 24, m. 35d.; 'County Court Indictment Roll', pp. 872–3; SC 2/254/3 m. 3, SC 2/253/2 m. 4d. As a juror, see SC 2/254/11 m. 4; as a witness, SC 2/254/15 m. 3; and as a pledge, SC 2/254/10 m. 7.

[5] SC 2/253/3 m. 10, SC 2/253/4 m. 1, SC 2/253/5 m. 10. Benedict, SC 2/253/12 m. 1.

[6] SC 2/252/13 m. 4, SC 2/253/4 m. 1, SC 2/253/5 m. 10d., SC 2/253/6 m. 3, m. 4d., SC 2/253/9 mm. 3–4, SC 2/254/8 m. 2d., SC 2/253/6 m. 3d., SC 2/253/7 m. 1. Common suit, SC 2/253/10 m. 4 – SC 2/254/6 m. 8.

he had died without heirs of his body. A few months later Robert's daughter, Agnes, entered a similar sized holding, but was not subsequently referred to under this surname: a few courts later this property passed to Robert son of John, Robert's nephew.[7]

Edmund son of Robert held an enclosure called 'Boterlandes' (Butterlands) in Sutton which passed to his son, Richard, on his death in 1383. Edmund served as a juror in the halmote, was responsible for three affrays and a rescue upon the bailiff in this township, and purchased wood from the forest.[8] Richard, however, made no appearances and the Sutton land passed to his sisters, Joan and Mary, in 1393. A 'John son of Edmund' was amerced for breaching the assize of ale in 1389 – the same year as another Robert Ashton began to be amerced for the same reason.[9]

ROGER SON OF WILLIAM BARKER

Roger was a resident of Macclesfield town and a tenant in Sutton. In the aftermath of the Black Death he entered his father's holding in Sutton, with a house and more than fifteen acres, rented at 10s. 0d. a year. This was granted to his pledge, John son of Adam Cloghes, until he reached full age; he was then to pay John 40s. 0d. and all reasonable expenses. Ten years later, in 1360, the property was entered by Roger Mascy. Before 1360 Barker had probably continued to live in Sutton, and was amerced three times for common suit in the portmote between 1357 and 1359, as well as once in the halmote in 1352. In the borough his holdings of around seven acres and a dwelling house included part of 'le Guneker', a hearth, pieces by the mill and three acres of new land in the Roewood. His three forges in the market place tell of his trade as a smith, and had presumably been passed on from his father. He disposed of the last

---

[7] Robert, SC 2/252/6 m. 1. As there were several people appearing under this name it is difficult to distinguish between them; see the family tree for a probable lineage. John, SC 2/252/6 m. 3d. and SC 2/252/13 m. 4d.; Agnes, SC 2/252/14 m. 3d.; Robert son of John, SC 2/252/14 m. 4. A John son of Roger was referred to in a suit against a Kettleshulme man in 1391, SC 2/254/12 m. 6d.

[8] SC 2/253/6 m. 3d., SC 2/254/4 m. 4d., SC 2/254/3 m. 3, SC 2/252/13 m. 4, SC 2/253/2 m. 3d., SC 2/254/1 m. 12, SC 2/253/7 m. 1.

[9] Joan and Mary, SC 2/254/14 m. 5d. John and Robert, SC 2/254/11 m. 4., and John's assault the previous year, SC 2/254/10 m. 6d.

of his holdings in Sutton when a further piece of just over an acre, on the side of 'Barkersruddyng', was surrendered in 1370. Four years later an unconcluded action by writ probably related to this land, and he brought three further inconclusive writs in the portmote. Later, in 1390, nearing his old age, he acquired more land in Sutton and entered all the land, nearly fourteen acres, that had formerly belonged to John son of Roger Mulnere. He held a tenement in Macclesfield in Wallgate, and in 1397 a burgage and other holdings in Macclesfield and Sutton, worth £5 per year, were alienated by him to John Macclesfield, senior, clerk; a plot near the market place also later passed to John through its surrender to other rent holders.[10]

Although Roger appeared in both the local courts it was only in the portmote that he played a really active role by serving as a juror, as well as serving in the indictment juries in the eyre. As far as offices were concerned, he was chosen as custodian of the assize of bread and meat on at least three occasions. He acted as a pledge a similar number of times in both courts: in the portmote this was frequently for prosecution, which included burgesses and outsiders, and in the halmote this was usually for entry-fines. He was present as a witness to several land transfers in the halmote for other townships as well as Sutton.[11]

In the portmote he had a dispute with William Bullynche. In 1363 Bullynche failed to prosecute a suit of debt against him, although in 1368 Roger served as his pledge. Ten years later Roger assaulted and wounded him in his back with a knife.[12]

Roger was involved in several further acts of violence and affray, which usually took place in Wallgate. In 1381 he again wounded a man, this time William Scot, by striking him in his back with a knife, and in 1382, with the help of John Leversegge, he was indicted for the killing of John Haywod; in the portmote he paid a fine of

[10] SC 2/252/2 m. 4d., SC 2/253/5 m. 10, SC 2/254/1 m. 12, SC 2/254/11 m. 5; SC 11/898 m. 1; 'John de Macclesfield Cartulary', fos. 67–8. Common suit, SC 2/252/5 m. 5, SC 2/252/8 m. 4d., SC 2/252/10 m. 4, SC 2/252/11 m. 3.

[11] c.1350–1396, SC 2/252/2 m. 4d. – SC 2/255/2 mm. 5–6. As a juror, see SC 2/254/9 m. 6, SC 2/255/2 mm. 5–5d.; as a pledge, SC 2/252/11 m. 6, SC 2/253/7 m. 2d.; and as a witness, SC 2/254/11 m. 5. He was a custodian of bread and meat in 1369/70, 1377/8 and 1391/2, SC 2/253/5 m. 8, SC 2/253/12 m. 2, SC 2/254/13 m. 6.

[12] SC 2/252/14 m. 5d.; Chester City Record Office, Earwaker MSS CR 63/2/338 m. 1; SC 2/253/12 m. 2d.

one mark (or 1½ marks) for bail until the eyre. After this he made no further appearances until 1387 when Nicholas Upton assaulted him with a stick. Later in the same year he drew his baslard upon John Mareschall, causing John to cut his hand, and in 1391 was involved in a brawl with at least four other men using sticks. He struck William Etkus, a chaplain of Robert, son of Robert, Legh, on his head and another former servant of Robert did the same to Roger. Another servant drew his knife upon him in 1393. This was reported at the same court as his amercement in a civil suit for detaining £10 from Peter Legh.[13]

There is little general evidence regarding his trade as a smith. His wife began brewing in 1374/5 and was amerced eight times over the 20 years following. In 1374/5 he was twice amerced 3*d*. for a trespass in the forest and for allowing his pigs to go into the park. He was indicted in 1385 for hunting hares and foxes in the Minns (Sutton common) and for being a common hunter.[14]

ROBERT AND STEPHEN BLAGGE

Robert was a mercer who sold both spices and bread in Macclesfield. He was amerced 6*d*. for an affray upon a servant in 1383, his first court appearance.[15] He played an active role in borough affairs through serving as a juror and in the offices of catchpoll and as a custodian of the assizes and market. It was his wife who was mostly responsible for selling bread, and she was amerced regularly after 1387 for breaches of the assize. This commercial activity extended to brewing for which she was occasionally amerced.[16]

[13] SC 2/254/3 m. 5; SC 2/254/4 mm. 6d.–7; SC 2/254/8 m. 1d.; SC 2/254/9 m. 6d.; SC 2/254/13 m. 7d.; CHES 25/22 m. 22; SC 2/254/15 m. 5.

[14] SC 2/253/8 m. 5d., SC 2/253/9 m. 5; CHES 25/21 m. 25. His wife, SC 2/253/2 m. 4 – SC 2/255/2 m. 6.

[15] *c.* 1383–1396, SC 2/254/4 m. 6d. – SC 2/255/2 m. 6. He was amerced for illegal weights in 1387, SC 2/254/9 m. 6. He, or another of this name, was described as the servant of Maud, widow of Robert Legh the elder, when presented by the foresters for cutting holly and hazel in Bollington wood in 1378/9, SC 2/254/2 m. 10.

[16] He served as a custodian of ale in 1386/7, 1389/90, 1393/4 and bread and meat in 1395/6, SC 2/254/7 m. 3, SC 2/254/8 m. 1, SC 2/254/11 m. 7, SC 2/254/15 m. 5, SC 2/255/2 m. 5; as a catchpoll in 1390/1, SC 2/254/12 m. 8; and served as a custodian of the market, Birkenhead Public Library, Macclesfield Collection, MA B/6/19. As a juror, see SC 2/254/10 m. 8. His

Stephen Blagge, who was probably a relative of Robert's, began to appear in the courts two years later than Robert. He also sold spices and bread, as well as cloth, although, in this instance it was Stephen rather than his wife who was amerced for breaches of the assize of bread. His wife concentrated on brewing ale, being amerced roughly once every two years, and this was probably sold from her husband's basement tavern in Wallgate.[17] He served as a portmote juror and as borough reeve, and received 2d. rent from a small tenement in Jordangate. He was indicted for taking wood from the forest, such as underwood in Shrigley common in 1383/4.[18] He was convicted of two assaults, striking a man with his bow in Wallgate in 1386, the year he served as reeve, and drawing his knife upon merchant Richard Burelles in Chestergate in 1391. Alice, his wife, assaulted another woman in 1389.[19]

THE BROCWALHURST FAMILY

Adam Brocwalhurst appears to have held land in Kettleshulme and Sutton and died around the time of the Black Death. The entry of his three daughters, Alice, Margery and Emma, into a messuage and nine acres of land in Sutton, rented at 5s. 0¾d., was recorded in the halmote in 1352. There are no subsequent references to them, under this surname, in the local courts. A John son of John *Brodehurst* entered a large and different holding in Sutton around this time, and several people of that name appear in this or adjacent townships and the borough.[20]

In 1350 his son, John, of Kettleshulme, was described as poor and unable to pay the 3d. fine for an unlawful hue. In the rental he is charged 3s. 4d. for the five acres he held in this township and in

---

wife (selling both simnel and wastel loaves), SC 2/254/11 m. 9 – SC 2/255/1 mm. 5d.–6d.

[17] c.1386–1395, SC 2/254/8 m. 1 – SC 2/255/1 m. 6. He was amerced, with Robert, for illegal weights in 1387, SC 2/254/9 m. 6. For bread (selling both cocket and wastel loaves), see SC 2/254/13 m. 6d. Alice's amercements for ale, SC 2/254/7 m. 3, SC 2/254/13 m. 6d., SC 2/255/2 m. 6.

[18] He served as reeve in 1386/7, SC 2/254/8 m. 1. His land-holdings, SC 2/254/13 m. 6d., 'John de Macclesfield Cartulary' fo. 197. As a juror, see SC 2/254/10 mm. 8–9; and for wood, CHES 25/21 m. 13.

[19] SC 2/254/8 m. 1, SC 2/254/13 m. 6d., SC 2/254/10 m. 9d.

[20] Adam, SC 2/252/4 mm. 4–4d. John, SC 2/252/3 m. 1. Brodehurst (1350), SC 2/252/3 m. 2.

Family Tree of the Brocwalhurst Family

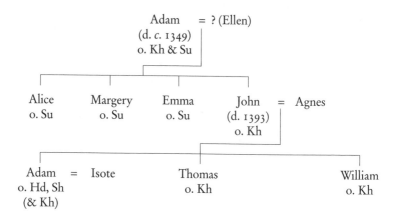

1356 he entered an enclosure and meadow formerly belonging to William Hanlegh at 9*d.* per year. In 1361/2 he and another man paid a fine following their conviction for refusing to serve as constables of Kettleshulme. He extended his holding in 1368 when he paid an entry-fine of 11*s.* 8*d.* for an enclosure and one acre of land while surrendering half an acre to Richard Godeson. Half this land was granted to his son, Thomas, in 1381 and a larger holding in the same township to Richard son of John Picford.[21] In 1373 a suit against him by forester John son of Richard Sutton in the portmote related to work or a service agreement. When his house was burgled *c.* 1392, by a man from Adlington, 4*s.* 0*d.* in money was stolen.[22]

The majority of the references to John are in connection with wood taken or purchased from Handley and Tods Cliff, and he appears more frequently than any other individual in this connection. As he was sometimes accompanied by William and Richard Hanlegh it is likely that his house was close to Handley pasture. His halmote payments and fines totalled around 19*s.* 0*d.*, and he

[21] From *c.* 1350 to his death in 1392/3, SC 2/252/2 m. 4d. – SC 2/254/14 mm. 5–5d. SC 11/899 m. 4; SC 2/252/7 m. 2d., SC 2/253/3 m. 10d., SC 2/254/3 m. 3, SC 2/252/13 m. 4d.

[22] SC 2/253/7 m. 2d., SC 2/253/12 m. 2d., Chester City Record Office, Earwaker MSS CR 63/2/338 m. 1. The burglary must have been shortly before his death, CHES 25/22 m. 26.

was additionally indicted on several other occasions. Most of these were for taking dead wood as well as for felling old trees, and his indictments included taking a cartload of wood. As John was pasturing a large number of animals some of this may have been used as fodder. His flocks of sheep – again the largest held by a tenant at this time – numbered about 100 head, and were grazed in Whaley and other commons throughout the forest.[23]

His occasional service as a pledge included acting for his wife, his sons, William and Adam, for Nicholas Brocwalhurst, and for the widow of Richard Hanlegh. He was responsible for both a hue and affray in Kettleshulme, while his pledge in the latter, John Werynton, unjustly raised the hue upon him. His neighbour, William Hanlegh, failed to prosecute a plea of trespass against him while a dispute with Benedict Hancokeson Persones in 1378/9 became more serious. He paid a fine of 1s. 0d. after going with his son, Thomas, in September 1378 to break Benedict's fold and remove a mare. In the following July he was guilty of an affray upon Benedict, who retaliated by striking him on his hands with a stick and drawing blood, with the help of his son, Edmund. In the same year John successfully prosecuted Adam Cok of Sutton in a lawsuit over the abduction of a foal.[24] His wife, Agnes, was involved in two disputes with their son, Adam, in 1372: she unjustly raised the hue against his wife, Isote, and Adam did likewise a few months later.[25]

John's son, Thomas, was guilty of an affray in Whaley in 1381, which was shortly after he entered a messuage and over 4½ acres of his father's land. Apart from his amercement for common suit in 1386, he is not subsequently mentioned until 1392 when he granted his land in Kettleshulme, by his attorney Geoffrey Dounes, to Thomas Adlynton, a cooper. In the same court Richard Hordren of Sutton was amerced for a false claim in a civil action for trespass. In 1393 John died and another son, William, succeeded to three acres of land; the lord also took John's heriot, a mare valued at

---

[23] For wood, see SC 2/253/1 m. 2, SC 2/253/4 m. 1d., CHES 25/19 m. 5; and pasturing, SC 2/253/7 m. 1; CHES 25/20 m. 71.

[24] SC 2/252/2 m. 4d., SC 2/253/3 m. 10d., SC 2/253/10 m. 4, SC 2/252/11 m. 5, SC 2/253/9 mm. 3–4, SC 2/253/12 m. 1–1d., SC 2/254/2 m. 4. As a pledge, see SC 2/252/4 m. 4, SC 2/253/3 m. 10d.

[25] SC 2/253/6 m. 3d., SC 2/253/7 m. 1. Agnes, or another of the same name, was involved in an affray with a woman in Wallgate in 1389, SC 2/254/10 m. 8.

only 1s. 6d. There are no references to this William, who alienated the land almost immediately to Edmund Dounes.[26]

Robert Brocwalhurst acted as a pledge for Thomas, son of John, for his entry-fine, and there are occasional references to Robert cutting wood, as in Shrigley moor in 1385. In 1391 he was pledged by Geoffrey Dounes and described as 'of Shrigley', and was probably, therefore, an under-tenant of the Downes family.[27] A Nicholas Brocwalhurst entered five acres in Whaley (formerly of Sibyl Hanlegh) in 1393 when he was pledged by Richard Pycford. He was twice amerced for ale in 1390 and 1395.[28]

Adam son of John Brocwalhurst acquired a close with a house in Hurdsfield in 1365, for which his father stood as his pledge. This used to belong to Marion daughter of Richard Heeth who had tried, and failed, to recover it by writ. While living there he unlawfully raised a hue and cut down green wood in Rainow common. Like his father, Adam was extensively involved in stock-keeping and was indicted, for instance, for pasturing 30 sheep in Sutton and Macclesfield commons in 1368–9. However, he was not regularly referred to in connection with wood from the forest. In 1375–6 he approved or enclosed one rood of land in Hurdsfield. In 1383 he granted his holding in Hurdsfield to Robert Worth of Tytherington, and later in that year he was amerced 6d. with 2s. od. damages, in an action brought by Geoffrey Dounes for the recovery of ten marks owed for land purchased in Pott Shrigley. In the following year he was amerced 4d. for unjustly taking pannage within Lyme, and Roger Turnour of Rainow was amerced after bringing a civil action for trespass. He made no further appearances in the courts.[29]

DENISE BROUNHULL

Denise, wife of Peter Brounhull, appears to have been a widow for most or all of the period. As a borough resident she was amerced

---

[26] Thomas, SC 2/254/3 mm. 3–3d., SC 2/254/7 m. 2, SC 2/254/13 m. 5d. William, SC 2/254/14 mm. 5–5d.

[27] SC 2/254/3 m. 3, SC 2/254/4 m. 5d., SC 2/254/6 m. 6d., SC 2/254/12 m. 7d.

[28] SC 2/254/12 m. 5., SC 2/254/15 m. 3., SC 2/255/2 m. 3.

[29] SC 2/253/1 mm. 2d.–3, SC 2/253/8 m. 3d., SC 2/253/12 m. 1; CHES 25/20 m. 43, m. 87; SC 2/254/3 m. 4, SC 2/254/4 m. 5d., SC 2/254/5 m. 7.

in nine of the years between 1349 and 1364 for brewing ale. Before 1364 she was amerced in the portmote for five hues or affrays and for one trespass, incurring fines totalling 4s. 0d. In addition the county court indictment roll records a more serious incident in 1356 when she conspired with Isabel, daughter of John Munshul, maid of Margery Shalcross, to assault and injure burgess Philippa, wife of Thomas Walker, at Sutton. After 1364, when her brewing ceased, she was amerced another 2s. 6d. for affrays and for trespassing in the park with her pigs, and in 1367 she was fined 3s. 4d. for being a common scold. In 1371–2 she paid a fine of 1s. 0d. for a trespass against Richard Walker and Margery, his wife, while she was also guilty of an affray upon Margery herself. In the same year she paid a 1s. 0d. amercement as a scold, she lay in wait to beat Parnel Shalcrosse with a stick, and Henry Mareschall, clerk of the steward of the manor, made an affray upon her. Two years later James Roulegh (possibly a relative of Robert Roulegh) was indicted for her abduction and rape in Gawsworth.[30]

ROGER BROUNHULL

Roger served as catchpoll of the borough in 1386/7, custodian of bread and meat in 1395/6, and regularly as both a juror and pledge in the portmote. He held a tenement in Wallgate with a small orchard attached. His involvement as both a plaintiff and defendant in actions of debt in the portmote, often with manor residents, is indicative of his income from trade.[31] The

[30] c. 1349–1375, SC 2/252/2 m. 3 – SC 2/253/8 mm. 5–5d. Ale, SC 2/252/2 m. 3 – SC 2/252/15 m. 4d. SC 2/252/5 m. 4d., SC 2/252/8 mm. 4–4d., SC 2/252/11 m. 3, 'County Court Indictment Roll', pp. 86–7, SC 2/253/2 m. 4d., SC 2/253/5 m. 8d., SC 2/253/6 m. 5–5d., SC 2/253/8 m. 5d., CHES 25/20 m. 72.

[31] c. 1366–1396, SC 2/253/2 m. 4 – SC 2/255/2 mm. 5–5d. His office-holding, SC 2/254/8 m. 1, SC 2/255/2 m. 5. His tenement, SC 2/254/11 m. 7. In 1373 he had been one of the deputies to stock-keeper Alexander Gaoler, SC 2/253/7 m. 1d. As a juror, see SC 2/254/12 m. 8, SC 2/255/2 m. 5; and as a pledge, SC 2/253/8 m. 5d., SC 2/254/9 m. 6d. His portmote suits involving debts, SC 2/253/3 m. 9d., SC 2/253/9 m. 5, SC 2/254/10 m. 8, SC 2/254/11 mm. 8, 9d., SC 2/254/13 m. 6d., Chester City Record Office, Earwaker MSS CR 63/2/338 m. 1–1d.

amercements of his wife, Joan, for brewing were as many as three a year.[32]

Roger took part in affrays or brawls on at least six occasions, and one of them involved the mayor, Richard Rowe, in execution of his office (prior to Roger holding office), three of which incurred the large fine of 1s. 0d. each. In 1375 he was fined for taking hares from the forest and he kept at least three working horses which were agisted there.[33]

WILLIAM SON OF MAUD BULLYNCHE

Maud herself was fined as a scold in 1359 and for an affray upon Alice wife of Walter Swordsliper in Jordangate in 1371. At the following court she failed to prosecute a civil action against Alice and Walter, and Walter stood pledge for her amercement.[34]

William was a burgess involved in both trade, as a fuller, and in some farming activity. His first appearance in the portmote was for carrying off turves in the borough. His holding in Hurdsfield, for a short time at least, included 'le Heghruddyng' which was a tenement with buildings, eight acres of land and two acres of enclosed meadow. This was recovered in 1367 by William Hayfeld, who successfully prosecuted a writ in the halmote. Ten years later Bullynche was amerced for his false claim after bringing a writ over the same land.[35] In 1367 he paid a fine after his cattle strayed on to the pasture and corn of burgess John Walker, while in 1375 six of his cattle also trespassed in the park. He purchased wood from the park, and elsewhere, and also kept pigs. In 1359 he was amerced 3s. 4d. for breaking the fold at the manor, and was one of ten men sworn as servants or deputies to stock-keeper Alexander Gaoler in the halmote in 1373. In 1382/3 he killed a hind, with his dog, at Danes Moss.[36]

---

[32] c. 1372–1395, SC 2/253/7 m. 3 – SC 2/255/1 m. 5d. (see, for example, SC 2/254/13 mm. 6–6d., m. 8d.)

[33] SC 2/253/5 m. 8d., SC 2/253/6 mm. 5, 7, SC 2/253/9 m. 5, SC 2/254/8 m. 1, SC 2/254/10 m. 8, Chester City Record Office, Earwaker MSS CR 63/2/338 m. 1. For his stock, see SC 2/254/4 m. 15d., SC 2/254/5 m. 5.

[34] SC 2/252/11 m. 4, SC 2/253/5 m. 11.

[35] SC 2/252/2 m. 3, SC 2/252/3 m. 1, SC 2/253/2 m. 3d., SC 2/253/3 m. 8, SC 2/253/12 m. 1d. His surname was often spelt 'Bullyng'.

[36] SC 2/253/8 m. 5d., SC 2/253/3 m. 9, SC 2/253/9 m. 11, SC 2/252/9 m. 7, SC 2/253/7 m. 1d., SC 2/254/1 m. 11d. Both William and his son, William, pastured draught animals in the forest in 1379/80, SC 2/254/1 m. 11.

Family Tree of the Bullynche Family

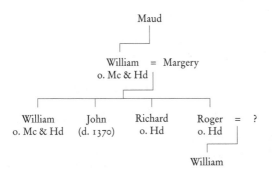

In connection with his economic activity he extensively used the portmote to bring civil suits, for, amongst other things, the detention of a pair of shears, woollen cloth and a brass pot.[37] He was responsible for several affrays and unlawful hues in Macclesfield, and at least one in Hurdsfield, between 1357 and 1372; in the borough he assaulted William Somerbache and William Stubbes, and he drew his knife upon Hugh Pulton, and was himself wounded in his back with a knife by Roger Barker in 1378. In 1368 he paid a fine of 2s. 0d. for an unspecified rescue upon the catchpoll.[38] Unlike other leading burgesses he appears to have showed little interest in running local courts, but the William Bullynche who served as a juror from 1385, and held office from 1389 may have been his son.[39] His wife, Margery, was convicted of affray in

---

[37] SC 2/252/9 m. 7, SC 2/253/1 m. 4d. William also brought civil pleas in the three Hundred after Eyre courts, SC 2/253/11 m. 4d.

[38] SC 2/252/9 m. 5, SC 2/253/4 m. 3d. (William Somerbache defaulted in two pleas brought against him more than three years earlier, SC 2/253/2 m. 4), SC 2/253/7 m. 2, SC 2/253/12 m. 2d., Chester City Record Office, Earwaker MSS CR 63/2/338 m. 1. He was responsible for an affray, an unlawful hue and a false presentment of a hue in Wallgate between 1360 and 1365, SC 2/252/12 m. 3, SC 2/252/13 m. 5, SC 2/253/1 m. 4.

[39] William served as a custodian of the assize of ale in 1389/90, as a custodian of the pavage in Wallgate in 1390, as a catchpoll in 1393/4. SC 2/254/11 m. 7, SC 2/254/15 m. 5; Birkenhead Public Library, Macclesfield Collection, MA B/6/19/55. He was a juror from 1385, SC 2/254/6 m. 5 – SC 2/255/2 m. 5d.

Wallgate in 1356, and was in her widowhood from c.1383, when she was amerced once for the assize of ale.[40]

William and Margery had at least four sons. In 1370 William was amerced 3s. 4d. for concealing the principal animal or heriot, worth 12s. od., of his son John. Richard approved one rood of waste in Hurdsfield and may also have died before his father as his brother, William, entered it only three years later, in 1370. Roger was in service to his father, who unsuccessfully sued him for breach of contract in 1370, and his father was guilty of an affray upon him in Wallgate the following year; Roger was also amerced as his pledge to prosecute in 1373. In 1371 Roger was accused in the halmote of unjustly breaking the fold to take nine horses. He may have lived in Hurdsfield where he shared a cow, worth 13s. 4d., with his brother, William, which was proved to have been unjustly detained by the son of another fuller in the halmote in 1372.[41]

As a burgage holder William son of William was amerced five times for non-appearance in the portmote between 1370 and 1372. He held one rood of land, rented at 2d., in Hurdsfield, which formerly belonged to his brother Richard, from 1370 until 1392, when he granted it to William Slegh. He brought a land action in the portmote in 1382 against William son of Roger Bullynche, while his mother, Margery, twice sued him by writ; in 1384, over a third part of two messuages and four acres of land, and in 1389. None of these were successful.[42]

THOMAS BUNNYNG

Thomas was an undertenant of Whaley who was convicted of theft from three residents in Whaley between 1380 and 1382: he broke the grange of Benedict Strynger and took one blanket worth 3s. 4d. and stole other goods on another occasion; and he took six capons from William Schore's house and two geese from William Menerell. In 1382 he was amerced 6d. for an affray upon another undertenant,

[40] SC 2/252/7 m. 3d., SC 2/254/4 m. 6d.
[41] John, SC 2/253/5 m. 8. Richard, SC 2/253/2 m. 3. William, SC 2/253/4 m. 1d. Roger, SC 2/253/1 m. 4, SC 2/253/2 m. 4, SC 2/253/7 m. 2d., SC 2/253/5 m. 10d., SC 2/253/6 m. 3.
[42] SC 2/253/4 m. 1d., SC 2/254/14 m. 4, SC 2/254/3 m. 5d., Chester City Record Office, Earwaker MSS CR 63/2/339 rot. 1, m. 2. Common suit, SC 2/253/4 mm. 3–3d. – SC 2/253/7 m. 2.

William Potte, and later in the year he killed Roger Filleson, a tailor, with a sword at nearby Taxal; for this, or the previous theft, he paid a fine of one mark, and was mainperned until the following eyre.[43]

RICHARD BURELLES

Richard was an active burgess who served as catchpoll in 1383/4, a custodian of ale in 1382/3 and of bread and meat in 1390/1, and as a juror in the portmote. He appears to have been a general merchant and had yard-sticks for measuring cloth and also sold bread.[44] He was involved in more than 20 lawsuits in the portmote and brought a further two in the halmote. Several of these suits were for debt and they reveal his economic links with the surrounding area; for example, with fuller William Bullynche, John Caton the parson of Gawsworth, Thomas Fitton of Pownall and William Dene of Adlington. In 1390/1 he was arrested, together with his servant, for a rescue upon Richard Kenworthey, the deputy serjeant of the peace, and in the following year he failed to prosecute an action of debt against Richard.[45]

He was involved in a number of violent incidents. Those who assaulted him included burgesses Stephen Blagge, who drew his knife in 1391, and Stephen Rowe, who struck him with a stick in 1394. His beating of Hugh Wyan (unidentified) in 1366 resulted in bloodshed. In 1362/3 Richard son of Thomas Sydynton was indicted for an affray upon him in Siddington. In 1366 Burelles was indicted for the death of John Harald (unidentified). His possessions at his arrest included corn in a barn worth £3, two (working) horses and a mare, a calf, two sheep, and a brass pot. He resisted arrest (for an unspecified offence), with Robert his servant, in 1391.[46]

[43] SC 2/254/3 m. 4, SC 2/254/4 mm. 4–5, 9d.; CHES 25/21 m. 6, m. 8d.
[44] c. 1375–1396, SC 2/253/8 m. 5 – SC 2/255/2 m. 5–6. His office-holding, SC 2/254/4 m. 6, SC 2/254/12 m. 8; Chester City Record Office, Earwaker MSS CR 63/2/339 rot. 1, m. 1. As a juror, see SC 2/254/10 m. 8–9. Bread, SC 2/254/13 m. 6d., SC 2/255/1 m. 5d.–6. Tourn, SC 2/254/9 m. 6.
[45] His portmote suits, SC 2/253/9 m. 5, SC 2/254/4 m. 6, SC 2/254/9 m. 6d., SC 2/254/13 m. 7d., SC 2/254/15 m. 5–5d.; and halmote suit, SC 2/254/12 m. 5d. His rescue, SC 2/254/12 m. 10.
[46] SC 2/254/13 m. 6d., SC 2/254/15 m. 6, SC 2/253/2 m. 4, CHES 25/19 m. 30, CHES 25/20 m. 25, m. 27; SC 2/254/12 m. 10. See Table 23.

In the autumn of 1395 William son of William Heuster failed to prosecute an action of covenant against him and he was amerced, together with his father (of Knutsford), who stood as his pledge. However, this or another dispute remained unresolved and in the following spring William, with the help of another man, lay in wait, ambushed and killed Richard at Hurdsfield. Shortly before his death, Robert Byran had been amerced twice in the portmote for unjustly presenting an affray between Richard and butcher William Pemberton in Jordangate. The executors of Richard's will were Agnes, his widow, and William Heuster.[47]

ISABEL WIDOW OF ROGER CLYFF

Isabel was a woman of relatively high status who appeared several times in the portmote between 1352 and 1372. She was the farmer of the common oven from 1359 to 1363/4 and the executrix of the wills of at least four different people in 1357/8. She was involved in lawsuits over the detention of a brooch, falsely claimed by Agnes Balle, and a sack by Roger Skot. She was amerced in only one year, 1355, for brewing ale. In 1355/6 an outsider was indicted for a theft from her house of roofing material worth half a mark. Her landholding, excluding burgages, included five small closes, at a rent of 1s. 9d., and over nine acres, at 6s. 4d., on the Boothgreen in the borough fields. It is likely, therefore, that she obtained some income by subletting.[48]

---

[47] SC2 2/255/2 mm. 5d.–6; CHES 25/22 mm. 50–51.

[48] c. 1353–1360, SC 2/252/5 m. 4 – SC 2/252/11 m. 4d.; she sued, unsuccessfully, William Bullynche in 1373, SC 2/253/7 m. 2d. As holder of the common oven, SC 6/802/15 m. 2d, SC 6/803/9 m. 3; and as an executrix, SC 2/252/7 m. 3. Her land, SC 11/899 m. 1–1d. She held a tenement in Wallgate and granted a nearby close to John Boyle in 1362, 'John de Macclesfield Cartulary', fo. 50–1. Prior to his death, Roger had held two forges in the forest. Isabel received two oaks, as fuel, from the Fence as gifts in 1358 from the Black Prince, B.P.R., iii, pp. 114, 315. Her suits, SC 2/252/7 m. 3, SC 2/252/8 m. 4, SC 2/252/9 m. 7d.; and theft, CHES 25/19 m. 8.

AMICE DAUGHTER OF THOMAS FLETCHER

Amice was the person most closely associated with petty crime and acts of violence in Macclesfield. In 1386 she granted two enclosures in Jordangate, held jointly with Margaret widow of Ranulph Whytlof, to another burgess, John Walkedene. This was the year when she was first referred to as the wife of burgess John Oldefeld. Amice, however, appears to have retained a high degree of independence, probably on account of her burgage holding, and brought civil actions under her own name in both the port-mote and Hundred after the eyre, such as the plea of debt against Richard Astbury of Rode in 1375.[49] Her husband was a butcher who was amerced as much as 2s. 3d. a year for offences against the assize of meat. He employed a female servant and kept at least two horses, which he was accused of illegally pasturing at night-time in 1389.[50]

When young, in 1355, Amice was convicted of illegally leaving the service of William Dounes. For a fourteen year period, between 1361 to 1375, she appeared in the courts as a typical ale-wife, and was amerced in nine of those years. She may have sold ale from her house, or was possibly the owner of a tavern, although in her last amercement she was described as a tranter; on five occasions she either refused to sell ale or sold it from unsealed measures. On three occasions, between 1361 and 1367, she was convicted of taking turves and fences from neighbours in the borough, while she also trespassed in the park and was accused of breaking the manor palisade.[51] She was described as a common scold on several

---

[49] c. 1355–1390, SC 2/252/6 mm. 1–1d. – SC 2/254/11 mm. 7–8. Her land, SC 2/253/6 mm. 5–5d.; and suits, SC 2/253/8 m. 6, SC 2/253/9 m. 5d. She was also sometimes referred to as Alice Fletcher; see, for example, CHES 25/21 m. 7.

[50] c. 1367–1390, SC 2/253/3 m. 9 – SC 2/254/12 m. 8d.; he, or another of this name, was also assaulted by Richard Spencer in 1396, SC 2/255/2 m. 6. SC 2/254/8 m. 1, SC 2/254/11 m. 9. The assize of meat, c. 1375–1382, SC 2/253/8 m. 5d. – SC 2/254/4 m. 6. John held burgages in Souterslane and Chestergate, 'John de Macclesfield Cartulary', fo. 197–8.

[51] Her service, SC 2/252/6 mm. 1–1d. Ale, SC 2/252/13 m. 6 – SC 2/253/9 m. 5. Her trespasses, SC 2/252/13 m. 5, SC 2/252/14 mm. 5–5d., SC 2/252/15 m. 5, SC 2/253/2 m. 4, CHES 25/20 m. 56.

occasions to the nuisance of the wives of burgesses Richard Walker, John Oselcok, Nicholas Upton and John Knokeden.[52]

The most notable features of Amice's career of crime were her nineteen appearances for affray, unlawful hue and assault. She was accused, for instance, of more than a dozen assaults, her victims including both men and women.[53] In 1371, for instance, fines of 3s. 6d. were imposed upon her in the portmote – a year when neither herself nor John were presented for breach of the assizes.[54] Amice was further prosecuted for theft, larceny and receiving of stolen goods, most frequently of poultry. This crime extended beyond Macclesfield town to the nearby townships of Upton and Alderley. Her reputation may have led to false accusations, and the claims made by three burgesses in 1371, regarding her theft of fences, turves and geese, were withdrawn. In 1372 she

[52] In 1366, SC 2/253/2 m. 4 (John Knokeden brought an action for debt the following year, SC 2/253/3 m. 9); in 1372, SC 2/253/6 m. 5; in 1376, SC 2/253/10 m. 5 (she was amerced after being sued for debt by Nicholas Upton and Ellen, his wife, six months later, and was convicted of the theft of a capon from Nicholas in 1387, CHES 25/21 m. 34, SC 2/254/8 m. 1d.); in 1385, SC 2/254/6 m. 5 (she also assaulted Richard Walker five years later, SC 2/254/11 m. 7d.); in 1386, SC 2/253/7 m. 3; and in 1388, SC 2/254/11 m. 9.

[53] Her convictions in the portmote were as follows. In 1367 she assaulted both Thomas Daukynson and her husband (or future spouse) John SC 2/253/3 m. 9d. Thomas and his wife sued her for trespass in the same year, and Thomas had served as her pledge when Amice was amerced for two unlawful hues in 1361–2, SC 2/252/13 m. 5. In 1371–2 she assaulted Cecily wife of Ranulph Upton, a burgess, and John Yrish, a labourer or servant, SC 2/253/6 mm. 5–5d. Ranulph falsely accused her of theft in the same month, CHES 25/20 m. 72. In 1376, Alice daughter of Hervey Taillour, SC 2/253/10 m. 5, and in 1377, both John Sclater, with a stick, and his wife on separate occasions, SC 2/253/12 m. 2. In 1378, Margot Machon, twice, with her hands and a tool, SC 2/254/2 m. 4d. She was indicted for assaulting burgess Richard Walker, with a stone, in 1384 (this, after Walker had successfully sued her for the assault, in a civil action for trespass, in the portmote). She was also convicted of assaulting Walker with her fist, in the portmote in 1390, when John Leversegge came to Walker's aid, CHES 25/21 m. 12, Chester City Record Office, Earwaker MSS CR 63/2/339 rot. 1, m. 2, SC 2/254/11 m. 7d.

[54] Those convicted in the portmote of assaulting her were Roger Bower in 1370, SC 2/253/5 m. 8; Adam Paver in 1373, SC 2/253/7 m. 3d.; Roger Dycon in 1377, SC 2/253/10 m. 5d.; and butcher William Pemberton, who struck her on her head with a bow in 1386, SC 2/254/8 m. 1.

was committed to gaol for receiving her maid after she had committed a felony, and she had her goods distrained, namely a brass pot, worth the high sum of 6s. 8d., four pigs and a stirk.[55]

DAVID GOLBOURN ('LE WALSHEMON')

In 1372 David and his concubine were described as common breakers of gardens in the borough. At this time he was a servant of Thomas Fitton and was indicted for the theft of oats, barley and rye worth 6s. 8d., capons and hens worth 6s. 8d., and geese, capons, hens and piglets worth another 3s. 4d. from Thomas at Gawsworth. For this felony he was subsequently gaoled.

David was another person who was involved in violence in the borough on a several occasions. After he had failed to prosecute a civil action for trespass against Henry Sclater in 1372, Henry made an affray upon him. In 1373 he was amerced 3d. for two affrays upon two men in Wallgate. In March 1375 an assault upon another Welshman resulted in a head wound and, if the indictment is to be believed, the near amputation of Matthew Walshe's hand with a baslard. This conflict again spilled over into the courts when, in the following month, Matthew was amerced for not prosecuting a suit of trespass against David. The last time he is mentioned was in September 1375, when a serjeant of the peace was acquitted of refusing to execute an order relating to David's transfer from Macclesfield gaol to Chester castle.[56]

MARGARET DAUGHTER OF ADAM HERVY

After the Black Death Adam's former holding of 1½ bovates in Sutton was held by William Hobeler until Margaret was of full age. While still in her minority she was in service in the borough, and

---

[55] Her thefts included geese and capons, loaves, hay and oat sheaves. She was indicted for receiving stolen goods, such as 3s. 0d. worth of woollen cloth from Alderley and barley bread and three bushels of barley taken from burgess William Sondebache by Adam Smyth of the same township. SC 2/253/7 m. 2, SC 2/254/8 m. 1d., SC 2/254/1 m. 1d.; CHES 25/20 m. 34d., m. 72, m. 85, CHES 25/21 m. 32, m. 37; 'County Court Indictment Roll', pp. 806–7. See Table 23.

[56] SC 2/253/6 m. 5d., SC 2/253/7 m. 2d., SC 2/253/8 mm. 5–5d.; CHES 25/20 m. 70, m. 81, m. 84; 'County Court Indictment Roll', pp. 806–7.

in 1354/5 twice broke half yearly agreements to serve Alice London and Roger Astbury. In that year she failed to prosecute a suit of debt in the portmote and in the following she incurred the large fine of 2s. 0d. for a serious assault.[57] There are no further references to her in the borough court and she must have succeeded to her land in 1359–60 when she was amerced twice for common suit in the halmote. This holding, which was rented at only 3s. 1½d., was held by the customary service of providing the stall for toll at Macclesfield fair; in 1382 she was amerced for failing to do this at the Barnaby fair. In 1367 she sued Margaret widow of Richard Sutton for the detention of an ox.[58]

The majority of Margaret's appearances in court relate to affrays in Sutton, and most of these concerned other women. In 1364 she was wounded when Maud Tylledoghter struck her on head, and in 1376 John Rode made an affray upon her; additionally, in 1374, she was indicted for striking Alice wife of Robert Dounes on the head with a stone. In 1385 she was wounded once again by Alice wife of Geoffrey Burgeys, who had the help of Alice Helegh and John Wosewall's widow, while in a separate incident in the same year she was mistreated by 'unknown' persons. In 1386–7 forester John Dycon twice wrongfully presented affrays involving Margaret, one with Richard Rode and one with Richard's servant, William. In 1390 William Togod unlawfully raised the hue upon her.[59]

Her daughter, Maud, also appears to have been in service in the borough, where she was described as a common breaker and burner of fences in 1389/90. Four years later she was accused of the theft of a winnowing-fan from John son of Robert Legh, of breaking and burning Roger Barker's fence and for being a scold with Roger's servant. In the same year Reginald Cook assaulted her, in Wallgate, and struck her upon her back.[60]

---

[57] She appeared in the portmote, c. 1354–1357, SC 2/252/6 m. 1 – SC 2/252/8 m. 4. Her land, SC 11/899 m. 2; suits, SC 2/252/6 mm. 1–1d., SC 2/252/7 m. 3d.; and affray, SC 2/252/8 m. 4.

[58] She appeared in the halmote, c. 1364–1390, SC 2/252/15 m. 3d. – SC 2/254/12 m. 5d.; and her amercements for common suit, SC 2/252/11 m. 5, SC 2/252/12 m. 2. Her land, SC 2/254/3 m. 3d.; and suit, SC 2/253/3 m. 8d.

[59] SC 2/252/15 m. 3d., SC 2/253/9 m. 3; SC 2/254/6 m. 6d.; CHES 25/20 m. 80; SC 2/254/8 mm. 3–3d., SC 2/254/12 m. 5d.

[60] SC 2/254/11 m. 7, SC 2/254/15 m. 5.

ROBERT HEYE

Robert was a burgess butcher who served as both custodian of ale in 1377/8 and as catchpoll in 1388/9. He rarely acted as a pledge and was more frequently referred to as a juror. His income as a butcher must have been sufficient to finance his frequent amercements for breaking the assize of flesh, which totalled at least £1 1s. 6d. in a period of 25 years. His offences included refusing, on several occasions, to have his meat tested, selling meat which was diseased, and for being a common regrator along with two other butchers. In one year alone, 1394–5, he was fined over 5s. 0d., 4s. 2d. of which was imposed within a three-month spell during the middle of the year. Rivalry or a dispute with fellow butcher Reginald Cook led to him drawing his knife against him.[61]

His wife, Joan, was a full-time brewer who was fined up to three or four times a year. These included, for instance, refusing to serve burgess Stephen Blagge and for selling weak ale. Her amercements between 1382 and 1396 totalled more than 5s. 0d. In addition, she was amerced twice for the assize of bread in 1383 and 1390.[62]

ROGER HURDESFELD AND AGNES HIS WIFE

Agnes was an ale-wife for nearly 40 years, and was amerced on at least 35 occasions. Although the reason for her offence was usually unspecified, she sold ale with unsealed and short measures on three occasions and twice refused to sell either from her house or to her neighbours.[63]

Roger was found guilty of a serious assault in Wallgate in 1358

---

[61] c. 1374–1396, SC 2/253/8 m. 5 – SC 2/255/2 m. 6. His office-holding, SC 2/253/12 m. 2, SC 2/254/10 m. 8. As a pledge, see SC 2/253/8 m. 5d; as a juror, SC 2/255/2 mm. 5–5d.; and the assize of meat, SC 2/253/8 m. 5d., SC 2/254/3 m. 5, SC 2/254/13 m. 8, SC 2/255/1 mm. 5–6. His affray, SC 2/254/4 m. 7.

[62] SC 2/254/4 mm. 6–6d. – SC 2/255/2 m. 5–6, Chester City Record Office, Earwaker MSS CR 63/2/339 rot. 1, m. 1. She paid as much as 1s. 4d. to 1s. 8d. for ale in some years (for example, SC 2/254/4 mm. 6–6d., SC 2/254/12 mm. 8d.–10d., SC 2/254/13 m. 6d., SC 2/255/1 mm. 5–6d.).

[63] c. 1360–1396, SC 2/252/11 m. 3d. – SC 2/255/2 mm. 5–6 (for example, SC 2/252/15 m. 5d., SC 2/254/9 m. 7d., SC 2/255/1 mm. 5–6d.).

and was one of seven men, including three chaplains, who were indicted in 1370 for assaulting a man; he was also the victim of an assault in 1372. Roger was central to the serious affray which broke out at the Barnaby fair in 1372, after which a group, led by mayor Richard Rowe, helped him escape arrest.[64]

JOHN JAYE / JOYE

John and his wife, Ellen, lived in the borough in the first half of the 1350s. In 1354–5 John was convicted in suits of trespass brought by smith William Botfysh and Roger Astbury, and was also found guilty of an unlawful hue in Chestergate. During this time Ellen was one of a small group of women who were indicted for taking excessive wages as carriers of water within the borough.[65]

In the halmote in the autumn of 1356 John was accused of trespassing in Handley wood and a fine of 12*d.* for trespass was imposed on Ellen in the portmote of the following day. After this they appear to have moved house, and John regularly incurred fines in the halmote for carrying off dead wood, sometimes in the company of others, from Handley between 1357 and 1363; these totalled 4*s.* 6*d.* In 1362 he incurred fines for overburdening the common pasture of Kettleshulme with four horses, and for raising a hue unlawfully in the same township.[66]

A possible relative, William Joye, held land worth 6*d.* in Yeardsley between 1351 and 1358, and William Dounes of Shrigley sought his service at Taxal in 1359. This William Joye, or another of the same name, was twice amerced for breaching the assize of ale in the halmote between 1377 and 1379.[67] Others of this surname lived in the north-east of the manor during this time.[68]

---

[64] SC 2/252/10 m. 4; CHES 25/20 m. 47; SC 2/253/6 m. 5d., SC 2/253/7 m. 3. See pp. 154–5 above.

[65] SC 2/252/6 m. 1, SC 2/252/7 m. 3; CHES 25/19 m. 4d.

[66] SC 2/252/8 mm. 4–5, SC 2/252/14 mm. 3. His fines, for example, SC 2/252/12 m. 2, SC 2/252/13 m. 3.

[67] SC 2/252/4 m. 4, SC 2/252/14 m. 3, SC 2/252/10 m. 5, SC 2/253/12 m. 1, SC 2/254/1 m. 12.

[68] William son of Roger Joye in Marple, SC 2/254/1 m. 12, and Robert Joye who was a tenant in Rainow, SC 2/252/12 m. 2.

HENRY AND NICHOLAS JOLYNET

Although Henry owned a forge in the borough, at 5½d. rent, he made only two appearances in the portmote. He served as a juror in the election at the great portmote of 1349, and was a pledge for his wife, Agnes, in 1362 when she was amerced for an affray in Jordangate. In the halmote he purchased a pig in 1349 and brought a suit against Richard Shepherd in 1358.[69]

His daughter, Agnes, who was probably in service, was a victim of an affray in the borough in 1372 and was amerced twice in 1374/5: for unlawfully raising the hue against Roger Brounhull's wife, when she was pledged by Nicholas Jolynet, and for carrying off wood from the park, when she was pledged by Roger Brounhull.[70]

Nicholas was presumably a relative of Henry, and served as a custodian of the assize of ale in 1356/7, when he was amerced for failing to carry out his duties. He made occasional appearances as a juror in the portmote and acted as a pledge and was one of the affeerers in the portmote in 1382. As well as the forge which had belonged to Henry, he held land in the borough's fields close to William Walker.[71] As far as trade was concerned he was amerced in 1371 for not producing his baskets and other measures to be tested at the tourn, and also for carrying off coal from the forest without licence. In 1383 he was one of six people who bought coal, for 14d., in the halmote. He also purchased wood and was further indicted for unlawfully taking it from the forest on several occasions.[72] His wife, Isabel, was amerced fourteen times for brewing in the borough between 1360 and 1377.[73]

---

[69] SC 11/899 m. 1; SC 2/252/2 mm. 3–4, SC 2/252/14 m. 5, SC 2/252/9 m. 5d.

[70] SC 2/253/6 m. 5d., SC 2/253/8 mm. 5–5d.

[71] c. 1353–1382, SC 2/252/5 m. 4 – SC 2/254/3 mm. 5–5d.; he, or another of this name, was also a defendant in a plea of debt in 1391, SC 2/254/12 m. 9. His office-holding, SC 2/252/8 mm. 4–4d., SC 2/254/3 mm. 5–5d.; his land, SC 11/898 m. 1d.; and service as a juror, SC 2/253/10 m. 5.

[72] SC 2/252/15 m. 4, SC 2/253/5 mm. 8–8d., 10, SC 2/254/4 m. 5d. He was fined 4d. for cutting wood in 1370, and was twice presented for vert in 1377–78, SC 2/253/5 m. 10, SC 2/253/10 m. 2d., SC 2/254/2 m. 10. He pastured two horses in the forest in 1379/80, SC 2/254/1 m. 11.

[73] The assize of ale, SC 2/252/11 m. 3d. – SC 2/253/12 m. 2; she, or another of this name, was also amerced in 1387 and 1395, SC 2/254/8 m. 2, SC 2/255/1 m. 6d.

EDMUND JUDDESONE OF HURDSFIELD

Edmund held four messuages and more than eighteen acres of land in Hordern, where he had assarted half a rood, and Little Hordern in Rainow. As a carpenter he purchased a number of wood cuttings.[74] His livestock included draught-beasts, such as oxen and horses, and sheep and pigs. In February 1372 he was one of ten men accused of demolishing a house of John Oldefeld, at Ormesby in Disley, and then unjustly raising the hue. From 1379 until 1387, his last appearance in the court records, he regularly served as a juror in the halmote, and also served in the eyre.[75]

His son, Thomas, who shared the family holding, was amerced for wounding another Rainow tenant and drawing blood with a stick, in 1372, and drew his knife upon John son of John Boller, of Bollington, in Jordangate in 1396. He was serving as a juror in the halmote in 1390.[76] Thomas, like his father, cut wood and pastured working horses, and other beasts, as well as up to 40 sheep in the forest.[77]

RICHARD KENWORTHEY

Richard was another burgess who held land in the manor-forest. This amounted to a small tenement in Sutton, for which he paid an entry-fine of 3d., and a parcel of land adjoining Macclesfield mill with ten square perches of 'new land'. His livestock consisted of a small flock of sheep as well as horses, pigs and over 20 cattle.

[74] c. 1359–1387, SC 2/252/10 m. 5 – SC 2/254/9 m. 4. He was also referred to as Edmund Hurdsfield. His land, SC 11/898 m. 3d., SC 2/252/13 m. 4d., SC 2/254/5 m. 8. As a carpenter, SC 6/802/17 m. 3. For taking wood, see SC 2/253/2 m. 2d., SC 2/253/3 m. 10d.

[75] For his livestock, see SC 2/253/5 m. 4, SC 2/253/9 mm. 9–10, 12, SC 2/254/1 m. 6, m. 11, SC 2/254/2 m. 10, SC 2/254/4 mm. 14–16. His indictment, CHES 25/20 m. 63d. As a juror, SC 2/254/1 m. 3d., m. 12 – SC 2/254/9 m. 4.

[76] His land SC 2/253/5 m. 11; affrays, SC 2/253/7 m. 1, SC 2/255/2 m. 6; service as a juror, SC 2/254/12 m. 5; and suit, SC 2/254/5 m. 8d. He was fined, along with four others, 100s. 0d. in the eyre of 1379/80, after they had stood pledge to produce William Lowe of Rainow, who was convicted of a felony in the previous year, SC 2/253/12 m. 6.

[77] For his wood and livestock, see SC 2/254/2 mm. 10–10d., SC 2/254/4 mm. 14–16.

He collected significant amounts of green wood, which again may have been for fodder.[78]

In terms of trade he was involved in baking, as was his wife, and he leased the common oven in 1372. Although rarely amerced for breach of the assize, he did pay 1s. 6d. for an illegal dry grain measure.[79] His wife, Margery, was a prolific brewer who was presented on 36 occasions in 33 years, incurring total fines of 18s. 7d., and in addition was amerced three times (1s. 3d.) for bread in 1360/1. She also incurred fines of 4s. 0d. for two unlawful hues in 1360 and 1363, and for being a scold in 1358, when Richard pledged her good behaviour on pain of 3s. 4d.[80]

The majority of Richard's portmote appearances were as a pledge, on more than 30 occasions, and as a juror, on at least 29. His pledging again seems to have been undertaken on a professional basis and was not concerned with relatives or neighbours, and it also extended to the Hundred court. In the portmote alone he was involved in over 30 suits, most of which were for trespass.[81] He held office, as reeve and custodian of the assize, and served as a juror in both the portmote and eyre. His status was above that of trading burgess and in 1390/1 he leased the stallage of the borough with forester John Sherd, and in the following year was deputy serjeant of the peace to Nicholas Vernon.[82]

[78] c. 1355–1396, SC 2/252/7 m. 3d. – SC 2/255/2 mm. 5–6. His land, SC 2/253/4 m. 2, SC 11/898 m. 2. See also his biography, Ch.Acc. (2), p. 152. For his livestock, see SC 2/253/8 m. 8, SC 2/253/9 m. 11, SC 2/253/12 m. 9d., SC 2/254/1 m. 11; and taking wood, SC 2/155/87 m. 5d., SC 2/254/3 m. 6.

[79] SC 2/253/6 m. 7, SC 2/252/14 m. 5. The assize of bread, SC 2/252/7 m. 3d., SC 2/252/13 m. 5d., SC 2/252/15 m. 5d., SC 2/253/7 m. 2, SC 2/254/3 m. 5.

[80] The assize of ale, c. 1359–1392, SC 2/252/10 m. 4d. – SC 2/254/13 m. 6d., m. 8d.; and bread, SC 2/252/12 m. 3. Her hues, SC 2/252/11 m. 4, SC 2/252/15 m. 4; and as a scold, SC 2/252/9 m. 7d. She was also fined in the county court for assaulting another woman in 1358, 'County Court Indictment Roll', pp. 144–5.

[81] As a pledge, c. 1362–1394, SC 2/252/13 m. 5d. – SC 2/254/15 m. 5d.; and as a juror, c. 1368–1393, Chester City Record Office, Earwaker MSS CR 63/2/338 m. 1, SC 2/253/7 m. 3 – SC 2/254/15 m. 5 (in eyre, see SC 2/254/2 m. 9d). For his suits, see, for example, SC 2/252/11 mm. 3–4, SC 2/254/11 m. 8, SC 2/254/12 m. 8d.

[82] He was a custodian of bread and meat in 1374/5, 1386/7 and 1388/9, ale in 1381/2, and reeve in 1361/2, SC 2/253/8 m. 5, SC 2/254/8 m. 1, SC 2/254/10 m. 8, SC 2/254/3 m. 5, Ch.Acc. (2), p. 152. He was deputy serjeant of the peace in 1391, SC 2/254/12 m. 10.

His son, William, was also a burgess although, unlike his father, he did not serve as either a pledge or juror in the portmote during this time. He served as custodian of ale in 1381/2. Although his wife, Margery, brewed once in 1359 she did not subsequently.[83]

His portmote appearances show his involvement in a number of affrays. He assaulted and wounded Robert Barker and Richard Bagger (both residents of lower status), with a stick, and Nicholas Upton, with a knife, between 1370 and 1377. In the halmote he falsely, and presumably maliciously, presented an affray between himself and John Leversegge in 1383 – John had previously pledged his father – and two years later another false presentment was made by Thomas Wattesone regarding William and Thomas' wife. In addition, he was arrested for carrying arms in the borough, with a group of four other men.[84]

He appears to have lived in Sutton Downes. His stock included horses and as many as 22 cattle, and he kept pigs and at least four sheep which were unjustly sheared by another man in the spring of 1388. In 1377 he was indicted, with two others and a servant, for killing a doe at Tegg's Nose brook. In 1383/4 he was presented by the foresters for cutting holly and hazel, presumably as fodder, was fined 2s. 0d. for taking a bee-hive, and 20s. 0d. for trespassing in the forest; his indictment in this year included hunting with nets and cords and three dogs, and for making a large fence around his garden. He was also indicted, the following year, for impounding the animals of at least six other tenants of Sutton as escapes in Coombs.[85]

In 1396 he was amerced for not appearing in the portmote, and in the same year Alice Rowe made a false claim in a land suit (probably in connection with his burgage holding) against him and his father, butcher Robert Heye and his wife and draper John Ibot.[86]

---

[83] c. 1361–1396, SC 2/252/13 m. 5 – SC 2/255/2 m. 6. Margery, SC 2/252/11 m. 3d. While serving as a custodian he purchased 4d. worth of chattels which formerly belonged to Ellen, daughter of Robert Carles, who was convicted of assault. Ellen was unsuccessful in her civil action for trespass against him the following year, SC 2/254/3 m. 5–5d.

[84] SC 2/253/5 m. 8, SC 2/253/7 m. 3d., SC 2/253/11 m. 2, SC 2/254/4 m. 5d., SC 2/253/4 m. 2, SC 2/254/6 m. 6d.; CHES 25/21 m. 23.

[85] CHES 25/21 m. 16, mm. 23–4. SC 2/253/10 m. 1, SC 2/254/10 m. 6, SC 2/254/5 m. 8d. For his livestock, see SC 2/254/4 mm. 13–16; and wood, SC 2/254/5 m. 5d.

[86] SC 2/255/1 m. 6, SC 2/255/2 mm. 5–6.

ROBERT KYNDER

Robert entered the tenement of 'Sparhaukesert', of 7½ acres, in Sutton with Marion, his wife, in 1353. Ten years later he acquired a small close at 1d. rent from Robert Holyncete (who had acted as his pledge for his previous entry-fine). He made few appearances in the courts, although he served as a halmote juror in a plea of land. In 1384, one year before his death, he was amerced 4d. for digging turves in Coombs.[87] Marion was twice amerced for the assize of ale in 1354 and 1363, and purchased her dead husband's heriot for 12s. 0d. in 1385. His son, Thomas, was amerced for failing to prosecute a civil action for debt in 1383, his only appearance in the court records.[88]

His tenement and other lands very likely passed to his son Robert, who was involved in several large-scale debts, including a third part of 62s. 0d. to Richard Rode and 17s. 3d. to Adam Kyngeslegh. The younger Robert appears to have been a shepherd and in 1388 had in his keeping 40 sheep which belonged to outsider Richard Mylynton, and unlawfully pastured them in Sutton. When they were returned they included two sheep of another Sutton tenant. Just before Christmas 1390 Robert was convicted of assaulting William Holyncete with a stick in Wallgate. Between 1388 and 1391 he was one of a group who were indicted of the theft of many livestock from Sutton, Kettleshulme, Whaley, Gawsworth and Buxton. After conviction for this offence his lands were forfeited, although he appears to have retained those which belonged to his mother, by pledge of Robert Holyncete senior and Reginald Dounes in the halmote court in 1392. However, in January 1394 Reginald took possession of Robert's lands, at a rent of 10s. 3d. and by a fine of 61s. 6d., following his recent hanging for these felonies.[89]

---

[87] His land, SC 2/252/5 m. 5d. (he gave the lord 2s. 0d. for licence to enfeoff Marion for life), SC 2/252/15 m. 2. As a juror, SC 2/253/2 m. 3d., SC 2/253/3 m. 10; digging turves, SC 2/254/5 m. 7; his heriot, SC 2/254/6 m. 6. For a summary of his appearances, see Table 9, pp. 59–60.

[88] Marion, SC 2/252/6 m. 3, SC 2/252/15 m. 2, SC 2/254/6 m. 6d. Thomas, SC 2/254/5 m. 7.

[89] As a shepherd, SC 2/254/10 m. 6. His debts and assault, SC 2/254/12 mm. 5–5d., m. 9; his thefts and land, CHES 25/22 m. 11, m. 13, m. 17–18; SC 2/254/13 m. 5, SC 2/254/15 m. 4. For taking wood, see CHES 25/22 m. 27. See Table 29, pp. 184–6 for his felonies.

JOHN LEVERSEGGE

John was both a burgess and substantial land-holder in the manor-forest. He held a burgage in Jordangate and a number of closes in the borough fields, including le Mulnefeld, as well as a bovate called Little Hurdsfield and part of Great Hurdsfield.[90] He lived in Macclesfield where he had weights to sell wool and a gallon measure. In 1396 he recovered £24-worth of woollen cloth and pottery from John Etwell of Nottingham in a portmote suit; John was also amerced, 3*d.*, for assaulting him and obstructing his way. He was often mentioned for taking wood from the forest, which included holly which was used as fodder.[91]

He served on the majority of portmote juries and also served on indictment juries in the eyre. He also served as a pledge on more than ten occasions in both the portmote and halmote. He had two household servants ('familiam suam'): Hugh Lether and John Hobbeson (see Richard Pope), as well as a maid. His wife appears only twice in the portmote for the assize of ale in 1383 and 1387.[92]

He was involved in several assaults and affrays. He was assaulted in a brawl, for instance, that involved fellow burgesses John son of Henry Sydsworth and Reginald Cook, a butcher who drew a knife on him; two men, Richard Stoke and Robert Barker, came to his aid and retaliated by striking Reginald with a knife.[93] But his conflicts

[90] *c.*1381–1396, SC 2/254/3 mm. 4d.–5 – SC 2/255/2 m. 5–6. His land, SC 11/898 m. 1d., m. 3d., SC 2/254/11 m. 8. His surname was frequently spelt Lyversegge.

[91] SC 2/254/9 m. 6, SC 2/255/2 m. 6. For his livestock, see SC 2/254/4 mm. 14–15, SC 2/254/5 m. 5; and taking wood, SC 2/254/8 m. 4d., CHES 25/22 m. 13.

[92] As a juror from 1382, SC 2/254/3 m. 5d. (for example, SC 2/254/4 m. 8d., SC 2/254/12 mm. 8–9d.); and as a pledge from 1381, SC 2/254/3 mm. 4–5d. His servants, SC 2/254/4 m. 6, SC 2/254/13 m. 6. His wife, SC 2/254/4 m. 6, SC 2/254/8 m. 2. Of his sons or relatives, Richard Leversegge held a burgage in Wallgate in 1400/1, 'John de Macclesfield Cartulary', fo. 52; and Thomas Leversegge was mayor in 1422/3, SC 2/315/15 m. 1.

[93] SC 2/254/6 m. 5d. He was convicted in the portmote of assaulting servant Richard Walker in 1391, when he struck him on his hand with a sword, SC 2/254/12 m. 9d.; in defending Richard Walker against Amice Fletcher in 1390, when he struck her with a stick, SC 2/254/11 m. 7d.; baker Thomas Spycer in 1394, when he threw him to the ground and struck in the back with a stick, SC 2/255/1 m. 5; and Agnes wife of borough

appear to have extended beyond local boundaries. Richard Pope, with others, twice broke into the house of John's relative, Robert Leversegge, and attacked his servants, and then abducted John's two servants after lying in wait for him. This abduction happened in March 1383 and followed John's fatal assault on John Haywod in the borough in the previous November.[94]

The county court indictment rolls reveal further details about these conflicts. His serious assault upon burgess Thomas Spycer was said to have broken both the lord's peace and his bail – he had been mainperned by the mayor on pain of £20. It is easy to see the burgess community being behind the accusations regarding his enclosing of part of their common wood pasture, the Fence, in Hurdsfield. He and two others (outsiders) were said to have seriously damaged the underwood of a man at Hurdsfield, consisting of ash and other small trees, with their swords (somewhat unlikely tools) and carried it off. His enclosure of this parcel of underwood led to Reginald Cook and three other men (including John Rossyndale son of Goditha Fitton) going to Hurdsfield to break and demolish the enclosure; this, however, was not mentioned in the county court record.[95]

ALICE AND WILLIAM LONDON

Alice, who may have been related to William, was amerced for breaches of the assize of ale in at least eleven years between 1352 and 1369. In 1349 she had her dry measure burned and between 1351 and 1353 her ale was said to have been weak. In the 1366 she refused to sell ale from her house, when she had some available, and in the following two years sold with unsealed measures. She

resident Richard Bedlem in 1395, whom he also threw to the ground, SC 2/255/2 m. 5. He unjustly presented an affray between Robert Heye and Robert Vernon in 1384, Chester City Record Office, Earwaker MSS CR 63/2/339 rot. 1, m. 2.

[94] He was accused with Roger Barker of killing Haywod. John was fined 10s. od. and Roger 13s. 4d. in the halmote, and they were mainperned until the following eyre. SC 2/254/4 mm. 6–7. John was later cleared in the county court, CHES 25/8 m. 15–15d.

[95] CHES 25/8 m. 43, CHES 25/21 mm. 34–34d. This appears to have been two or three years after the assault and disturbance with Reginald. He stood as a pledge for Reginald, along with William Slegh, when he failed to prosecute a suit in the portmote around this time, SC 2/254/10 m. 9d.

hired a maid and in 1354 Margaret Hervy broke a service agreement with her.[96]

William appeared only once in the portmote, in 1351, when he was fined 1s. 0d. for an unlawful hue in Jordangate. Later in the year he was fined in the eyre for committing an offence against the statute of labourers.[97]

MILLICENT DAUGHTER OF MICHAEL

Millicent was perhaps typical of many of the single women living in the borough at this time. In terms of trade she was amerced four times for brewing, and once for baking, in 1372–3 and 1377. Her livestock included a pig, and she was amerced twice for trespassing in the park and once for carrying off dead wood.[98]

ROBERT MIDDELTON

Robert was a retainer of Peter (and John) Legh, and played an important part in their political rivalry and conflict with the younger Robert Legh of Adlington. The county court records the events of 1376 when John Legh was rescued from Chester castle and subsequent attempts were made by armed men to murder, intimidate and eject Robert Legh, his servants and supporters, from their lands.[99] These events followed an order in the earl of Chester's name that Peter, John and Maud Legh, together with Richard and Robert Middelton, should seek arbitration in their dispute. However the court records that they nevertheless went to Adlington and maimed Robert Legh's bailiff, damaged his harrows and ploughs, and killed his cattle, and also ejected his tenants from their lands at Poynton. Although they had lain in wait to murder Robert Legh they do not appear to have caught up with him. In October two servants of Peter and John met with Robert Middelton, John Legh,

---

[96] The assize of ale, c. 1352–1369, SC 2/252/4 m. 6 – SC 2/253/3 m. 9, Chester City Record Office, Earwaker MSS CR 63/2/338 m. 1 (see, for example, SC 2/253/2 m. 4, SC 2/253/3 m. 9). Her measure, SC 2/252/2 m. 3; and maid, SC 2/252/6 m. 1d.

[97] SC 2/252/3 m. 4d., SC 2/252/4 m. 1.

[98] SC 2/252/15 m. 5, SC 2/253/7 mm. 2–3, SC 2/253/8 m. 5, SC 2/253/9 mm. 5–5d., SC 2/253/12 m. 2.

[99] 'County Court Indictment Roll', pp. 578–9, 876–7.

Daykyn Wryght and his servant at Butley from where they rode to Whaley and murdered the prosperous local tenant and ally of Robert Legh, William Joudrel.

The local courts record a number of other violent attacks by Middelton, including two in 1375–6. In the first he assaulted and injured an under-tenant of William Joudrel, Joan wife of John Hickesone of Hawkhurst, by hitting her on the head with a sword pommel in Disley, with the aid of three other unknown men. In the second he entered the house of Richard Stele in Macclesfield at night-time, along with one other person, where he seriously wounded burgess merchant Robert Thorbald, who was said to be in peril of death as a result. Two other indictments refer to attacks in 1374 and 1383: in the former, with John Sherd and William son of Robert Sherd, on Roger Hokerlegh (probably a tenant of Geoffrey Dounes) and his wife, who were wounded at Bollington; in the latter, the victim was Robert Fyket at Bosley who was struck with a stick on his arm.[100]

ROGER OLDHED

Roger was an under-forester and agister living in the south-east of the manor, near Wincle.[101] He had a house at Homeldon, which was subsequently acquired or purchased by Edmund Homeldon, and approved five acres of waste nearby as well as another three acres of the former Midgley vaccary by a fine of 12s. 0d. in 1390. All his land and tenements at Midgley, held for a rent of only 2s. 0d., were surrendered and re-entered in the halmote in 1394, with the remainder going to his daughter Agnes. Further land, of around ten acres at Over Midgley, was held by another daughter, Ellen, between 1363 and 1375.[102] Roger's land at Over Midgley

---

[100] SC 2/253/9 m. 3–5d., m. 14; CHES 25/20 m. 83, m. 96, CHES 25/21 m. 11.

[101] c. 1351–1396, SC 2/252/3 m. 1 – SC 2/255/2 m. 4. He was an under-forester and agister in the 1357 forest eyre, CHES 33/9 m. 36.

[102] His land, SC 2/252/13 m. 3d., SC 2/253/2 m. 3d., SC 2/253/4 m. 2, SC 2/254/12 m. 5d., m. 6d., SC 2/255/1 m. 7. William Clewlowe acquired or purchased another messuage and seven acres in Sutton from him in 1363, and he granted one acre of new increment to Adam Kyngeslegh, at the same court as Ellen's grant to Adam in 1375, SC 2/252/14 m. 4, SC 2/253/9 mm. 3–4.

included a house and extensive pasture rights.[103] In total, Roger assarted around eight acres. None of these holdings, as former demesne, were included in the manor rental.

As a forest official Roger made presentments of animals pastured in the forest. In addition he paid many fines or amercements for wood he had taken from Handley and elsewhere in the forest. The halmote, for example, records payments of 8s. 8d. in a three year period between 1382 and 1385. It is likely that much of this wood was for fodder for his livestock.[104] He made few appearances in the local courts, although he acted as a pledge to several Sutton tenants for debts to Adam Kyngeslegh between 1389 and 1394. These debts may have related to rents from sublet land, and Roger himself owed 17s. 7d. to Sutton tenant John son of William Oldefeld, as well as smaller debts to other local residents in the 1390s. William Wynge of Macclesfield, for instance, brought actions for debt against him in the portmote and then ten years later in the halmote.[105] Otherwise, however, he did not actively contribute to the running of the courts.

In June 1385 seven outside men, including one from Adlington, lay in wait to kill or mistreat him near Broomycroft, and were indicted instead for stalking and killing a red deer with their swords. Roger assaulted William Stubbes in Wallgate in 1376 and Maud Stubbes in the same street in 1390. Two years later he drew his knife on a tenant in Sutton. He was indicted for the abduction of Agnes daughter of John Narowdale in Newcastle, Staffordshire, in 1376.[106]

---

[103] He had a house at Over Midgley with a meadow for 12d. rent a year, with the right to keep twelve cows grazed twice yearly, for 2d. in both summer and in winter, as well as sheep and one mare and its offspring, at 2d. a year, within the bounds as follows: from 'Knottyok' up to 'le Consichemosse', 'le Crest de Taggetlonghegge', 'le Whavandemedowe', 'Wyldeborsherd', 'le Boure de Alstaneshed', and then up to 'Davenhed'. SC 2/253/7 m. 10.

[104] SC 2/254/4 mm. 14–16, SC 2/254/5 m. 5, m. 8d., SC 2/254/6 m. 6d. See, for example, Table 4.

[105] He also owed 10s. 0d. to Adam Kyngeslegh in 1394, SC 2/254/6 m. 5, SC 2/254/10 m. 7, SC 2/254/12 m. 6, SC 2/254/13 m. 4, SC 2/254/15 mm. 4–4d., SC 2/255/1 m. 8, SC 2/255/2 m. 3d.–4.

[106] CHES 25/21 m. 25. His affrays, SC 2/253/9 m. 5d., SC 2/254/11 m. 7d., SC 2/254/13 m. 5. Agnes, SC 2/253/12 m. 10. He was fined after his indictment for an unspecified trespass in 1380, SC 2/254/1 m. 1.

RICHARD POPE

Richard was one of John and Peter Legh's 54 armed and war-like retainers who sought to eject Robert Legh, the younger, from his tenements in the dispute over the wardship of James son of John Legh. He was indicted in the county court, with his son, Ralph, and four others including a man from Tatton, for twice breaking into Robert Leversegge's house at night in 1377 and 1383, and beating and then killing his servant at Wolstancroft. This must have been the result of a vendetta against this family, as Pope next went with his son and abducted two of John Leversegge's servants in the fields of Macclesfield, after lying in wait for them at William Bullynche's barn.[107]

ALICE WIDOW OF RICHARD RAVENOWE

Alice is referred to as a widow throughout the period. She held a small amount of land in the borough fields which included a one-acre close called 'le Hegandacre' and possessed another one of a similar size by the 1380s. In 1360 she entered another close of land in the halmote, of around 1½ acres, called 'le Bykersheye' in Sutton.[108]

She lived in the borough where she employed maids, such as Emma Thorbald and Agnes Clay. In 1359 she was amerced for her false claim after suing William Snowball, a leather-craftsman, over a work agreement. In 1361 William Osebourn made a false claim against her in a plea of land, and she came to an agreement with John Walker over two debts owed to Richard Tonge. She started brewing in 1364, nine years after her first appearance, and continued to do so for eleven years, until 1374. In 1366 William Bullynche and his wife were found guilty of a trespass against her, for which they owed 3s. 4d. in damages. There are no further references to Alice in the courts, apart from a failed action for land brought

---

[107] 'County Court Indictment Roll', pp. 872–3; CHES 25/8 m. 15d.; SC 2/254/4 m. 6d.
[108] c. 1355–1381, SC 2/252/6 m. 1d. – SC 2/254/3 m. 5. Her land, SC 11/899 m. 1, SC 11/898 m. 1d., SC 2/252/12 m. 2.

falsely against her and John Walker by Ellen, widow of Adam Mottrum.[109]

WILLIAM SCHORE

William was a servant of Robert, son of Robert, Legh, in 1391, and relative by marriage of William Joudrel. In the halmote in 1376 he purchased William Joudrel's heriot, at 13s. 4d., and brought a writ of right, with Agnes his wife against Roger son of William Joudrel for a third part of William's lands and rents of 40 messuages and 300 acres of land. In the halmote, William acted as a pledge to local tenants on a small number of occasions, including land entries by Roger Joudrel.[110] He does not appear as a tenant in the rentals. In 1355 he had been indicted of taking a pair of *waynblades* from John Sutton's house in Hawkhurst.[111]

William was involved in a number of violent incidents, some of which related to the wider conflict involving the Legh family. In 1354 he was one of four people who killed Robert Walker at Upton. In 1375, the year before Daykyn Wryght helped murder William

[109] Her servants, SC 2/252/6 m. 1d., SC 2/252/10 mm. 4–4d., SC 2/252/11 m. 4d.; and suits, SC 2/252/13 m. 5, SC 2/253/1 m. 4d., SC 2/254/3 m. 5. The assize of ale, SC 2/253/2 m. 4 – SC 2/253/8 m. 5.

[110] c. 1376–1396, SC 2/253/10 m. 4 – SC 2/255/2 m. 4d. As Legh's servant, CHES 25/22 m. 8. As a pledge, in 1376 and c. 1382–1385, SC 2/254/3 mm. 3d–4, SC 2/254/4 m. 4d.–5, SC 2/254/5 m. 8d, SC 2/254/6 m. 6d. Agnes may have been the widow of Robert Discher, and had previously held a third part of these lands with her sister Margery daughter of William Joudrel, SC 2/252/2 m. 4, SC 11/899 m. 4. No conclusion to the suit is given.

[111] CHES 25/19 m. 14. Hawkhurst, in Whaley or Disley, passed from John Sutton, after Adam Kyngeslegh and Thomas Stathum, to William Joudrel in 1376, and William's lands were entered by Roger, his son, the following year. SC 2/252/14 m. 3d., SC 2/253/3 m. 10d., SC 2/253/8 mm. 3–3d., SC 2/253/10 m. 4. The full holding, rented at 15s. 8½d. a year, included a house at Hawkhurst, a close called 'le Stykymyre' next to Hockerley, a hedged enclosure near 'Brocwalhurst', and a close called 'le Wallekerre' in Kettleshulme. The house was occupied by John Hickesone of Hawkhurst in 1375, when his wife, Joan, was attacked by Robert Middelton, SC 2/253/9 m. 3. John's son, John, was living here c. 1383/4, SC 2/254/5 m. 8d. (it is not mentioned in the rental). As William Schore recovered a debt against John Hickesone in court in 1380, it is possible that William held and sublet this tenement after William Joudrel, SC 2/254/2 m. 3d.

Joudrel, Schore took his brother Adam, and others, to John Davenport's house at Bramhall with the intention of killing or mistreating
Daykyn and John's other servants, and when the hue was raised
he fled to Poynton. In this he was said to have had the counsel
and support of Robert Legh, John Mascy, the parson of Stockport,
and Henry Mareschall – some of the most powerful people within
Macclesfield Hundred. In 1377 he was amerced 1s. 8d. for wounding
John Hancokeson del Persones in Whaley and was later indicted
of another assault against him in the same township.[112]

JOHN SERLE

In 1362 John was amerced for common suit in the portmote, but
from the late 1360s or early 1370s he held two messuages and over
ten acres of land, at 7s. 1d. rent, in Disley.[113] This property appears
to have passed to his son Henry, who was amerced between 1379
and 1382 for common suit, and subsequently to another son,
Richard, in 1383. Prior to this, Richard had been in service to
Ranulph Bulkylegh. In 1387 the land then passed to John's
daughters, Alice and Maud, who granted it back to their father a
few months later. Maud served as a maid to local undertenant
William Hode, and William Dounes had claimed the service of
Alice.[114] John was found guilty in three separate halmote suits, two
for debt and one of trespass, against Geoffrey Dounes between
1377 and 1383. He also served as a pledge for William Dounes.[115]

John was involved in a series of offences. In 1362 he was one of
five men, aided by three others, who were indicted for forcible
entry of the manor-house of Bollin. In 1383 he was indicted for
taking animals and depasturing the corn of divers tenants in Disley
over the previous six years (or prior to his re-entry to the tenement).
In the same year he was said to have stolen, with the aid of two

---

[112] CHES 25/19 m. 8, CHES 25/22 m. 8; 'County Court Indictment Roll',
pp. 786/7; SC 2/253/12 m. 1d.
[113] Common suit, SC 2/252/13 m. 6. His land, SC 2/254/1 mm. 12–13d.,
SC 2/254/2 m. 3, SC 2/254/4 m. 4d., m. 5d.
[114] Henry and Richard, SC 2/254/1 mm. 12–13, SC 2/254/2 m. 3, SC
2/254/4 mm. 4–4d. Alice and Maud, SC 2/254/8 m. 2d–3d, SC 2/254/9 m.
4, SC 2/254/6 m. 6d.
[115] SC 2/253/10 m. 4, SC 2/254/2 m. 3d., SC 2/254/4 m. 5d., SC 2/254/8
m. 2d.

outside men, two oxen, two cows and a horse at Bramhall. His wife, Margery, was struck by another woman with a stick in Disley in 1381.[116]

THE SLEGH FAMILY

This was one of the most important families in the borough in the half-century following the Black Death. Both John and his brother Richard held office in the 1350s, and both were actively involved in the process of the courts. Neither was presented for any hues or affrays.[117]

To take John first, he was elected borough-reeve in 1349 and regularly served as a juror in the portmote, although rarely as a pledge. His land-holdings included a close in Wallgate, three other small closes worth 3½d., and, at one time, land in both Shrigley and Hurdsfield.[118] Alice, his wife, was an active brewer who was amerced in eight of the thirteen years between 1355 and 1368. She was also amerced for an affray in Chestergate in 1367.[119] Their son, John, who rarely appears in the courts, held over eight acres of land in the Roewood and at least one acre in the borough fields.[120]

Richard Slegh served as a custodian of ale in 1350/1 and as mayor of Macclesfield in 1359–63, 1366, and 1369. Although less active as a juror he acted as a pledge in a professional capacity and served over 60 times in the portmote and twice in the halmote. He held

---

[116] At Bollin they were accused of abducting ('rapuerunt') Margaret, widow of Hugh Chaderton, and carrying off her goods to the value of 13s. 4d., CHES 25/19 m. 30. CHES 25/21 m. 1, m. 6, SC 2/254/4 m. 8d. Margery, SC 2/254/3 m. 3. In 1352/2, John, or another of the same name, had been bailed at the eyre for a felony, SC 2/252/5 m. 8.

[117] John, c. 1349–1377, SC 2/252/2 m. 3 – SC 2/253/10 m. 5. Later appearances, such as serving as a pledge in 1388, SC 2/254/10 m. 8, most likely referred to his son. Richard, c. 1350–1373, SC 2/252/3 m. 4 – SC 2/253/7 mm. 2–3.

[118] As reeve, SC 2/252/2 mm. 3–3d; and as a juror and as a pledge, SC 2/252/3 m. 4, SC 2/252/4 mm. 6–6d., Chester City Record Office, Earwaker MSS CR 63/2/338 m. 1. His land, SC 11/899 m. 1, m. 3d.

[119] The assize of ale, SC 2/252/7 m. 3 – SC 2/253/3 m. 9. Her affray, SC 2/253/2 m. 4d.

[120] For his land, see SC 2/252/13 m. 5d., SC 2/252/15 m. 4, SC 11/899 m. 1d., SC 11/898 m. 1d, SC 2/254/13 m. 8d.

Family Tree of the Slegh Family

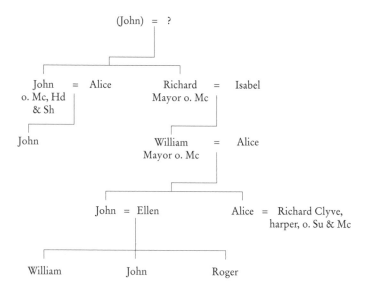

burgages in both Wallgate and Souterslane, and owned some land adjoining that of his brother.[121] He was twice amerced for the false presentment of hues, and paid 3s. od. for cutting down two oak trees in 1373.[122] Isabel, his wife, had received a third of an acre and 2s. od. rent in dower, which she recovered from William, her son, in a portmote suit in her old age. She was a brewer between 1372 and 1376 and briefly returned to brewing in 1391 – a couple of years before her death.[123]

William, son of Richard, also served in office and was described

---

[121] As mayor, SC 2/252/15 m. 4, SC 2/253/2 m. 4, 'John de Macclesfield Cartulary', fos. 37, 40, 50, 60, 110–12, 172–3; and as custodian of ale, SC 2/252/3 m. 4. As a portmote pledge, c. 1352–1373, SC 2/252/4 m. 6 – SC 2/253/7 m. 2d (eight times in 1352/3 SC 2/252/5 mm. 4–4d); and as a halmote pledge in 1356 and 1365, SC 2/252/7 m. 2d, SC 2/253/1 m. 2. His land, SC 2/252/15 m. 4, SC 2/253/4 m. 3d, SC 2/254/13 m. 8d.

[122] His false presentment of hues, SC 2/252/12 m. 3, SC 2/253/4 m. 3d; and wood, SC 2/253/7 m. 3d.

[123] SC 2/254/12 m. 8d. The assize of ale, SC 2/253/6 m. 5d. – SC 2/253/10 m. 5, SC 2/254/13 m. 6d. She died in 1393/4, SC 2/254/15 m. 6.

in 1374/5 as both catchpoll and reeve, and was reeve in 1377/8. He was mayor in 1375, 1390–1 and 1396–8.[124] He frequently acted as a pledge in the portmote, although not on the same scale as his father. He was more involved in the running of the courts and regularly served as a juror. In the halmote he served as both a pledge and as a witness to land transactions.[125] His livestock included horses and pigs. His regular taking or purchasing of wood, timber (including oak and birch) and holly may have contributed to their fodder, and during an eight-year period, for instance, he made payments of at least 15s. 0d. for this purpose. In terms of trade he was amerced once for the assize of bread in 1381.[126]

He held substantial land-holdings in the borough and those which formerly belonged to his father were granted to him in 1370. These included several burgages which were, in turn, granted to his daughter, Alice, on her marriage in 1392. He also held a 12½ acre enclosure called 'le Halleheye' next to the Fence, which had formerly belonged to Jordan Macclesfield.[127] In Hurdsfield he held

---

[124] He appears in the portmote, c.1362–1394, SC 2/252/13 m. 6d. – SC 2/254/15 m. 6; and in the halmote, c.1379–1396, SC 2/254/1 m. 12 – SC 2/255/2 m. 3d. His office-holding, SC 2/253/8 mm. 5–5d., m. 8d., SC 2/253/10 m. 5, SC 2/253/12 m. 2, SC 2/254/12 mm. 5d.–6d., mm. 8–9, SC 2/254/13 m. 6; 'John de Macclesfield Cartulary', fos. 44–7, 50–1, 56, 59, 115.

[125] As a portmote pledge, c.1366–1378, SC 2/253/1 m. 4d – SC 2/253/12 m. 2, and three times in 1383 and 1388/9, SC 2/254/4 m. 7, SC 2/254/10 mm. 8–9d. As a juror, c.1386–1389, SC 2/254/7 m. 3, SC 2/254/8 mm. 1–1d. – SC 2/254/11 m. 7. As a halmote pledge, five times between 1382 and 1385, SC 2/254/4 m. 4 – SC 2/254/6 m. 6d. As a witness, see SC 2/254/14 m. 5; he was one of William Birchels' two attorneys in 1395, SC 2/255/1 m. 7.

[126] For wood, see SC 2/253/8 m. 8d., SC 2/253/9 m. 5, SC 2/254/2 m. 10; and his livestock, SC 2/253/9 m. 10, SC 2/254/4 mm. 14–16. The assize of bread, SC 2/254/3 m. 5.

[127] His grant to Alice consisted of two closes, one with a house and a garden, in Wallgate, half a burgage in Chestergate, half a burgage near the common oven, and half a burgage in Souterslane. Further land, including a close over the Boothfield, between Richard Rowe's and John Leversegge's land, was granted to him by Richard son of John Morton in 1392. SC 2/253/4 m. 3d., SC 2/254/13 mm. 7–8; SC 11/898 m. 1d.

a close of eight acres of land and two acres of meadow called 'le Heghruddyng', and asserted a further 2¼ acres.[128]

His amercement of 1s. 0d. for an affray in Wallgate in 1362 was his first court appearance and the only one involving violence, although he was later amerced on another two occasions for unlawfully presenting affrays. He was also involved in the affray at the Barnaby fair in 1372, when John Chorlegh of Wilmslow drew a knife on him, and he was fined 2s. 0d. in the eyre in 1377 for a trespass. In 1388 he was assaulted in Rainow and burgess Reginald Cook acted in his defence.[129]

Alice, his wife, brewed ale regularly and was amerced in fourteen of the twenty years between 1372 and 1392. In one year, for instance, her total amercements were 2s. 2d.[130] Their daughter, and heiress, Alice, married Richard Clyve, harper, round about 1392. There are no references to Clyve in the portmote before this, but two years earlier, in 1390, he enclosed an acre of waste at Ridge in Sutton. After 1394 he started to appear as a portmote juror. Alice, like her mother, was also an ale-wife whose amercements began shortly after her marriage in 1394.[131]

---

[128] This land formerly belonged to William Bullynche and was granted by William Hayfeld to Slegh in 1379, after Hayfield had recovered it by a plea of land in the halmote. He was given another rood of land nearby by William son of William Bullynche in 1392. SC 2/253/2 m. 3d., SC 2/254/1 m. 12, SC 2/254/14 mm. 4–4d., SC 11/898 m. 3d.

[129] SC 2/252/13 m. 6d., SC 2/254/4 m. 6d., SC 2/254/11 m. 7, SC 2/253/7 m. 3, SC 2/253/12 m. 10, SC 2/254/9 m. 5.

[130] The assize of ale, SC 2/253/7 mm. 2–3 – SC 2/254/13 m. 6d., m. 8d. (for example, SC 2/254/9 m. 6–6d., SC 2/254/11 m. 9).

[131] SC 2/254/13 m. 8d, SC 2/254/15 mm. 5d.–6, SC 2/255/1 mm. 5–6d. His assart, SC 2/254/12 m. 5d. He is referred to as Richard Harper of Clyve in the portmote and Richard Clyve, harper, in the halmote. Alice and Richard received her father's land in July 1392. In August John Togod, a smallholder of Sutton, broke into Richard Harper's house at night-time in Sutton and beat Ellen Wevere (an undertenant) with a stick in her leg and other parts of her body, SC 2/254/14 m. 4.

THOMAS STANYSTRETE
AND WILLIAM CALVERHALE

William son of John Calverhale held a ten acre close of 'old' land in Rainow after the Black Death. He served as a pledge four times in the halmote between October 1349 and January 1350, and was amerced for pasturing his animals on land taken into the lord's hands in 1355, his last appearance in the court records.[132] His land was entered in 1361 by his son, Robert, who made few appearances in the courts. In 1378 his daughter, Joan, entered 4½ acres of 'new' land, which had formerly belonged to Robert Joye, in Rainow.[133]

In 1366 Thomas Stanystrete paid a fine of 3s. 4d. to espouse William's widow, Margery, and in 1380 entered a 9½ acre close of 'old' land in Rainow, near or adjacent to that formerly held by William. This was called 'Calrall' (Calrofold) and was granted to him by Thomas Shryglegh, who had recovered a debt of 1s. 6d. against him in the halmote in 1375. In 1379 they quitclaimed all right to lands in Pot, which Margery had held in dower from William Potte who died around 1363. His livestock included at least seven cattle, six bullocks, two horses, fourteen sheep and two pigs.[134]

Nicholas Upton was indicted for two assaults on Thomas between 1372 and 1374, beating and wounding him in Rainow, when Adam Haregreve was Upton's accomplice, and assaulting him with a stick in Hurdsfield. In 1382 he was amerced 9d. in three separate pleas of trespass in the halmote against Robert Calverhale. A plea of debt in the halmote between Thomas and Robert Thorbald, in the same year, led to amercements of 1½d. each, which were imposed upon Thorbald, as a burgess, in the portmote. In the early 1390s Stanystrete served as a juror in the halmote.[135]

---

[132] His land, SC 11/899 m. 3; service as a pledge, SC 2/252/2 m. 4; and pasturing, SC 2/252/6 m. 3.

[133] Robert's land, SC 2/252/12 m. 2d.; and suits in 1359 and 1368, SC 2/252/10 m. 5, SC 2/253/3 m. 10d. Joan, SC 2/253/12 m. 1d.

[134] SC 2/253/2 m. 2. Thomas paid an entry-fine of 9s. 4d., SC 2/254/1 m. 12; SC 2/253/8 m. 3d. SC 2/254/2 m. 3, SC 2/252/14 m. 4. The rental also refers to half an acre of 'new' land brought into cultivation in 1361/2, SC 11/898 m. 3d. His livestock, SC 2/254/1 m. 6, m. 11, SC 2/254/2 m. 10, SC 2/254/4 mm. 14–16.

[135] CHES 25/20 mm. 80, m. 83. His disputes with Calverhale, SC 2/254/3 m. 3d; and Thorbald, SC 2/254/4 m. 4, m. 6. As a juror, SC 2/254/14 m. 4, SC 2/252/15 m. 3.

There were a number of other crimes associated with the family. In 1367 Margery was amerced for an affray in Rainow, and in 1369 Thomas was amerced for another in Macclesfield. In 1380 Margery was fined 3s. 4d. for a felony. In 1383/4 a number of accusations were made, some of which led to convictions. Thomas was amerced 1s. 2d. in the halmote for carrying off acorns from Lyme at the time of pannage, and for digging turves in Coombs and 'Longlachemore'. Margery and Joan, aided probably by Thomas, were indicted for stealing ewes at Rainow, while Margery was accused of receiving other property stolen by Joan. These included clothes, linen and woollen cloth from residents in Whaley and Shrigley, and 20s. 0d. in money from Robert Joye in Rainow. When the foresters came to arrest Joan, who was living with them, she could not be found and her possessions, which included three cows, two bullocks, and five yearling calves, were sold.[136] In that year Thomas also acknowledged another debt of 8s. 0d. to Thomas Shryglegh. The following year Joan was amerced 6d. for failing to prosecute a plea of land against Robert Joye.[137]

ROGER STOKE

Roger was convicted of five serious affrays between 1362 and 1367, four of which were in the borough and one was in Bollington, and he was amerced the high total sum of 7s. 6d. In addition, he was indicted for an assault upon burgess Nicholas Jolynet. In 1370 he was amerced another 6d. after wounding a woman in Chestergate with Alice Hondedoghter le Mulward, his concubine; he used his baslard, and Alice a stick. In 1371 another affray occurred as he attempted to take Richard Rowe's horse from his house; for this, he was fined 1s. 6d. In this year he was also amerced 3d., together with three others, for being a common fisherman within the forest. He was the victim of a brawl, along with John Wryght, in the summer of 1375 and died a few months later while serving as a custodian of ale. This event must clearly have affected his

---

[136] Chester City Record Office, Earwaker MSS CR 63/2/338 m. 1d.; SC 2/253/2 m. 3d., SC 2/254/1 m. 13, CHES 25/21 mm. 8–8d.
[137] SC 2/254/5 mm. 7–8, SC 2/254/6 m. 6d.

family's standard of living as his wife and daughter, both named Alice, paid a fine for unlawfully carrying off dead wood.[138]

His son, Richard, also committed several acts of violence. In 1375 he was amerced 1s. od. for wounding John Wryght, and drawing blood, shortly after the affray involving John and his father. In 1385 he came to the aid of John Leversegge, by striking Reginald Cook with a stick after Cook had drawn his knife. In 1389 he hit Alice Wosewall, again with a stick.[139]

Another son, John, aided in the homicide of Thomas Bunbury, who was killed with a knife by Robert, the servant of Roger Walker, in 1376. In 1380 John was indicted, along with borough residents William Stubbes and William Hayfeld, for burglary by breaking the doors and windows of Ranulph Neuton's house at Macclesfield, who chased and arrested them. The following year Annabel Lether struck him with a stone on his back in an affray.[140]

JOHN WALKER

John served as catchpoll and coroner for Macclesfield and a juror in the portmote. His holdings included two closes, one of which was in Godiaslane, and these contained hay, corn and turves. He appears to have been involved in the cloth trade, and was probably, as his name suggests, a fuller. He brought at least nineteen suits in the portmote and owed jointly, with Roger Bower, 20s. od. to Beatrice Mascy. He was involved in stock rearing and employed a shepherd.[141] Another of John's servants was Richard Walker, who was described as a 'schermon' in 1378. This Richard was sued by Edmund Dounes over the detention of woollen cloth.[142]

---

[138] SC 2/252/13 m. 6d., SC 2/252/15 m. 4, SC 2/253/1 m. 2, SC 2/253/2 m. 4d., CHES 25/20 m. 26, m. 53d., SC 2/253/4 m. 3d., SC 2/253/6 m. 3, m. 5. SC 2/253/8 m. 5d., SC 2/253/9 m. 5.

[139] SC 2/253/8 m. 5d, SC 2/254/6 m. 5d., SC 2/254/11 m. 7.

[140] SC 2/253/9 m. 14d., SC 2/254/1 m. 10d., SC 2/254/3 m. 5.

[141] c. 1360–1381, SC 2/252/12 m. 3 – SC 2/254/3 m. 5, and in 1391/2, SC 2/254/12 m. 9d., SC 2/254/13 m. 6d. He was catchpoll in 1372/3, SC 2/253/1 m. 2, and serving as coroner in 1375 and 1379, SC 2/253/9 m. 14d., SC 2/254/1 m. 5. His land, and service as a juror, SC 2/253/10 mm. 5–5d., SC 2/253/12 mm. 2–2d. His debt, SC 2/253/8 m. 5; and shepherd, SC 2/253/5 m. 8.

[142] c. 1372–1390, SC 2/253/6 m. 5d – SC 2/254/11 mm. 7–7d. SC 2/253/12 m. 2d, SC 2/254/11 m. 9. Denise Brounhull was convicted of an affray

Like other burgesses John pastured his livestock within the forest and obtained holly and other wood as a fodder; in a five-year period, for instance, he paid 10s. 0d. for green wood or timber, and a further 1s. 0d. for fruit from the orchard at the manor-house of Macclesfield. In addition he held some pasture land within the borough fields.[143] He was involved in five affrays in a 30 year period between 1361 and 1391.[144] His wife, Ellen, was a brewer between 1371 and 1378.[145]

WILLIAM WHITEHULL

In 1363 William was convicted for allowing his cattle to trespass in Handley after William Dounes and the other lessees had brought a suit in the halmote. In 1375 he took possession of a close at the Ringstones in Whaley. This tenement, of around thirteen acres, passed to Richard, his son, and Katherine, daughter of Roger Mottrum, in 1381. He must have then held some land as an under-tenant, and in the following year he was convicted of detaining 7½d. rent from another under-tenant, William Hode; at the same court William Hode was amerced twice for falsely claiming a larger amount, and for burning Whitehull's fences. This was the second civil action brought against him by William Hode in the halmote, while William also owed other more substantial debts. These included 11s. 0d. to Geoffrey Dounes, jointly with his son Richard, and 1s. 6d., with carpenter Richard Egge, to Adam Olyver.[146]

His son, Richard, took possession of a messuage called 'Ormesty' in Disley in 1371 and ten years later quitclaimed all right to a tenement in this township called 'le Bothum', just prior to entering

against Margery, his wife, and of a trespass against Richard and Margery in 1371/2, SC 2/253/6 mm. 5–5d.
[143] His timber included oak and birch trees cut down in the park. SC 2/253/6 m. 5d., SC 2/253/7 m. 3d., SC 2/253/9 m. 5, SC 2/253/3 m. 9. His livestock included at least two horses, SC 2/253/12 mm. 8–9.
[144] SC 2/252/13 m. 5, SC 2/253/4 m. 3, SC 2/253/11 m. 2, SC 2/254/12 m. 9d.
[145] SC 2/253/6 m. 5 – SC 2/254/2 m. 4d.
[146] c.1363–1386, SC 2/252/15 m. 2 – SC 2/254/8 m. 3d (for later amercements for ale see n. 149 below). His trespass, SC 2/252/15 m. 2. His land, SC 2/253/8 m. 4, SC 2/254/3 m. 3. His dispute with Hode and debts, SC 2/254/3 m. 3d, SC 2/254/4 mm. 4–5d.

his father's holding in Whaley. He also acquired another enclosure, of around six acres, in Whaley called Little Bromhall in 1387. Like his father, Richard also incurred some substantial debts, including 15s. 0d. with his brother, William, to Richard Kyngeslegh in 1393. He was amerced for striking Agnes Sutton, with his fists, in Macclesfield in 1381.[147]

The majority of the appearances in the courts of both William and Richard related to the taking or purchase of wood, which included various trees and loppings such as curved pieces, 'spyres' and 'grayves'. As these were sometimes said to have been for the work of others it seems likely that they were carpenters; in c. 1390/1, for instance, William was indicted with carpenter Richard Egge for taking and selling an oak from Disley common. In total William made payments in the halmote of more than 20s. 0d.[148] Additionally, both Richard, in 1389, and William, between 1392 and 1395, were amerced for the assize of ale.[149]

---

[147] SC 2/253/5 m. 10, SC 2/254/3 m. 3, m. 5, SC 2/254/4 m. 4, SC 2/254/8 m. 2d, SC 2/254/14 m. 5d.

[148] His payments included 8s. 8d. in 1378 and 10s. 2d. in 1383–4. Richard paid 9s. 0d. in 1382–3; see Table 4. SC 2/253/12 m. 1d, SC 2/254/4 m. 5d., SC 2/254/5 m. 8d.; CHES 25/22 m. 4. This appears to have been timber rather than fodder, as neither William or Richard appear in the lists of escapes. They did, however, keep pigs, SC 2/254/5 m. 4.

[149] The assize of ale: Richard, SC 2/254/11 m. 4; and William, SC 2/254/14 m. 4 – SC 2/255/2 m. 3. This William may have been Richard's brother.

Appendix Two: Analysis of Appearances in the Courts of Manor and Borough, c. 1349–96

(A) KEY

Column One : Name

General Terms

br.	brother of	sen.	senior
d.	daughter of	serv.	servant of
h.	heir of	sis.	sister of
jun.	junior	w.	wife of
o.	of (a place)	wdw.	widow.
s.	son of		

Names (Modern Equivalents)

Ad.	Adam	Isb.	Isabel
Al.	Alan	Jam.	James
Alc.	Alice	Jn.	John
Alx.	Alexander	Jord.	Jordan
Bend.	Benedict	Margt.	Margaret
Col.	Colin	Mich.	Michael
Dav.	David	Mrgy.	Margery
Den.	Denise	Md.	Maud
Edm.	Edmund	Mth.	Matthew
Gff.	Geoffrey	Nch.	Nicholas
Glb.	Gilbert	Pet.	Peter
Ham.	Hamon	Rb.	Robert
Hecok	?	Rch.	Richard
Hen.	Henry	Reg.	Reginald
Herv.	Hervey	Rg.	Roger
Hgh.	Hugh	Rnph.	Ranulph

Rph.	Ralph	Th.	Thomas
Sbl.	Sybil	Wll.	William
Sim.	Simon	Wlt.	Walter
Stph.	Stephen		

Column Two : Land

This records rentholding according to the following categories:

1	30s. and over (44 acres and over)
2	15s.–29s. 11d. (22 to 44 acres)
3	6s.–14s. 11d. (9 to 22 acres)
4	2s.–5s. 11d. (3 to 9 acres)
5	up to 1s. 11d. (3 acres and below).

The above key is based on the standard rent of 8d. per acre for assarted land. Although it takes into account where possible the small proportion of land rented at 4d. per acre there will inevitably be some inaccuracy. Land held within the borough is indicated by 'B' to denote burgage holdings and by 'b' for land rented by outsiders or land in the fields and territories.

Column Three : Halmote (Hal) and Portmote (Port)

The aim of this column is to show an individuals' involvement within the local community, and can be used, therefore, for identification purposes. It also denotes status. The criteria for each number were:

0	to denote fewer than 5 appearances in the court.
1	to denote landholding (either as an entry or as an amercement for not appearing for common suit). Where this is the only 'appearance' the (1) is given to indicate probable non residence.
1–3	to denote the number of Appearances, whereby 1 for 5–9, 2 for 10–19, and 3 for 20 or more.
1–2	to denote service as a juror, whereby 1 for 1–4 times, and 2 for 5 or more times.
1–2	to denote service as a pledge, whereby 1 for 10 or more times and 2 for 20 or more times.
1	to denote evidence of local office-holding.

1   to denote service as a witness to land grants and charters on
         5 or more occasions.

This gives a maximum mark out of 10. Additionally 'w' and 'f' reveals
that a wife or other family member also appeared in the courts.

Column Four : Business (Bus.)

Although similar to the number given above this identifies what
an individual most frequently appeared for and includes suits,
affrays and land entry. Those in italics indicate a larger number of
appearances.

Key:

a   affrays and hues (3+)

j   juror (2+ for Halmote and 3+ for Portmote)

l   land entry or exchange (3+)

pl   pledge (5+)

st   suit (10+)

v   fines or purchases relating to wood, or vert (3+).

Column Five : Stock

This indicates the number and type of animals held, as illustrated
by the fines made for escapes or for grazing (foggage and herbage).

Key:

e   an escape fine under 1s.,

E   an escape fine 1s.–1s. 11d.,

EE   an escape fine 2s. and over

x   for 1–2 animals

X   for 3–5 animals

XX   for 6 or more animals

whereby 'h' is for working horses, 'f' for foal; 'c' is for cows; 'o'
is for draught-beasts and oxen (including bullocks, steers and heifers)
with OOO for 20 or more and OOOO for 40 or more.

As the number of sheep was not always indicated they are summarised by 'S' unless the numbers were under 5 (s), over 40 (SS),
over 60 (SSS), or 100 or more (SSSS).

Unfortunately this information is incomplete and is available, in a limited form, for only a quarter of the years during the period.

Column Six : Wood (W.)

This indicates the frequency of fines for or purchases of wood in the local courts, whereby 'w' is for under five, 'W' is for more than five and 'WW' is for more than ten. As they do not include the numerous indictments or attachments for vert these can only provide an indication of the wood taken. Most wood was probably cut as green foliage for use as fodder.

Column Seven : Origin

This section lists both the place of residence or origin of people, and summarises their land-holdings. Brackets indicate probable origin.

Vill Key:

Adlg	Adlington		Man	Manor (not known)
ass	assart		Mc	Macclesfield (Borough)
Bg	Burgess		Mdg	Midgley
Bs	Bosley		mkt	market
Bt	Bollington		Mp	Marple
Bu	Butley		nr	non resident
Chg	Chestergate (Borough)		Out	Outsider
Ddstr	Dedestrete (Borough)		ov	oven
Ds	Disley		Pby	Prestbury
Dw	Downes (Sutton)		Pt	Pott
Ed	Eddisbury (Rainow)		-r	rentholder (with several
flds	fields (Borough)			holdings)
Gw	Gawsworth		Ra	Rainow
Gdl	Godiaslane (Borough)		Sbch	Sandbach
Glh	Galtrehill (Borough)		Sh	Shrigley
Hd	Hurdsfield		St	Stanley
Hnd	Hundred		Stl	Souterslane (Borough)
Hord	Hordern (Rainow)		Stckpt	Stockport
hse	house		Su	Sutton
Hlst	Hollinset		Tx	Taxal
Hy	Handley (Lyme)		Ty	Tytherington
Jg	Jordangate (Borough)		Up	Upton
Kh	Kettleshulme		Wh	Whaley (and Yeardsley)
lsd	leased		Wo	Worth

Column Eight : Notes

This section summarises information on these people, primarily in connection to office and trade.

Key for Office:

Ags	Agister	Lab	Labourers (Justice of)
Arch	leader of the archers in Macclesfield hundred	lsd	leased
		Man	Manor
Bff	Bailiff	mil	mill
Chap	Chaplain	off	borough office
Chmb	Chamberlain	Prk	Parker (or Park)
clk	clerk	Rctr	Rector
Crn	Coroner	Rdr	Rider (of forest)
Cstd	Custodian	Rv. Bl.	Reeve of the chantry of
cstbl	constable	Mary	the Blessed Mary
Dep	deputy	serv	servant
esc	escapes	Shff	Sheriff
esch	escheator of Cheshire	Sjp	Serjeant of the Peace
felon	guilty of a felony	Stckm	Stockman
For	Forester	stlg	stallage
frm	farmer (ie. lessee)	U-	Under
fulm	fulling mill	Stwd	Steward
Glr	Gaoler	Vcr	Vicar
hbg	herbage	Vrdr	Verderer
Just	Justice	vlln	villein
knght	knight	wfs	waifs
Kp	Keeper	Wodw	Woodward

Key for Trade:

Ale:

for the borough (b.):

3–4	(ale),
5–8	(alew): a small number of amercements,
9+	AleW

for the manor (m.):

3–4	(ale),
5+	Ale *or* m. AleW.

General Trade:

bchr	butcher	lthr	leather-craftsman
bkr	baker	Lyme	frequent fines for
cblr	cobbler	wood	purchases of wood
chlnr	blanket-maker		from this area
chmb	chamberlain	mrcr	mercer
clth	cloth-seller	milr	miller
coalm	coal mine	shp	shop holder
copr	cooper	smth	smith
cptr	carpenter	tavern	tavern holder
drpr	draper	thshr	thresher
frg	forge holder	tlr	tailor
fulr	fuller	tnr	tanner
glvr	glover	(w)	wife
hcks	huckster	wol	wool (seller)
haftm	haft-maker	work	a fine for work or
hrpr	harper		service
labr	labourer	wvr	weaver

(B) ANALYSIS OF APPEARANCES

Name	Cat	Hal	Port	Bus	Stock	W	Vill	Notes
Achard, Rch.	4	3w	3wf	l, st	h	W	Su, (Mc)	(b. ale)
Achard, Ellen d. Rch. serv. Jn. Boyle	—		2	a		w	Mc	serv
Adamsone, Rg. (o. Bs)	—	o				w	Bs	
Adamsone, Wll. (o. Bt)	5	1	o		P		Bt	
Adamsone, Rch. s. Wll.	—	o	o				(o. Bt)	
Addesheved, Rb.	3	4w		j	PP/SS HH/ OOO	W	Sh	
Adlynton, Th.	4	1			OO		Kh	copr
Adlynton, Wll. o.	—	1w						m. Ale
Aleyn, Ad. (o. Su)	u	ow	o		P/h/E	w	(Su)	
Alayn, Jn. (o. Ty)	—	1w	o		(e)		(Ty)	
Alayn, Jn.	3	2			P	w	Ra	
Alayn, Hen. s. Jn.	3	1					Ra	
Alayn, Jn. s. Jn.	3	1	(o)		p		Ra	
Aleyn, Margaret d. Jn.	3	1					Ra	
Alayn, Rch. s. Jn.	3	1					Ra	
Alcok, Jn. (le Deye)	4/b	4w	2f	pl, l, v	h/E		Ra	Stckm
Alycok, Jn. (o. Bt)	—	o			E		(Bt)	
Alcok, Margery	—		o			w	Bg	serv
Alcok, Rch.	5	1				w	Bt	cptr
Alcok, Rg.	2/B	5	4	st, l	h/o/p	w	Su, Ra	Mayor, b. AleW
Alderley, Agnes d. Wll.	b		—				Mc	
Alderlegh, Rg.	—		1				Mc	
Aleynson, Th., (o. Herdewykwall)	B		3				Bg	
Amelyn, Rch.	4	1w					Ds	
Andertoun, Gff.	—		1				Mc	
Anker, Jn. (s. Rch.)	3	(1)	(1)		h		Ds, nr	
Anker, Rch.	2	o					Ds St	

Name	Cat	Hal	Port	Bus	Stock	W	Vill	Notes
Anker, Margaret d. Rch.	2	-f					Ds, nr	
Archer, Jn.	4	2			H/O		Su	
Archer, Jn., jun.	3	(1)					Su	
Archer, Wll. (o. Su)	4	4wf		l	SS/O		Su	cstbl
Archer, Agnes d. Wll.	4	(1)					Su	
Ashton, Bend. (s. Rg.)	2	7wf	o	l, j, a	S/P	w	Kh, Wh, Ds, lsd. Hy	(m. ale)
Ashton, Edm.	4	3wf		a	H/OO/p	w	Su	
Ashton, Rch. s. Edm.	4	1			p		Su	
Ashton, Joan d. Edm. & Mary sis.	4	(1) (1)					Su	
Ashton, Rb.	—	3wf				w	Bg	off
Ashton, Rb.	3	3wf		l, v		(W)	Kh	m. Ale
Ashton, Agnes d. Rb.	4	(1)					Kh	
Ashton, Jn. s. Rb.	4	1f			(p)		Kh	
Ashton, Rb. s. Jn.	4	1		v		w	Kh	
Ashton, Rg.	3	6wf	o	l, pl	p	w	Kh, Wh	(m. ale)
Ashton, Wll. s. Rg.	2	3f		l	o/s/E	w	Wh, Kh	
Ashton, Jn. s. Wll.	3	1					Kh	
Ashton, Wll. s/h. Wll.	2	1					Wh	
Astbury, Rg.	4/b	1	5f	st		W	Su, Hd	(b. alew)
Astbury, Jn. (s. Rg.)	B		2f				Gdl	
Astbury, Agnes(d. Th.)	—		3			W	Mc	AleW
Astbury, Margt. (d. Th.)	b		—				Mc	
Averil, Wll.	—		1w				Mc	(wol)
Bagger, Rch.	—		2w		h/p	w	Mc	bchr
Bagylegh, Ad.	5	1			P/h		Su	
Bagylegh, Rch.	—	1		pl				
Bagylegh, Rb.	B		ow				Gdl	(ale)
Balle, Wll. s. Wll. s. Ad. (Hepphales)	4	1					Su	
Balle/doghter, Agnes	—		3f	st, a			Mc	AleW
Balleson/doghter, Alc.	—		3f	a			Mc	AleW
Balledoghter, Amy	—		1f			w	Mc	(ale)

Name	Cat	Hal	Port	Bus	Stock	W	Vill	Notes
Balleson, Rch.	B		of				Wg	
Balleson, Rg.	B	o	3w	pl, *a*			Wg	off, tlr(alew)
Bargh, Rb.	u	(o)						vlln
Bargh, Margaret d. Ad.	4						Su	vlln
Barker, Amy d. Th.	—		3	*st*			Mc	AleW
Barker, Rb.			1			w	(Mc)	off
Barker, Rg., s. Wll.	2/b	5	9w	*pl*, l j, *a*	O	w	Mc, Su (£5-r)	off, smth b. AleW
Barwe, Rb. (o. Mc)	—		1				Mc	
Baskervyle, Rb.	4	(1)					*nr*	
Batemon, Jn. s. Rg.	4	1					Su	
Batemon, Jn. s. Ad.	3	6		pl, j	p	w	Su	
Batemon, Ellen d. Jn.	3	(1)					Su	
Batemon, Rb.	3	4w	o	pl, st	P/o		Su	
Batemon, Rg., s. Jn.	2	2		l	PP/o		Su	
Baxster, Margery			1			w	(Mc)	(ale)
Bedlem, Rch.			ow			w	(Mc)	
Bedulf, Rg.	B	1	6w	l, a, j	PP	w	Jg, Gdl	off
Benet, Wll. (o. High Lee)	3	2w			e		Su/Ra	tlr
Benet, Agnes d. Wll	3	o					Ra	
Bentelegh, Hen.	3	1					Wh	
Bentelegh, Jn.	2	3		*l*	p	w	Wh	
Bercrofte, Hen.	4						Bt	
Bernewell, Jn.	B		4w	j			Bg	Mayor
Birchels, Wll. s. Wll.	4	1					Ra	
Blagg, Jn. s. Th.	3	1					Su	
Blagge, Rb.	(B)		6w	*j*		w	Bg	off, mrcr, (w)bkr(ale)
Blagge, Stph.	B		6w	*j*		w	Bg	off, mrcr, bkr (ale) tavern, Wg
Blag, Rg. (o. Bs)	—	o				w	Bs	
Boller, Jn. (o. Bt)	4	3wf	o	st	H/O	w	Bt	haftm
Boller, Jn., jun.	—	o	o				(Bt)	
Bolynton, Ad.	4/B	2	o		EE		Kh, Chg	

Name	Cat	Hal	Port	Bus	Stock	W	Vill	Notes
Bolynton, Dav.	—		1				Mc	
Bolynton, Md. wdw. Wll.	5	o					Bt	
Bolynton, Rph.	—		2				Mc	
Bolynton, Rph. (o. Sh)	3	1w					Su	
Bolynton, Wll. (s. Ad.)	B	o	(1)w				Chg	
Bosedon, Jn., s. Edm.	1	7w	o	*l, j*, pl	O/P/h	W	Great Hd, Ra	
Bosedon, Jn. s. Jn.	2	1					Ra	
Bosedon, Jn., s. Rch.	3	1f					Su	
Bosedon, Rg., s. Ad.	b		2				Mc	
Bosedon, Th. s. Mrgy. Shalcross	3/b	3w	3	pl	E	w	Su, Hd, Mc	(m. ale)
Bosedon, Th. s. Jn.	(2)	(1)					Ra	
Bosedon, Th. s. Jn. s. Rch.	3	1f					Su	
Bosedon, Th. s. Rch.	5	1f	o				Su	
Boterale, Ad.	(u)	ow						m. Ale
Boterale, Hen.	(u)	1w				w		m. Ale
Botfysh, Jn.	B	-f	1				Chg	
Botfysh, Rch.		ow				w	(Mc)	
Botfysh, Wll. & Alice w.	5/b	ow	6wf	*st*, pl *a*(w)		w	Bg	off, smth, AleW
Boure, Th.	5	1w					Su	
Bouker, Wll. (o. Ds)	4	4w		v	OO/h	W	Ds, Wh,	
Bouker, Jn. s. Wll.	—	o						*felon*
Bower, Rg.	—		2w		h	w	Mc	(alew)
Boyle, Jn. & Isb. w.	B	o	5w		o/p	w	Jg, Wg, Gdl	off (w)bkr(ale)
(Boyll, Wll.	5						Su	vlln)
Bradburne, Jn.	4	1w					Ds	
Brocwalhurst, Ad.	5	3wf	o		P/OO/h	W	Hd, Kh	
Brocwalhurst, Jn.	3	7f	o	*l*, pl, *v*, a	P/OOO/ SSSS/H	WW	Kh	cstbl (*Lyme wood*)
Brocwalhurst, Alice, Emma, Margery d. Ad.	4	(1)					Su	
Brodehurst, Jn.	—	2w		j	PP/O		Man	

Name	Cat	Hal	Port	Bus	Stock	W	Vill	Notes
Brodehurst, Jn. s. Jn.	3	1f				w	Su	
Brocwalhurst, Th. s. Jn.	4	2f			p		Kh	
Brocwalhurst, Wll. s. Jn.	4	1f		l	OO/p	w	Kh	
Brocwalhurst, Nch.	4	1					Wh, Kh	
Brodehurst, Ham.	4	1f					Su	
Brodehurst, Wll. s. Ham.	4	1f			H/(p)	w	Su	
Brocwalhurst, Rb. (o. Sh)	(u)	o					(Sh)	
Brocelhurst, Sewel	—		1	st			Mc	*work*
Brok, Rch.	(u)	1w				w	(Man)	
Bromhale, Rch. (o. Mp)	—	o				w	Mp	(w)wvr
Bromall, Rch. s. Rch.	(3)	1					(Ds)	
Bromyleghs, Maud	—		1				(Mc)	(ale)
Bromyleghs, Ell. d. Md.	—			a			(Mc)	(ale)
Bromylegh, Wll. o. Over Alderley	4	o	o				Su	
Bromyleghs, Wll. s. Wll.	4	1					Su	
Broud, Wll. s. Rb.	5	1					Su	
Brounhull, Agnes	—		2					AleW
Brounhull, Den. wdw. Pet.	—		3	a				AleW
Brounhull, Jn.	(B)		(1)				nr	Chap
Brounhull, Rch.	—	o	1				(Mc)	(Chap)
Brounhull, Rg.	(B)		7w	st, pl a, j	H	w	Bg	off, AleW
Brugge, Herv.	(b)		(1)				nr	
Brugge, Sim.	(b)		(1)				nr	
Bulkylegh, Rnph. (Lucy w.)	5	2wf	1w	a	S/PP/ OO/H	w	Su, (Mc)	m. & b. AleW
Bulkylegh, Wll. s. Rnph. 'o. Oteworth'	B	of	of		p		Mc, (Su)	off
Bullynche, Wll. & w.	4/b	3f	7wf	st, a, j	O/h/P		Bg, Hd	off, fulr
Bullynch, Rch. s. Wll.	5	1f					Hd, Mc	
Bullyng, Wll. s. Wll.	5/b	1f	1f		o	w	Hd, Mc	(off)
Bunder, Rb.	3						nr	
Bunnyng, Th. (o. Wh)	(u)	o			p		(Wh)	

Name	Cat	Hal	Port	Bus	Stock	W	Vill	Notes
Burelles, Rch.	B	o	6w	st, a, j	h	w	Bg	off, clth(bkr)
Burgeys, Gff.	—	ow	5wf	a, j	P	w	Bg	off, AleW(bkr)
Buyll, Th.	3						Bt	
Bydulph, Rg.	(B)		2				Bg	off
Byler, Wll.	5	1w					Ra	
Bynges, Cecilia	—		1					(ale)
Bynges, Hgh.	B		1w		o		Mc(by mkt)	
Byrade, Rb. (o. Ty)	(B)		1				(Mc)	
Byran, Ellen	—		2	st, a			Mc	
Byran, Hen.	2/B	3	o			w	Su, Hd, Wg	
Byran, Hen. s. Hen.	4	1					Hd	
Byran, Nch.	2	7wf	o	pl	PP	w	Hd	U-Bff
Byran, Jn., s. Nch	5	2w			h/o/p		Hd	
Byran, Rb. (o. Mc)	3/B	7	6–7	j, pl		w	Bg, Hd	off
Byran, Rg. (o. Bt)	—	1w		a		w	Bt	
Byrcheles, Hen.	-/B	(1)	(1)				Chg, Man, nr	
Calverhale, Wll.	4	2wf	o		S/e		Ra	
Calverhale, Joan d. Wll.	5	1			OO/C		Ra	
Callerhale, Rb. s. Wll.	4	2			e		Ra	
Carles, Rb.	(B)		3wf	a(w)	p	w	Bg	off, tlr, AleW
Carter, Gff. (o. Bt)	—	o					Bt	
Carpentar, Th. s. Jn.	5	1					Hd	
Carter, Th.	(B)		1w			w	Bg	off, AleW
Cartewrught, Jn. (o. Mc)	—		1		P		(Mc)	
Cartwrught, Rb. s. Jn.	—		1		O		Mc	
Cartwright, Jn. (o. Ty)	—	1	o			w	(Ty)	
Cartewryght, Jn. s. Hen.	4	1					Ra	
Caton, Jn. (s. Ad.)	-/b	(1)	4				Mc, Hd	ChapGw
Caton, Wll., br. Jn.	b		4wf				Bg	
Cayrugge, Jn.	—		o			w	Mc	cblr
Chadkyrk, h. Wll.	(B)		(1)				nr	Chap
Charge, Rch.	—		1				Mc	(w)(wol)

Name	Cat	Hal	Port	Bus	Stock	W	Vill	Notes
Chaumpeyn, Rch.	3	2w			h/o		Su, Bt	U-For, frm coalm
Chaumpayn, Rch. s. Rb.	—	2w					Up	
Chaumpayn, Rb. (s. Hgh.?) —			2w	a			Mc	
Chaumpayn, Th.	—	1					Up	U-For
Chaumpayn, Rch. s. Th.	3	1					Up	
Chaunpayn, Wll.	—	2w		v	e	W	(Kh)	
Chaumpeney, Gff.	—	2					Mp	mil, m. Ale
Chauntrell, Jn., o. Stockport	(u)	1					Kh	
Chester, Abbot o.	b		(1)				nr	abbot
Chorlegh, Hgh.	(5)	(1)					Ra	
Chorlegh, Jn., o. Shotstall	3/b	1					Wh, (Mc)	
Chorlegh, Wll.	-/b	1	1wf	pl	e			Kp Man & Prk
Clayton, Wll.	b	1	o	v			Mc-r	frm wfs
Clewlowe, Rch.	3	4			S/p	w	Su	
Clewelowe, Wll. (br. Rch.)	4	1			O/S/P	w	Su	
Clerk, Rch.	—		1			w	Mc	off, cblr
Clerk, Rb.	b		2			w	Mc	
Clokspoke, Ad.	B		3f	a			Stl	(w)wvr
Cloghes, Bend. (s. Jn.)	—	1wf	o		E/p			
Clowes, Sbl. d. Bend. s. Ad.	4	(1)					Su	
Cloghes, Jn., s. Ad.	(4)	2w			OO/h/s		Su	
Cloghes, Rch. (br. Wll.)	5	1			p		Su	
Cloghes, Ellen d. Rch.	5	(1)					Su	
Clowes, Sarah d. Wll. (sis. Rch.)	3						Su	
Clowes, Th., s. Rg.	3	3	(o)	l	OO/H/P	w	Su	
Cloghes, Wll. s. Jn.	4	1					Su	
Clowes, Wll. (s. Rch.)	3	4wf	(o)		O/P/h		Su	cstbl
Clulowe, Edm., s. Wll.	—	o	o		h/o		(Su)	
Clyf, Jn. (& Ellen sis.)	3/B	2	4-5	pl	o		Bg	
Clyf, Isb. wdw. Rg.	b		2	st			Mc	

Name	Cat	Hal	Port	Bus	Stock	W	Vill	Notes
Clyve, Rch. & Alc. w. (d. Wll. Slegh)	B/5	I	2w				Su, Wg, Chg	hrpr (alew)
Coquina, Jn.	3	I					Su	
Cok, Ad. (s. Jn.)	3	4	o	pl, a, v	S/H/ OO/p	W	Su	
Cook, Alx.	3	o					Su	
Cook, Hgh.	(B)		2				Bg	bchr
Cok, Jn.	3	3w	-w	l	e		Su	(w)wvr
Cook, Reg.	B	o	5w	st, a		w	Gdl	off, bchr, AleW
Combermere, Abbot o.	3	I					Wincle	abbot
Colt, Th.	u	o						vlln
Coton, Jn., Margery w.	2	3w		pl	E/P		Su	
Coton, Wll.	—		2w	pl			(Mc)	
Cooper, Rch. (o. Kh)	(u)	ow			OO/P	w	(Kh)	
Court, Col. (br. Rch.)	u	o			o/p	w	(Ra)	
Court, Rch. (o. Ra)	5	I	o		O/H/s/p	w	Ra	
Craven, Rb.	u	I w			e		Man	
Cressmyle, Th.	—	I		v		W		(Lyme wood)
Cresswall, Jn.	I	10wf		l, pl, j, st, v	H/c/s	W	Su, Ed, Ra	For frm esc & mil, Crn
Ad. serv. Jn. o. Creswall	4	I			O/h		Ra	serv.
Crouther, Rch., o. Barthomley	3	1wf					Su, (Ed)	
Croumon, Wll.	4	I					Ra	
Cryour, Rb. (o. Su)	u	(o)w					(Su)	
Dale, Wll. (o. Mc)	B	(o)	7wf	st, pl, j, a		w	lsd. Gdl, Stl, Chg	off, mrcr, mil (ale)
Dale, Wll., (o. Stckpt)	—		I				Mc	
Dande, Rg. (o. Ds)	u	I		a	h/p		(Ds)	
Daukynsone, Th.	B	o	6w	pl		w	Gdl	off, cblr(ale)
Dausone, Rch.	u	I				w	Sh	cstbl
Davenport, Jord.	-/B	4f	3w		e	w	Hnd, Dstr	For
Davenport, Rph.	b		(I)				nr	knght
Davenport, Th.	b	o	(I)				nr	

Name	Cat	Hal	Port	Bus	Stock	W	Vill	Notes
Davenport, Jn. s. Th.	4	1					Su	
Dawe, Jn.	—	ow		v	e/p	w	(Su/Bs)	
Dawe, Wll. s. Jn.	3	1					Su	
Dayfox, Ad. s. Rch. s. Th.	4	3	o	st	p		Su	
Dayfox, Rg. s. Rg. s. Th.	4	1					Su	
Dene, Wll.	3	1w					Wh	
Denyas, Hen.	-/b	1wf	4w				Bg, Mp	off, glvr (b. alew)
Depelache, Jn.	4	1	2				Mc, Kh	
Discher, Rb., Agnes w. (& Margery d. Rg. Joudrel)	3	1		l			Wh	
Doket, Jn.	4	1w					Wh	tnr & glvr
Doket, Jn. s. Jn.	4	1					Wh	
Downes, Edm.	(4)	8f	o	j	H/O		Wo Tx, Kh	For
Dounes, Edm. s. Edm.	(4)	1f				w	Kh	
Dounes, Nch., s. Edm.	b		(1)f				nr	
Dounes, Wll. s. Edm.	3	1f			(o)		Kh, Wh	
Dounes, Gff. (o. Sh)	(3)	9f	3f	pl, st, v, l, j	SS/H OO/P	w	Sh, Bt, Mc, Ra	frm stlg Glr
Dounes, Hgh.	3	3w		pl, l	O/EE		Su, Ra	frm stlg & mil
Dounes, Margaret d. Hgh.	3	(1)					Su	
Dounes, Nch. s. Hen.	5	1			e/p		Su	
Dounes, Nch.	2	3	(1)				Kh, (Mc)	served Gascony
Dounes, Reg. (s. Edm.)	2	8wf	2f	pl, j	OO/h		Su	Prk, (Mayor), mil
Dounes, Rg., s. Nch.	4/b	5	1	j	E		Mc, Kh	
Dounes, Rb. (o. Su)	5	3w	o	v, a	o/p	W	Su	
Doune, Th. s/h. Hen.	—	o						Chmb
Dounes, Wll. (o. Sh)	1/b	8	2f	pl, st, v, l	S/PP/h		Su, Sh, Ra Kh, Bt frm Hy, Bt	Vrdr, Ags
Dounes, Rb. s. Wll. (o. Sh)	1/b	7	2f	l, pl			Sh, Su, Ra, Kh, Bt	(For) Dep Stwd 1400

Name	Cat	Hal	Port	Bus	Stock	W	Vill	Notes
Dounes, Wll. s. Wll. (?)	/b		1f				Mc-r,Sh	
Dounes, Wll. (o. Tx)	/b	2w	1				Tx, Wo, Up, (Mc-r)	
Dimbell, Jn. s. Jn.	3	2					Su	
Dunbull, Jn. s. Wll.	3	2f					Su	
Dunbull, Th. s. Wll.	5	1f					Su	
Dunbull, Wll. s. Jn.	4	2f			OO/H/p		Su	
Dunbull, Wll. s. Wll.	4	2f					Su	
Doncalf, Hen.	—		1w				Mc	(alew)
Duncalf, Jn.	—	o			SS/p/o	W		
Dykeson, Jn. (o. Ra)	3	2wf		l	HH/ OOO/p	w	Ra	tlr
Dikeson, Rb. s. Jn.	4	1f			(h)		Ra	
Dycon, Jn., s. Rg.	5	6f	o	st, j, pl, v	OO/h	w	Su	frm esc
Dykon, Rg. s. Jn. (o. Su)	(2)	3f	1	l, st, a	(p)		Su, Wh	For
Dykon, Jord. s. Jn.	(4)	1w			E		Su	
Dyconsone, Th. s. H. (o. Mp)	—	o					(Mp)	
Dyot, Hen.	4/B	1w	8w	pl, j	P		Su, Mc-r	off, bchr, AleW frm stlg
Edam, Th, s. Wll. (o. Sh)	u	o		st	h/p	W		
Egge, Rch.	u/b	o	1		P	w	Ds	cptr
Elynsone, Rch. s. Wll.	b		(1)w				(Mc)	
Eves, Rch.	5	2w			EE/h/p		Ra	
Eydale, Jn. o. (br. Rch.)	(u)	o			S/OO /h/p	w		
Eydale, Rch., sen.	4	1wf					Su	cblr
Eydale, Rch., jun.	4	4wf		st, l	S/e/P	w	Su, Wh	Rv. Bl. Mary
Eydale, Rb. s. Rch.	3	2f			S/p		Ra	
Eydale, Wll. s. Rch., jun.	4	1f					Su	
Falghes, Th.	2	3		l			Hd	
Fall, Jn. (o. Ds)	u	o				w	(Ds)	
Fall, Jn. s. Jn.	4	1					Wh	
Falle, Rb.	u	1					(Ds/Wh)	(w)wvr

Name	Cat	Hal	Port	Bus	Stock	W	Vill	Notes
Falle, Th.	(u)	o			HH	w		(wol)
Fall, Wll., s. Sarah	5	1f					Wh	wol
Falle, Ellen d. Wll.	5	(1)					Wh	
Falyngbrom, Jn. (Jn. Agnesone Starky)	B	o	4wf	j		w	Wg, Chg	off
Falybron, Rg.	4/B	1	7	pl, st	e	w	Ra, Bg-r	
Fayrefe[o]ld, Rg.	(u)	o			O/h/p		(Su)	
Flecher, Jn. & Mrgy. w.	4–3	1w		l		w	Wh	
Fecheler, Jn.	—		ow				Mc	AleW
Felyppesmayden, Emma	—		1				(Mc)	(alew)
Ferour, Jn. (o. Mc)	—		3				Mc	
Fleccher, Amice w. o. Jn. Oldefeld	—		3f	st, a			Mc	AleW
Flech, Hen.	—		2f	a	p		Mc	
Fleccher, Rnph. s. Hen.	—		2f	a	h		Mc	
Fletcher, Rch.	—		1		e		(Mc)	
Fletcher, Wll. (o. Ds)	4	3w			p		Ds	m. Ale
Flectcher, Th.			o			w	(Mc)	
Flynt, Rch. (o. Mp)	—	(2)					Mp	
Flynt, Rch. s. Wll., sen.	4	1w	o		e/p/s	w	Su	
Flynt, Margery w. Rch.	5	1					Ra	
F'ogge, Th.	b	(1)					nr	knght
Foliot, Gff.	(B)		2w	st			Bg	off, AleW
Forster, Jn. (o. Saltersford)	—	o						(m. ale)
Fox, Alice	4	o					Su	vlln
Foxwist, Rb.	—	2	o				(Su)	For
Foxwyst, Edm. s. Rb.	5	1			p		Su	
Frenche, Pet.	—	o	1w	j			Mc	(ale)
Frenche, Wll.	5/B	4	6w	pl	SS/HH/ O/p	W	Su, Bg	off, AleW
Frere, Wll.	—	o	1w	st				(ale)
Frodesham, Jn. (o. Mc)	3	2	1f	a	h	w	Su, Mc	
Furiynale, Rch.	(u)	o			s/e/p			
Fylle, Jn.	—	o			O/h		(Bs)	
Fyton, Pet., s. Rch.	3	(1)w					Wh, nr	

Name	Cat	Hal	Port	Bus	Stock	W	Vill	Notes
Fyton, Rb. s. Pet.	3	I					Wh	
Fytton, Th. s. Pet.	3						Wh	
Fytton, Th., o. Pownall	4	3	o				Ds	For
Fyton, Th., o. Gawsworth	-/b	(1)f	2				Wg, Hnd	For
Gappe, Glb.	—	I		*v*		W	Hnd	(*Lyme wood*)
Gardener, Nch.	2	5	o	*v*, l, pl	H/O		Su, Ra	frm esc
Gardener, Rb.	3	6	o	*l, pl*, st	OOO/h/p	w	Su, Ra,Bt	
Gaoler, Hen.	3	5wf	*pl*		e		Su	
Gaoler, Hen.	—		3w				Mc	(alew)
Gaoler, Hen. (Gaoler, Hen., *several*)	—		1w				Mc	bchr
Jayler, Hen. s. Hen.	B		1f				(Gdl)	
Gaoler, Alx., s. Hen.	(4)	6wf		l, j	s/H/O/P		Su, Ra	U-For, Stckm
Jayler, Rch., s. Alx.	3	3f					Su, Ra	
Jayler, Jn.	—		I				Mc	
Gatiler, Al.	—		2w				Mc	off, AleW
Gaze, Jn.	—	o			OO/h			(Chap)
Geneson, Wll.	(b)		(I)				nr	
Geppeson, Wll. *Geffeson*	u	1w		*v*	h/o/p	w	(Sh)	
Geppeson, Jn.	B		3–4	st			Jg	
Gilbert, Edm. s. Jn. s. Wll.	(3)	I					Ra	
Glover, Jn., o. Butley	B		I				Mc(1366–9)	
Glover, Wll.	—		ow					
Godemon, Jn. (o. Su)	3–4	2			o/p	w	Su	
Golbourn, Dav. (*Walsh*)	—		I	*a*			(Mc)	
Goldeson, Rch.	3	2		l, v	O/h/p	w	Kh	
Goldesmyth, Edm.	—	2		*a*			Mc	
Gore, Jn.	4	I			h/p		Su	
Gore, Rg.	4	2					Sh	
Grene, Ellen	—		2				(Mc)	(AleW)
Grene, Jn. (o. Bt)	—	o			H	w	(Bt)	
Grene, Rch., s. Ad.	4	6	2	*pl*	(h)	w	Ra	(m. ale)

Name	Cat	Hal	Port	Bus	Stock	W	Vill	Notes
Grenes, Rb.	—	of			S/e			
Grene, Wll.	u	ow			(h/o/s)	(W)	lsd. Ra	
Grene, Wll. (o. Bt)	—	1		a			(Bt)	
Grenelache, Wll.	u	o					Sh	
Grosvenour, Rb. s. Rph.	3	(1)					Kh, nr	
Gumbeltoth, Jn.	(B)		3	a	h	w	(Bg)	
Hadfeld, Wll. o. (o. Mp)	—	o					Mp	
Halle, Agnes d. Wlt. & Alice sis.	4	(1) (1)					Ra	
Halle, Rg. s. Jn., o. Somerford	4	1					Su, Ed, Ra	
Hally, Jn. (o. Su)	3/b	2w	1w				Su, Mc	
Hanlegh, Hen.	-/B	of	1				Mc	Chap
Hanlegh, Rch.	3	2wf		v	e	W	Kh	
Hanlegh, Jn., s. Rch. & Sybil w.	3	2wf		v	o	w	Kh, Wh	
Hanlegh, Wll. (br. Wll.)	3	4f	1	v, l	e/p	WW	Kh, Wh, Mc-r	ChapTx
Hanlegh, Hen. s. Wll.	B	o	2				Wg	Chap
Hanlegh, Jn. s. Wll.	3	1f					Kh	
Hanlegh, Wll. s. Wll.	3	1f					Kh	
Harfot, Nch. s. Rch. &, Margaret sis.	4	(1) (1)					Ra	
Haregreve, Ad.	4	3		a		w	Bt	*work*
Hargreve, Agnes	5	1				w	Bt	
Hargreve, Rch.	4	1w	(o)		h	w	Bt	
Harper, Rch. (see *Clyve*)								
Harpere, Hgh.	—		1				Mc	
Harper, Rb.	—		1	*a*			Mc	
Harstoneslegh, Jn.	B		4wf				Chg	off
Hasty, Rb.	5/b	o	2w		p	w	Bg	mrcr, Alew
Haukeshurst, Rch.	(u)	o			S/PP			
Haukesert, Jn. (s. Rch.)	b		(1)			W	*nr*	*work*
Hayfeld, Wll.	3-4/B	2	7w	*j*, v, st	o/P	W	Hd, Ra, Jg	off, cptr, AleW

Name	Cat	Hal	Port	Bus	Stock	W	Vill	Notes
Hayne, Jn.	(B)		2wf		P		Bg	off, AleW
Hayneson, Edm. (s. Reg. Mercer)	B		4wf			w	Chg	bchr, AleW
Hayneson, Rb.	(B)		2				(Bg)	
Haywod, Jn., o. Over Alderley	4	1w	o		(e)		Su	
Haywode, Wll. s/h. Jn.	4	1					Su	
Hegynbothum, Amy	—	1						m. AleW
Helay, Ad. (o. Bs)	—	(1)			e		Bs	
Helegh, Ellen wdw. Rg.	—		2				Mc	AleW(bkr)
Helegh, Jn. s. Ad.	B		2w				Stl	cblr
Heley, Rch. (o. Su)	u	o					(Su)	
Helegh, Rb.	—		ow		P	W		
Helegh, Th. (Chap)	4/B	o	6wf	st, pl			Bg	off, AleW
Henshagh, Alice, &	4	(1)					Su	
Isabel d. Jn. s. Hen.		(1)						
Henneshagh, Hgh.	4	1					Su	
Henneshagh, Pet.	(u)	o			e/p		(Su)	
Henneschagh, Rch.	—	o	1				Mc	
Henneshawe, Wll.	B		1				Dstr	
Hendbury, Hen.	—	1w			(e)	w	(Su/Out)	
Henresone, Jn.	—	2			p	w		(m. ale)
Henreson, Th. (o. Wh)	3	6w		j, pl	P	w	Wh, Kh, lsd. Hy	m. Ale
Hephales, Ad. s. Ad.	4	3		v, j	O/PP	W	Su	
Hephals, Th. s. Ad.	3	3					Su	
Hephales, Jn.	—	3			h	w	Dw, Hd	Chap
Heppal, Jn.	(B)		7w	j	P		Bg	off, shp, bchr(alew)
Hephales, Jn. s. Ad.	4	1			e		Su	
Heppales, Jn. s. Hgh.	3	1					Ds St	
Heppal, Margery d. Hgh.	3-4	(1)					Su	
Heppal, Wll. (o. Su)	3	3		pl			Su	
Hephals, Ad. s. Wll.	3	1					Su	
Hephales, Wll. s. Wll. (jun)	3	2					Su	

Name	Cat	Hal	Port	Bus	Stock	W	Vill	Notes
Herdmon, Th. s. Hen.	3	1			e		Wh	
Herdmon, Th.	4	1					Su	
Herdwykwall, Jn. s. Rch.	4	1					Su	
Hervy, Margt. d. Ad.	5	2		*v*			Su	
Hervy, Rch.	4	1			p		Su	
Hervy, Wll.	—		1		e		Mc	
Hesketh, Ad.	2/b	1	1	a			Hd, Mc-r	
Heye, Rb.	(B)	o	6w	pl, j, a		w	Bg	off, bchr, AleW
Hickesone, Jn. (o. Hawkhurst)	u	owf					Wh/Ds	
Hobeler, Wll.	u	2f	-w		e		Ra	
Hode, Wll. (o. Ds)	u	2w		*a*, st	p	w	Ds	
Hodnet, Alice d. Wll.	5	(1)					Ds	
Hokerlegh, Rb. s. Nch.	3	1					Wh	
Hokerlegh, Rg. & Alina w.	3	3w		*st*	h/P	w	Bt	*scold*
Holyncete, Jn.	5/B	2wf	4w	*v*, pl	E/p	w	Bg, Su	off, (b. ale)
Holyncete, Rb.(s. Jn.), sen.	2	1wf	of	*pl*, st, l	OO/h/PP		Su	Rv. Bl. Mary
Holyncete, Edm. s. Rb.	u	of		l	h		Ra	
Holyncete, Jn. s. Rb.	2	3w	o	*l*	O/h/P	w	Su	
Holyncete, Jn. s. Rb., jun	3	1f					Su	
Holyncete, Rb. s. Rb.	3	4f			h	w	Su	
Holyncete, Wll. s. Rb.	3	1f					Su	
Holyncete, Jn. s. Th.	3	1	o				Ra	
Holyncete, Wll.	2	5f	(o)	*j*	E/p		Su	
Holyncete, Jn. s. Wll.	3	4w	o	st, *l*, pl	e/P		Su	
Holyncete, Rb. s. Wll.	4	1f			h/p		Su	
Holyncete, Wll. s. Wll.	3	2f			P		Su	
Holynworth, Wll.	u	1					Ds	cstbl
Homeldon, Edm.	3/b	6	o	*l*, pl, v, j	S/OO/h/PP	W	Su	U-For, Rv. Bl. Mary
Homeldon, Ellen d. Edm.	3						Su	

Name	Cat	Hal	Port	Bus	Stock	W	Vill	Notes
Honford, Jn. s. Hen. o. Handforth	3	1f	1				Ds, Su, *Hnd* Mc-r, *nr*	
Honford, Jn. s. Jn. s. Hen.	3	1f					Su	
Honford, Jn. s. Wll.	—	1				w	(Man)	
Hopkynsone, Wll. (o. Su)	u	o			OO/h		(Su)	
Hordren, Rch. (o. Hord)	3	3w	o	st	SS/O/h/p	w	Su (Bs)	
Hordren, Th. s. Hen.	4	1					Kh	
Hordren, Wll. (o. Bs)	—	1			S/OO/H	w	Bs	
Hordren, Stph. s. Wll.	—	o		a			(Bs)	
Horeston, Emma d. Jn.	5	(1)					Ds	
Hot, Hgh.	2	1w					Su	
Huetteson, Ad. (o. Bs)	—	o	o		OO/h		Bs	
Hogh, Ad.	—	ow					Bt	
Huggesone, Jn. (o. Mp)	—	o					Mp	
Hugsone, Rb. (o. Mp)	—	ow					Mp	m. Ale
Hogsone, Jn. (o. Shadeyard)	—	o			PP		(Su)	
Hugsone, Wll. (Lowe)	—	o		v	E/h	(w)	(Mp)	
Hugsone, Wll. (s. Ad.)	—		1w	a			(Mc)	milr
Hulcokes, Glb. (o. Hollinset)	(u)	3	o	pl, st	h/o/p		(Su)	
Hulm, Wll. s. Rb.	5	2wf					Up	
Hurdesfeld, Jn.	—		1	a			Mc	mrcr
Hurdesfeld, Rg.	—		2w			w	Mc	
& Agn. w./wdw.			2					AleW
Hurle, Wll. & Margery w.	2–3	1			OO	w	Pt Sh	
Hurlebot, Jn.	—		2w		h		Mc	
Hurteheven, Rch. (o. Bt)	4–3	2f			S/OO		Ra	
Hyde, Jn. (s. Rch.)	(u)	2w		*v*		W	(Wh)	
Hyde, Th.	(3)	2w		pl		w	(Wh)	Vrdr
Hyde, Rch. s. Th.	—	1w		v			(Man)	
Hyde, Th. s. Th.	3	2		*l*			Ds, Wh	
Ibot, Jn., o. Offerton	(b)		1				Mc-r	drpr
Jackson, Rb. (o. Tx)	—	o			OO/h		Tx	(m. ale)

Name	Cat	Hal	Port	Bus	Stock	W	Vill	Notes
Jackson, Rb.	3	1wf			p		Ds, Wh	tlr
Jaksone, Jn. s. Rb.	(u)	of				w	(o. Ds)	
Jankynsone, Mrgy. d. Rb.	4	o					Ra	
Janny, Jn.	—	o					Bs	
Janny, Rch.	(4)	4f	owf	pl, st	h		Bt, (Bs), Mc	U-For,(b. alew)
Janny, Th. s. Rch.	—	of			e		Bt	
John, Margery d. Rch. s.	4	(1)					Su	
Jolion, Jn.	(B)	-w	4w		h/o	w	Bg	off, lthr, b. & m. AleW
Jolynet, Hen.	5/b	o	2wf				Mc	smth
Jolynet, Nch.	5/b	o	2w	j	h	W	Mc	off, smth
Joneson, Al.	(B)	(o)	2	j			Bg	(off)
Joneson, Wll.	(b)		(1)				nr	
Joudrel, Jn.	—	ow			P		(Mp)	
Joudrel, Wll.	1	6f		l, pl, st	E/p		Ds, Wh, Kh	
Joudrel, Rg. s. Wll.	1	(2)f	l				Ds, Wh, Kh nr	
Joudrel, Margery d. Rg. (& Rb. Discher)	2	o					Ds	
Joye, Jn.	—	2		v	(e)	WW	(Kh)	
Joye, Rb. & (Joan) w.	3	4w		l	S/O/p		Ra	
Joye, Rg.	—	owf					(Mp)	(w)wvr(m. ale)
Joye, Wll., s. Rg. (o. Mp)	—	o					Mp	
Joye, Wll.	3	4					Wh	
Juddesone, Edm. (o. Hd)	3	5f		j, v	S/OO H/p	W	Ra(Hord)	cptr
Juddesone, Th. s. Edm.	4	2f			SS/h	W	Ra	
Juddesone, Rg. o. Chelford, Mrgt. w.	b		(1)w				lsd Wg, nr	
Juddesone, Rg. s. Rg. o. Astle	—		ow				(Mc)	
Kempe, Jn., sen.	(u)	2f		v	OO	W	(Ds)	
Kenworthey, Hgh.			ow			w		

Name	Cat	Hal	Port	Bus	Stock	W	Vill	Notes
Kenworthey, Rch.	5/B	1f	9w	st, j, pl	h	W	Bg, Su	off, AleW, (bkr) frm ov
Kenworthey, Wll., s. Rch.	4/b	3w	3w		S/OOO/ h/p	W	Bg, Su	off
Kenwrek/Ken, Th.	(B)		5w	j	P		Bg	off, bkr, AleW
Knokeden, Jn.	—	o	2w	pl		w	Mc	off, frm ov
Knyght, Rch.	(B)	o	7w	j, pl	h/p	w	Bg	off, tlr
Knight, Wll.	—		2w		p	WW	Mc	
Kynder, Rb. (o. Su)	3	3wf			S/PP	w	Su	
Kynder, Rb. s. Rb.	4	3f					Su	*felon*
Kyndour, Nch.	B	o	2w		(p)	w	Dstr	
Kyngeslegh, Ad. Clerk	2/b	5	3	l	H/O		Su, Ra, Wh, Kh,Mc-r	wol esch1361 Just Lab, Shff Flint 1383
Kyngeslegh, Rch.	b	2	I				Mc-r	clk
Kyrkehouses, Th.	—	ow	o		S/P			
Kysse, Rb. (s. Jankyn)	(u)	o	o		O/h/p	w	(Ra)	*work*
Lache, Agnes	—		I					AleW
Lauton, Hgh.	(B)		4w	pl			Bg	off, smth
Lee, Bend.	—	5			hf/o/p	W		Bff
Leghes, Jn. s. Jn.	—	(I)					Mp	labr
Legh, Rb. (d. c.1370)							Adlg	Dep Stwd, Rdr, Just Lab
Legh, Rb. (d. 1382)	(3)	-f	-wf	v	(OOOO/ h)	W	Adlg, Ra frm Hy, Bt	Stwd Arch
Legh, Rb. (d. 1408)	—	—	—				Adlg	Shff
Legh, Jn. s. Rb.	(2)	7w	I	l			Su, Ra, Hnd	Stwd
Legh, Pet. (s. Rb.)	—	6f			HH/O/C		Ra, Hnd	Stwd
Legh, Wll., knight	—	3	o				Adlg	Bff, Rdr
Lepere, Rb.	—	I		v		W		(*Lyme wood*)
Lether, Anable			I				(Mc)	(ale)

Name	Cat	Hal	Port	Bus	Stock	W	Vill	Notes
Lether, Hgh. serv. Jn. Leversegge	B		o				Stl	
Leve, Stph. Rector o. Horsemonden	b	o	3		p		Mc-r	Chap
Lever, Hen., w.	4	1w					Wh	
Levehale, Wll.	4	1					Su	
Leveresegge, Jn.	2/B	6	9w	pl, j, a, st	OOO/h	w	Hd, Jg, Wg, Gdl	wol
Lighthaseles, Rg.	—	o					Mp	
Loges, Jn.	—		2				(Mc)	
Lounesdale, Wll.	—		2	a			(Mc)	
London, Alc.	—		2				(Mc)	AleW
Lord, Rb. (o. Bt)	4	1			h/p	w	Bt	
Lowe, Rg. (o. Su)	(u)	1		(j)	(o)		(Su)	
Lowe, Rg. (o. Bt)	—	ow			h		Bt	
Lowe, Rg. (o. Ra) & Ellen w.	5	3wf		l	SS/OO/ h/p	(w)	Ra	
Lowe, Wll. s. Rg.	4	4f	o	l, v	SSS/OO CC/h/P	W	Ra, (Mc)	
Lowe, Wll. s. Jn.	3	5w		l, j	h/P	w	Ra	
Lowe, Jn. s. Wll. s. Jn.	3	1					Ra	
Lowe, Th. s. Rg.	4	1w			o		Bt	
Lowe, Th. (o. Bs)	—	o					Bs	
Lowe, Wll. (o. Mc)	4/B		6w	j			Hd, Mc-r	off, b. AleW, bkr
Lowe. Th. (s. Wll.)	B	o	o			w	Jg	
Lowe, Wll., sen.	3	3w			S/E/o		Ra	
Lowe, Wll. s. Wll.	(4	1)					Ra	
Lyard, Jn.	—		1w				Mc	(ale)
Lymnour, Jn.	B		1w			w	Wg	AleW
Lyncrofte, Rch. & w.	4	2wf					Ra	
Lyncrofte, Rch. s. Rch.	4	1f					Ra	
Lynster, Wll.	B	1	8w	pl, st		W	Stl, Dstr Chg, flds	off, lthr/ cblr, (alew)
Lytchtt, Rg.	—		1				Mc	

Name	Cat	Hal	Port	Bus	Stock	W	Vill	Notes
Mabbeson, Herv.	3	2f	o	l	EE/p		Su	
Mabbeson, Jn. s. Herv.	4	1f			(p)		Su	
Herveysone, Rch. (s. Herv. Mabbeson)	3	of	o		e/p		Su	
Macclesfield, Jord.	B		2f				Mc, Hd, Up Sh, Ds	Mayor
Macclesfield, Jn. s. Jrd.	1/b	2f		l			Hd, Sh, Up	Mayor
Macclesfield, Isb d. Jn.	1	(1)					Hd, Sh, Up	
Macclesfield, Jn. sen. clerk (*Alcok* ?)	1/B		4f	st, pl	e		Mc-r, Hd, Up, Sh, Ds	
Maggesone, Glb.	u	1			e	w		(w)wvr
Mareschall, Hen.	(3)	5w	o	l			Su	Bff, clk
& Maud w.							Ed, Ds	Sjp
Mareschall, Jn. (o. Mc)			1	a				Chap
Marler, Rch.	—	o	1w					(ale)
Masy, Rch.	(3)	1					Su	knght
Maysone, Jn. (br. Pet.)	—	o			OO/h			
Mayson, Pet. (o. Bs)	—	ow			s/h		Bs	*work*
Masonn, Rb.	(5)	ow	(o)				Bt, (Mc)	
Maykyn, Hgh., o. Butley	—	o			PP		(Bu/Bt)	
Maykyn, Jn.	(B)		5w	pl			Bg	off, bchr, AleW
Maykyn, Rb. (s. Jn.)	B	o	3w	a, st		w	Bg(by oven)	
& Denise w.				a(w)				
Maynwaryn, Wll.	3	1					Su, *nr*	
Maynwaryng, Rnph. s. Wll.	b	-f	of				(Mc)	
Maynwaryn, Wll. s. Wll.	2/b	1	of				Su, Mc	
Menerell, Wll. (o. Wh)	u	1w			p		Wh	bchr, m. AleW
Mere, Rch. (o. Bt)	—	1wf	o	a			Bt	
Michael, Milicent d. Alc.	—		o					*poor, hcks*

Name	Cat	Hal	Port	Bus	Stock	W	Vill	Notes
Mill, Rch. s. Mich. o. the	5						Su	
Miller, Wll. (o. Ra)	4	1					Ra	
Morton, Rch. o. Parva Morton	1/b	2	1w	l			Hd, Sh, Mc	
Mottrum, Ad.	-/b	6wf	2w	pl	p		Hnd	Bff, Glr
Mottrum, Jn., s. Ad.	3/2	4f	1	pl	E/h/p	w	Su, Mc	Bff
Mottram, Edm.	3	1					Su	
Mottrum, Jn. s. Rg.	3	1f					Su	
Mottrum, Rg., s. Sim.	(5)	6w		j, pl	e	w	St	For, m. Ale
Mottrum, Rph. s. Rg.	(4)	1f					Ds St	
Mulnere, Jn. s. Hen./ Hannesone (o. Pt)	5	2			h/p	w	Sh	
Mulnere, Rch.	(b)	(o)	2w		h/p		Mc	AleW
Mulnere, Rg.	3/B	1w	2wf				Mc, Su Chg, Wg, Gdl	
Mulner, Jn. s. Rg.	2	1					Su	
Mulner, Jn. (o. Su)	u	2			p		Su	
Mulnere, Th. (s/h. Rg.)	B	o	2f				Mc	
Mulnere, Rph. s. Rg.	B		(1)f				Wg	
Mustardmon, Jn.	—	o	o		h	w	(Mc)	
Nelleson, Rch. serv. Th. Wodehous	—	1	2					Dep Glr, (wol)
Neuton, Nch.	3/b	1	3	pl	e		Su, Up, Mc	off, Dep Glr
Neuton, Pet.	3/b	1	3wf	pl	(e)		Mc, Ds, Wh	
Neuton, Jn. s. Pet.	5	1					Wh	
Neuton, Rph.	-/b	1	3				(Mc)	clk, U-Bff, serv Glr
Newton, Rch.	—		owf	a			(Mc)	
Neuton, Rch. s. Rch.	—		of	a			(Mc)	
Neuton, Rch. s. Th.	3	1					Su	
Neuton, Wll. o. (s. Th.)	—	ow			OO		Bs	
Newenham, Jn.	—	1					Stwd	
Nichol, Agnes d. Wll.	5	(1)					Ra	

Name	Cat	Hal	Port	Bus	Stock	W	Vill	Notes
Nicholas, Hen. s. Wll. s.	5	I					Su	
Nicholas, Rch. s. Rb. (o. Ds)	u	o					(Ds/Su)	
Nog, Wll.	—		2				Mc	chlnr
Nol, Ad.	B	-f	(1)w				Wg, *nr*	
Nol, Jn.	4	I					Su, Bs	
Norman/Northman, Bend., o.'Pylatecroft'	3/b	4	o	*j*	O/h/p		Su	Rv. Bl. Mary
Norman, Rg., s. Wll.	(u)	I					Su	
Normonhull, Rg.	3	I					Su	
Oclegh, Jn.	(B)		1w				(Bg)	
Odam, Rph.	5	I					Ra	
Oldefeld, Hgh.	4	I			o/P		Ra	
Oldefeld, Jn. s. Jn.	u	of		v			Su	
Oldefeld, Jn. (o. Mc) Amy w. (*see Fletcher*)	B		3w	*pl, a*	h		Wg, Gdl	bchr, AleW
Oldefeld, Jn., s. Wll.	3	7f	o	pl, v	H/O/PP	W	Su	lsd. esc
Oldefeld, Wll. s. Hen.	3	3w		*l*, a	S/o/p	w	Su	
Oldhed, Rg.	3	6wf	o	*l, v,* pl	h/p	W	Su, Mdg	Ags
Oldhed, Ell. d. Rg.	3						Su, Mdg	
Olereshed, Hen.	4	2					Wh	
Olrecete/Olershed, Jn. s. Hen.	4	2					Ds	
Olerenshawe, Jn. s. Rch.	3	1w					Wh	(w)wvr
Olyver, Wll. (o. Wh)	(5)	2wf		l	S/O/P		Wh, lsd Hy	(w)wvr, mil
Olyver, Ad., s. Wll.	5	2f					Wh	
Ones, Rch.	3	1w			p		Ra	
Orme, Rg. & (Marion) w. (& Th. br.)	3	4w	o	*j*	S/OO/ h/PP	W	Ra	
Osebourn, Wll. s. Bend.	4	I	o				Ra	
Oselcok, Jn.	B		5w	j		w	(Dstr)	off, bkr, AleW
Oselcok, Th.	(B)	o	7w	*st, pl,* j		w	Bg	off, bchr, AleW, shp
Parfay, Nch. (o. Su)	2/B	5w	o	pl	o/P		Su, Chg	

Name	Cat	Hal	Port	Bus	Stock	W	Vill	Notes
Parker, Jn.			I	a			(Mc)	
Parmonter, Rb.	(B)	o	5w	*pl*, j	P		Bg	AleW
Paynesley, Jn.	(u)	I			OO/h/p	w	(Su)	
Pedlegh, Jn. (o. Hd)	(u)	o			(o)			
Pedlegh, Jn. (o. Ra)	(u)	o			(o)			
Pedlegh, Th.	—		I	a			(Mc)	
Peiton', Jn.	—	Iw					Ds, Hnd	For
Pekke, Al. (s. Rb.)	3–4	I					Su	
Peek, Nch. s. Jn.	5	I					Ds	
Peket, Rch. (o. Bs)	—	2w		v	S/OO/h		Bs	
Pemberton, Wll.	(B)	o	3w	st		w	Bg	bchr, AleW
Penk, Hgh.	—		2w				Mc	
Perkynsone, Rg. s. Rg.	4	I					Su	
Perkynsone, Rb. (o. Bs)	—	If			OOO/e	w	Bs	
Perkynsone, Jn. s. Rb.	—	of			S		Bs	
Persones, Bend. (Hancokeson)	4	3f		a	E/p	W	Ds	tlr
Persones, Rb., s. Hen.	3	2f		pl		w	Wh	
Persones, Jn., s. Rb. (Hancokeson/Robynsone)	4	3f			P		Wh	bchr, m. Ale
Pierson/Peter, Al.	B	I	7wf	*pl*, st	SS/O/h/ P	W	lsd. Chg	Mayor, bchr, frm stlg, (w)wol(ale)
Pereson, Jn. (o. Ra)	4	Iwf		l	s/H/O/p	W	Ra	
Pierson, Th. s. Jn., serv. Al. Pierson	—		I				Mc	
Peresone, Rch. s. Jn.	4	If				w	Ra	
Peter, Jn. s. Rg. s.	4	-f					Su	
Peter, Rg. s. Rg. s.	4	I			p		Su	
Petton, Rch. s. Jn.	(5)	(I)						
Pevere, Marion	—		3	a, st			Mc	(AleW)
Pikford, Rch. s. Jn., sen.	4	2w			e/P	w	Kh	
Pipere, Rch.	—	o					(Ty)	
Playtour, Rb. (o. Mp)	—	o					Mp	
Plont, Rnph.	4	3wf			S/O/h/p	w	Ra	

Name	Cat	Hal	Port	Bus	Stock	W	Vill	Notes
Plont, Jn. s. Rnph., sen.	4	1f					Ra	
Poker, Th.	b		(1)				nr	
Pomhale, Wll. & w. (d. Th. Walker)	(b)		(1)w				Mc	
Pot, Hen. o. (s. Jn.)	3	1f					Ra	
Potte, Margery d. Rch.	4	1					Ra, Sh	
Pot, Rb., s. Ad.	3	2			e/P		Sh	
Potte, Nch. s. Rb.	3	1					Sh	
Potte, Th.	3	1wf			e/p	w	Sh	
Potte, (six) d. Th.	3	(1)					Sh	
Potte, Wll., s. Rch.	3	4		a	p		Pt Sh	
Potte, Wll. (o. Pt)	(u)	o			h		(Pt)	
Potte, Wll. (o. Wh)	(u)	o		a			(Wh)	
Prestall, Jn.	—		ow				(Mc)	
Prestall, Rch.	(B)		2w				Mc	off, (ale)
Prestbury, Hen.	—	1	o	v, pl			(Hnd)	wfs
Prestbury, Hen.	(B)		4w	j		WW	Bg	off, (alew)
Prestbury, Rch.	(B)		3wf	pl			Bg	off, cblr
Prestbury, Hgh. (s. Rch.)	—		1w				Mc	(ale)
Proudiyng, Rch.	(u)	1wf			h/E/p			
Prounyng, Wll., s. Rch.	u	1f		a	OO/h/p		Su	
Pulton, Hgh.	(B)		2wf				Bg	AleW
Pygot, Hen. & w.	—	1w			p		Bt	
Pygot, Jn.	b		o			w	Mc-r	
Pygot, Rch.	b		1				Mc-r	VcrPby
Pygot, Wll.	—	2			e		Hnd	Vrdr, Cstd Pby
Pykemere, Anable	—		2					AleW
Pylatecroft, Rg. s. Rg.	4	1					Su	
Pymme, Hgh. s. Rg.	5	1					Ra	
Pymme/Pymmeson, Jn. (Spencer)	4/B	(o)	1w				Ra, Mc, Gdl, Glh	bchr
Pymme, Jn. (o. Bs)	—	o	o				Bs	
Pymme, Hgh. s. Rg.	5	1					Ra	
Pymyng, Jam.	4	1	l				Kh	(w)wvr

Name	Cat	Hal	Port	Bus	Stock	W	Vill	Notes
Pynk, Dav.	4	I					Su	
Pyper, Wll. (o. Su)	(u)	o			p			
Rathebon, Rnph., o. Rushton	3	I					Su	
Ravenowe, Alc. (wdw. Rch.)	5/b	I	2	pl		w	Su, Mc	(b. alew)
Ravenowe, Agnes d. Jn. s. Wll. & Maud sis.	5	(I) (I)					Ra	
Ravenowe, Jn. s. Wl. s. Jn.	5	I					Ra	
Ravenowe, Nch.	(B)	o	Iw			w	(Bg)	off, AleW
Redych, Rch. (o. Stckpt)	b	o	o				(Mc-r)	For, Chap
Redych, Th., s. Rch.	4	If					Ds	
Redyshagh, Nch. s. Jn.	4						Ds	
Reveson, Jn. (o. Bs)	—	ow	(o)		(e/p)		Bs	
Revesone, Wll. (o. Bs)	—	o			OO/H		Bs	
Richard, Rch. s.	4	I					Ra	
Robert, Jn. s. Jn. s.	3						Su	
Robynsone / Robartson Rg. Williamsone	u	2					Su	
Rode, Jn.	—	o	ow	a		w	(Mc)	
Rode, Rch.	5/B	I	6w	j	OO/h	w	Bg	off
Roger, Rg. s.	(u)	I		j	S/O/P/h	w		
Roker, Bend.	4	2wf					Wh	
Roker, Margery d. Bend.	4	(I)					Ds, Wh	
Roker, Wll. s. Rb.	4	2					Ds	
Roket, Th.	(u)	o	o		S/p			
Rossyndale, Jn., knght	(3)/b	2	5	st, pl	(h)/p		Su, Mc-r	Chap
Rouland, Jn.	—	o					Bs	Chap
Rowe, Rch. (s. Wll.)	4/B	I	Iow	pl, j, a	O/P	w	shp-r	Mayor, AleW
Rowe, Stph.	B	o	5w	a, st			Jg	Mayor
Rowe, Th. (s. Wll.)	(B)	o	Iw				Mc	
Rowe, Wll. (o. Wh)	u	o					Wh	
Rudischagh, Nch. s. Jn.	4	I					Ds	
Rushton, Rg. (s. Ad.) o.	4	If					Su	

Name	Cat	Hal	Port	Bus	Stock	W	Vill	Notes
Ruyll, Th. (o. Bt)	—	ow			e/p		(Bt)	
Sadeler, Wll.	B		2w		h/p	w	Dstr	
Sailliour, Jn.	—		1	*a*		w	(Mc)	
Sayllour, Wll.	—		2	st, a			(Mc)	Chap
Salter, Rch.	—	ow						m. Ale
Schagh, Jn.	—	o		v, st, a	e/p	w	Mc	VcrPby
Scoles, Rch.	(u)	o					(Sh)	
Serle, Jn. (o. Ds)	3	2wf			P		Ds	
Serle, Rch. s. Jn.	3	1f					Ds	
Suell, Alice d. Wll.	3	(1)					Ds	
Sewall, Herv. (Bagger)	4/B	2w	5wf	*st, pl,* l	e	w	Su, Chg	off, bchr, AleW
Sewale, Rch. s. Rch.	3	1					Su	
Seynesbury, Wll.	4	1w					Kh, Wh	
Shalcross, Jn.,	—	o			SS/OO/h		Tx	RctrTx
Shalcrosse, Rch.	5	1					Kh	
Shepherd, Jn. (o. Ra)	3	1w			e		Sh, Ra	
Shepherd, Th.	5	1				w	Ra(Hord)	
Shepherd, Wll. (o. Bs)	—	o			S/OO/e		Bs	
Shepherd, Wll. s. R. (o. Pt)	5	1					Ra	
Sherd, Rch. (s. Hgh.)	—	4f		*j*	e		Ds	For, coalm
Sherd, Jn., s. Rch.	2	8w	1	*pl, st,* l *v, j, a*	P	w	St/Ds lsd. Hy	For, coalm, (m. ale), frm stlg
Sherd, Rg. (o. Bt)	—	1		pl			Bt	
Sherd, Th. (s. Edm.)	B		4w	a			Chg	off, (ale)
Sherd, Wll. (br. Rg.)	—	2			p		Ds	m. Ale
Scherth, Hgh. (s. Jn.)	—	2f				w	Ds	
Schore, Wll.	—	2w		pl	OO/PP		(Ds/Wh)	
Shoteswall, Wll.	3	3		l	s		Wh	
Shotelsworth, Jn.	—	o			P	w	Mp	
Shrygelegh, Jak	b		(1)				*nr*	
Shryglegh, Rb.	3/b	8f	1f	*l, pl, a, v*	h/o/P	w	Sh, Ra, Mc, lsd. Hy	U-For, coalm

Name	Cat	Hal	Port	Bus	Stock	W	Vill	Notes
Shryglegh, Jn., s. Rb. (d. 1374/5)	2/B	6f	3f	j, l, pl	E/Hf		Sh, Su Dstr, Stl	
Shryglegh, Rb. s. Rb.	4	1f	o		o		Ra, (Mc)	
Shryglegh, Th., s. Rb.	2	1of	3	l, pl, j, st, v	SSS/OOO/hf/P	W	Sh, Ra, (Mc) lsd. Hd	
Shryglegh, Jn. s. Th. o.	2	3	1			w	Sh, Ra, Mc	
Shydyort, Jn., s. Jn. o. Wincle	3	7	o	j, pl	O/h/p	w	Su	
Skot, Rg.	(B)	o	2w	st			Bg	AleW
Scot, Wll.	(B)	o	3	a	p	w	Bg	
Slak, Ellen	—		1	a				
Slegh, Jn. (br. Rch.)	4/B	o	6wf	j		w	Wg, Gdl Hd, Sh	off, AleW
Slegh, Jn., jun.	B		1f				Wg, Chg	
Slegh, Rch.	B	o	9wf	pl			Wg, Stl	Mayor, (alew)
Slegh, Wll., s. Rch.	3/B	5w	1owf	pl, l, j	h/o/p	WW	Hd, Chg, Gdl, Stl, Wg, mkt	Mayor b. AleW
Smale, Wll. (o. Sh) sen/jun ?	u	o			S/e/p	w	Su	
Smert, Rb.	—		1				(Mc)	
Smyth, Jn. (s. Wll.)	B	o	4w		(h)/P	w	Chg	off, AleW
Smyth, Jn., jun.	—		ow				(Mc)	
Smyth, Rch. (s. Hgh.) & Margaret w.	(3)	1w	o		h	w	Bt, (Ra)	
Smyth, Rb. (o. St)	(u)	o					(Su)	
Smyth, Wll. (o. Su)	(u)	1	o		O/p		(Su)	
Snelleston, Th., & Isabel w., o. Snelson	5/b	o	2		SS/p		Mc	
Snowball, Wll.	B	o	3			w	Dstr	lthr
Somerford, Jn.	5/B	1w	4w	j		w	Wg	Bff, Glr smth (b. alew)
Somonour, Agnes	—	o	1					

Name	Cat	Hal	Port	Bus	Stock	W	Vill	Notes
Sondebache, Jn. (o. Bt)	—	(o)					Bt	
Sondebache, Ph.	—	o			H			Dep Sjp
Sondebache, Wll.	5/b	1	4wf	st	OO/h	W	Bg, Hd	(b. ale)
Souter, Rb.	—	ow	3w	a, st			Bt, Mc	b. AleW, mower
Spark, Rch.	B		(1)f				Wg, Gdl	
Spark, Ad. (s. Rch.)	5/B	o	4w		e/h	W	Chg, Gdl, Dstr, shp	off, AleW, (bkr)
Sparky, Wll., s. Rch.	5/B	o	7w	st, j	P	W	Dstr, Jg	off, clth, AleW, (bkr)
Spencer, Rch.	B	(o)	8/9	j, pl			Chg	off
Spycer, Wll.	—		owf				(Mc)	
Spycer, Th ... (s. Wll.)	(B)	o	3w	st, a	h	w	Bg	bkr(& w)
Sprag, Amice d. Margt.	5	(1)					Wh	
Stachard, Hen.		o	o			w		
Stafford, Ad., s. Rb.	4	1					Ds	
Stanlegh, Gff.	3	1					Ds	
Stanlegh, Jn., s. Gff.	3	(1)					Ds, nr	
Stanlegh, Wll. s. Gff. (o. Sutton)	3	1					Ds	
Stanlegh, Rch. & w.	—	o		pl			Bt	
Stanlegh, Rch.	5	2					Ds	(w)wvr
Stanystrete, Th.	4	5wf	o	st, v	S/OO/H/p	W	Ra	
Stare, Pet.	B		3wf	st	o	W	Bg	AleW
Starky, Agnes serv. Rg. Falybrom	—		2					AleW
Starky, Joan	—		3					AleW
Starky, Rch.	4	1wf			O/h/p		Ra	
Stathum, Th.	2	1w					Kh, Wh	
Staykhull, Rb.	4						Ds	
Stele, Edith wdw. Jn.			2					AleW
Stele, Rch. & w.	—		2w		p		Mc	AleW, cblr
Stevensone, Jn. s. Th.	—	1					Wodw Bt	
Stikewynd, Isote wdw. Ad.	—		1					(ale)

Name	Cat	Hal	Port	Bus	Stock	W	Vill	Notes
Stodherd, Rch., br. Th. s. Hen.	—	of					(Su/Bs)	
Stodherd, Hen.	4	1f			H/O	w	Su	
Stoke, Rg.	—	o	3wf	a		w	Mc	off
Stoke, Rch. s. Rg.			ow	a		w	(Mc)	
Stoke, Wll.	—	o	o				Out	frm wfs
Stones, Nch., o. Wh	3	5wf		j	O/P		Wh	(d)wvr
Stones, Wll., s. Nch.	2	2f		l	p		Wh	
Stones, Agnes d. Wll.	3	(1)					Wh	
s. Rph. & Sarah sis.		(1)						
Stopenhull, Wll. s. Rg. & Alice w.	3	(2)f			(S)/p	w	Ra	
Stopenhul, Wll.	3	4w		l, j	O/p		Su	
Stopenhall, Rch. s. Wll.	3	1f					Su	
Strangweys, Jn.	b	(1)					nr	
Strynger, Bend.	3	3		j	p	w	Wh	
Stubbes, Jn. (s. Ad.)	4	1			e		Su	
Stubbes, Th., Maud w.	4	1wf					Su	
Stubbes, Wll. (s. Ad.) & Mrgy. w.	3/B	2w	6wf	j, st, l	H/o/PP	w	Su, Jg, flds	off, b. AleW
Stubbes, Jn. s. Wll.	B		2w				(Jg)	
Stubbes, Maud d. Wll.			2	a, st(w)			Mc	
Styeker, Wll. (o. Ra)	u	(1)w			O/h/p		Ra, nr	
Sutton, Edm.	B		ow				Wg, flds	
Sutton, Jn., sen. (d. 1362)	1	5wf		pl			Su, Ds, Wh	For
Sutton, Jn. s. Rch., jun.	1/b	8	1	j, st, l	EE/h/p	w	Su, Hd Ds, Wh, Mc, Mdg	For
Sutton, Th. s. Jn.	3	1f					Su, Ds	
Sutton, Jn. (o. Barleighford)	—	2			P		(Su)	
Sutton, Margaret d. Wll. (& Mgry. d. Hgh. Dounes)	3	(1)					Su	
Sutton, Rch. s. Rch.	3	3f		st	p		Su	

Name	Cat	Hal	Port	Bus	Stock	W	Vill	Notes
Sutton, Jn. s. Stph.	(1)	2f		j	e	w	Su	
Sutton, Jn. s. Rg., s. Stph.	2	3f			e/p	w	Su	frg
Sutton, Rch.	—	2f	(o)	pl	O/p	w	(Su)	
Sutton, Th.	4	1w					Su, Ds	
Swanshogh, Th.	—	o			S/P	w		
Swayn, Hen. s. Wll.	4	1					Kh	
Swayn, Rch. s. Wll.	5	1					Wh	
Swetenham, Th.	b	o	(1)w				Chg, nr	
Swecook, Hen.	—	(o)w						m. AleW
Swettok, Rch., & Isabel w./Jn. Oldefeld)	3	2		l			Su	
Swettok, Wll. (s. Hen.)	—	o			OO/h		(Bs)	
Swordsliper, Ad.	—		1w	st		w	Mc	AleW, bkr
Swordsliper, Jn. (o. Mc)	—		o				(Mc)	
Swordsliper, Rch. o. Hockerley	—		ow			w	(Mc)	poor
Sydebothum, Th. (s. Rch.)	—	o						(wdw)m. AleW
Sydsworth, Jn., s. Hen.	4/B	2	5w	a, j	O/e	w	Bg, Su	off, (b. ale)
Symeson, Jn.	—		4w				Bg	off, bkr
Symeson, Wll. (o. Wh)	u	1				w	(Wh)	(m. ale)
Taillour, Hecok.	b		(1)		h		nr	
Taillour, Hen. (o. Mc)	—	o	1		e	w	(Mc)	
Taillour, Alice d. Herv.	—		2	a				
Taillour, Jn. (o. Mc)	—		o				(Mc)	
Taillour, Jn. s. Wll.	4	1			s/h/PP		Su	
Taillour, Isabel d. Jn.	3						Su	
Taillour, Wll. s. Jn. (o. Sutton)	(u)	o					(Ra)	
Taillour, Jn., o. Chelford	4	1					Su	
Taillour, Rch. (o. Bt)	—	o			o/p		(Bt)	
Tailour, Rch. (o. Kh)	4	1			(h)	w	Wh	
Taillour, Rch. (s. Hen.)	—		o		h		Mc	(w)wvr
Taillour, Rb. s. Jn.	4	(o)					Ra	
Taillour, Rb., o. Chorley	b	o	(1)w				nr	

Name	Cat	Hal	Port	Bus	Stock	W	Vill	Notes
Taillour, Wll. (o. Bt)	4	1w			o/(h)		Bt	m. AleW
Taillour, Wll., o. Hockerley	—	2		a			Wh	
Tervyn, Th., Chap	—	o					Out	frm wfs
Thatcher, Wll., s. Rb.,	4	1			(e)	w	Su	
Thatcher, Rg. s. Wll.	4	1					Su	
Thorbald, Jn.	—		of		p		(Mc)	
Thorbald, Rb.	B	o	4w	st, a	h/o	W	Dstr, Ty	off
Thorneycroft, Rch., sen.	-/B		(1)				Hd, Dstr-r	
Togod, Jn. (o. Su)	4	1			OO	W	Su	
Togod, Jn., sen. & w.	3	3wf	(o)	l, v	P		Sh, Wh	
Togod, Jn. s. Jn. (o. Sh)	4	1wf					Sh	
Togod, Wll. & w.	4	4wf			H/p	w	Su	
Tonge, Rch.	—		1w				Mc	
Torkesay, Rb.	—		2w	st	o		Mc	(ale)
Treveyn, Wll.	3	1					Ed-r	Chap
Turnour, Rph.	—	o					Mp	
Turnour, Rb. (o. Mp)	—	o			(e)		Mp	
Turnour, Rg., Ellen w.	4	2			h/p	w	Ra	
Turnour, Rg. (o. Wh)	u	1			(H)/p	w	(Wh)	(m. alew)
Turnour, Th., (s. Wll.)	—	o					Bt	
Turnour, Wll. (o. Ra)	u	o	o		s/O/P		(Ra)	
Turnour, Wll.	B		5w	j			Chg	off, AleW, bkr
Tydnak, Wll.	4	2		l	h/P		Su	
Tydrynton, Ad. s. Rg.	3/B	3f	5w	v	e/p		Kh, Jg	off
Tydrynton, Wll. s. Ad. s. Rg. (o. Normanwood)	3	3		st, a	OOO/ p/h	w	Kh	
Tydrynton, Hgh. s. Hen.	—	3		a, v	h/P/H	W	(Ty)	
Tydrynton, Jn.	b		1				Mc-r	VcrSbch
Tydrynton, Rch. s. Hgh.	—	1w		st			Ty	
Tydrynton, Wll. s. Hen.	4	1			OO/h/p		Su	
Tydrynton, Wll. s. Rb.	—		1	st			(Mc)	
Tyllesone, Rch. (o. Ra)	3	3w		l	OO/H/P		Ra	tlr

Name	Cat	Hal	Port	Bus	Stock	W	Vill	Notes
Tynker, Jn.	4	2wf	(o)	l	p		Wh, Ds	
Tynker, Sim. s. Jn.	4	1f					Wh	
Tynker, Th., s. Jn.	2	1f		*l*	p		Wh, Ds, Ra	
Typpyng, Marion (w. Rg.)			3				Mc	AleW
Unwyn, Jn. sen.	o	ow					(Mp)	m. Ale
Unwyn, Rch. s. Jn.	—	of					(Mp)	(w)wvr, (m. ale)
Upton, Edm.	1	3wf				w	Hd, Ra	
Upton, Nch. s. Edm.	1/B	2wf	6w	*j*, l	E	w	Hd, Ra, Wg, Gdl	wol, b. AleW,
Upton, Rnph.	b		2w			w	Mc	off, cptr, bkr(alew)
Upton, Wll. s. Th. s. Rnph.	5	1					Ra	
Verdon, Jn.	—	o						Dep Glr
Vernon, Hgh.	b		(1)				nr	
Vernon, Nch. (s. Rb.)	b	(o)	2			w	Mc-r	
Vernon, Rb. (s. Hgh.)	—		3w	st, pl, a		w	Bg	(bkr)
Vernon, Rg., sen.	b		(1)f				nr	
Vernon, Jn. (s. Rg.)	—		1w				Mc-r	
Vernon, Rch. s. Jn.	—		1				Mc-r	
Walkedene, Jn.	5/B	o	6–7w	*j*, pl			Jg Lyme(ass)	off, (ale)
Walker, Alice	—		2					AleW
Walker, Hen.	B		3	st, j	H		Mc(by gaol)	
Walker, Jn.	B	o	7w	st, pl, a	e/PP	W	Gdl	off, Crn, (alew), fulr
Walker, Rch. (o. Mc) serv. o. Jn. Walker	—		2w	st	h/p	w	Mc	
Walker, Rch. (o. Wh)	u	o					(Wh)	
Walker, Rb. (s. Ad., o. Wolstancroft)	(B)		2				Bg	frm fulm
Walker, Th.	(B)	(o)	5w	st, pl			Bg	off, (w)bkr(ale)
Walker, Wll. (o. Haywood)	B	(o)	6–7w	pl			(Chg)	off, AleW

Name	Cat	Hal	Port	Bus	Stock	W	Vill	Notes
Walle, Jn.	4	I					Su	
Walsh, Wll.	u	(o)w						(alew)
Wassen, Rb. s. Jn. s. Wll.	3/4	I					Kh, Ra	
Watteson, Rch., o. Woodford, Mrgy w. (& Alc. w. Rch. Eves)	5	Iw			h		Ra	
Watteson, Rg. (o. Ra)	u	4w		j	S/E	w	Ra	
Watson, Rch., s. Wll.	(u)	o			p	w	(o. Ds)	m. Ale
Watteson, Th., s. Wll. Downes (o. Su)	3	3w		l	s/H/ O/p	w	Su (Su)	
Watson, Agnes d/h. Th.	3	o					Su	
Werynton, Jn.	5	3w		a	OO/H/P	W	(Kh)(ass)	
Werynton, Rb.	(u)	o			HH/o			m. Ale
Westedysh, Th.	b	o	(I)				nr	
Wetenhale, Wll. s. Wll.	4	I					Wh	
Whychode, Mth.	—	o						frm wfs
Whyke, Jn.	—		3wf	st			Mc	
Whyks, Wll. s. Jn.	—		of				Mc	
Whitehull, Wll. (s. Rg.)	3	4f		v, st	P	w	Wh	(m. ale)
Whithull, Rch., s. Wll.	3	2f		l	p	w	Wh, Ds	
Whitlegh, Rch.	—	o	o				(Mc)	
Wilberham, Rnph.	4	Iw					Ds(ass)	
Wilcok, Mrgy. d. Rph.	3						Wh	
Wilkynsone, Ad. s. Ad.	—	I					Bs	
Wilkynson, Th.	—	ow			OO		(Mp)	(m. alew)
Willeson, Jn. (o. Su)	(3)	2w			E/P	w	Su	
Willeson, Isabel d/h.	3	(I)					Su	
Willesone, Wll. s. Jn.	—	o			h			m. Ale
Wode, Hen. (o. Sh)	(u)	ow					(Sh)	
Wode, Hen. (s. Wll.)	3	2				w	Hd	
Wode, Jn.	—	Iw						m. Ale
Wode, Rg.	—	ow						(w)wvr, m.Ale
Wodecok, Ad. (s. Rg.)	—	o	o		PP			(Rg)wvr, fulr
Wodecok, Jn.	—	of			OO/e/p		(Bs)	

Name	Cat	Hal	Port	Bus	Stock	W	Vill	Notes
Wodecok, Jn. & Alice w.	4	ow					Su	
Wodehous, Jn.	—	o	I				(Mc)	
Wodehous, Th.	(5)	I	o				Su	U-Bff
Wodehous, h. Th.	2	(1)					Su	
Worth, Edm. (o. Ds)	2	4wf	o	j	p		Ds	
Worth, Rb., (o. Ty)	3/b	4f	4w	l, v st, pl		w	Hd, Bt, Mc	U-Bff, Glr
Worth, Th. s. Rb. (o. Ty)	(4)/b	1–2f	o			w	Bt	
Worth, Th.	(5)	2					Up	For, frg
Worth, Wll. (o. Bt)	—	1w		st			(Bt)	
Worth, Wll. (o. Hd)	(u)	o			(h)		(Hd)	
Worth, Wll. (o. Su)	(u)	2w		st	(h)	(w)	(Su)	
Worth, Wll. (o. Ty)	—	o					Ty, (Bt)	
Wosewall, Jn.	—	ow	1w	a	h	w	(Mc)	
Wrenche, Rb.	(B)	o	3w			w	(Bg)	off
Wrught, Al. (o. Bt)	—	o					Bt	
Wryght, Rch. (s. Jn.), (o. Su/Brodehurst)	—	2			e/p		(Su)	
Wryght, Rch. (s. Th.)	—		2w	a			(Mc)	
Wryght, Th.	—	o			S		(Su)	
Wyan, Hgh.	—		o		e		(Mc)	
Wylot, Th.	—	o	I				Mc (-r)	Cstd Pby
Wylot, Wll., o. Foxtwist	b	o	3w	j			Mc-r	
Wynge, Wll.	—	1f	2w		h/o/P	W	Mc	AleW(bkr)
Wynkil, Stph. s. H.	4	1f	o		h		Su	thshr
Wytlof, Rnph.	B	o	6wf	pl, st			Jg, Dstr-r	off, (alew)
Ydenchale, Rch.	4	I					Ra	

Index

(Excluding Appendix Two)